STO

OVERSIZE

REFERENCE

r
913.031028
Ar2
oversize
2165903

W9-CBE-209

Archeology under Water

An Atlas of the World's Submerged Sites

CONTRIBUTORS

J. Barto Arnold III
Director of the Underwater Archeological Research Section,
Texas Antiquities Committee

Professor George F. Bass
Professor of Anthropology, Texas A&M University;
President of the Institute of Nautical Archeology,
Philadelphia, Pa

Dr Carl O. Cederlund
Keeper of Maritime Archeology,
National Maritime Museum, Stockholm

Wilburn A. Cockrell
State Underwater Archeologist and Administrator,
Florida Department of State

Angela C. Evans
Archeologist, Department of Medieval and
Later Antiquities, British Museum, London

Dr Nicholas C. Flemming
Principal Scientific Officer,
Institute of Oceanographic Sciences, Wormley, England

Jeremy N. Green
Curator of Maritime Archeology,
Western Australian Museum, Fremantle

Professor Michael L. Katzev
American School of Classical Studies, Athens;
Vice-president of the Institute of Nautical Archeology,
Philadelphia, Pa

Colin J. M. Martin
Director of the Institute of Maritime Archaeology,
St. Andrews University, Scotland

Robert F. Marx
Marine archeologist, Satellite Beach, Florida

Dr Ian A. Morrison
Lecturer in Geography, Edinburgh University

Keith W. Muckelroy
Assistant Keeper, Archeological Research Centre,
National Maritime Museum, Greenwich, England;
Archeology Adviser, British Sub Aqua Club

Dr Anthony J. Parker
Lecturer in Roman Archeology, Bristol University

Dr Ulrich Ruoff
City Archeologist, Zurich, Switzerland

CARTOGRAPHER
John Flower

Preceding page: A diver
recovering a Roman
amphora, or wine jar,
from the wreck site of a
Roman freighter at
Madrague de Giens, off
the south coast of France
(pp. 54-55).
Right: A diver inspecting
a large storage jar
discovered on the Bronze
Age site at Sheytan
Deresi in south-west
Turkey (pp. 46-47).

Archeology under Water

An Atlas of the World's Submerged Sites

General Editor
Keith Muckelroy

McGraw-Hill Book Company

NEW YORK · LONDON
St. Louis · San Francisco · Hamburg
Johannesburg · Mexico · Toronto

The general editor and contributors
dedicate this atlas to

Dr. Joan du Plat Taylor,

founder secretary of the Council for
Nautical Archaeology and first editor of
The International Journal of Nautical Archaeology,
in recognition of her exceptional services
in fostering maritime archaeology
and assisting diving archaeologists throughout
the world.

ALLEN COUNTY PUBLIC LIBRARY
FORT. WAYNE, INDIANA

© Russel Sharp Ltd. 1980

All rights reserved. No part of this publication may be
reproduced, stored in a retrieval system, or transmitted,
in any form or by any means, electronic, mechanical,
photocopying, recording, or otherwise, without the prior
written permission of the publisher.

First published in the United States of America in 1980
by McGraw-Hill Book Company, New York

First published in the United Kingdom in 1980
by McGraw-Hill Book Company (UK) Limited, Maidenhead, Berkshire

This book was designed and produced by
Russel Sharp Ltd.
66 Woodbridge Road
Guildford, Surrey GU1 4RD

Text editor: David Lambert
Designer: Tony Truscott

Text set by SX Composing Ltd., England
Printed in Hong Kong by Dai Nippon Printing Co. (HK) Ltd.

Library of Congress Cataloging in Publication Data
Main entry under title:

Atlas of archeology under water.

  Bibliography: p.
  Includes index.
  1. Underwater archaeology.   I. Muckelroy, Keith
1951–
CC77.U5A84   930'.1'02804   79–18380
ISBN 0–07–043951–6

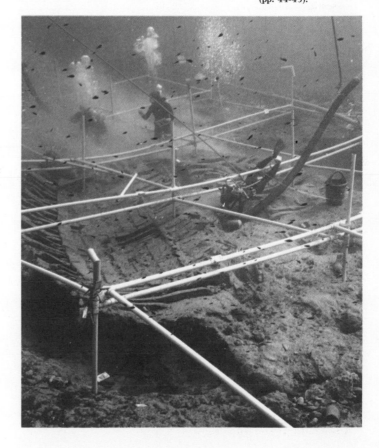

Below: Excavation and
surveying in progress on
the 4th century BC
merchantman discovered
off Kyrenia in Cyprus
(pp. 44-45).

Contents

2165903

Prologue

Right: A diver using the underwater 'telephone booth' on the site of the 4th century AD wreck at Yassi Ada. This piece of equipment enabled divers to both talk to each other easily and communicate with the support vessel on the surface (pp. 38-39).

Since World War II, the development of convenient and efficient subaquatic equipment has opened a new world to archaeologists. For tens, if not hundreds, of thousands of years man has exploited the sea: living beside it, fishing in it, and voyaging on it. But until recently, any of his tools, materials, or foodstuffs that happened to fall below the waves were lost for all time. Seabed sediments preserved many drowned artifacts, but archaeologists had no way of studying these where they lay. Fishermen and dredger crews occasionally hauled up an interesting object by chance, but no one knew anything of where it had come from. The aqualung has changed all that.

In the three decades of work embraced by this atlas, the first generation of diving archaeologists has begun to develop techniques of exploration and excavation, and to appreciate the full scope of a new archaeological resource. Maritime archaeologists investigating early ships, naval activity, and maritime trade can now pursue questions that their land-bound predecessors were forced to ignore. To help solve the problems raised by the archaeologists' work, scientific and technical specialists undertake new lines of research and develop new kinds of equipment. And the newly recognized needs for protection and responsible control of sites under water pose hitherto unforeseen demands on public policy and international law.

All these factors and more recur through this book in the context of individual sites. In many cases you will find no tidy solutions or well-rounded conclusions for the problems involved. With a discipline barely 30 years old, few projects have actually been carried through to completion, and specialists have not had time to reach considered solutions to many operational, research, or legal problems. This atlas is thus very much an interim statement, allowing the reader a chance to assess the current state of the art.

We have chosen the title and format of an atlas for a number of reasons, but above all because this format gives plenty of scope for site plans and distribution maps. Both are vital for putting our subject in perspective. Archaeology under water has long been notorious for occasional finds of spectacular treasure – so much so that many a wreck reported to the media immediately becomes a "treasure ship." But, to the archaeologist, the discovery of financially valuable objects is not the whole story, or even the most important part of it. He is concerned chiefly with context: a grouping of discovered objects that suggests all had been in use at the same time; or their arrangement across a site, indicating the organization or operation of a ship or harbor. Thus we can best achieve a genuinely archaeological balance by relating illustrations of finds (both spectacular and commonplace) to plans and maps of the sites that the finds came from, and by making these plans and maps preeminent features.

Incidentally, to the student of the past, the commonplace is at least as interesting as the spectacular: finds of everyday clothes and utensils give him a better overall view of a vanished society than gold and silver ornaments or exotic jewelry. Many of the sites we shall consider therefore involve ships or structures that were by no means outstanding.

To return to the importance of context in archaeological research, one of our principal aims is to justify the time and effort archaeologists devote to it. For this reason we include several detailed accounts of how particular sites have been analyzed, or patterns of sites in a region interpreted. Context can be investigated on any scale, from the relationship between two objects on one site to the relationship between groups of sites across the world. Only in the light of such investigations can the reader understand the logic behind the techniques and approaches adopted by an archaeologist in tackling a site.

An atlas is a book with a geographical theme, and the concept of context also involves relationships in space. Understandably, then, besides stressing maps and plans, many contributors describe the surveying methods they use. In the course of the text, you will learn about a variety of surveying systems, ranging from simple rulers and tapes to electronic rangemeters and stereo-photogrammetry (the production by machine of measured drawings from stereo pairs of photographs). Perhaps more than any other activity, it is this devotion to surveying and recording that distinguishes the archaeologist from the commercial salvor or treasure hunter.

This is not to say, of course, that all archaeological investigations achieve the same high standards in site recording. Poor underwater visibility or fast currents may force the director to compromise. Also his own interests help to determine the standard he aims for: like all sciences, archaeology thrives on differences of opinion. Moreover, the director's experience influences recording: most of our authors show how their techniques have become more accurate and efficient over the years, and all would admit there is always room for improvement.

The wide range of sites and projects that we cover builds up a broad picture of how and where underwater archaeology has evolved. This approach needs no extensive editorial commentaries or signposting. However, a few of the main themes are worth highlighting here.

A glance at the many site plans clearly shows the variety of sites available to the archaeologist under water. Wreck sites form the largest category, but there are great differences in the size and complexity of the vessels involved, and in the degree of destruction they suffered. On one hand we find vessels like the Swedish warship *Wasa* (p. 82), raised substantially intact in 1961; at the other extreme there are wrecks like that of the *San Esteban* (pp. 102–9) of which very little survived. But shipwrecks are not alone under water: Section V (pp. 132–77) discusses a wide range of other objects that have become submerged. Some of these, like Paleo-Indian burials in Florida or Neolithic villages in Switzerland, were drowned by natural processes. Others, such as the lake-dwellings of Scotland or harbors anywhere, were always intended to be at least partly submerged.

The geographical spread of the sites discussed is also striking. This reflects not so much where remains lie under water as where there are divers to find them. Only in affluent Europe and North America are there enough people using the seafloor recreationally or commercially for many sites to be found. And only in these same areas is society able and willing to sponsor this branch of archaeological research. However, the 1977–79 wreck excavation at Mombasa in Kenya (p. 125) suggests that this bias may be less marked in the future.

Our allocation of space to different periods of the past is also notably biased. Two of the four central sections concern shipping in just a few centuries. Thus Section II (pp. 32–61) deals with Mediterranean seafaring in the last centuries BC and the first centuries AD, although with outliers in the Bronze Age and medieval period. Section IV (pp. 102–31)

covers shipping outside Europe from the sixteenth through the eighteenth century AD. This period also dominates the second half of Section III (pp. 82–101). Prehistory and the medieval period in general are poorly served. In the course of the text, several authors explain this uneven coverage, chiefly in terms of the preservation and recognition of sites under water. There are signs that future investigations will help to remedy the present chronological imbalances.

A glance through the projects described in this atlas will also reveal something interesting about the development of archaeology under water. Well over half of the projects began in the 1970s. In many regions, and for many topics, nothing seems to have been achieved before 1970. The development of the subject is still gaining momentum, and there is every sign that the 1980s achievements will outshine those of the 1970s.

This sense of flux and continuing development in underwater archaeology is carried through to the institutional and legal provisions described in the course of this book. Some states have established comprehensive arrangements for dealing with their underwater cultural heritage; others have done nothing. In some countries, research under water is seen as one of the most exciting new developments in archaeology; in others, it is regarded as academically disreputable. The result is a rather confused overall picture.

So far, we have been discussing archaeology under water as if it were a self-contained subject with a discipline of its own. But in fact most of us in the field would not see it that way. We are just archaeologists who happen to reach our sites by diving instead of by driving or walking. The history of the subject, its environmental constraints, and its fieldwork techniques are all peculiar to archaeology under water, but they alone do not make it an independent discipline. General approach, standards of accuracy, methods of interpretation, and many other features are common to all branches of archaeology and override all operational differences.

If we subdivide archaeology at all, we find the only academically valid subdivisions are those based on topics studied. Thus archaeologists may specialize in the study of the Palaeolithic (Old Stone Age) period, or burial customs, or Near Eastern cities. Archaeology under water may constitute a part of many of these subdivisions. In some instances its contribution is substantial. Thus with maritime archaeology, the study of the remains of ships and seafaring, most of the evidence must come from under water, so that the characteristics of underwater archaeology heavily influence this subdiscipline's scope and potential. In other instances, as with landscape studies in the Alps or in Scotland (pp. 148–61), the contribution of underwater archaeology is more peripheral. In the course of this atlas we touch on many branches of archaeology, although the archaeology of ships is obviously dominant (pp. 24–131).

Since archaeology under water represents a cross section through archaeology in general, we shall incidentally touch on many of the principal features of the parent discipline. We have already mentioned some generally applicable topics such as the importance of context in archaeology, or the relationship between particular sites and general research problems. In the ensuing sections we shall also encounter more specific archaeological concerns, like the interpretation of pottery assemblages (pp. 98–99), the use of ethnographic evidence in interpreting remains (p. 88),

Left: A diver surveying the area around a large iron anchor from the wreck of the Spanish Armada supply ship *El Gran Grifon* (1588). The anchor, which is in the left foreground, now lies among boulders in about 25 meters of water (pp. 94-95).

or the place of conservation in archaeology (pp. 108–9). In effect, we present in passing a microcosm of archaeology in the late 1970s.

The general plan of our atlas is designed to highlight simultaneously as many of these themes and concepts as possible. With archaeology under water defined principally in terms of its working environment, it makes good sense to start with some of the problems faced by diving archaeologists, and the techniques they have developed to achieve their objectives.

In the following sections, dealing with specific sites, we move from objects that arrived under water by accident to those originally placed there. First we examine ships and shipwrecks (pp. 31–131). Broadly speaking these three sections relate wreck sites by age and place. Beginning with classical wreck sites in the Mediterranean also means that we start with the pioneering excavations of Professor George Bass and his colleagues.

In Section V (pp. 132–77) we finally leave the topic of shipwrecks, and move on through a series of submerged sites of other types. We begin with settlements and burials that were originally dry, and end with harbors: structures always meant to be in water. In Section VI (pp. 178–87) the general editor seeks to tie together some important strands in the various contributions, not by repeating the general themes already set out in this prologue, but by concentrating on one topic of central importance in all aspects of archaeology: preservation.

No volume of this type can ever hope to be comprehensive, and undoubtedly many important sites have not received the attention they deserve. Some were still under investigation at the time of writing, and it was too early to summarize what had been found. Other omissions are sites standing alone in time or place, without parallel discoveries that would help us to use them to illustrate general themes. In the last analysis we have tried to make the selection representative rather than all embracing, giving at least a balanced view of the whole subject.

Some readers may be surprised at the absence of nineteenth- and twentieth-century finds. Since the development of the aqualung, divers have undertaken a great deal of work on early steamships, American Civil War gunships, World War I battleships, and even World War II aircraft. But while such enterprises are interesting, and sometimes furnish useful displays for museums, they are not archaeology. As an academic discipline, archaeology interprets the past on the basis of surviving objects; it becomes redundant at that point in the past after which surviving records, descriptions, plans, and drawings of contemporary objects can tell us more about the culture of the time than we can learn by digging up a few relics. For most of the societies dealt with here, the onset of industrialization and modern-style bureaucracies in the early 1800s marks the cut-off point.

At the opening of each section the general editor has inserted a brief introduction explaining how that section is organized, and introducing the respective authors. Each of our contributors is active in fieldwork and archaeological research associated with our subject. These introductions and the overall plan of the atlas should help the reader to appreciate the broad significance of the sites; the adventure of their exploration, and the beauty or interest of the objects recovered will emerge from the pages that follow.

Right: Divers breaking up coral encrustation to uncover material on the site of *Nuestra Senora de los Milagros* off the Yucatan peninsular in Mexico (pp. 118-119).

SECTION I
Techniques and Approaches

Before we look in detail at the sites themselves and some of the general historical themes they relate to, it is worth closely examining the practicalities of archaeology under water. The archaeologist's first task is to get to the seabed, so we begin our first section by considering the problems of diving. From there we move on through the sequence of activities involved in a comprehensive site investigation. There is a change of emphasis on p. 24, where we focus on shipwrecks—the type of underwater site most studied by the archaeologist. An introeuction to wreck sites, the opportunities they present, and the challenges they pose, sets the scene for the ensuing three sections.

This section has been written by Keith Muckelroy, the general editor of this atlas. His descriptions are firmly based on his experience of work on over a dozen sites in British and Mediterranean waters. As Archaeology Adviser to the British Sub-Aqua Club, he is particularly experienced in communicating basic ideas and techniques to amateur divers. At the same time, as a graduate in archaeology and a pioneer in developing the theory of maritime archaeology, his presentation is firmly rooted in the disciplines of archaeology.

The diver and his problems

On land or under water, archaeological survey and excavation is labor-intensive. Since on all underwater sites the work is done by divers, success or failure depends on their capabilities. We shall thus start this brief survey of the techniques of archaeology under water by looking at the problems faced by those who work submerged. We will consider these under two heads: the expense of these operations, and the insuperable limitations common to all divers.

First there is the cost and sheer complexity of gear required. While a land archaeologist needs only a jeep or a truck to get him to a site, his diving colleague is encumbered by a great deal of equipment. Besides a boat, he needs a compressor, diving suit, air supply, mask, and fins. All of this costs a good deal to buy, transport, and insure.

Basically, there are two types of underwater life-support equipment. One is scuba (self-contained underwater breathing apparatus) involving a tank of high-pressure air carried on the diver's back. The air travels to the mouth via tube and automatic regulator. Scuba gear has the advantage of leaving the diver self-contained and free to swim about without restriction. But no dive can last longer than the air supply. The alternative is a small compressor on the surface, pumping air at medium pressure through a hose and regulator to the diver down below. These units are generally cheaper than scuba systems, and they can feed divers air indefinitely. Their most obvious disadvantage lies in the hose-restricted operating range. However, if you are working for weeks on one small site this limitation may not matter.

Having used up much time and money getting to his site, the underwater archaeologist can spend far less time per day there than his colleague on dry land. Should the site lie deeper than 10 meters (33ft) he must stay down no longer than the limit set forth in decompression tables. These are designed to minimize the risk of decompression sickness, a potentially killing condition known as "the bends." The bends can occur when nitrogen that had dissolved in the blood under pressure at depth comes out of solution during ascent, forming bubbles that block veins and arteries. According to tables published by the Royal Navy, no one making even a simple dive to 15 meters (about 50ft) should stay down for more than 80 minutes, while for a depth of 35 meters (115ft) the limit is 15. You can slightly extend these bottom times by pausing for several minutes at depths of 6 and 3 meters (20 and 10ft) during ascent, but this may introduce other diving risks. In any case, such times involve much less than the 8 or more hours per day that you could easily spend on a land site.

Even in water too shallow to make decompression a problem, diving time may have to be brief. The two main reasons are limited air supply – this chiefly affects scuba divers, of course – and the effect of cold upon the body, which loses heat much faster in water than in air. Heat loss can drain away stamina faster than almost any other factor. In a temperate climate, even in summer, a diver wearing a standard wet suit (in which water is allowed to seep within the suit) is unlikely to manage more than about $2\frac{1}{2}$ hours under water at a stretch, or to average more than 4 hours' total per day for work lasting several weeks. He can increase these periods to some extent by using a dry suit (into which no water should enter). But dry suits cost more than wet suits and can prove cumbersome.

For these and other reasons, the cost per man-hour on an underwater site may be 5–20 times as high as it would be on land. But the problem goes deeper than that, as we see when we turn to the actual performance of people who work under water. A diver may accomplish only half as much work in an hour as he would get through on the surface. Psychological studies and common experience tell us that performance slumps in an alien environment, and the bed of the sea or a lake is a very different place from the one our bodies were intended for.

Visual problems result from the differing refractive indices of air and water: viewed through a diver's face mask, underwater objects seem distorted. Then, too, most face masks restrict the field of view. Moreover, because water filters out the red end of the color spectrum, the underwater world can seem curiously blue. At the same time all you can hear is your own breathing. Objects feel strange to the touch, and your directional sense is often upset (especially in murky water) by lack of a natural horizon and by the apparent absence of gravity. Training and experience help you combat the effects of these distortions and distractions but you can never dismiss them entirely.

From the archaeologist's viewpoint, the worst problem is reduced ability to observe. Psychological studies have proved that divers have difficulty maintaining full alertness to more than one set of observations. This means that if their first concern is safety (as it must be), their archaeological

Opposite, below: A diver in standard hard-hat diving apparatus. Although this equipment has been available since the 1830s, it is clumsy and expensive, and is rarely used nowadays in archaeology under water.
Below: Three types of diver, the heavily weighted hard-hat diver being contrasted with mobile aqualung divers. The one on the right is supplied by a hose from the surface, while the one on the left uses scuba (self-contained underwater breathing apparatus) equipment – his air supply is compressed in cylinders on his back.
Right: A scuba diver swims across an undisturbed mound of amphorae (pottery jars), which betrays the site of a classical-period wreck.
Below, right: A diver with surface-demand mobile diving equipment carrying a massive wooden lodging knee across the sea bed.

work will suffer. A related problem is the difficulty of recalling information acquired in one environment when you enter another. This is one reason why diving archaeologists record all they can while actually on the spot.

Despite all these snags, underwater archaeological work is, of course, possible. It is also not so demanding or dangerous that only he-men should attempt it. Any reasonably fit person between the ages of 16 and 60 can do it with due care and instruction, and women actually have a few physiological advantages. Indeed, a fair proportion of leading diving archaeologists are female. But no one should think of literally taking the plunge without a full course of tuition from a recognized diving club or school. Finally, just becoming a diver does not make you an underwater archaeologist. His (or her) work involves a battery of skills, as the next few pages show.

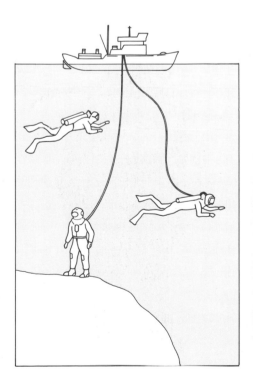

Finding a site

"First find your site" would seem to be a reasonable instruction to any archaeologist embarking on a new project. In fact most underwater sites probably come to light as chance discoveries by divers and others who are not archaeologists at all. The experts enter only later, drawn by news of the discoveries. To some extent this sequence of events reflects the relative youth of underwater archaeology, and, in most countries, a lack of specialist professional teams undertaking systematic research. But it seems likely that chance discoveries will always be important under water as indeed they have remained on land.

Many of the accounts in this book, however, demonstrate that teams have found a number of important sites because they deliberately went out looking for them. Such detective work can take two forms: studying documents in archives, and systematically searching the seafloor. So far as ships are concerned, archival documents cover only relatively modern wrecks, dating from about AD 1500 onward. Even then archives often cover only vessels that attracted special notice, for example, through their size or the nature of their cargo. As recently as the Napoleonic period, bureaucratic organizations produced detailed accounts only of naval vessels and the ships of major trading bodies such as the various

East India companies. Very often, surviving correspondence or court records from the vicinity of a wrecking will prove the most revealing source of information. After all, for an isolated community, a shipwreck could be the most exciting, disruptive, and profitable happening for many years.

Sites described in old documents may thus lead on to actual searching of an area of seabed. But this work can have other origins — for example, in a comprehensive survey of a region, or in seeking the find-site of important objects dredged up by chance. But before the diving archaeologist sets out to search any area he must carefully assess the work this could involve: objects that his team discovers may need immediate and expensive survey and excavation in order to protect them from plundering; then, too, sites with known locations may have a greater claim upon the team's time and resources than sites still to be found. Deciding which area to work must involve choosing the one that promises to add most to our knowledge of the past.

The search itself may include any or all of a whole group of tools and techniques. The quickest way to scan a large seabed area is by means of electronic remote-sensing devices. There are two main classes of such instrument. The first group includes echo sounders and side-scan sonars. Both record the shape of the seabed, and are useful on a generally flat bottom from which remains may protrude. Sub-bottom profilers are rather different in that they record the various strata below the seabed. The second class of remote-sensing devices consists of magnetometers and other metal-detectors that reveal metal objects as anomalies (or variations) in a local magnetic field. These instruments have proved particularly useful for finding post-medieval vessels, with their stores of cannons, anchors, and other large metal objects. A fine example is the search for the *San Esteban*, which sank in 1554 off Texas (pp. 104–05).

The obvious alternative to electronic devices is the facility widely known as the "Mark I Eyeball." However, plain visual search is often laborious and slow. In shallow waters visibility is rarely more than 50 meters (165ft) and often nil. This seriously limits the area that divers can cover. Nevertheless, wherever the search area is relatively well defined, and electronic devices

An aqualung diver laying a line across kelp-covered seabed in preparation for a systematic search.

are unsuitable or unavailable, divers can accomplish a great deal by disciplined, systematic searching. See, for example, the searches on the Bronze Age site at Salcombe (p. 64) or those on the Spanish Armada site in Blasket Sound, southwest Ireland (p. 94).

An important substitute for a visual search is the use of photographic or video systems, either towed behind a surface craft or mounted on some kind of submarine. Although less sensitive and flexible than the human observer, such equipment is better than a diver in that it does not tire and cameras can produce permanent pictures.

In both electronic and visual search, the major problem is often not so much how to make and record observations as knowing where you are when you do so. An effective search program is one where no area is scanned twice or missed altogether, and to achieve this you must know exactly which part of the area you are scrutinizing at any moment. In small-scale visual or metal-detector searches of limited areas you may thus have to devote a great deal of time and effort to laying buoys and control lines. For larger areas you may manage with standard optical or radio-navigation systems, although it is often necessary to establish a local electronic position-finding system founded on specially established transponders (radio or radar sets that respond to an external signal by emitting their own). In many instances, the problem is not so much tracking the surface craft as establishing the position of the sensing device trailing behind it at the end of several hundred meters of cable.

However you do it, searching a large area of seabed is expensive and time-consuming, and therefore justified only in special circumstances. But there are some shortcuts. Where relatively recent wrecks are concerned you can often save a great deal of time by uncovering clues in the kinds of archival sources already described. For non-documented sites you will find that a careful study of local conditions (tides, currents, and sediment patterns) may help to show which areas are most likely to contain wrecks.

Searching need not be limited to finding previously unknown sites; a systematic search around the core of a known site under investigation is usually worthwhile, too. Some projects have been left incomplete because those concerned did not bother to look far away from the deposit first found; in some cases, divers have missed the heart of a site in this way.

There is still scope for finding new ways to improve search techniques. But the most sophisticated electronic aids will never replace the experienced archaeological diver. In the end, only his or her personal inspection of underwater remains can confirm that the search has found its objective.

Above: A powered sledge, such as this Rebicoff Pegasus machine (above), allows a diver to inspect a larger area of seabed than he could otherwise cover swimming on his own.
Right: A diver-controlled metal detector being used within a shingle-filled gully.

Surveying under water

This atlas includes many site plans showing the various forms archaeological evidence may take under water; captions and text help to explain for the reader how archaeologists interpret this evidence. Together with the objects recovered, the plans, sections, and diagrams of an underwater site are the archaeologist's chief source of information about it. Costly and time-consuming it may be, but detailed, accurate, on-site recording is a vital part of any genuine archaeological project and one that most plainly separates it from the simple salvage operation. Our contributing authors outline the survey methods used on their various sites. Here, I shall simply introduce the main principles.

Once an archaeologist has identified a site and decided to study it, his first task is to undertake a pre-disturbance survey. His aim is to make an exact record of the surface appearance of the site before removing anything. This should reveal the extent and significance of the remains and help the archaeologist to decide how best to tackle them. In many cases, this survey is a self-contained program: only afterward will the archaeologist know whether further work is worthwhile. The pre-disturbance survey that produces well-documented evidence to justify his own hopes and expectations for the site also helps the archaeologist win backing from potential sponsors and other supporters. If excavation does go ahead, surveying and recording will then continue throughout the operation.

The first thing to establish in a survey is what to record. No one records absolutely everything, and the definition of what to include and what to ignore depends on the purpose for which you are making the survey. On an archaeological site under water, you are unlikely ever to need to record the size and location of each pebble, let alone each grain of sand; but obviously wherever a ship's hull survives you should carefully record its lines. In intermediate cases only judgment and experience can tell you whether you ought to make a precise record — for example, of each nail hole and potsherd. The decision must depend upon the sort of questions the appropriate specialists are likely to ask; thus only an archaeologist at least conversant with such questions has the necessary judgment to direct the survey.

Closely linked to this problem of what to record is another: how accurately to record it. There is no such thing as perfect precision: any drawing or model will involve approximations, especially where you are representing a three-dimensional object in two dimensions. This is especially true of scale drawings, where even the thickness of a pencil line can raise difficulties. On a site plan produced to a scale of 1:20 (a realistic example for a large site), a pencil line 1 millimeter wide will be equivalent to a great gash 2 centimeters ($\frac{3}{4}$in) wide on the site

Above: In producing a detailed map of a small area a superimposed grid can be of great assistance. Here the diver is using a graduated rod to record the depth of a feature below the grid.
The problems of surveying a site in murky water are well illustrated by this photograph (left) taken on the *Mary Rose* site in the Solent near Portsmouth, southern England. The other end of the tape, behind the photographer, is probably invisible to the surveyor. Strapped to his left arm is a white plastic noteboard.

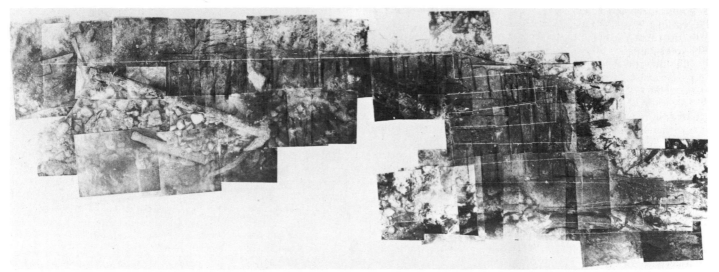

itself, making nonsense of any attempt to measure distances to, say, the nearest centimeter. Ideally, levels of accuracy should be determined by the purpose that the plans will serve, but what is ideal is not always practicable. Where there is any doubt, the archaeologist should err as far as possible on the side of too much detail, or too high a level of precision. Information can always be discarded, but if excavation destroys an unrecorded feature or measurement, then that is lost forever.

So much for the general approach. The first actual task in any survey is to establish a framework within which everything can be related. The standard procedure is to cover the site with a grid or lattice of squares, either physically laid out with tapes or scaffold poles, or indicated by datum stakes or pitons placed to mark the principal points. The accuracy of the whole survey depends on extremely accurate measurements between the corners and main intersections of this grid, since a small error made here will affect every subsequent reading. For such long-distance measuring under water the best aids are sonic range-meters or graduated tension wires as used in civil engineering, but such expensive equipment is rarely available. Failing this, direct measurement with standard tape measures is often the only answer. Restricted visibility under water usually rules out optical instruments like theodolites, such as land-based archaeologists will generally use.

Within such a framework, however established, you have to fit all the data required. This usually means striking a balance between the use of photography and drawing. Photography is more objective and generally quicker, but suffers from the optical distortion inherent in the use of a lens (no matter how fine), and cannot discriminate between variations in texture and hardness. Moreover, poor visibility, low light levels, reduced visual contrast, and color imbalance further limit the

use of photography under water. Drawing by hand permits more discrimination, so that the resulting image contains only relevant information. But drawing is also subjective: liable to reflect what the observer wants to see rather than what is actually there. It is also slow, a serious handicap where diving time may be restricted. Stereophotogrammetry (plan-making by computer from stereo-photographs of the site) provides an intermediate option. Although less flexible and speedy than ordinary photography, it does give accurate plans, and archaeologists use it increasingly. Photomosaics, composite pictures built up of many overlapping photographs, are

widely used under water in order to combat low visibility, but suffer from more extensive distortion than ordinary photographs. They may give a good general impression of a site, but are generally too inaccurate as a basis for detailed recording.

From what you have read you will see that each plan in this atlas reflects the techniques used by a particular investigator, and his views on which aspects of his site were important. In the hands of an experienced and intelligent archaeologist, the results can be most informative and revealing. But try to be critical of the work involved: inspect each offering carefully in the light of how it was made.

Above: Once the main outlines of a site have been measured in, further details can be recorded photographically and added to the plans at a later date. Where the visibility under water does not allow a structure to be encompassed in one shot, a number of photographs can be linked together in a photomosaic such as this. The wooden remains here represent part of the hull of the *Dartmouth*, a Royal Navy vessel sunk in 1690 (see pp. 28-29, 100-01).

Left: Surveying continues as excavation proceeds. Grid lines subdivide this site into squares, and each amphora (pottery jar) is given a numbered tag so that it can be identified at every stage.

Excavation strategy

If asked what archaeologists actually do, most people would say: "dig." By now you will have grasped that they do a great deal more than that. Nevertheless, excavation is their most spectacular activity, under water as well as on land. Maritime archaeologists probably spend even less of their working time digging than their land colleagues do. This is because of the additional time spent in preparations for diving.

In the next sections you will find a great deal about the tools, techniques, and procedures used on different sites. Here it is worth making the general point that the several unusual machines and other devices used by diving archaeologists are selected not by whim but to meet the requirements of strategy. By archaeological strategy I mean the procedures adopted as part of a program planned to achieve a given set of objectives. In practice, of course, an archaeologist may have to modify his program as work proceeds and reveals unexpected findings or problems.

Once the archaeologist has completed his pre-disturbance survey of a wreck and decided to excavate, he must choose where to begin and how much to do. These decisions involve weighing up not only the results of the survey, but also the excavation's objectives. These may range from recovering all artifacts and other evidence contained in a site, to answering specific

questions about the remains; for instance, establishing their date, or identifying the woods used in building the ship. Archaeologists generally dislike partial excavation because this damages a site while yielding incomplete and thus possibly misleading results. However, financial and other constraints often mean that partial investigation is the only kind possible. When this is so, the archaeologist must evolve a strategy that helps him achieve his objectives in a way that harms the site as little as possible.

We can investigate further the problems of determining an excavation strategy by considering the example of the *Mary Rose*, Henry VIII's warship which sank in 1545 in the silts of the Solent channel off the southern English port of Portsmouth. In 1971 all that you could see of the newly rediscovered hull were a short and a long line of oak posts jutting from the seabed — and converging almost at a right angle. The wreck posed three major questions. First, was this really the *Mary Rose*? Second, how much of the hull had survived? Third, what was its condition?

After clearing the lines of posts, as far as possible without digging major trenches, the excavators decided to concentrate on the corner, the only outstanding feature that they could see. Bearing in mind the likely fragility and importance of any ship's con-

tents, they confined excavation to the outside of the vessel, hoping to reveal enough to confirm her identity. The team spent no less than five years extending and exploring the large trenches around this corner before the position became fully clear; they learned that this was the stern port corner, with the sternpost rising obliquely through it and much of the rudder still attached. The vessel lay heeled over 60 degrees to starboard and, although only a few meters of the port side remained, the starboard side promised to be substantially complete. The visible structure seemed in excellent condition, so the next question was whether the rest of the ship was equally sound. Establishing that this was so took up the next two years. First, the team cut extensive trenches around the bows and along the port side. Later, as the situation became clearer, they made exploratory excavations inside the hull.

This carefully developed strategy produced enough evidence to permit project archaeologist Margaret Rule to plan a complete excavation of the wreck and its contents, culminating in recovery of the hull itself. Graduating from partial to total excavation, her strategy accordingly switched from the digging of deep, narrow external trenches to opening up large parts of the ship's interior. The team tackled this level by level, uncovering the remains in reverse

order to that in which they had been buried.

Obviously, each site is unique, and what was appropriate on the *Mary Rose* may apply nowhere else. However, that example demonstrates many situations commonly met with in the partial or complete investigation of wreck sites where the hull is largely intact.

Archaeologists face a very different problem on sites where the remains are widely scattered and little or no wooden structure survives. Here the wreck-bearing layers of mud or sand are often not very deep, and the most efficient procedure is to clear an area at one edge of an apparent concentration of material, and then work your way across the site, digging a broad trench, and dumping soil on the ground you have already excavated. But this method is valid only where there are no more than three or four different layers of sediment, and no extensive buried structures that should be seen at one time in plan rather than in section.

On scattered sites, searching beyond the main area of wreckage is especially important in order to ensure that you miss no important remains. On a large site, with several main groups of artifacts, it is often wise to begin by cutting exploratory trenches across several such groups. These should give some idea of the extent of the

Right: Uncovering the hull remains of a Roman freighter off the southern coast of France. The cargo of amphorae has already been removed from the right-hand part of the site.

deposits and help you, early on, to decide whether you need modify your methods of survey or excavation, or indeed whether to continue at all. By no means all sites live up to expectation, as Professor George Bass shows in describing the remains at Sheytan Deresi in Turkey (p. 46).

Whatever strategy the archaeologist chooses, he must express it clearly enough for site workers to know what they are meant to be doing, and why. He must also

set it forth honestly in the final publication, so that readers can understand the evidence acquired and assess its scope and limitations. Such formal planning should be a feature of all archaeology, but it is particularly important in underwater projects, where the chief archaeologist must delegate much to subordinates, and each hour on site is expensive. The maritime archaeologist cannot afford to open new trenches "to see what's there," or "just to check I'm right."

Opposite: A model showing the operations on the site of the *Mary Rose* during the first few seasons of excavation. The expedition's catamaran is moored over the site, while on the seabed the line of timber-heads marks the port side of the Tudor warship. Outside the vessel, below her stern, metal poles delimit two excavation areas, with an airlift tethered over one of them.
Right: A diving archaeologist excavating among the wreckage of the Spanish Armada vessel *La Trinidad Valencera*.

Excavation tools and techniques

A whole arsenal of digging aids lies at the disposal of the underwater archaeologist who has planned his strategy and secured the cash and people for excavation. Most of these machines and tools have their parallels on land, although in many ways the underwater excavator is actually better served than the land-based archaeologist.

At the simplest level, though, the maritime archaeologist needs no tools at all. Where the land archaeologist delicately removes sediment with a trowel, hand brush, paintbrush or teaspoon, the underwater excavator can often shift sediment merely by fanning with his hand. He fans gently or vigorously according to circumstances, but always operates on the material indirectly through the medium of the water. This is a more subtle and sensitive procedure than anything possible on land, and allows the experienced worker carefully to uncover and interpret a complex series of deposits. When you disturb a layer containing mud, stones, artifacts, and ecofacts (seeds, bones, etc.), individual items tend to break up or sort themselves out according to density. Fine particles float away, undermining stones and pebbles so that these roll downward. The result is to leave the interesting material exposed.

While this approach is essential for excavating many types of sediment, from light silts to heavy gravels, there are situations where it does not work. With closely compacted clays that will not readily go into suspension, the best method is generally to use the mason's trowel, as you would on land. At the other extreme, you must manually remove large pebbles and boulders. Removal of this type of deposit appears in our photograph of a gully on the *Gran Grifón* wreck site (p. 95): the excavator dumped stones in a large net laid out behind him, and frequently lifted the net by means of an air-filled bag in order to drop the stones off site.

An underwater situation with no close parallel on land occurs where corrosion products from some ferrous object have invaded the nearby seabed and any artifacts within it, creating a solid composite mass. Such concretions can be very hard, and breaking them with hammer and chisel can be extremely laborious, slow, and difficult to achieve with care. Some archaeologists solve this problem by means of very small explosive charges, each of 20–40 grams (about $\frac{3}{4}$–$1\frac{1}{2}$ oz). Carefully applied to the right type of concretion, explosions simply shake it and destroy its cohesion without damaging its contents. Because the spatial relationships of objects in the resulting lump remain undisturbed, you can then excavate the whole deposit in the normal manner. In the past, though, treasure hunters have used considerably larger, more destructive,

charges for breaking open sites in order to remove any valuables as quickly as possible. Thus among archaeologists the use of explosives remains controversial.

Once the archaeologist has dissected an area, and collected all the finds and other evidence that this can yield, he may be left with much spoil to remove before work can continue. On land, workers shift spoil by means of buckets or wheelbarrows, or (on very large, well-funded projects) by light railway. Under water, too, the simple bucket has its uses. But the major aids are water dredges (also called hydrolifts) and airlifts. Both are basically pipes 5–20 centimeters (2–8in) in diameter, designed to suck up spoil and transfer it across the seabed for any distance required. In a dredge, the propulsive force is a jet of water pumped down from the surface and directed along the tube; in an airlift, compressed air injected at the bottom of a tube rises and expands, creating considerable suction.

I cannot overstress the fact that these are primarily tools for removing spoil, not for recovering artifacts. Archaeologists now reject as unacceptable the once-common practice of excavating deposits with airlifts, and screening out the artifacts in trays on the surface. Such a procedure inevitably jumbles up objects that had been lying at various levels and distances apart, and destroys fragile materials altogether. Similar

objections apply to the use of a propwash, as is fairly common in America (p. 117); this suffers from the additional snag that you cannot directly control its force from the seabed. The only situation where archaeologists may justifiably use airlifts or prop-

washes directly on undisturbed sites is where they must remove thick layers of sediment known to be archaeologically sterile. (This parallels using a mechanical excavator to remove large quantities of topsoil from a land site.)

As with the removal of spoil, the recovery of archaeological objects may also present problems. While you can simply place potsherds, pieces of glass, or animal bones on trays, as you would on a land site, other items may be too heavy or fragile for such treatment. Air-filled bags are the best tools for raising heavy objects like boulders. Fragile artifacts must be carefully packed into sealed containers for the hazardous journey up through the water, past the often turbulent surface, and back to the shore by boat. Often, the best padding available is sediment from the site itself. Pieces of ship's structure and some other items can be both heavy and fragile and need bracing and padding before you can lift them with safety.

Opposite: An excavation in progress; an airlift rises from the gully floor to take away the lighter spoil, while the net to the left receives larger boulders. Note the baseline along the far gully wall.
Above: Using air-filled lifting bags to raise a Spanish bronze gun; both heavy artifacts and heavier types of spoil are best lifted in this way.
Right: A pattern of small explosive charges laid out on top of an area of iron concentration. Once blown, they should allow the archaeologists to dissect the deposit in the usual way, without having damaged any of the artifacts contained within it.

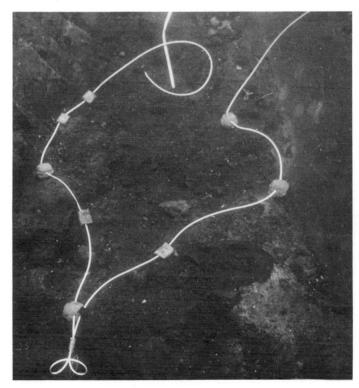

Although many excavation and recovery problems are greater than those faced by the land-based archaeologist, shifting loads by airlift or lifting-bag is much easier and quicker than trundling a wheelbarrow or hauling the ropes of a hoist. Then, too, divers can readily cross a site without fear of damage to delicate or fragile structures, since they need never touch the bottom (on land, you need to lay duckboards and gangplanks to achieve this). In many ways, then, underwater excavation is much less hard work than excavation on land. This helps to compensate for the general problems that diving involves and contributes to the impressive achievements of some teams.

Archaeologists under water

Over the past few pages, I have given an outline of the main aspects of an underwater archaeological investigation. I deliberately stressed two themes: first, the need for detailed stage-by-stage planning geared to finding answers to specific questions; second, the supreme importance of accurately recording discoveries before disturbing them. To any land archaeologist all this is routine practice, so why the fuss? The reason is the slow acceptance of these standards in maritime archaeology — a subject established only since the 1940s. On these two pages we briefly look back at its development, traced mainly through some of the leading pioneers, and discover some of the ways in which today's maritime archaeologists came to work under water. In a subject this new, everyone active in the field so far can be labeled "first generation." In fact, our contributors include a reasonable selection of the English-speaking pioneers.

Professional divers, using specialized and complex equipment, have been with us for well over a century. But only the wartime invention of the aqualung gave ordinary people the chance to work freely under water without undue exertion or excessive training. Nevertheless, it was military and commercial concerns that first took up the idea of archaeological work on the seabed. The Undersea Research Group of the French navy became the first body to attempt an excavation under water; under the direction of Commandant Jacques-Yves Cousteau, one of the inventors of the aqualung, the group in 1952 investigated a Roman wreck site off the islet of Le Grand Congloué near Marseilles. Other members of this group, notably Philippe Tailliez and Frédéric Dumas, subsequently explored a number of wrecks off the French Mediterranean coast during the 1950s. They recovered much interesting material. But some of them became increasingly conscious of the need for direct archaeological supervision on the seabed (p. 53).

One of the spurs to action behind these projects was the increased popularity of diving as a recreation in the emerging affluent society. Sports divers were removing much important ancient material as souvenirs or for profit. But archaeologists came to see club divers not only as a threat but also as a potential reservoir of labor for research. In their turn, many divers in a number of countries came to realize that a responsibly conducted investigation could be much more interesting and challenging than simple looting.

In Britain, divers from around Portsmouth and Southampton in Hampshire have produced a notable example of this attitude. Under the direction of Alexander McKee, in 1965 they launched Project Solent Ships, which directly led to the discovery of the Tudor warship *Mary Rose*; her excavation and recovery became the biggest underwater project attempted in British archaeology. In Ireland, years of searching by members of the City of Derry Sub-Aqua Club bore fruit with the discovery in 1971 of the Spanish Armada galleon *Trinidad Valencera*. In the years that followed, these divers provided the work force for extensive excavations (p. 96). In southern France, the divers of the Agde Underwater Archaeological Research Group, led by Denis Fonquerle, have discovered and excavated many important prehistoric and classical sites. In North America we can see the same spirit of amateur endeavor in the excellent site work undertaken by members of the

Left: A diving archaeologist setting up a camera on a prepared frame ready for stereophotogrammetry (p. 17). Practical skills are required of such researchers as well as standard academic accomplishments and the ability to dive. Opposite: Excavation is a skill required of any archaeologist. Here, the diver is defining the limits of a cargo of amphorae that has already been labeled and gridded out.

Newfoundland Marine Archaeology Society, notably at Bay Bulls, Trinity and Conche.

Among those who entered underwater archaeology from academic backgrounds, by no means all have come from archaeology itself. Dr. Nicholas Flemming (p. 162) who undertook his first archaeological survey in 1958, is a professional oceanographer. Dr. Ian Morrison (p. 132) is a lecturer in geography. To these people archaeology remains a subsidiary interest, but it has become the main employment of some others, for example, Jeremy Green (p. 120), who entered the field through research in underwater instrumentation. A new discipline such as this benefits greatly from contributions from a variety of backgrounds. However, since about 1960 a number of archaeologists have also emerged who are prepared to dive in the course of their research. For some, as with Margaret Rule of the *Mary Rose* project, or George Bass (p. 32), in southern Turkey, the stimulus was involvement with one important site. For others, like Dr. Anthony Parker (p. 50), research in an aspect of economic archaeology led naturally to a consideration of the evidence from sites under water.

Whatever their backgrounds, how do people working in this field find themselves placed today? In some countries – for instance, France, Italy, and Greece – there are national marine archaeological services with their own professional staffs. Some states in the U.S.A. have set up similar bodies; among our own contributors, W. A. Cockrell (p. 138) and J. Barto Arnold III (p. 102) serve in such agencies. Certain governments delegate the responsibility for sites under water to national maritime museums; thus in Sweden, Dr. Carl Cederlund (p. 78) heads an underwater research unit in the museum at Stockholm. A few universities have sponsored research departments to work in this field. Well-established examples include the Institut d'Archéologie Mediterranée at Aix-en-Provence in southern France, directed by professors André Tchernia and Patrice Pomey, and the Institute of Maritime Archaeology at St. Andrews in Scotland, with Colin Martin (p. 90) as director. But in most universities, maritime studies form no part of the ordinary archaeological courses, and there is no sponsorship for underwater work. Similarly there is no governmental sponsorship of the subject in some major maritime countries.

Thus, with local exceptions, diving archaeology remains generally unrecognized as a profession. Indeed, in many countries we may question whether the academic establishment yet fully accepts underwater archaeologists as a subgroup in the archaeological profession. This scarcely need surprise us in view of the newness of the subject, the wide range of backgrounds of its practitioners, and its dependence on equipment and methods not familiar to the average archaeologist. However, the pioneering stage is past, and further progress depends on the intensive development of improved tools and techniques allied to a number of well-conceived long-term research programs. This progress can come only if those archaeologists who go under water receive the same recognition and support as their dry-land colleagues. This atlas to a large extent summarizes the achievements of the first generation of such people and in so doing makes the case for fostering the second generation.

Shipping in the past

As we noted in the Prologue, the first and largest group of sites discussed below is shipwrecks. Before looking at individual sites, then, I shall devote a few pages to considering the special position of ships and seafaring within archaeology.

Ships have always been especially important, being the largest and most complex objects produced in most societies before the industrial revolution. As means of transport, they remained unrivaled until the advent of aircraft. In other spheres, only mining has occasionally approached ship-construction and operation in terms of technical and organizational complexity, quantity of natural power harnessed, and numbers of workers employed.

In effect, boats (and later ships) formed the "leading edge" of the technologies of most preindustrial societies from the Mesolithic (Middle Stone Age) period onward. Finds of more than 10,000 year-old fish remains from Mesolithic sites in northern Europe show that the inhabitants had the ability to reach deep waters, several kilometers offshore. We presume their craft were either skin boats or wooden dugouts. Either type was more complex than any other Mesolithic structures and we know of no other Mesolithic product that would have taken so long to make or have involved so many people and so many kinds of tool. The subsequent development of metal tools no doubt enabled craftsmen to produce more complex and sophisticated vessels, like those carved on rocks in Bronze Age Scandinavia.

Turning to early civilizations, we find advances in shipbuilding proceeding hand in hand with the growth of towns and cities, and the development of monumental buildings. The pyramids, temples, and obelisks of ancient Egypt are themselves witnesses to the size and sophistication of the river craft in which men transported massive building stones from quarries. Then, too, the refinement of classical Greek architecture is mirrored by the elegance and efficiency of the oared warships with which Greek city-states preserved their independence. Later, the immense scale of Roman civic buildings and engineering works paralleled the merchantmen of more than 1,000 tons employed to carry grain from Egypt to Italy. Finally, in the post-medieval period, the age of transoceanic exploration and colonization became possible through a revolution in naval architecture that left shipbuilders unsurpassed among manufacturers for skill and their demands upon materials (especially timber) and labor.

Ships and shipping have also made a powerful social impact. You see one aspect of this in the creation of a specialized seafaring group within a society and sometimes of a whole seafaring community, with its own peculiar customs and conventions. The development of such seafaring cultures plainly depends on a certain degree of economic development, permitting a division of labor between communities, and methods of exchange enabling such groups to trade to their mutual advantage. We do not know when this situation first arose, but it could have happened as early as the Stone Age. Nevertheless, a mutual mistrust and misunderstanding between seafarers

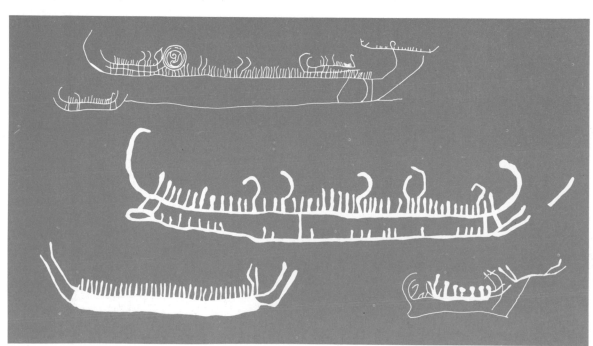

Left: The log-boat recovered in 1863 from Giggleswick Tarn in Yorkshire. Examples of vessels of this type are known from all periods between Mesolithic times and the onset of industrialization. Artists have portrayed boats, ships, and their equipment throughout the ages, reflecting their continuing importance, and providing historians and archaeologists with valuable information. During the Bronze Age in Scandinavia, boats and their crews were frequently depicted in carvings made on bare rock outcrops (left). Later, the ancient Greeks sometimes decorated their fine tableware with representations of ships. On the example shown here (above, right), there is a high-sided merchantman to the left, and a low, sleek warship to the right. In more recent times, artists have celebrated both the wealth and the power arising from a successful shipping industry. The former is reflected in the eighteenth-century woodcut (right) from the Netherlands, showing a fleet of Dutch East Indiamen. Naval might is represented in the nineteenth-century engraving (above, right) of a carronade on the upper deck of HMS *Victory*.

and their rural or urban neighbors often led to the seafarers' isolation and hence a lack of contemporary written evidence about them. This makes archaeological study of such groups especially important.

Besides creating seafaring social groups, ships and shipping have had a broader social impact. Among more primitive groups, the cooperative effort of building a boat may trigger a series of reciprocal obligations with a variety of economic, political, or religious consequences. In the Athens of the fifth century BC, national security depended on the trireme warships and their oarsmen. The latter were recruited from among the citizenry, who thus acquired the political influence to produce the world's first democracy. In imperial Rome, the emperor's control of the grain ships and the distribution of their cargoes helped maintain his power.

Perhaps the greatest impact of the ship has been economic. For Stone Age societies, the ability to go to sea to fish added considerably to food resources. Once metal-working emerged, long-distance exchange of ores, manufactured goods, and food-stuffs nourished the growth of widely separated economic systems, encouraged some to specialize, and led to regional dependence on imported products. For example, in the fifth century BC, Athens relied on seaborne grain imported from the Black Sea area; and, later, imperial Rome would have starved without Egyptian wheat. For heavy objects and bulk cargoes, shipping remained the only effective means of transportation until the arrival of the railroad; even in the sixteenth century AD, transporting goods by water was 25–50 times cheaper per ton per mile than shifting goods by road. For transportation overseas ships remained unrivaled until the advent of the aircraft.

Besides distributing foods and other materials, ships have helped disseminate ideas. In recent years, archaeologists have reacted against the old notion of the (largely seaborne) diffusion of civilization from a Near Eastern nucleus. Instead, they have seized on clear evidence for the local and independent inventions of such basic skills as agriculture and metalworking. But this, too, could be an oversimplification, and long-distance seaborne contacts may have at least contributed to the development of European civilization.

While ships have helped to spread discoveries from place to place, improvements in nautical technology have also led to new inventions in other fields. Thus there is a clear connection between eighteenth-century advances in casting cannons for the Royal Navy, and the development of efficient cylinders for steam engines.

Despite their crucial role in so many kinds of cultural developments, ships and shipping have not until recently attracted their fair share of archaeological attention. There were two main reasons. One was the sheer lack of information about old vessels before underwater excavation became possible. The second reason for neglecting this important branch of archaeology was the low status and inwardlooking nature of seafaring peoples in most societies. This made them less attractive subjects for study than urban or agricultural communities. Technical advances and changes in social attitudes have at last begun to change this.

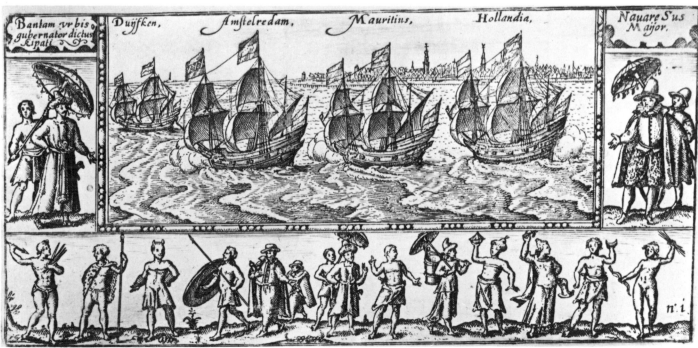

The formation of wreck sites

A ship is an organized assemblage of objects and materials designed to perform certain functions. When she is holed or capsized, this organization begins to break down. She may sink to the seabed intact or arrive there in pieces. Either way, over the centuries, waves, currents, and marine creatures may break up and scatter the remains of the vessel. Because archaeologists are ultimately interested not in wrecks but in the ships these once were, their principal task is untangling such disorganization.

To help you grasp what this may involve we shall now look at the two groups of processes that can affect a vessel and her contents during and after shipwreck. The first group comprises what we may call extracting filters because these tend to remove or destroy objects, as it were, filtering them out of the wreck site. The second group of processes simply rearranges items within the wreck assemblage. Because rearrangement makes it difficult to understand how and why the items are related to one another (that is, it distorts the message coming through to us), we may label these processes scrambling devices.

There are three extracting filters. The first operates during shipwreck, when the mechanical forces of winds, waves, and currents may make certain objects break loose from the ship and float away. This dispersal affects some substances more than others. Often, cargo and ballast are heavy

and sink. Wood, the most plentiful material on old vessels, may sink or float according to its variety and whether or not it is waterlogged; but most of the wood that sinks does so because it is weighed down by overlying, heavy, high-density objects. Lightweight wooden ships without ballast may drift off, as may pieces of wood that break from a stricken vessel.

Once a wrecked ship has sunk to the seabed, the second extracting filter comes into play: chemical and biological agents set to work to degrade and destroy various objects. Those made of certain substances will simply disintegrate, but the rate and intensity of destruction largely depend upon local chemical conditions.

Salvage work is the third type of extracting filter operating to remove objects from a wreck site. It is surprising how much men could recover with grapnels and free diving, even thousands of years ago, and archaeologists should always bear this in mind. However, they can usually recognize a site too deep to have attracted salvage disturbance. Of course, for some relatively recent wrecks, there may be detailed documentary evidence of the salvage recovered.

Within limits, archaeologists can usually assess the general effects of all these extracting filters; but with scrambling devices – those processes that rearrange bits of a wreck – the calculations can be more complex. You cannot readily watch wrecking and seabed movement (the two processes

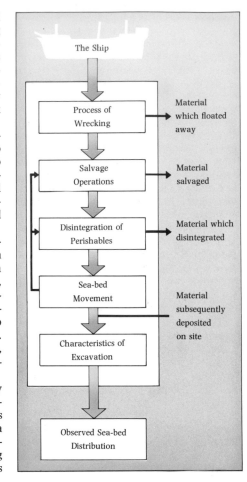

The Ship

Process of Wrecking → Material which floated away

Salvage Operations → Material salvaged

Disintegration of Perishables → Material which disintegrated

Sea-bed Movement → Material subsequently deposited on site

Characteristics of Excavation

Observed Sea-bed Distribution

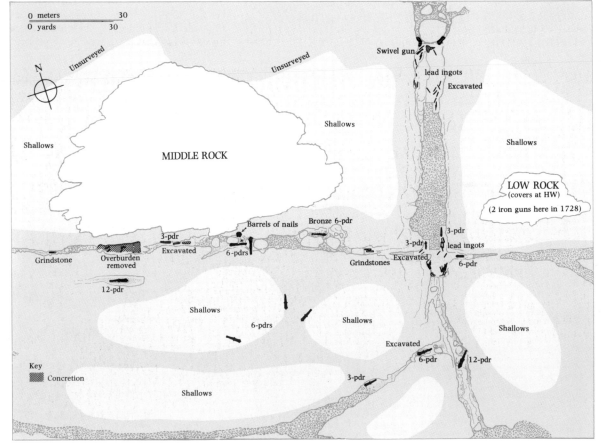

Above: A flow diagram showing the development of a wreck site, from functioning ship to a scatter of objects on the seafloor.

Left: A map of the wrecksite of the *Adelaar*, a Dutch East Indiaman lost in 1728. With the scanty remains confined to narrow gullies, this represents a highly scattered site. Contrast this with the structural integrity of a wreck precisely a century older, the *Wasa* (opposite). This photograph was taken shortly after she was raised in 1959.

Above, opposite: A classical Mediterranean amphora mound photographed after archaeologists had sectioned it. Note the wooden hulk remains to the right, formerly protected by the cargo.

involved) as they happen, and there are few general principles that help you to grasp how these processes have affected an individual site. Often, the best clue to how a wreck occurred is the spread of remains across the site, related to the wind direction or tidal regime at the time the shipwreck took place, if this is known. Surviving archives and local folk traditions about the wrecking can also be helpful, as they were for the *Kennemerland* (p. 124).

You might expect oceanographers or geomorphologists to help explain how seabed movement has affected the different bits of a wreck. Unfortunately, these scientists tend to study the movements of large masses of material, as in sandbanks and beaches, while we need to know the behavior of individual items. The only solution is to study local prevailing winds, tidal flows, and so on, and to deduce the likely ways in which these may have affected a site. The kinds of plant that grow on a site can give you a good idea of the extent to which it suffers from strong water movement. Finally, you can check the overall picture by laying an experimental deposit of objects of different substances and seeing how water movement affects them over several seasons. The snag here is that the behavior of your tracers depends on weather conditions that may not match those just after the original wrecking. Also, such tests take no account of the profound effect of the "big storm": the severe gale that may occur only once a century.

The sites that we shall describe have suffered to varying extents from these filters and scrambling devices. Their effects have obviously been least severe where the ship and her contents remain substantially intact. But even the *Wasa* (pp. 82–83) had lost much material from seventeenth-century salvage operations, and most wrecks have lost large structural sections, especially from the upper parts. Thus much of the upperworks and all the port side are missing from the *Mary Rose*, Henry VIII's warship sunk in the mud off Portsmouth in Hampshire.

Mediterranean waters hold many examples of a type of site on which a part of the hull may be preserved. Known as the amphora mound, this type occurs when a stricken ship loaded with wine jars or oil jars sank into deep water. Currents piled seabed sediments around the wreck, producing a characteristic mound. Sea creatures ate away any wood exposed to open water, but amphorae protected the hull bottom, although this often became flat-

tened out and otherwise distorted. The French diving pioneer Frédéric Dumas recognized and described this type of wreck during the 1950s. Particularly common along the south coast of France, examples also occur throughout the Mediterranean, as at Yassi Ada, Turkey (pp. 36–39) and Kyrenia, Cyprus (pp. 40–45).

Ships with ballast or heavy cargo of almost any kind can settle, and be partly preserved, in a similar manner, provided sediment soon covers the structure. A good example is the *Dartmouth* site, on the west coast of Scotland (pp. 100–101), where about one third of the lower part of the starboard side has survived.

Substantial remains of wooden structures are much less likely to survive if the vessel breaks up on the surface, and only heavy objects drop to the seafloor. Obviously, this happens frequently. Here, we shall meet examples including prehistoric cargoes (pp. 62–65), classical traders (p. 60), and Atlantic galleons (pp. 102–19). These show that we can still glean a great deal of archaeological evidence from even the most scattered and fragmentary remains. The wreck of the Dutch East Indiaman *Adelaar* (p. 126) on the exposed, rocky, western coast of Barra in the Outer Hebrides off Scotland represents a truly disorganized site; heavily depleted by natural forces and contemporary salvage. Nevertheless, Colin Martin's excavations of 1972–74 have revealed a good deal about the ship, her armament, and her cargo. Examples like this drive home the fact that studying the process of wreck formation is an essential step toward interpreting a wreck site and understanding the ship that this represents.

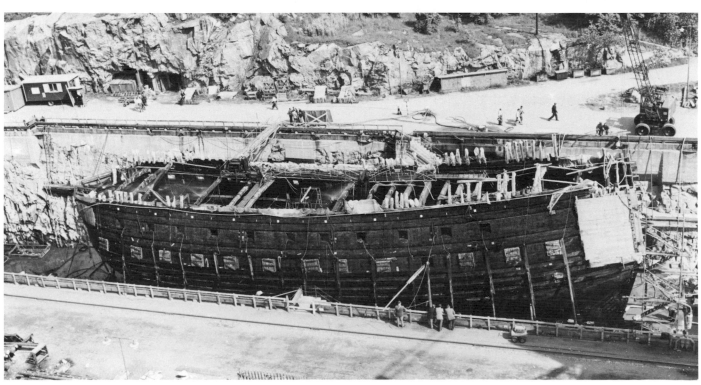

The interpretation of wreck sites

On any archaeological site, the excavator is interested chiefly in two things: content and context. On a wreck site, this means what you can find of the original vessel, and what relationships you can discover between the various pieces. You must then interpret this information in the light of what you know about the processes that created the wreck site (p. 26).

We can consider a wreck site's content under three heads. First, and most obviously, there will be evidence concerning the original vessel and her equipment. Even a small section of structure may be enough to enable the archaeologist to reconstruct hull lines and other structural details. I discuss some of the principal considerations involved in such studies on the next two pages (pp. 30–31).

Some commentators have objected to archaeologists' seeking to deduce overall traditions of naval architecture from wreck-site evidence. These critics argue that wrecked ships are unlikely to be typical of their time and place. They would point out that the *Wasa* (pp. 82–83) sank (and survived) because she possessed a design fault, or that our knowledge of Dark Age and early medieval shipping is unhealthily dependent on grave-ships (pp. 68–73). Furthermore, whole classes of vessel may seldom enter the archaeological record; one particularly significant group are the oared

warships of classical antiquity. These were lightweight, and carried little or no ballast or stores. When holed, they therefore tended to float until recovered or smashed to pieces. Our only examples are two vessels excavated by the British archaeologist Honor Frost at Marsala in western Sicily; both appear to have been deliberately rammed into the sand. The lack of comparable finds elsewhere means that we cannot include a detailed account of such early warships in these pages. But while these biases undoubtedly affect our evidence, most are easy to spot and can be allowed for. Experience suggests that the most important single cause of the loss of ships is human error, and there are no reasons to suppose that any one type of vessel has been more subject to this than others. Provided we exercise general archaeological caution, there seem no good reasons to reject wreck sites as a basis for the study of shipbuilding traditions.

The second element in a wreck's content will be material reflecting the vessel's original purpose: cargo in a merchantman, and armaments in a warship. Finds on an individual site can thus give archaeologists insights into contemporary economic trends. Several examples appear in this book, for instance, relating to Bronze Age trade in the Mediterranean (pp. 32–35) and the English Channel (pp. 62–65), and to classical-

period trading across the western Mediterranean (pp. 50–59).

Finally, a wreck's contents are likely to reflect something about the society on board: the way of life of the officers, crew, and passengers. We have already noted (p. 25) how seafaring communities have not attracted scholarly attention to the same extent as their landbound contemporaries, so this evidence has considerable research potential. Projects such as the reconstruction of the amenities on the

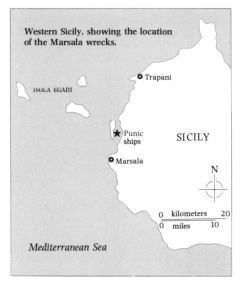

Western Sicily, showing the location of the Marsala wrecks.

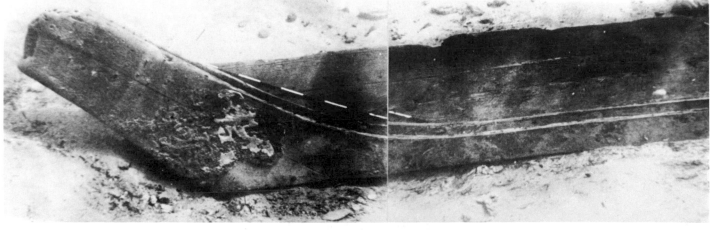

A number of wrecks were found buried in the sand at Motya near Marsala. Opposite: the stern part of one was particularly well preserved, and is shown in the upper picture during excavation. On another vessel the prow and stempost had survived, together with two "tusks," intended to hold a projecting ram. This is shown in the lower picture, on which you can also pick out a Punic letter (the WAW) painted on the nearer "tusk" just to the left of the fifth nailhole from the left. This may have been a builder's mark. Above: A collection of bone dice from the wreck of the Dutch East Indiaman *Kennemerland* (1664).

seventh-century Yassi Ada ship (p. 36) point the way to future progress in this field.

Context — the archaeologist's second major concern — may also involve him in a wide range of studies. For example, the type of social reconstruction just mentioned is possible only if the excavators have carefully recorded the seabed locations of every object. Generally speaking, the more dis-

organized the remains, the more complex the analysis needed for their interpretation. When a hull is substantially intact, the excavator only has to locate everything with reference to the structure. The cargo will be in the hold, the stores in the boatswain's locker, the officers' possessions in the aft cabins, and so forth.

Difficult analytical problems arise, however, when the remains are more scattered. Comparing the locations of different groups of objects may mean that the archaeologist has to use sophisticated methods of spatial analysis. Dr. Parker (pp. 60–61) shows how such a study led to the disentangling of several wrecks on one site in Marzamemi Bay off Sicily. I present below a similar analysis of the remains of the seventeenth-century frigate *Dartmouth*. Here we are seeking patterns we can relate to the lie of the vessel when she broke up, as evidenced by the hull remains. Of course, at some sites the scattering is so confused that no system of analysis will ever sort out the evidence; the *Adelaar* site (p. 27) probably falls in this category.

With its natural emphasis on maps and plans, this atlas is concerned above all with context. A glance through the contributions below should be enough to show that, to an archaeologist, interpreting a site's context matters as much as acquiring its entire content.

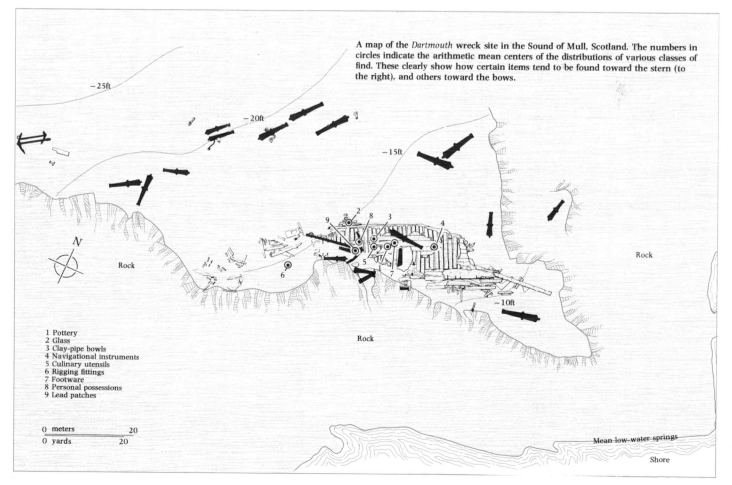

A map of the *Dartmouth* wreck site in the Sound of Mull, Scotland. The numbers in circles indicate the arithmetic mean centers of the distributions of various classes of find. These clearly show how certain items tend to be found toward the stern (to the right), and others toward the bows.

1 Pottery
2 Glass
3 Clay-pipe bowls
4 Navigational instruments
5 Culinary utensils
6 Rigging fittings
7 Footware
8 Personal possessions
9 Lead patches

0 meters 20
0 yards 20

The interpretation of ship remains

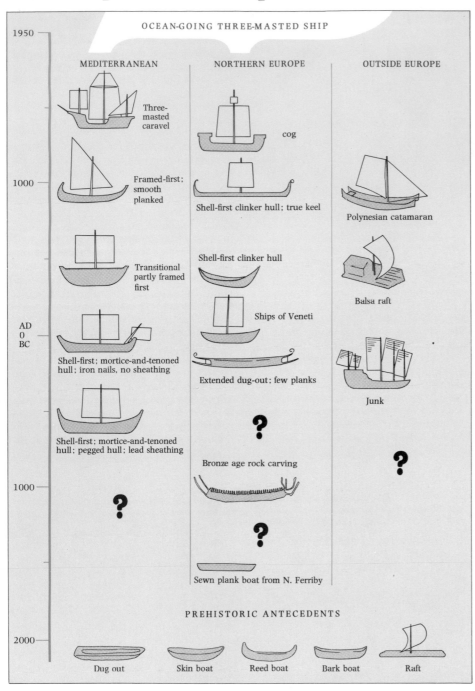

OCEAN-GOING THREE-MASTED SHIP

1950

MEDITERRANEAN

NORTHERN EUROPE

OUTSIDE EUROPE

Three-masted caravel

cog

1000

Framed-first; smooth planked

Shell-first clinker hull; true keel

Polynesian catamaran

Transitional partly framed first

Shell-first clinker hull

Balsa raft

AD
0
BC

Shell-first; mortice-and-tenoned hull; iron nails, no sheathing

Ships of Veneti

Shell-first; mortice-and-tenoned hull; pegged hull; lead sheathing

Extended dug-out; few planks

Junk

1000

?

?

Bronze age rock carving

?

?

Sewn plank boat from N. Ferriby

PREHISTORIC ANTECEDENTS

2000

Dug out   Skin boat   Reed boat   Bark boat   Raft

Ships' hulls are complex structures and many of those from previous centuries were built in ways unfamiliar to modern man. For that reason, old hull remains present particular difficulties in interpretation. This is despite the fact that certain features, such as lateral symmetry and the need for fair lines, allow the skilled investigator to reconstruct a complete vessel from as little as 10% of the whole. In the past, researchers have frequently made mistakes by assuming that early shipbuilders used modern methods and concepts. The American nautical archaeologists Frederick H. van Doornick, Jr., and J. Richard Steffy have shown by their exhaustive studies on the hulls from Yassi Ada, Kyrenia, and Serçe Limani (pp. 36–49) that only meticulous observation and recording of every feature can reveal the tools and techniques used.

Despite all the difficulties, such research is now possible, thanks to the development of archaeology under water. The sheer number of sites, and the preservation of timbers on many of them, allows us to contemplate the development of detailed histories of ship construction in various regions. Much of this would have been inconceivable even a decade or so back. The approximations and ambiguities of the accompanying time chart, and its European emphasis, indicate how much remains to be found. Despite this, it represents a creditable monument to the first few decades of excavation under water. For certain periods and places, we are now able to identify and comprehend distinctive shipbuilding procedures in some detail. I describe the main features of three of these procedures on the opposite page in order to help you to understand them where they occur in the accounts that follow.

Left: A time-chart giving a general impression of the principal types of craft being used over the past four thousand years in the Mediterranean, northern Europe, and elsewhere. In various ways, the craft shown can be seen as developments from the five simple boat forms shown at the bottom, all of which were probably in use in earlier prehistoric times.

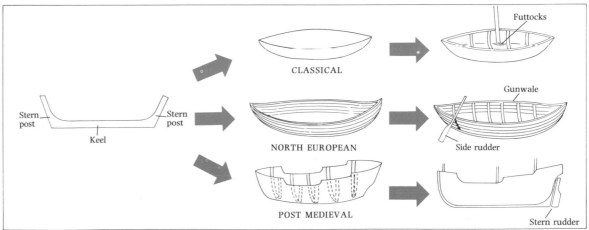

Futtocks

CLASSICAL

Stern post   Stern post

Keel

Gunwale

NORTH EUROPEAN

Side rudder

POST MEDIEVAL

Stern rudder

Below, left: A schematic representation of three methods of boat-building which were widespread in the past. In every case, the boat builder began by laying down the keel, and attaching stem and stern posts to it. (left). In the upper sequence, a shell of smooth planking is seen at the next stage, before internal frames and other fittings are finally added. This procedure was used, for example, in the Mediterranean in classical times. In the central line a shell of clinker planking is created instead, as done, for example, in northern Europe in Viking times. In the lower sequence, by contrast, the ship's frames have been set up before the planking is added, a procedure generally used in Europe in recent centuries.
Right: A series of drawings and sections of boat and ship elements, showing the location and function of all the technical terms in naval architecture used later in this Atlas.

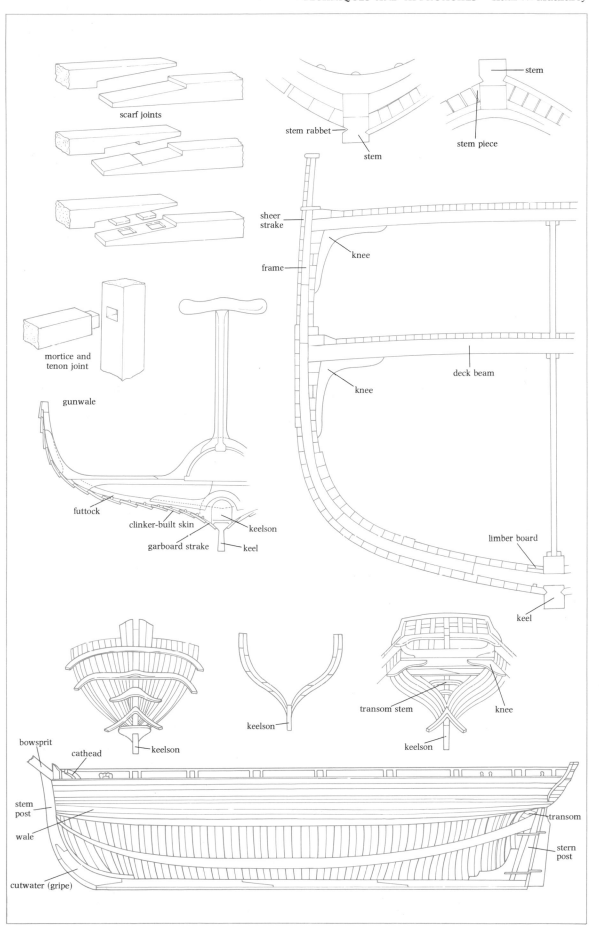

scarf joints

stem

stem rabbet

stem piece

stem

sheer strake

knee

frame

knee

deck beam

mortice and tenon joint

gunwale

limber board

futtock

clinker-built skin

keelson

garboard strake

keel

keel

transom stem

knee

keelson

keelson

keelson

bowsprit

cathead

keelson

stem post

wale

transom

stern post

cutwater (gripe)

Mediterranean Wreck Sites and Classical Seafaring

We begin our tour of specific sites and themes with classical shipwrecks in the Mediterranean. This is appropriate because collectively they form the earliest group of sites that we shall meet. Moreover, the Mediterranean saw the first underwater excavations, and the evolution of many of the basic tools and techniques of underwater archaeology.

Our first contributor is Professor George Bass, an American archaeologist who played a major part in these developments. While researching at the University of Pennsylvania, Bass was invited to direct the excavation of the Bronze Age site at Cape Gelidonya in Turkey. He learned to dive and, by personally directing the work on the seabed, achieved the first fully

recorded excavation under water. After that first season in 1960, he led further projects off the south coast of Turkey. In 1973 he established the Institute of Nautical Archaeology (of which he is president) to advance his own and his colleagues' researches; he is now based at Texas A&M University.

Maintaining a chronological sequence of investigations, we interrupt the Bass excavations with six pages contributed by Professor Michael Katzev, vice-president of the Institute of Nautical Archaeology. Professor Katzev describes the excavation of the fourth-century BC Kyrenia ship, a landmark in the development of techniques by this team. Professor Katzev is now attached to the American School of Classical Studies in Athens.

Next we turn to the western Mediterranean, where hundreds of wreck sites have been discovered, and investigated with widely varying degrees of competence. It seemed appropriate to invite Dr. Anthony Parker to consider some of the broad historical themes illuminated by so much material. A lecturer in the department of classics and archaeology at Bristol University, England, Dr. Parker became involved in this subject when research into the economy of Roman Spain made him realize that wreck sites could provide new insights into ancient production and distribution. He has directed several investigations of wreck sites off eastern Sicily.

A pioneering excavation off Turkey

The investigation of wreck sites in the 1950s had left much to be desired because of the absence of any diving archaeologists controlling work on the seabed (p. 52). In 1960 we set out to demonstrate that higher standards were possible, with the excavation of the oldest shipwreck then known, at Cape Gelidonya in southwest Turkey. I and several fellow archaeologists learned to dive specifically in order to participate in this work, and together we achieved the first total excavation of an ancient Mediterranean wreck.

Notes taken from Turkish sponge divers had led the American photojournalist Peter Throckmorton to the site in 1959. He found a mound submerged at an average depth of 27 meters (90ft) between two islands in a chain extending from Cape Gelidonya. Sample finds suggested a uniquely ancient site, and the University of Pennsylvania Museum accordingly sponsored an expedition for its excavation in 1960.

We found that the ship had settled on an uneven bottom with little sand to cover and protect her wooden hull from shipworm. Thus only small fragments of wood survived. Possibly ceiling strakes (p. 31), they lay under the well-preserved brushwood dunnage, or "cushioning," on which heavy cargo rested; wooden pegs fastened some of the fragments to a piece showing signs of scarf joints (p. 31). But the precise function of none of these pieces is certain. Drawings of the wood made on the seabed and later published may lead to an accurate interpretation when future excavations reveal more of Bronze Age construction techniques. Fascinatingly, both dunnage and hull fragments match those described by Homer in his lines on the departure of Odysseus from Calypso's island.

We dated the ship from the brushwood's radiocarbon content and by stylistic analysis of pottery on board. Both studies point to 1200 BC ± 50 years.

We could only estimate the vessel's size from distribution plans of cargo; these suggest a length of 9 or 10 meters (30–33ft).

Site plans reveal, too, that most of what we believe to be the crew's personal possessions lay at one end of the wreck, representing perhaps a cabin area or some kind of living quarters. Here we found a cylinder seal of the type carried by most Near Eastern merchants; five scarabs (stone beetles used as talismans); an oil lamp; two stone hammers or maceheads; a whetstone; stone polishers; and several sets of polished stone balance weights (mostly of the iron ore hematite).

Above: Setting up the camp site on the beach near Cape Gelidonya; this was the team's home for three months.
Right: The only cylinder seal recovered from the wreck, showing one of the three male figures that were drawn on it. This one is wearing an Egyptian-style costume.

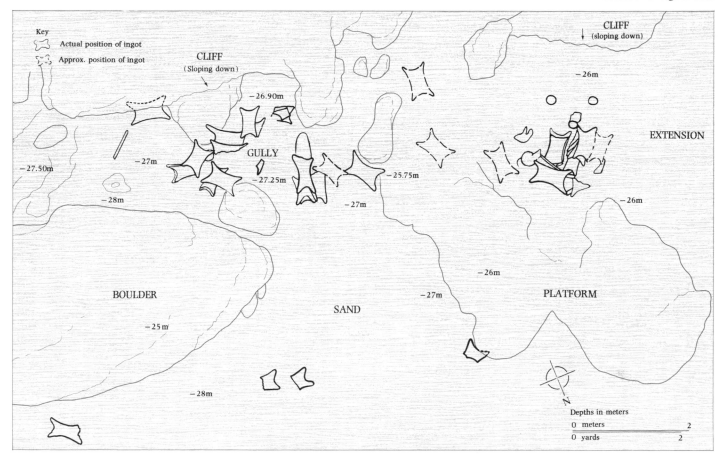

All these and two stone mortars found elsewhere on the wreck are of Syro-Palestinian origin; similar Syro-Palestinian artifacts have been found on Cyprus, which could have been the source of some of those on board. It is harder to determine the origins of unworked crystal from the "cabin" area and its bronze implements — razor, punch, spatula, needles, and chisels. Nevertheless, the evidence strongly suggests a Near Eastern, probably Canaanite, crew.

Olive stones in the same area represent a meal taken on board, but a single knuckle-bone from a sheep or goat may have provided "divine" guidance at sea, for men who tossed it as we now toss dice.

The bulk of the ship's preserved cargo comprised 34 four-handled ingots of nearly pure copper, averaging 25 kilograms (55lb) apiece; disk-shaped copper ingots weighing about 3 kilograms (6lb 9oz); flat, oval ingots, at least one of which is bronze, weighing 0.5–1.5 kilograms (1–3½lb); residue from tin ingots, probably rectangular in shape; broken bronze tools including axes; adzes; plowshares; pruning hooks; a spade; chisels; knives; and bits of bronze-casting waste.

Most of this cargo, weighing altogether about a ton, was encased in marine concretion up to 15 centimeters (6in) thick. We plotted individual masses of concretion under water, using triangulation with meter tapes stretched from iron spikes driven into the seabed around the site. We added details

Above: A plan of the wreck site at Cape Gelidonya, showing the distribution of copper ingots.
Above: An archaeologist drawing the features in a lump of concretion at Cape Gelidonya, preparatory to lifting it from the seabed.

of these concretions to our plans with the help of underwater drawings and photographs, including a crude photomontage made with a hand-held camera. Then we used hammers and chisels to break separate concretions into manageable pieces weighing up to 100 kilograms (220lb). Next, we raised these to the surface with air-filled balloons or by cable and winch. Back on land we fitted the broken lumps together, and recorded them in detail. Then we carefully freed the cargo from its stony matrix. This work revealed ingots still stacked as they had been in the ancient hull, and scrap bronze and bits of copper ingots packed in wicker baskets. We carefully recorded each step in this dissection so that our plans should show the position of each artifact as we found it on the site.

What we had found was scrap bronze destined to be remelted and recast, along with copper and tin to be amalgamated into new bronze. Stone hammers, a whetstone, and stone polishers from the "cabin" area suggest that a tinker may have been on board; a large, flat, fine-grained stone found on the site could have been his anvil. We did, however, find one obvious metal-working tool, a bronze swage, at the opposite end of the wreck, far from the other intact tools. Perhaps this too was part of the scrap cargo. Taken together, this ship and her cargo had far-reaching archaeological implications, some of which I discuss overleaf.

Lessons from a Bronze Age wreck

No matter how carefully you organize archaeological excavation on land or under water, this work is not an end in itself; nor is the simple identification and publication of excavated finds. Only when you interpret archaeological discoveries in relation to their historical and cultural context do they gain their full meaning.

But interpretation can be tricky. Thus the Cape Gelidonya wreck that we have just examined was evidently Canaanite in origin; but we should not use this solitary find to infer that the Canaanites had an overseas trade network. Nevertheless, a study of objects found at Cape Gelidonya has led to a fruitful reexamination of similar discoveries made previously around the central and eastern Mediterranean. The resulting reevaluation of these finds has strengthened theories of Bronze Age trade that few people accepted at the time of the Cape Gelidonya excavation.

Most prehistorians used to hold that Mediterranean maritime trade was largely in the hands of Mycenaean (late Bronze Age Greek) merchants, at least between 1400 and 1200 BC. The supposed proof for this was Mycenaean pottery found from Sicily and mainland Italy to the Levant, usually at coastal sites, or cities connected to the sea by rivers. People naturally assumed that Mycenaean wares had reached these places on board Mycenaean ships.

The earlier centuries of late Bronze Age trade, between 1600 and 1400 BC, had been more difficult to explain. In that period, Mycenaean pottery seems to have been the chief Aegean import in the Levant, but contemporary Egyptian paintings of Aegean peoples usually depict not Mycenaeans but Minoans from Bronze Age Crete (or *Keftiu*, as the Egyptians called that island). However, Egyptian painters also sometimes labeled typical Syrians as derived from Keftiu, suggesting a complex internationality of foreign contacts. By the fourteenth and thirteenth centuries BC, Keftiu had come to matter less to the Egyptians, but large quantities of Mycenaean pottery now reached Egypt and centers along the Syro-Palestinian coast. It was this boom in Mycenaean imports that led prehistorians to postulate a Mycenaean trading empire. Semitic maritime activity, the scholars thought, flowered only in the following Iron Age, under the impetus of Phoenician sailors.

Researchers interpreted further archaeo-logical evidence accordingly. When archaeologists excavating Bronze Age Greek sites found cylinder seals of the types Semitic merchants used to carry, they tended to regard them as souvenirs picked up by seafaring Mycenaeans. Mycenaean merchants returning from the Near East had also supposedly brought back the Canaanite jars found by archaeologists in Greece. When four-handled copper ingots like those of the Cape Gelidonya wreck turned up in Sardinia or mainland Greece, experts argued that they had been made of Cypriot copper but imported in Mycenaean hulls. Part of the reasoning for this last hypothesis rested on fifteenth-century BC Egyptian representations of four-handled copper ingots brought to the pharaoh by men from Keftiu. These pictures drove archaeologists to the conclusion that ingots of that type were always "Aegean" or "Mycenaean" in character, a notion that ignored the fact that Minoans had been linguistically and culturally distinct from Mycenaeans.

A study of the Cape Gelidonya ingots led to a search through Egyptian art that eventually revealed 16 representations of such ingots. Only the two fifteenth-century

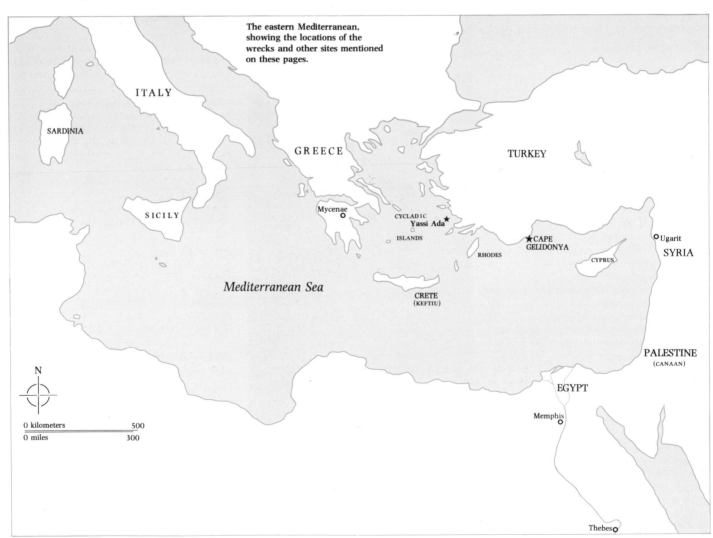

The eastern Mediterranean, showing the locations of the wrecks and other sites mentioned on these pages.

ITALY

SARDINIA

GREECE

TURKEY

SICILY

Mycenae

CYCLADIC
ISLANDS

Yassi Ada

RHODES

★ CAPE GELIDONYA

CYPRUS

Ugarit

SYRIA

Mediterranean Sea

CRETE
(KEFTIU)

PALESTINE
(CANAAN)

EGYPT

Memphis

N

0 kilometers   500
0 miles   300

Thebes

examples had any link with Crete, and in both we find hieroglyphs identifying as North Syrians the men carrying the ingots. Similar ingots depicted in the fourteenth and thirteenth centuries also seem to be Syrian in origin; in one picture the painter even showed the Syrian ship that had brought the ingots to Egypt. Therefore by the time the Cape Gelidonya shipwreck happened, Egyptians plainly considered four-handled copper ingots to be Syrian items of trade.

So much for the origin of the metal used for making tools. As for the implements themselves, we think that the broken bronze tools of the Cape Gelidonya cargo had been made on copper-rich Cyprus, where archaeologists have found identical tools, and molds for casting them. Some scholars once argued that such tools had had their origins in Bronze Age Greece, and that Mycenaean colonists had introduced them into Cyprus. Once again a study of the Cape Gelidonya cargo has led to a re-evaluation of existing evidence. A search for the earliest examples of such implements showed that archaeologists had found most prototypes in the Near East. Thus Near Eastern not Mycenaean seafarers probably influenced Cypriot bronze work.

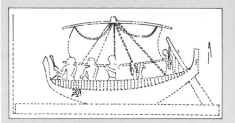

Two scenes from a painting in the tomb of Nebamun at Thebes in Egypt. Nebamun, who was a doctor, is being visited by a rich Syrian, whose boat is shown here (left). This is one of the few surviving pictures of a Bronze Age boat in the eastern Mediterranean.

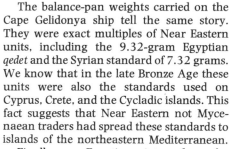

Among the gifts presented by the Syrian (right) was a large, almost rectangular, copper ingot, similar to the type found at Cape Gelidonya. These pictures illustrate the kind of trading network, apparently in the hands of the Syrians, in which the vessel wrecked at Cape Gelidonya was involved.

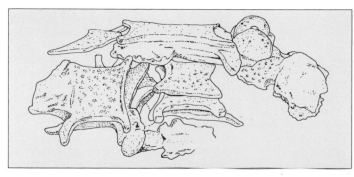

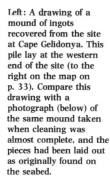

Left: A drawing of a mound of ingots recovered from the site at Cape Gelidonya. This pile lay at the western end of the site (to the right on the map on p. 33). Compare this drawing with a photograph (below) of the same mound taken when cleaning was almost complete, and the pieces had been laid out as originally found on the seabed.

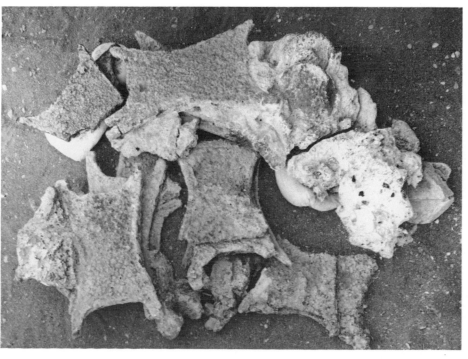

The balance-pan weights carried on the Cape Gelidonya ship tell the same story. They were exact multiples of Near Eastern units, including the 9.32-gram Egyptian *qedet* and the Syrian standard of 7.32 grams. We know that in the late Bronze Age these units were also the standards used on Cyprus, Crete, and the Cycladic islands. This fact suggests that Near Eastern not Mycenaean traders had spread these standards to islands of the northeastern Mediterranean.

Finally, one Egyptian picture from the fourteenth century BC shows an entire Syrian or Canaanite merchant fleet trading in an Egyptian port. Yet no Egyptian work of art depicts one Mycenaean ship, a strange omission if Mycenaeans truly held a maritime monopoly.

This brief summary of research stemming from the Cape Gelidonya excavation suggests that Semitic maritime trade in the late Bronze Age Mediterranean was much more active than we used to think. This interpretation does not mean we need deny that there were Mycenaean settlements on Rhodes and the coasts of Italy and Asia Minor, or that Mycenaeans had a commercial center in Canaanite Ugarit. We need not even deny that there was widespread Mycenaean seaborne commerce. But the new evidence shows the dangers of using a single imperishable commodity – in this case, pottery – to suggest theories of ancient trade. Theories thus devised ignore the goods that must have flowed to Greece in return for Greek export wares. Unfortunately, excavations in Greece have revealed few traces of these imports. Presumably they included raw materials such as copper and ivory, worked by local artisans in ways that left no clues to the nationalities of the ships that had brought those raw materials to Greece. If this is so, it explains why Near Eastern cylinder seals are the only trace of visits that Semitic merchants paid to Greece.

Recording a Byzantine merchantman

Nowhere has the importance of mapping a site in minute detail been more clearly demonstrated than in our excavation of the seventh-century Byzantine shipwreck at Yassi Ada. This was the first full excavation and interpretation of an ancient sunken vessel and the second project we undertook for the University of Pennsylvania Museum. The remains lay in 37 meters (120ft) of water off the low flat rock of Yassi Ada ("Flat Island") off southwest Turkey. In four seasons of work, 1961–64, we uncovered the flattened hull remains from underneath a cargo of amphorae, and tested a variety of mapping aids, including plane tables, wire grids, scaffolding photo towers, and stereophotography. Over 2,000 sharpened bicycle-wheel spokes were used to skewer down fragments of wood that might otherwise have been swept away by currents. Thereafter, it took 15 years to complete the post-excavation analysis of finds, the preparation of reconstructions on paper of the ship's hull, and the compilation of a final report.

Preparing these reconstructions on the basis of the evidence from the surviving 10% of the hull was the daunting task tackled by Frederick H. van Doorninck, Jr., later in collaboration with J. Richard Steffy.

Van Doorninck's findings concerning the galley alone are so extensive as to almost defy summary. The positions and angles of roof-tile and hearth-tile fragments in the wreck showed him which had remained on the galley's sloping floor when the ship listed to port on the seabed, and which had spilled outward when the vessel's port side eventually collapsed. Positions of the fragments suggested that the missing galley floor had stood somewhat above the turn of the bilge, where this has been reconstructed. Distribution patterns of the tiles and cargo further revealed that a bulkhead, now also missing, had separated the galley from the ship's hold, and that a "cooker" comprising a firebox or hearth made of tiles and iron bars had stood on the galley's port side. Pantiles and cover tiles had formed the galley's roof and the distribution of their fragments suggested to van Doorninck that the "roof had been more or less intact when the ship came to rest on the seabed."

As van Doorninck points out: "Despite a random element in the seabed distribution of the objects from the galley area (due to random movement during the process of wreck formation), significant patterns in their distribution do emerge."

Thus we now know that most of the utensils used for preparing and cooking food had been stored on the port side of the galley, just forward of the firebox or hearth. The locations of some 80 small finds between two of the ship's frames indicate the presence of some kind of storage place for valuables, probably a cupboard, in the forward part of the galley on the starboard side. Here were kept coins; weighing implements; glass; fine metal vessels; carpenter's

tools; and other items. Of the two dozen lamps on board it seems that the crew had kept those in use (the ones with fire-blackened nozzles) with the cooking utensils, but had stored new lamps with the valuables.

Strongly underlining the importance of mapping *everything* on a wreck is the history of our iron concretions. An iron object dropped into the Mediterranean can acquire a coating of marine concretion in a year. Over the centuries this coat builds up until it may be many centimeters thick. The original iron inside this concretion gradually corrodes until it almost disappears, leaving the concretion as a hollow mold. If you cut open a concretion and clean the mold you can then fill this with liquid rubber or a similar substance, to cast a perfect replica of the original iron object.

For four summers we plotted the positions of more than a hundred shapeless lumps of concretion, with no idea what, if anything, they contained. When we eventually opened them and produced our casts, we made remarkable discoveries. For one thing we discovered the ship's carpenter's tools, including an ax; adzes; a hammer-adz; a claw hammer; chisels; gouges; drill bits; dividers; files; an awl; assorted knives; and nails and tacks. All these the carpenter had stored in the forward galley "cupboard." We also found the tools used by the boatswain in foraging ashore for water and firewood. These tools were axes; a pickax; pruning hooks; and a shovel. The boatswain had kept them in an after storage area near the grapnel for his boat. Other concretions revealed the iron bars used in the construction of the firebox, and even some of the nails and bolts that had been used in construction of the vessel's hull.

Clues at least as unpromising as the concretions enabled van Doorninck to build an image of the vessel's almost vanished form. Deck, hatch, oars, and mast had all disappeared. All that van Doorninck had to go by were items like a scoreline scratched by the Byzantine shipwright on a timber; an angle of a nail or bolt hole; a tiny cutting in a wood fragment; the distances between frames. Yet from these he reconstructed the lines of the ship; the level of her deck; the position of her main hatch; the positions of the steering oars; and the probable position of her mast.

In the end we had the picture of a ship of 60 tons burden, about 21 meters (69ft) long, with a length-to-width ratio of four to one. Her keel, sternpost, and, probably, her stem were of cypress. On this framework, the shipwright had built up a hull bottom of pine planking, working in the Greco-Roman "shell-first" manner (p. 30). But he had used mortise-and-tenon joints spaced nearly a meter apart, loose fitting, and not pinned with treenails as on earlier vessels. In an early stage of hull construction he had therefore had to start installing his elm frames, or ribs, to which the strakes were fastened with iron nails. Experimental models show that he had probably installed short floors after just a few strakes had been completed. Next, he had added more strakes, then longer floors. Above the waterline level, however, he had erected the rest of the ship's skeleton and simply fastened on the remaining planking strakes, omitting mortise-and-tenon joints altogether. In other words, he had built his ship largely in the "ancient manner" below the waterline, and in the "modern manner" above it. This provides evidence for an important stage in the evolution from ancient to modern hull construction.

We have this fairly accurate picture of a seventh-century Byzantine ship entirely because of careful mapping on the seabed. Before this excavation, our only knowledge of ships dating from this period came from old but inexact illustrations and ambiguous references.

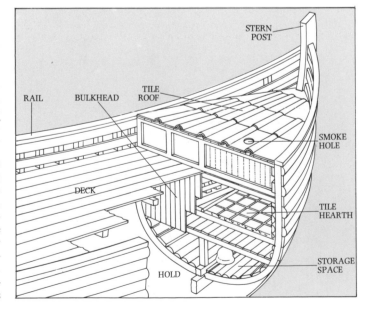

Left: A reconstruction of the galley area at the stern of the Byzantine merchantman. It was roofed with alternating flat and curved tiles. The tile hearth lay on the port side; its precise form remains conjectural.

STERN POST

RAIL BULKHEAD TILE ROOF

SMOKE HOLE

DECK

TILE HEARTH

STORAGE SPACE

HOLD

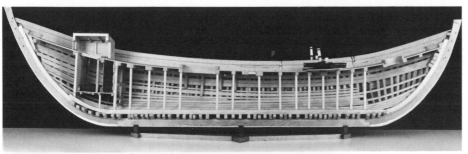

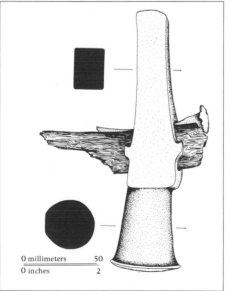

Above, top: A model of the merchantman, built by J. Richard Steffy. It shows clearly her framing and internal layout, including the stern galley (to left).
Above, center: A diver surveying some of the vessel's timbers on the seabed.
Left: A drawing of an iron metal-working hammer, one of the many tools recovered by taking casts from the iron concretions lifted from this wreck.
Right: The plan of the wood from the vessel's hull as recorded on the seabed at Yassi Ada. The stern of the ship is toward the bottom of the page.

0 millimeters 50
0 inches 2

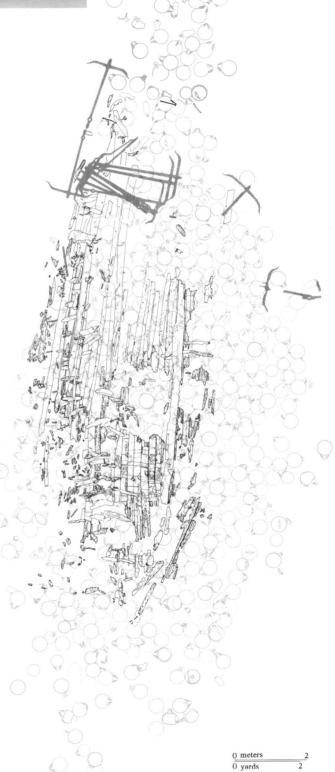

0 meters 2
0 yards 2

Improved techniques on a late Roman wreck

The excavation of another of the wrecks discovered by Peter Throckmorton at Yassi Ada in the late 1950s represented a landmark in the development of techniques for underwater archaeology. The project has also given us fresh insight into ship construction in the fourth century AD, although we have not yet achieved a full reconstruction of the hull.

The University of Pennsylvania Museum excavated much of this wreck in 1967 and 1969; but in 1974 the Cyprus War cut short a planned concluding campaign by the Institute of Nautical Archaeology. By the late 1970s work remained unfinished, with additional relics from the ship still lying under sand downslope from the excavated area.

We spent the 1960s seasons largely developing methods of scientific excavation in clear water. In this we profited from our experiences with the seventh-century Byzantine wreck (p. 36). But we also hoped to better that performance.

Excavating the Byzantine wreck had taken four summers and cost about $100,000. Studies of diving logs and field notebooks showed that we had done the work in 211 diving days, spending 1,243 man-hours on the seabed in 3,533 individual dives. The notebooks revealed, too, that we had split the actual working time as follows: 64% removing sand and shell overburden by airlifts and hand fanning; 19% making a plan of the site; 11% removing and raising cargo amphorae, ballast stones, and small finds; 4% bringing hull remains to the surface; and 2% on other activities such as pinning excavated wood in place, anchoring the diving barge, and covering the wreck protectively with sand when each summer season ended.

We reasoned that if we could excavate the fourth-century site — a site of comparable size — in two summers instead of four, we could save on annual expenses such as transportation of staff and equipment, insurance, barge and equipment mainten-ance, rental of local vessels, and camp construction.

There seemed to be two ways of increasing our efficiency. One was doubling the number of man-hours spent on the seabed. We accomplished this partly by raising the number of divers (mostly graduate students of archaeology) to about two dozen. We also designed a submersible decompression chamber (SDC) that worked without the support of a large, costly surface vessel. By allowing four divers at a time to decompress in dry comfort for an hour or more, the SDC permitted longer daily dives.

The second way of increasing our efficiency was to raise productivity during each man-hour on the seabed. To this end we obtained an airlift about 25 centimeters (10in) in diameter, and mounted it on 20 meters (66ft) of track laid along the deeper side of the sloping site. Hand fanning and a high-pressure water jet blew sand overburden between the rails of the track and the airlift then sucked up the sand.

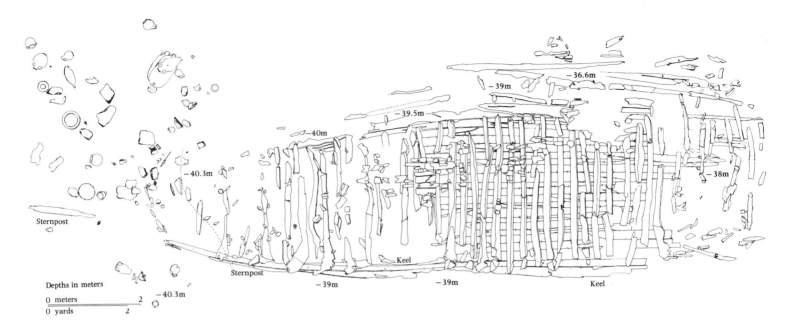

Sternpost

Depths in meters

0 meters   2
0 yards   2

−40.3m
−40.3m
Sternpost
−39m
−39m
Keel
Keel
−40m
−39.5m
−39m
−36.6m
−38m

The same scaffolding of stepped grids of angle iron that we had used on the seventh-century wreck served to support an improved photo tower for mapping cargo. At the same time, stereophotographs taken from the two-man submarine *Asherah* enabled us to make three-dimensional maps of parts of the wreck. But we mapped most of the wooden hull remains with stereophotographs taken measured distances apart by a camera slid along a horizontal bar floated over the site. We used a mapping instrument to process the resulting photographs.

To make cargo removal more efficient we built a lifting basket big enough and strong enough to take many amphorae at a single time, and equipped this basket with one or more balloons, each with a half-ton lifting capacity.

Other aids that made us more effective included an improved metal detector, from the Research Laboratory for Archaeology, Oxford; and a newly designed underwater "telephone booth," to improve communications between divers and between the seabed and the support barge above. Lastly, decompression on pure oxygen frequently allowed longer dives, even without the SDC.

Many of our innovations have now themselves been superseded, but they all worked at the time. Although the fourth-century wreck lay even deeper than its seventh-century neighbor, by the end of two summers we had spent 1,200 man-hours on the site. Even so this proved inadequate for total excavation. Two factors were to blame. One was sand overburden, which was much deeper than we had expected. The other problem was part of a later shipwreck that we found overlying part of ours, hampering the excavators' work.

Even so we made considerable progress. We learned that our ship had had 1,100 amphorae. This cargo stopped abruptly near the stern, probably against a bulkhead separating the hold from the ship's galley. There we found the expected cooking-, pantry- and tableware along with a steel-yard, badly corroded coins, glassware, and lamps (one bearing the mark of an Athenian lamp-maker known to have flourished late in the fourth century).

Frederick van Doorninck reports a mostly cypress hull, with white-oak keel and live-oak treenails for fastening frames to strakes. The hull measured nearly 19 meters (62ft) long, with a length-to-beam ratio of approximately 3:1. Construction was typically Greco-Roman, with mortise-and-tenon joints secured by oak pegs and used at least up to the second pair of wales. Long iron nails held frames to wales, and bolts held some frame floors to the keel, and wale ends to the stem- and sternpost.

Large gaps between mortise-and-tenon joints, loose fit of tenons in their mortises, and increased use of iron fastenings all point toward later developments in ship design as exemplified by the seventh-century Yassi Ada hull. Appreciation of the full significance of these findings must await completion of the excavation, full reconstruction of the hull, and publication of a final report. Nevertheless, it is already clear that, with this wreck, nautical archaeology has added one more link to the chain of evidence for evolution from Greco-Roman to modern ship construction.

Opposite, above: A diver working on the planking of the ship at Yassi Ada, after the cargo had been removed.
Opposite, below: Plotting the amphorae of the ship's cargo before recovery. The amphorae have all been tagged, and a grid frame is being used.
Opposite: A diver swims into the submersible decompression chamber (SDC) after working at a depth of 33 meters (110ft).

Left: Tracing the outline of one of the ship's frames recovered from the site at Yassi Ada. Above: A plan of the fourth-century-AD wreck at Yassi Ada, showing the wooden hull remains together with the debris from the galley in the stern (to the left).

Assessing a chance find near Kyrenia

In 1965 Andreas Cariolou was diving for sponges off northern Cyprus. A sudden squall hit his boat, and its anchor began to drag. Watching the anchor as it bumped over the flat seabed, Cariolou found himself distracted by an unfamiliar mound. He momentarily abandoned the anchor to examine it more closely. What he saw was a cluster of ancient amphorae, a discovery which so impressed Cariolou that he used up the rest of his air supply to inspect the site. By the time he surfaced, the storm had shifted his boat some distance away, and in his haste to join it he had no opportunity to take precise bearings. However, the significance of discovering an ancient shipwreck was not lost on him.

Cariolou determined to relocate the site. He took every available opportunity to dive in the area in search of the pottery. Two years later, his persistence was rewarded: he rediscovered the mound and pinpointed its position. Subsequently he often returned to admire the beauty of his find. But realizing its archaeological potential, and that nothing should be disturbed, he took care to leave the mound intact and kept his knowledge of its location secret from those who might violate and plunder its contents.

In the autumn of 1967 I led a team of underwater archaeologists seeking ancient shipwrecks along the coast of Cyprus. We had been invited to the island by Dr. Vassos Karageorghis, the director of antiquities. We found the battered remains of several ships, but not until our group met Cariolou were our expectations fully realized. Appreciating the mission's seriousness and experience, Cariolou agreed to show us his discovery.

We dived in open water less than 2 kilometers (1.2mi) northeast of Kyrenia, and 1 kilometer (0.6mi) offshore. There, at a depth of 30 meters (98ft), we glimpsed the forgotten mound of almost 100 amphorae, which rose from an eelgrass-covered floor of sandy mud. Most were still stacked in neat rows, apparently untouched since they had been loaded on board ship; plainly then, this was not simply a collection of jetsam. However, the mound measured only about 3× 5 meters (10× 16ft). Was this the sunken relic of a small lighter, or the tombstone of some ancient merchantman?

To answer this question we undertook a month-long survey. First, team members stretched a cord grid over the site. Then we used a thin metal rod gently to probe the soft overburden around the visible pottery. Working systematically meter by meter along the grid, we recorded where the rod met no resistance and where something hard stopped it short. In this way we determined that the entire cargo actually occupied an area 10× 19 meters (33× 62ft). This suggested that indeed a fair-sized merchant ship had sunk near the ancient harbor town of Kyrenia.

Next, the team carefully surveyed the area with a metal detector developed by Jeremy Green of the Research Laboratory for Archaeology and the History of Art at Oxford. This instrument located nine metallic concentrations beneath the sand. We plotted the position of these deposits by triangulation, measuring from three fixed points on the visible mound. Then, using a proton magnetometer designed by Dr. Edward Hall, director of the Oxford laboratory, we found that two of these metallic concentrations consisted of ferrous material. Of course, at that stage we could not say what actual artifacts these deposits represented. But, tantalizingly scanty though it was, the information did help to fill out our knowledge of the wreck's orientation and dimensions.

We neither moved nor removed anything during this survey. Nevertheless, we managed to make an accurate, measured drawing of the main type of amphora found in the mound. We showed this drawing and some photographs to Virginia Grace, specialist on amphora styles at the Agora Excavations of the American School of Classical Studies in Athens. She was able to provide perhaps the

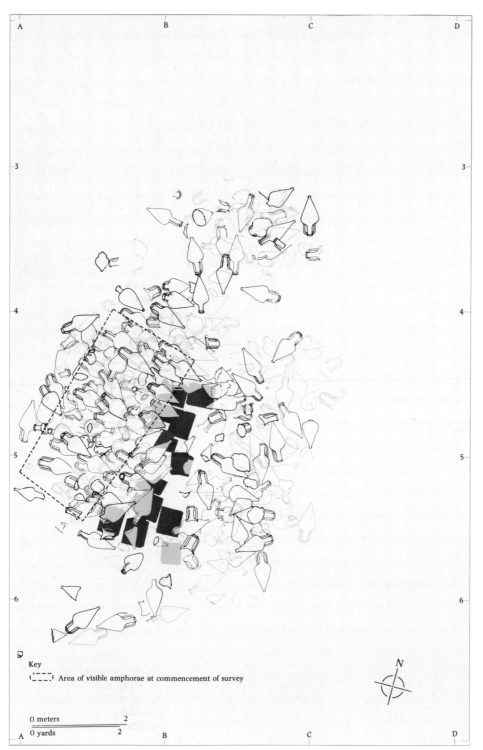

Key

|_ _ _ _| Area of visible amphorae at commencement of survey

N

0 meters   2
0 yards   2

single most important piece of information in the survey: someone had made the amphorae on the island of Rhodes in the last third of the fourth century BC. This meant that the ship had sunk during the lifetime of Alexander the Great or one of his immediate successors.

The techniques, tools, and expertise brought together for this survey represented a new procedure for inspecting a wreck site before its excavation. The methods that we used provided enough information to cut out much of the guesswork usually involved in approaching an underwater site. For example, knowing the approximate dimensions and axis of the wreck (which lay at a considerable angle to the line suggested by the visible amphora mound), archaeologists could design and position a permanent grid system that would cover the entire wreck area and need no subsequent repositioning. Also, our knowledge that the ship had settled on a soft bed of fine sandy mud in the late fourth century BC gave rise to the prospect of finding the first well-preserved hull from the classical period of Greek civilization.

Before we began excavation, however, we had to spend a great deal of time and effort in planning and preparation. First, we needed to obtain an excavation permit from the government of Cyprus; because they thoroughly appreciated the project's potential, the Cypriot authorities readily gave their permission. We also had to raise enough funds to meet the expedition's expenses; a host of American foundations, corporations, and individuals willingly contributed dollars. We had to buy and transport to the site equipment ranging from tiny, inexpensive, rubber O-rings to a big and very costly four-man recompression chamber. But most importantly, we had to sign up a crew of experienced and qualified individuals. Besides archaeologists, divers, and conservators, we needed photogrammetrists, draftsmen, artists, photographers, mechanics, electricians, doctors, and student trainees. Fortunately, all the positions were easily filled, many by volunteers. Indeed, more than 40 people from 10 countries eventually gathered together in Kyrenia. The problems of logistics (housing, feeding, and transporting the project's personnel) were solved with the help of local villagers. By June 1968 the excavation work was ready to start.

Opposite: A plan of the site at Kyrenia showing the distribution of amphorae and grain mills as they appeared after the initial clearance of overlying sand and weed. Note how small an area was actually exposed when Cariolou first saw the site.

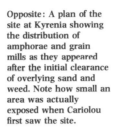

Top: Kyrenia from the air.
Left: The amphorae mound before survey began from above (upper), and with one of the team (lower).
Right: A diver using a prototype underwater metal detector on the Kyrenia wreck site.

A cargo from the age of Alexander the Great

Recording and recovery of material from the Kyrenia ship took place during the summer of 1968 and 1969. Our working platform was a flat-decked barge. We dived in teams of up to six individuals equipped with either scuba or surface demand gear (p. 12). Each team dived twice a day, which enabled every member to put in 70 minutes' working time on the bottom. A "telephone booth" set beside the wreck served as safety refuge and communication center.

First we fixed a grid of plastic piping over the site, to divide it into 3-meter (10ft) squares. Then we began excavating square by square, removing overburden chiefly by four airlifts, with a range of diameters to provide a range of power. We used a plastic label to tag each object, and plotted the positions of small objects by manual triangulation, using as fixed points the corners of the grid. To map large objects a diver "overflew" the site twice daily, taking a pair of stereophotographs for each square of the grid. These photographs were then analyzed, and the data transferred to plans. Once we had plotted their positions, we raised the objects: lighter ones by hand, others by winch and davit on the barge.

The major cargo comprised about 400 amphorae stacked in two layers. Those on one side were neatly aligned, those on the other lay scattered untidily. This showed that the ship had settled on her port side and her starboard side had subsequently collapsed so that the pots spilled out. Most were Rhodian, but a number of Samian examples

suggests another port of call on the ship's last voyage. A single Palestinian example and some others may have been picked up at some island emporium. Originally, the resin-coated Rhodian amphorae must have contained wine that had long ago filtered out and been replaced by sand. In removing the sand from the amphorae we discovered some fragmentary organic material. More

surprising still was the discovery, after we had raised most of the amphorae, of dense clusters of almonds inside the hull. In all, we recovered almost 10,000 almonds; a secondary cargo, most of which had been stowed on board in sacks.

Beneath the amphorae lay 29 millstones in four rows, aligned fore to aft directly above the keel. Weighing more than 1,650

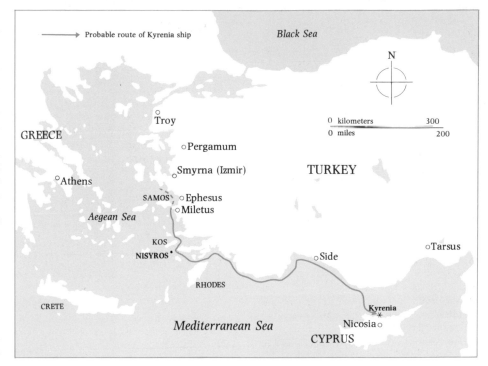

Above: A map of the eastern Mediterranean showing the probable last route of the Kyrenia ship, and the ports whose products were represented within her cargo.
Left: The site after most of the cargo had been removed. The spattern of scaffold grids across the site aided in site survey and helped control the excavation. In the foreground a diver is using a small airlift, while in the background a colleague makes notes.

kilograms (3,635lb), surrounded by fist-size stones, and bedded in gravel and beach sand, these millstones formed part of a mass of material that had served as the ship's ballast. However, originally such blocks were intended for hopper-type grain mills. Made of a volcanic stone similar to that quarried in antiquity on the island of Nisyros, they were probably the remnant of a larger consignment most of which had already been sold off during the voyage.

Concretions in the ship's stern proved to be the remains of another part of the cargo. When we sawed open these shapeless lumps we discovered molds left by the now decomposed iron objects around which the concretions had formed. Using a polysulfide rubber compound, we made casts from these molds, and obtained rubber replicas of the originals. These proved to be 30 iron blooms (masses of wrought iron produced by smelting iron ore).

From the remains of fore and aft cabins we recovered the crockery used by the sailors on the Kyrenia ship's last voyage. We found a variety of black-glazed plates, bowls, cups and pitchers. Identical sets of four, of items including pitchers and saltcellars, suggest that four sailors had manned the Kyrenia ship. In addition to pottery and wood, the crew had used copper vessels and utensils including a large cauldron with loop handles, and a ladle with a handle ending in an elegant swan's head.

There was bountiful evidence of the food the sailors had eaten. They had presumably consumed some of the wine and almonds on board. They had certainly dined on fish, for we discovered more than 300 small lead weights in two piles where the nets had last been stowed. Rounding out the mariners' diet, the excavators also recovered garlic, olive stones, grape pips, and fig seeds. But whether they cooked on board or went ashore for this purpose remains uncertain.

We recovered only seven bronze coins; two are too badly corroded to be legible but the other five date from the last decade of the fourth century BC. This information, together with the style of the Rhodian amphorae and the black-glazed pottery, and the carbon-14 date of 288 ± 62 BC for a sample of almonds, suggests that the ship sank about 300 BC.

After removing cargo, ballast, and small finds, the team faced the challenging task of mapping the amazingly well-preserved hull. Precise plotting of the position of each fragment where it lay seemed crucial for the ship's eventual reassembly. Photogrammetry was again our most valuable tool; but we also used a large template to check the recording of the hull's configuration, and manual triangulation for smaller wooden objects. Individually interesting finds from around the superbly cut maststep comprised a pulley block, several belaying pins, and toggles: all part of the ship's running

Above, left: Almonds recovered from inside the hull. They have been preserved in polyethylene glycol (PEG), and are shown spilling from a modern bag.
Above: A selection of pottery vessels from the crew's quarters, and (left) the ship's ballast of 29 millstones, as revealed by the removal of two layers of amphorae.
Below: A drawing of a Rhodian amphora from the cargo.

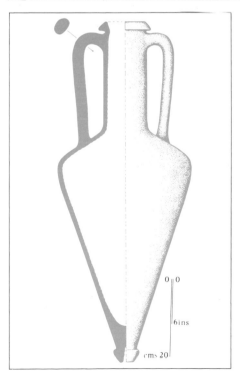

rigging. In the stern cabin, which doubled as spare sail locker, lay more than 160 lead brail rings, fragments of two- and three-strand line, and several deadeyes — objects collectively employed for raising a sail.

We hoped that we could raise the ancient hull intact. But the wood was like soft, soggy bread, and thin plates of lead sheathed the hull's exterior, making the mass too delicate and heavy for this. Therefore we had to separate the hull into manageable pieces. This meant minutely labeling each piece. Once plan and labeling were complete, we removed the pieces individually to trays that were then carefully ballooned to the surface. We lifted almost five tons of waterlogged wood in this fashion.

Beneath the hull the excavators made a last remarkable find: eight iron spears, some bent from impact. We had found no spears in the hull, or any valuable objects, or sailors' personal effects. All this suggests a pirate attack, followed by the looting and scuttling of the Kyrenia ship more than 22 centuries ago. Alas, we can never know the fate of her mariners.

The study and conservation of an ancient hull

In raising the timbers of the Kyrenia ship we had two objectives: first, to study the hull in order to gain a clearer idea of its construction and design; second, to reassemble the hull as a museum exhibit.

Both studies depended at first on keeping the waterlogged wood constantly wet. After washing the pieces, we laid the trays of wood in a large concrete basin built inside a Crusader barrack in Kyrenia Castle. Here we regularly changed the water, and added an antimicrobial agent. This treatment made sure the wood would not dry out and crack, warp, or shrink, and kept it safe from bacterial attack.

We sent samples of wood to laboratories for analysis. Besides stressing the obvious fact that the timbers were riddled by shipworm, analysis showed that they had lost almost all their cellulose content and would certainly shrink drastically if dried out. Analysis also revealed that the hull's keel, strakes, and frames were of Aleppo pine, but that tenons used in the hull's construction were of oak. Radiocarbon analysis of one of the strakes gave a date of 389 ± 44 BC, suggesting that the Kyrenia ship had seen service through most of the fourth century.

Our next step was photographing and making detailed full-scale drawings of each piece of wood from both sides. We also catalogued all the timbers. Thus we insured against loss of information should the wood suffer during preservation.

After more than a year of experiment, we decided the best way to keep the wood stable in shape and size would be by soaking in a solution containing polyethylene glycol (PEG), and gradually increasing its concentration to almost 100%. In 1971 we began large-scale treatment of the wood in specially made tanks of galvanized steel, coated inside with fiberglass, and equipped to heat and circulate the PEG. Treatment time needed for different timbers depended on their condition, type of timber, and cross-sectional dimensions. The strakes took about 8 months; keel, wales, and frames, 14 months; and the massive maststep, 24 months in solution. When we removed the timbers we let them dry and cool slowly to room conditions. We succeeded in maintaining the dimensional integrity of 99% of the pieces.

After stabilizing the timbers at ambient humidity and temperature, we had to remove surplus PEG that had congealed on their surfaces. This laborious task involved thousands of pieces of wood; but the results yielded fresh information on how the ship was built as saw, adz, and awl marks came to light. This job complete, the conserved timbers were ready for reassembly.

During the various phases of conservation, ship reconstructor J. Richard Steffy had sought to draft the ship's lines. Working from the plan we had made of the hull during excavation, full-scale drawings of each piece, and our detailed catalog of the wood, he produced a set of preliminary drawings. Construction of a 1:5-scale wooden research model then led to revisions. These showed the Kyrenia ship to have been a wide, shallow vessel 14.7 meters (48ft 2in) long; 4.3 meters (14ft 1in) abeam; and 1.4 meters (4ft 7in) in draft.

We also built a fiberglass model to the same scale. Equipped with dual steering oars and a broad square sail fitted with guide rings for brail lines, she was destined for sea trials. These revealed that in a following wind the Kyrenia ship might have made 4–5 knots (7–9 km/h). Because her mast was set relatively far forward amidships, with one edge of the sail swung around and brailed-up, she could also have made amazingly good headway while pointing as close as 6 points off the wind.

The Kyrenia ship had been built in the shell-first manner (pp. 30–31). Better to appreciate this technique of construction, we built a full-scale 2-meter (6ft 6in) section of hull aft amidships. For this replica

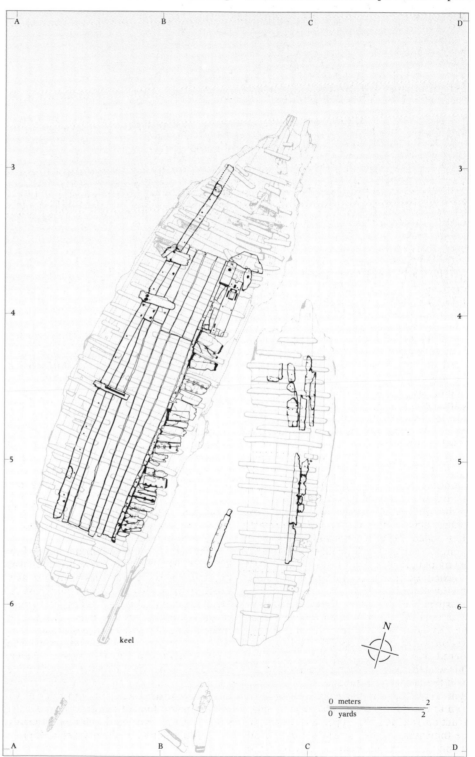

keel

0 meters 2
0 yards 2

N

Opposite: Plan of the hull remains of the Kyrenia ship, showing both the internal framing and the external planking. Compare this seabed plan with the reconstructed hull shown opposite.
Left: The ship's maststep during treatment in a PEG bath in Kyrenia Castle, where the hull was finally reconstructed.
Left, below: A full-size reconstruction of the midships section of the Kyrenia ship, from which the team learned much about the building techniques used, before attempting a full reconstruction of the original.
Below, right: A 1:5 scale model of the ship during a sea-test in the bay off Kyrenia.

our team used materials and tools similar to those of the ancient shipwright. They adzed the pine keel, and chiseled mortises into the lower faces of its rabbets. After shaping the garboard strake (the plank next to the keel), they cut mortises in its lower edge to match those in the keel. Then they joined garboard to keel by oak tenons inserted in the mortises, using pegs to lock these tenons in place. In this way they built up the hull strake by strake. Once they had completed the shell, they adzed the pine floors, frames, and top timbers to fit the shape of the hull, and secured all in place by copper spikes driven through treenails. They added limber strakes and stringers for strength, then placed limber boards and ceiling planks over the frames. Finally they attached plates of thin lead sheathing to the exterior of the hull.

Experience gained in these reconstructions enabled us to proceed to reassemble the Kyrenia ship from the preserved, original wood. In October 1972 we laid the curved, rocker-type, 10-meter (33ft) keel. This was the most exacting challenge of all, for if the keel's curvature were off by more than 1 centimeter, the error would have been at least 10 times greater when reconstruction reached the upper wale. Each of the thousands of pieces required individual attention. Mortises, tenons, and pegs had to

be aligned before planks could be joined. We had to match nails in frames with nail holes in strakes before we could accurately set and secure the frames within the hull.

Slowly, painstakingly, the reassembly of the Kyrenia ship progressed; but each day we were struck anew by the skill and craftsmanship of the ancient shipwright. Evidence also came to light of major hull repairs on at least three occasions, reinforcing the supposition that she had seen many years of service. Fortunately, about 70% of the ancient hull had survived, and after more than a year's work we could insert the last piece to the oldest seagoing hull yet recovered.

What we see is a merchantman of slightly less than 30 tons burden. Well built, she was nevertheless a "tramp" vessel of her day. Trading through the Aegean and eastern Mediterranean, she had called at Samos, Nisyros, Rhodes, and perhaps Kyrenia, to take on and discharge cargoes as varied as wine, millstones, almonds, and iron. She had undoubtedly made many similar voyages throughout the lifetime of Alexander the Great, and indeed for several generations of mariners. But luck ran out on her last crew of four. Sometime around the year 300 BC we think pirates suddenly ended the sailing life of the Kyrenia ship.

An enigmatic site from the Bronze Age

Our next site lies near Sheytan Deresi, a river on the north coast of Kerme Bay, in southwest Turkey. It is not a true wreck site in that there is no direct proof that a ship was ever wrecked there. But we found plenty of pottery fragments, and before we raised them we made an exact plan of their positions. This plan, as you will see, poses more questions than it answers.

In 1973 a survey team from the newly formed Institute of Nautical Archaeology visited the site, led there by team member and former sponge diver Cumhur Ilik. Seven years earlier Ilik had seen two "huge jars" lying at a depth of 33 meters (108ft). We photographed and raised both "jars": a mixing bowl (krater) and a storage jar (pithos). We also left lead diving weights to mark the two cavities where the jars had lain. Moving artifacts out of context before drawing a measured plan made us uneasy but this was the next to last day of our survey, and we feared someone might steal the jars before we could come back to mount a full excavation.

What little evidence we had made dating difficult. The first estimate put the site in the middle Bronze Age on the basis of a single sherd, one of several scattered around the krater and pithos; publications of the survey results mistakenly revised this date upward to the Iron Age or even later. Nevertheless, the sand around the pottery was deep enough to make us think it might hide a well-preserved hull of early date and importance.

The Cyprus War delayed our return to the site, but in the fall of 1975 we launched a full-scale excavation. Our lead weights remained in place, so we were able to plot the positions of the original "jars" on the site plan we now started. We made this plan with a combination of underwater photographs and drawings, using for control a light metal grid of rigid two-meter (6ft 7in)

squares placed over the area of the original finds and extended in all directions as excavation proceeded outward.

We discovered under the sand separate concentrations of sherds that we assumed marked the remains of individual ceramic vessels, mostly large storage jars including amphorae. But when we had raised, cleaned, and mended these sherds we discovered something rather disconcerting. Although most of the fragments of any one vessel had been close together, sometimes a single fragment lay mixed with another group 10 meters (33ft) or more away. Yet in places rock ridges would have prevented currents from shifting stray sherds from one group to another. Moreover, the groups of sherds lay too deeply buried for divers to have disturbed them in modern times.

Problems of distribution involved more than the displacement of individual scraps over short distances. In shallow water near the rocky shore we found thick sherds similar to those excavated 75–100 meters (235–330ft) away. Also, one intact pithos lay 30 meters (98ft) from most of the other pottery and higher on the slope. Partial burial in sand suggested that this jar had not been moved recently, yet inside lay sherds at least one of which joined perfectly a fragmentary pot found with the distant main mass of cargo.

Another mystery was the lack of all trace of the ship that had carried this strangely

scattered cargo. We sought the ship in vain: removing sand down to bedrock over the entire excavation site. We also probed the sand for wood for a considerable area around.

What had happened was probably this. A sudden, violent wind had whipped down the valley through which Sheytan Deresi ("Devil Creek") flows (such winds still occur). This gust had caught and capsized the ship as she rounded the point near where we found the pottery. Most of her cargo of, perhaps empty, jars sank straight to the seabed, where some broke and others settled intact. Other jars floated off before sinking, and at least one ended up against the rocky shore where the ship herself may have broken up. Later, an octopus made its home in one jar, bringing sherds from distances of up to 30 meters (98ft). (Divers familiar with that creature's habits know that this last hypothesis is not just possible but probable.) But would an octopus have carried a single sherd from one group of sherds to another when neither seemed suitable for a home? Questions remain. That we had overlooked little evidence emerged in the Bodrum Museum, where restoration work proved that almost all recovered sherds fitted together to form nearly complete vessels.

These vessels help us to date the lost cargo to about 1600 BC, making it about four centuries older than the Bronze Age

Below: The eastern Mediterranean, showing the locations of the sites at Sheytan Deresi and Serçe Limani.

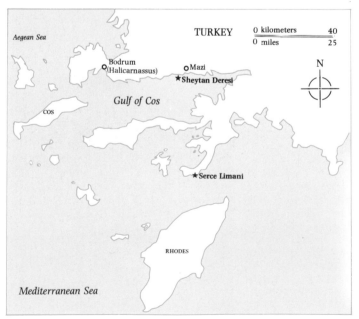

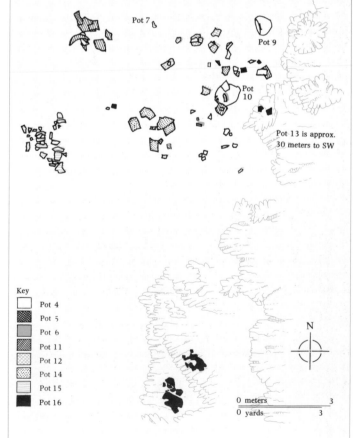

Pot 7

Pot 9

Pot 10

Pot 13 is approx. 30 meters to SW

Key

	Pot 4
	Pot 5
	Pot 6
	Pot 11
	Pot 12
	Pot 14
	Pot 15
	Pot 16

0 meters 3
0 yards 3

N

Aegean Sea

TURKEY

0 kilometers 40
0 miles 25

N

Bodrum (Halicarnassus)
Mazi
★ Sheytan Deresi

Gulf of Cos

COS

★ Serce Limani

RHODES

Mediterranean Sea

wreck at Cape Gelidonya (pp. 28–31). Three squat, belly-handled amphorae find their closest parallels in level IVb of the relatively near inland site of Beycesultan. A pair of one-handled jugs parallel many found in Troy VI, in northwest Turkey. Three tall amphorae with clay "rivet heads" on their necks resemble Middle Minoan III vases from Crete, especially Knossos. It is harder to date the three two-handled *pithoi* and four handleless *pithoi*, all nearly a meter high, and the *krater* raised in 1973. For all but the handleless *pithoi* we can find vague Aegean parallels from around 1600 BC, and no better parallels for later dates. If we had excavated these separately we might have put the *pithoi* without handles as late as the sixth century BC, but since we are sure they belonged to the same cargo as the rest of the pottery, we must assume that they, too, are from around 1600 BC.

This cargo's mixture of Anatolian and Aegean characteristics increases our knowledge of the period when pottery from Crete was arriving by ship on the western coast of Anatolia: an import trade revealed by land excavations at Miletus. The Sheytan Deresi pottery was perhaps a local product, manufactured at a still unknown site. A small coasting craft was probably shipping it from one village to another when she went down.

A diver with a *pithos* (SD 13 – see distribution plan opposite), illustrating the appearance of the site as found. Below: Pithos SD 13 after clearance. Opposite, right: The distribution of complete vessels and sherds across the site at Sheytan Deresi. Note how most of the broken vessels are represented by a main concentration of sherds, with one or two pieces lying some distance away. The complete *pithos* (SD 13) lays 30 meters (100ft) away from the main site; the numbers listed with it refer to the items found inside it.

An eleventh-century shipwreck lying 33 meters (108ft) deep inside Serçe Limani ("Sparrow Harbor") was just one of many wrecks in this small bay on the southwestern coast of Turkey opposite Rhodes. In 1977 the Institute of Nautical Archaeology chose to excavate this particular site for a special reason.

Among unanswered questions facing nautical archaeologists were those of how, when, where and why frame-first, or skeletal, hull construction had become widespread in the Mediterranean. In the 1960s, excavations at Yassi Ada (pp. 36–39) had proved that the change from earlier Greco-Roman shell-first construction was a slow evolutionary process still not completed by the seventh century AD. Amphorae found with the Serçe Limani wreck in 1973 had shown that this was medieval, so we believed that excavation might add valuably to our knowledge of the development of nautical technology.

The hull was so important that we laid special emphasis on mapping its remains. But our techniques were simpler than those of our former surveys, largely thanks to the development of a new wide-angle lens for underwater cameras. We profited still more from the fact that those keeping the plans were graduate students of nautical archaeology at Texas A&M University, where they had become well versed in ancient hull construction and reconstruction under Frederick van Doorninck and J. Richard

Steffy. This team thus understood wood remnants better than its predecessors. Steffy and van Doorninck concluded, for example, that hull reconstruction required far fewer seabed elevation measurements than we had used before because most hull analysis would occur after divers had brought wood fragments to the surface. A simple metal grid of two-meter (6ft 7in) squares laid over the site at Serçe Limani sufficed for photographic controls, and we found photo towers and stereophotography unnecessary. But we did use sharpened bicycle spokes to pin hull fragments to the seabed until we had plotted their positions by a series of undistorted photomosaics. Then we carried the fragments to land on specially prepared trays and placed them in holding tanks until chemical conservation treatment began.

Our second campaign, in 1978, did not quite complete excavation, but we gained enough data to determine that this ship had been 16 meters (52ft) long, nearly flat bottomed and full in cross section, with a beam-length ratio of 1:3. Her builders had both nailed and treenailed planking to a framing system heavier and stronger than any among our previously excavated ships. Skeletal built throughout, the hull indicated that at some point between the seventh and eleventh centuries AD the transition to a "modern" construction of seagoing vessels was complete. Who deserves credit for this most important development in the history

of seafaring? Perhaps the change came about by a mixture of cultural influences.

This particular ship was almost certainly an Arab merchantman. Some of her cargo comprised Byzantine amphorae bearing Greek graffiti, and some of the coins on board were also Byzantine Greek, but most or all of the utensils used by the crew and possible passengers were of Islamic origin. These utensils included typical glazed dishes and bowls, some decorated in imitation of Chinese T'ang dynasty wares, and gargoulettes, or jugs with filters in their necks, possibly of Egyptian manufacture. Glass bottles, cups, pitchers, and bowls, found intact in the living quarters at either end of the ship, were also Islamic, although we do not yet know if all came from Persia, Syria, Egypt, or Iraq, or a combination of such places. At least one of several bronze buckets bore an Arabic inscription, as did a number of Islamic glass weights and gold coins.

It was from the glass weights (glass disks used in weighing precious commodities) and bronze coins that we derived the date of the wreck. The latest of four glass weights studied in 1977 was from the time of the Fatimid caliph al-Zahir (1020–35), overlapping the Byzantine emperor Basil II (976–1025), to whose reign several coins can be attributed.

Within a few months of the end of the 1978 season, a reconstruction of the ship was under way, based on seabed plans of hull remains and cargo, and a study of wood fragments undergoing treatment. We found that as you moved from stem to curving sternpost, you would first come to a pair of iron Y-shaped anchors carried ready for use in the bow, where fire-blackened cooking pots, ceramic tablewares, glass vessels, and two wooden combs suggest the presence of small living quarters.

Just aft of this living area, in the forward quarter of the ship's hold, we found no evidence of cargo, dunnage, or inner hull planking. This suggested that any cargo carried here had been light and perishable. Six spare anchors, like those in the ship's bow, were stowed in the hold immediately forward of amidships.

Removable planking lined the after half of the hold. Here the crew had stowed the cargo in two categories. The forwardmost cargo comprised terracotta wine amphorae and other vessels collectively so light that the area had been heavily ballasted with beach rock. The remainder of the cargo consisted of several tons of broken glass destined for remelting and manufacture into new glass items. Deformed and un-finished vessels among the broken glass suggest rejects from a glass factory.

A large area of the stern devoted to living quarters contained intact glass and pottery vessels; amphorae; bronze and copper vessels; sets of balance-pan weights; silver and gold jewelry; lead weights for fishing

nets; and a variety of iron swords, lances, javelins, and an ax. The swords were sheathed in wooden scabbards and one sword blade, possibly Indian, had a bronze hilt decorated with ornate birds.

Careful screening of the mud contained in pottery vessels revealed traces of food: peaches; olives; lentils; grapes (or wine); fish; fowl; and animal or animals so far unidentified. Several of the amphorae are still sealed, and await examination.

When the excavation is complete and experts have analyzed the artifacts, we should have a detailed picture of an eleventh-century trading venture: from the design of the ship to the economics of the voyage and daily life at sea.

Opposite: A plan of the wreck site at Serçe Limani, as exposed at the end of the first season of excavation in 1977. It shows the dispersal of the cargo, which included pottery, glass, and other items, the ship's eight iron anchors, and parts (labeled) of the wooden hull.
Above: The team's barge moored above the wreck site at Serçe Limani. Note the therapeutic decompression chamber and support equipment amidships.
Above, right: A selection of the intact glass vessels recovered from the site.
Right: Divers surveying and excavating at Serçe Limani.

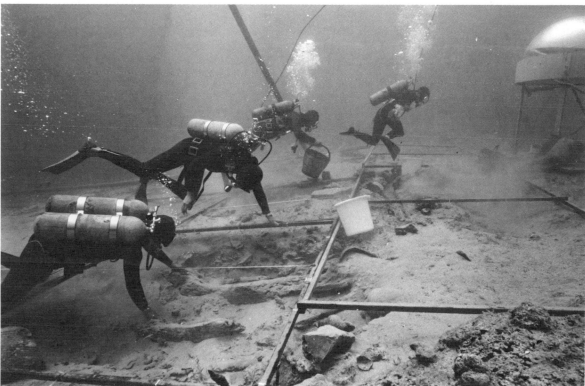

Roman wrecks in the western Mediterranean

Until the end of World War II the whole world held a mere handful of known ancient shipwrecks. Most represented chance finds of ships or boats abandoned in harbors or rivers that subsequently silted up. Since World War II the development of scuba diving has brought to light many new sites, and scuba divers are still finding more. By the late 1970s about 630 wrecks datable to before AD 1500 had been reported from the Mediterranean; this substantial sample represents an important addition to our knowledge of the ancient world, although some historians still undervalue its significance. Like most archaeological samples, though, this one is not truly random, and therefore calls for careful analysis.

The great majority of these ancient Mediterranean wrecks – 538 of the 630 – lie in the western Mediterranean. Reasons for this distribution include the early growth of sports diving in that area; the accessibility of its coasts to large centers of population; and a genuine (albeit ill-organized) West European interest in antiquity or antiquities. Then, too, some of the western Mediterranean's coasts that divers find the most attractive favor the discovery of well-preserved wrecks: the Costa Brava, French Riviera, and southern Corsica are examples of such shores. Lastly, a few areas, for instance, off Cartagena (Carthago Nova) in Spain or southeast Sicily, have been intensive surveys. Conversely, few sites are known from the largely inaccessible coasts of Morocco or Algeria. In eastern Italy and southern Spain shelving coasts and poor visibility make the coasts unsuited to diving and wreck discovery.

Of the 538 known wrecks, three-quarters (407) date from the Roman Republican and early to middle Empire periods (300 BC-AD 300). Earlier shipwrecks are uncommon (the oldest sites explored by divers are Etruscan wrecks of the seventh and sixth centuries BC); and post-Roman wrecks remain astonishingly rare. If we divide the whole Roman era into four periods (listed A to D), we get this distribution of finds:

A	300–150 BC	68
B	150–1 BC	130
C	AD 1–150	142
D	AD 150–300	67

Wrecks appear to show an increase in frequency during the early Empire (C), but this increase would probably be negligible if we knew the exact date of the 30 wrecks simply reported as "Roman" and here arbitrarily assigned to this period.

The concentrations that appear when these sites are plotted on a map are interesting. In period A (and indeed other periods), southern France shows a relatively dense distribution, due chiefly to locally more intensive diving and reporting of sites; in Sicily, on the other hand, the concentration represents the activity of Punic (i.e. Carthaginian) and Greek shipping. Period B, in contrast, shows the full development of Roman wine exports to Gaul and Spain. Economic activity in the Adriatic also appears, and, around Cartagena, a cluster of shipwrecks containing ore or ingots emphasizes the importance of the Spanish mines.

In period C, the map illustrates the emergence of Spain as a source of food and other products for the towns of Gaul and Italy, and for the expanding, permanently garrisoned European frontier of the Empire. The widespread distribution of Roman wrecks in the upper Adriatic may be due to a similar effect on trade exerted by the Roman center of Aquileia and the Danube frontier. The relative absence of wrecks in western Sicily may be due to the comparative unimportance of olive-oil exports from North Africa at this time.

Period D includes the troubled half century about AD 235–285, when political uncertainties may have caused a collapse of some supply arrangements. This period shows a notable decline in number of sites, and, by inference, in traffic. The number of wrecks in western and southern Sicily and around Malta is due to the importance of exports from Africa; also several of the southern Italian sites reflect the supply of marble and other goods from Greece and Asia Minor. The cluster of sites in central Italy, however, conceals a special factor — the abandonment of several vessels in the harbor of Portus (now under Rome Airport).

How far does this archaeological evidence affect our previous view of Roman economic life? In some respects, of course, the evidence is partial or biased, but it may also offer a corrective. For instance, many of these cargoes are made up mostly or entirely of amphorae. This fact gives us a clearer impression of the importance of trade in foodstuffs, especially wine, than we get from either surviving literary sources, which focus on the exceptional more than the humdrum, or from land archaeology, which tends to overstress the significance of pottery trade. Domestic pottery is indeed frequently found in shipwrecks, but in most instances it is just part (usually a small part) of a main cargo of amphorae.

Archaeology also helps to reveal the scale of ancient commerce. The 300- to 400-ton ship found at Madrague de Giens in France, and the possibly 600-ton wreck at Albenga in Italy confirm ancient authors' claims for the considerable size of cargo ships — claims once thought fantastic. What is more, such discoveries indicate that the export of wine from Italian vineyards – a trade closely linked with Roman territorial expansion — was run by merchants and shipmasters who operated at a highly commercial level.

Finally, there are Roman items that tend to be found only below the sea. On land, ingots may be melted down, quarrymen's rough work finished off, or fragile seals broken; in a shipwreck, all may survive, and, more than that, survive in a context that tells us their date, origin, and destination. The underwater archaeologist thus has a unique contribution to make to the history of Rome and her empire. The next pages examine in detail individual wrecks and what they can tell us about different aspects of Rome's seaborne trade.

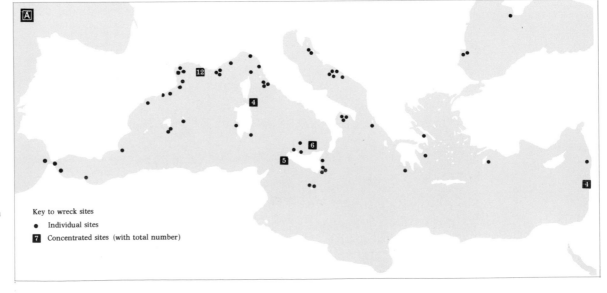

Four maps of the Mediterranean, showing the distribution of known wrecks of the classical period.

Key to wreck sites
- • Individual sites
- **7** Concentrated sites (with total number)

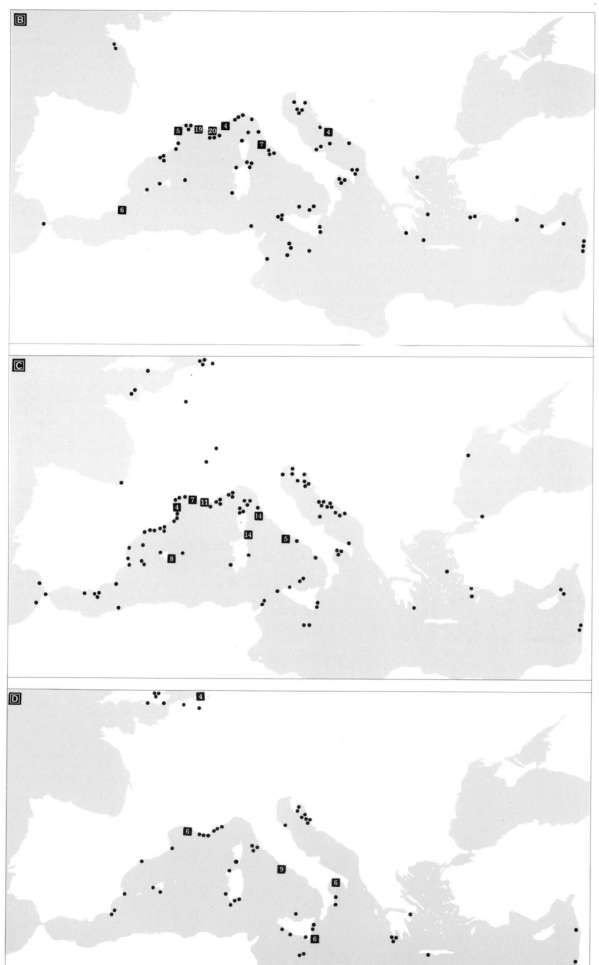

Roman merchantmen rediscovered

In the 1950s the rapid development of scuba diving in the western Mediterranean soon resulted in the discovery of many well-preserved shipwrecks. Official interest in underwater archaeology was slow to develop, though, and so were techniques of field excavation. The results of excavations in Italy and France during the 1950s thus hardly justified the optimistic enthusiasm of their respective proponents, Nino Lamboglia and Fernand Benoît.

Commandant Philippe Tailliez, the conscientious excavator of the first-century-BC Roman wreck on the Titan reef off southern France, lamented the absence of an archaeologist from his otherwise meticulous operation. At Grand Congloué island near Marseilles, Benoît was unable to control the operations of the divers, led by Jacques-Yves Cousteau. As most archaeologists now recognize, the regrettable result was that two wrecks were treated as one. In Italy, shortages of funds and of interested archaeologists meant that Lamboglia could not finish his excavations at Albenga, Spargi, or Punta Scaletta. Many more sites in Italy, France, and Spain have been destroyed by looting. In Spain, too, underwater archaeology has been slow to develop, and an Italo-Hispanic team never completed excavation of the very important site at el Sec in Majorca.

In these countries and elsewhere in the western Mediterranean the situation has improved in recent years, not least with the growth of expert, well-informed, amateur groups. In Spain, divers led by Federico Foerster have carried out substantial projects, notably at Cala Pedrosa; while, in France, François Carrazé and Jean-Pierre Joncheray have won impressive results from a number of sites.

A look at two Joncheray excavations near Anthéor in southeast France shows something of what we can learn about Roman cargo ships despite heavy looting in the 1950s and 1960s. The first excavation was on the Chrétienne C wreck, a site originally discovered in 1954. Three seasons' work recovered many small finds and relics of the plundered cargo, and exposed and recorded the ship's hull.

The cargo comprised amphorae of the so-called Greco-Italic form. None was stamped but, like the later pots from Madrague de Giens, each was sealed with a cork disk held in place with a cement seal stamped with a Roman name: C(ai). Teren(ti) M. . . . These pots had probably contained wine, and their form (together with other pottery evidence and a coin) date the wreck to 175–150 BC.

Joncheray's team found plenty of shipboard material. There were tools including a hammer, nail lifter, mallet, and rigging spike; also a spear. The ship's equipment featured a pulley block, two sounding leads, three lead-stocked anchors, and more than a dozen tile fragments. Many of these items, a good deal of pottery, some stores, amphorae, an oil lamp, and some hazel nuts lay on or close by the hull. The excavation plan shows the amphora cargo occupying the center of the ship, some kind of living area at the stern, anchors secured at the bows, and a working space and more living accommodation in the forecastle, probably sheltered by a tiled roof.

The ship had settled on her starboard side, which survived only in part, broken in two. Nonetheless, the timber was well enough preserved to show that construction had involved only a few nails, all of iron. Further study even suggested a reconstruction. The Chrétienne C vessel had been a fairly small ship, 15.5 meters (51ft) long, and she had held a mere 500 amphorae. Yet when she sank she was still fairly new. Thus she seemingly represents an early stage in the Roman wine trade.

The second wreck we shall look at here

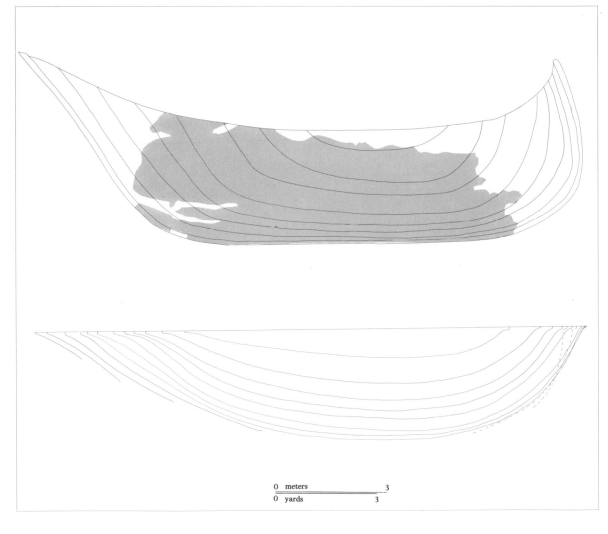

Left: Plan and profile of the vessel whose remains were uncovered at the site of La Chrétienne C. The shaded area represents the section actually recovered; the other lines are conjectural.
Opposite, above: Two maps showing the locations of the sites discussed on these pages. The nearer depicts the whole of the coast of southern France from the Rhône estuary to the Italian border, while the farther shows in detail the area around Agay. The latter demonstrates clearly the profusion of ancient wrecks on the reefs of Le Dramont and La Chrétienne.
Opposite, below: A detailed plan of the remains on the site known as Dramont D. The scarcity of cargo between the bows (right), where the amphorae were stowed, and the stern, which contained grinding bowls, shows that looters have been active. Three iron anchors were also found near the bows.

0 meters 3
0 yards 3

lies 53 meters (174ft) deep on a flat, muddy bottom, 500 meters (1,640ft) southwest of Île d'Or. Several ancient wrecks occur close to this one, which archaeologists know as Dramont D. The site was discovered in 1964, and Georges Delonca and Jean-Pierre Joncheray led the divers who excavated it between 1969 and 1972. Despite the considerable depth the team made a plan of the cargo and retrieved numerous objects, but left the hull unexcavated.

The excavators found the cargo coated with a hard, limy crust overlaid by a belt of fine mud in which they could see a trench dug by looters. These had removed all the central part of the cargo by 1969. Built up over four seasons, the site plan shows that this was a relatively large ship: the cargo covers about 18× 5 meters (60× 16ft). The wreck is contemporary with that of Port Vendres B, described elsewhere in this section.

Detailed study of small finds again showed what the inside of the ship must have looked like. At the northern end, a "galley" area had contained several Syrian amphorae (for water?), a Spanish amphora containing fish sauce for cooking, a jar of flour, and three amphorae, one of which held resin. A high shelf had seemingly supported a

variety of pots, and an ax and billhook may have hung from a bulkhead. Three iron anchors from the same end of the site suggest that this was the bows. The stores, then, had been in the forecastle. Unlike Chrétienne C, Dramont D lacked tiles or slabs to suggest a roof or a hearth; but cups, jugs, and bowls from the forecastle area suggest that people once ate food there. Toward the stern lay another area with cooking and eating wares – some fire blackened – as well as a basket of hand tools, and nails. This was evidently a separate cabin or mess; but again no roof tiles were found.

The cargo proved varied. Toward the stern lay a consignment of mortaria (grinding bowls) of two types. All had been stowed

according to size. The stamps on them show that they came from Italy, probably Campania. Toward the bow lay two kinds of amphora. One kind, of Greek form but unknown origin, had contained dates (the skins and outer part of the stones survived). The other amphorae were also Greek, maybe from Rhodes. They had held figs, of which the seeds remained. Plainly, Dramont D represented a cosmopolitan ship, with shipboard stores and equipment from southern Spain, Italy, and Syria; a cargo of figs from the Aegean; dates presumably from Africa (Cyrenaica?) and mortaria from Italy. This variety of goods is a testament to the peaceful conditions of the middle of the first century AD.

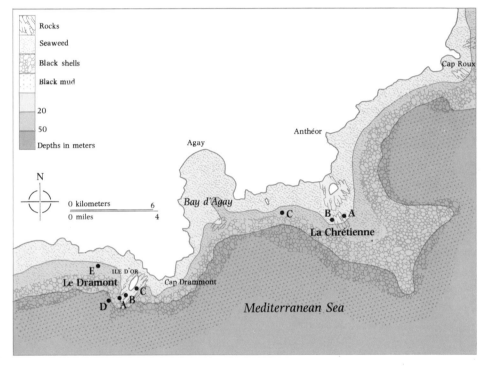

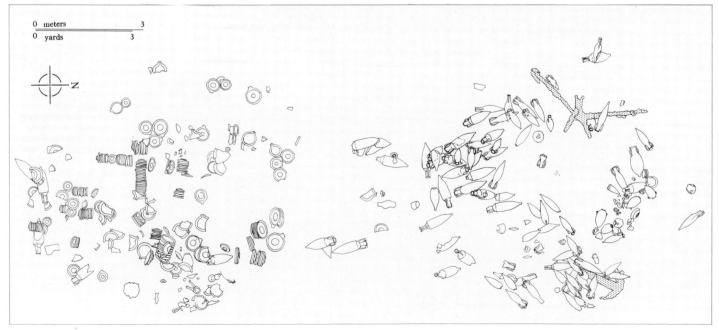

New light on an old wine trade

Pottery amphorae served in the Mediterranean region as the normal containers for wine and foodstuffs (barrels were used in the Po Valley and north of the Alps). These big pots were permeable, but there were ways of making them leakproof. People rubbed the insides of olive-oil amphorae with olive lees, which leave a trace detectable only by chemical tests. They used bitumen or rosin to line amphorae holding wine and some other liquids. This lining often survives in wrecks, and, with traces of the original contents, helps to show what each amphora contained.

The earliest wine cargoes date from the sixth century BC. During the next three centuries Etruscans, Greeks, and Carthaginians all carried on the trade. The first Roman enterprise, indicated by Latin inscriptions scratched on wine amphorae, appeared in the first half of the third century, but the great expansion of Roman wine exports came in the second half of the second century BC.

One effect of the increased investment resulting from the expansion of Roman power in Greece, Asia Minor, and North Africa was an increased export of wine from the Italian regions of Etruria, Latium, and (probably) Campania. Carefully bottled in corked and sealed amphorae, these fine wines were much in demand in southern France after the establishment in 118 BC of the Roman province of Gallia Narbonensis, where viticulture had not yet been introduced. Roman and other Italian merchants not only thronged the Roman provinces but also set up trading posts in Britain and other

barbarian lands outside the empire. Wine exports from Italy reached their peak in the mid-first century BC. But by the end of the century they had collapsed under competition from traditional wine areas such as Rhodes or Cnidos (in southwest Asia Minor) and from new vineyards in Spain and Gaul.

The pleasure of drinking good wine is enhanced by fine utensils. Thus the cargoes of Roman wine ships usually included fine pottery cups (the black-glaze "Campanian" ware). Sometimes other consignments were carried, too: millstones, nuts, lamps, coarse pottery, olive oil.

Until the reign of Augustus (31 BC– AD 14), there was no safe land route from Italy to southern Gaul; the markets for wine thus stimulated a large maritime traffic, and, indeed, many of the Roman vineyards were well placed to ship their wine by sea. This must be the main reason for the numbers of Roman wine shipments found wrecked off southern France. Indeed, until recently they made up most of the best-known sites in the western Mediterranean. Many are well preserved, and our knowledge of Roman seagoing ships springs largely from the Roman wine-ship wrecks known as Grand Congloué A and Chrétienne C (which are discussed elsewhere in this section); Dramont A; Planier C; and (a more recent discovery) Madrague de Giens. The last one is especially interesting.

The Madrague de Giens site lies 350 meters (1,150ft) off the north side of the Giens Peninsula, some 20 kilometers (12mi) southeast of Toulon. French naval divers

found it in 1967. All they could see of the wreck – in contrast to a substantial amphora mound (p. 26) – were a few amphorae in a sandy patch surrounded by thick eelgrass. Following salvage excavations and probe and magnetic surveys, four seasons of research excavation took place under the direction of André Tchernia and Patrice Pomey. From the painstaking excavation has emerged a dramatic picture of the structure, size, and cargo arrangement of a Roman wine ship of the mid-first century BC.

The cargo consisted of thousands of amphorae of the type archaeologists call Dressel 1B. They held traces of wine and many bore the stamps of P. VEVEIVS PAPVS and his colleagues or servants, whose kiln site we know lay near Terracina in Latium, south of Rome. Almost 600 amphorae have so far been raised from the trench 7 meters (23ft) wide excavated across the center of the site. They were stacked in the hold in four ways, and many had been cushioned by rushes and heather. It seems there were originally three or four layers of amphorae, numbering 6,000– 7,000, with a total weight of 300–350 tons.

The pots richly rewarded study. Before filling, the shippers had lined each with pitch, and carefully stopped its mouth with a cork, on which they had placed a plaster seal impressed with distinctive marks. There were three types of mark, matching the three slightly different varieties of pot shape found on the site. But the potter's stamps, applied before the amphorae had been fired, show no such correspondence. This brings home the fact that the cargo

Opposite, above: The western Mediterranean during the Roman period, showing the sites of some of the wrecks of wine carriers mentioned above.
Left and opposite: Two views of the large Roman freighter excavated at Madrague de Giens. The left photograph represents an overview of the site, showing the survey grid in position, and the amphorae tagged in readiness for lifting. The other picture gives a view along the floor of the vessel, from which the cargo has already been removed, and shows a section through the pile of amphorae still in its original position.

was of considerable value: the wine came from the famous Caecuban area, and each producer or shipper had taken care that his wine should reach the customer in good condition, and under his own mark. Incidentally, since the plaster seals on this kind of amphora had to be broken in order to pour out the wine, very few survive intact on land.

Other components of the Madrague de Giens cargo were pine cones prized for their edible nuts; cups, plates, and further items of black-glaze ware; other fine tableware; small jars that had held some kind of liquid; and casseroles and dishes of red coarseware. The last group is especially interesting, for it suggests that this type of coarse pottery was not made by romanized natives in Gaul as

archaeologists used to believe, but was an export from Italy.

The cargo removed, experts could study the hull of the ship herself. The wood proved well preserved, but there was no intention to raise the whole vessel. Instead, divers sawed off a piece of the keel for study on land. Together with detailed underwater recording, this showed that the ship was of "mixed" construction (p. 30): the builders had erected the shell and skeleton alternately. This came as a surprise for a ship of this date, bearing in mind the slow development of such techniques during the Byzantine period, revealed by the work of the Institute of Nautical Archaeology (see p. 38).

After they had carefully laid down and shaped the keel, the shipwrights had fitted the first three strakes on each side, held together with mortise-and-tenon joints. They had added some of the whole frames, bolting them to the keel. Next they had pinned battens between the frames; this in turn enabled them to attach more frames and the half frames. Using treenails, they had added planks to the framework, building up the sides edge-to-edge. Lastly they had inserted the futtocks. There were, in fact, two layers of bottom planking, and the ship was decked and internally fitted with stanchions, or upright supports. The outside of the hull was waterproofed with two layers of waxed or tarred blanket and a sheathing of lead. The selection of wood (mostly elm, oak, walnut, and fir), and the detailed care devoted to the construction, are most impressive. The sinking of so well prepared a vessel must have been a major disaster.

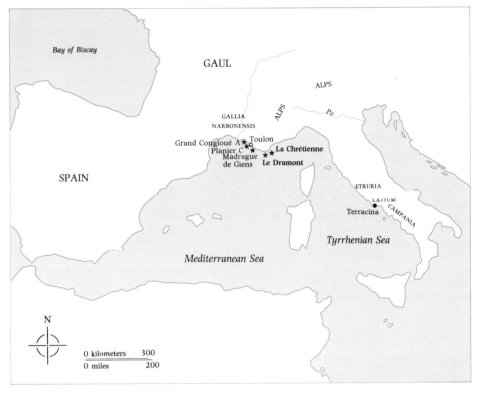

Rome's seaborne trade with Spain

The Romans established their rule in Spain late in the third century BC. It took them two centuries to complete their conquest of the whole Iberian Peninsula, but the south (Hispania Ulterior, later called Baetica) early became one of their wealthiest provinces. Rome's main motive for conquest was probably the silver/lead mining area around Cartagena. Indeed, silver and lead found in the fourth-century BC Punic shipwreck at Porticello in southern Italy very likely originated in that part of Spain. No Roman wreck has yielded silver, but lead ingots marked with the names of Roman lessees commonly crop up in wreck groups of the first centuries BC and AD. In the second half of the first century AD, however, export of Spanish lead seems to have slumped in competition with British and other mines.

Copper, too, was abundant in southern Iberia: in the Mons Marianus (Sierra Morena) mountains of Baetica, and in Lusitania farther west, especially at Vipasca (Aljustrel in southern Portugal). It was these deposits, above all, that must have drawn early voyagers from the eastern Mediterranean—voyagers who left signs of their presence about 700 BC in the wreck hoard discovered at Huelva in southwest Spain. Underwater archaeology shows that the traffic in copper certainly flourished under the early Roman Empire. Incidentally, while the lead ingots are of standardized form and weight, copper ingots are more varied; they also bear informative inscriptions.

Tin is the third metal to be found on Roman shipwrecks. There were no known Roman tin ingots of Spanish origin before 1972, when divers found the Port Vendres B wreck off southwest France. (More of that wreck in a moment.) The tin ingots vary greatly in shape. Many were cast in a decorated or inscribed mold, and all are marked with several stamps, including that of an imperial servant probably stationed in southern Lusitania to collect dues from the tinners.

Apart from mineral resources, much of Spain yielded foodstuffs. Many regions produced wheat, livestock, wine, and olives; Baetica in the south and eastern Tarraconensis in the east proved especially fertile. Then the coast of Baetica and Lusitania were noted for fishing and fish-sauce manufacture. Moreover, Baetica had a fine outlet to the sea for its products in the Baetis (Guadalquivir): unlike many Mediterranean rivers this one flows all the year.

The establishment of peace by Augustus, partly depending on a permanent frontier army posted along the Rhine and (eventually) in Britain, resulted in a demand for all these products that Spain was ideally placed to satisfy. Numbers of shipwrecks dating from Augustus's reign hold the remains of cargoes of fish sauce and olive oil from Baetica. Spanish trade plainly dominated the western Mediterranean by the middle of the first century AD, when wine, too, began to be exported from Tarraconensis. Despite competition from Africa, olive oil remained a major export until the second half of the third century AD (although trade in other products declined after about AD 100). Other products, such as fine pottery and glass, bulked out the early imperial cargoes from Spain.

Locations of known shipwrecks show that there were two main routes. One struck out past the Balearic Islands, and ran between Corsica and Sardinia toward Ostia and other ports of Italy. The other route followed the coast of eastern Spain toward the Rhône, and by transshipment and portage continued on to the Rhine and Britain.

Port Vendres B illustrates many aspects of Spain's export trade. This wreck lies in the harbor of Port Vendres, just north of the French-Spanish border. The site is in 6 meters (20ft) of water and only 35 meters (115ft) from the shore. This is one of the best dated of ancient shipwrecks: inscriptions on the tin ingots forming part of the cargo are not earlier than AD 41–42, while the other archaeological material is typical of the period AD 40–50. The cargo of amphorae evidently broke up when the ship sank but many of the sherds retain informative Latin inscriptions. These give details of the estate that produced the contents, the weight and sometimes the nature of the contents, and the name of the merchant who shipped them.

As I write, the site has been only partly excavated by Dalt Colls, with the support of the French underwater archaeology service. But we can already see that the ship sank aligned from northwest to southeast. On the western side of the excavation lie oil amphorae and most of the tin ingots, to the east lie *defrutum* and fish-sauce amphorae. Mentioned in three painted inscriptions from the wreck, *defrutum* was a sweet wine made from fruit juice boiled down to one half its volume. The fish-sauce amphorae—still contain mackerel bones. The ship carried a consignment of fine, color-coated pottery made in Baetica. But en route she may have called at a northeastern port, such as Tarraco or Emporiae. We can guess this from distinctive pear-shaped amphorae and glass bowls found in the wreck, together with a coin of Ilerda (Lérida).

The olive-oil amphorae almost all bear the stamped initials of the owners of the potteries that made them. We have not yet traced the remains of a kiln producing any of these stamps, although we do know the kilns of many other potters who worked in what is now southern Spain. But the close date given by this wreck to the stamps on sherds and ingots adds much to our understanding of Rome's trade with Spain.

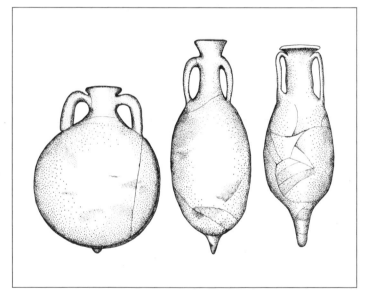

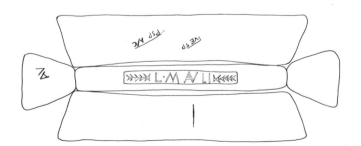

Opposite, above: Drawings of the two faces of the tin ingot number 18 from the Port Vendres B wreck. Below them is one of the stamps from another ingot, bearing the name L VALERIUS.
Left: The three types of amphora found on the Port Vendres B wreck. They are 0.72 (28in), 0.89 (35in), and 0.95 (37in) meters high respectively.
Below: An "exploded" drawing showing the top and sides of a lead ingot from the wreck at Ses Salines, Majorca. It was 0.465 meters (18in) long and weighed 33 kg (72lbs 12oz). The mark along the top is that of the founder, Lucius Manlius; the stamps on the sides are imperial control marks.
Opposite, top: Map showing the frequency of find-spots and quantities of amphorae discovered bearing the marks found on the oil amphorae from the Port Vendres B. wreck.
Right: Plan of the Port Vendres B wreck site, showing the distribution of wood, iron, bronze, ingots.

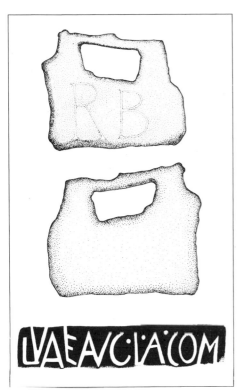

MEDITERRANEAN WRECK SITES AND CLASSICAL SEAFARING · Dt Anthony Parker

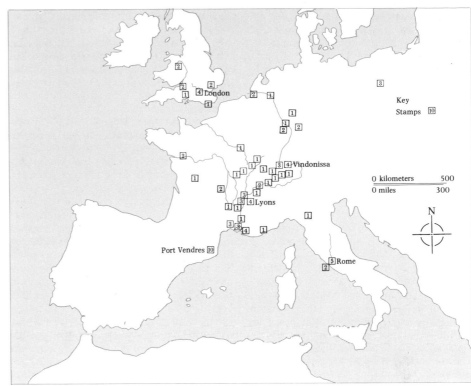

Key

Stamps [10]

0 kilometers   500
0 miles   300

N

London

Vindonissa

Lyons

Port Vendres [10]

Rome

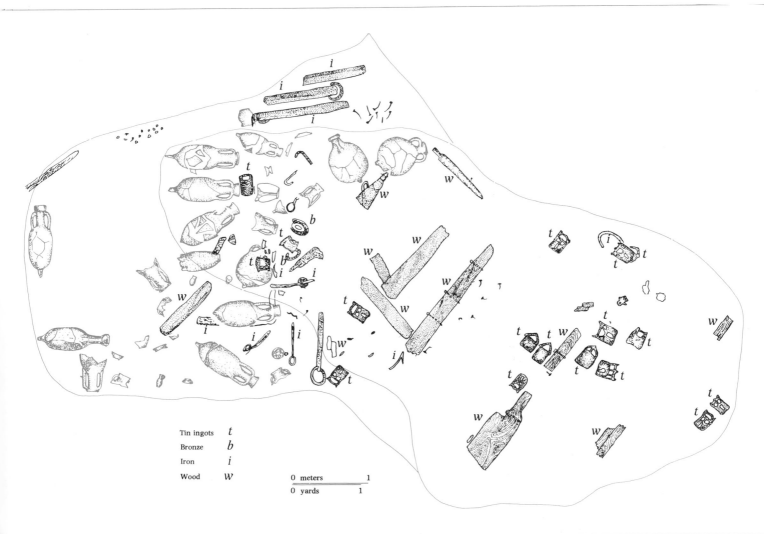

Tin ingots   *t*
Bronze   *b*
Iron   *i*
Wood   *w*

0 meters   1
0 yards   1

57

Marble by the shipload

In ancient Egypt, the pharaohs had exploited the splendidly colored granite from Aswan and fine basaltic stones from the Eastern Desert to erect columns, obelisks, and sculptures. In Greece, too, people later came to prize fine building stone. For instance, they quarried white marble from the Aegean island of Paros and from mainland Attica, and transported it for use in statues and important buildings.

The Romans inherited this taste for special stones derived from quarries in the eastern Mediterranean. The first emperor, Augustus, boasted that he found Rome brick and left it marble – a claim that has a factual basis. Of course, political motives drove Roman emperors to build like this. The difficulty and cost involved in finding, quarrying, shifting, and working exotic marble only served to underline the power and generosity of the leaders who bestowed fine stone structures on the Roman public. On a smaller scale, the well-to-do Roman of the second century AD onward wanted the best marble he could buy for the carved sarcophagus in which he would be buried. Then, too, marble veneers found widespread use for floors and wall decoration.

Some of the blocks quarried and shipped by the Roman emperors were truly huge. The biggest were the already old Egyptian obelisks brought to Rome to adorn the circuses. In at least one example this meant the special building of an outsize cargo vessel. After all, even an architectural column or a lintel (as in Trajan's Forum or Hadrian's Pantheon) might weigh 120 tons. No block that massive has yet been discovered under water. Nonetheless, some sunken Roman marble cargoes are substantial. Several loads total more than 300 tons, and the largest recorded block, a column of Attic marble from Marzamemi A, a wreck in southeast Sicily, weighs 40 tons.

Inscriptions on columns and blocks found on land help to show us how Romans organized the imperial quarries and stockpiled stone at Ostia and Rome; but we know much less about how stone was shipped by sea. However, divers have discovered a range of marble cargoes, some large, some small. Most wrecks of marble carriers have also produced amphorae and other pottery. In some places, at Camarina in southern Sicily, for example, the columns may have been only part of the cargo. But more interesting is the fact that sunken marble can answer questions that land-based marble finds have largely left unanswered.

People knew that Roman masons cut columns to standard sizes at the quarries, and architects adjusted buildings to fit slight irregularities of column length. But to what extent were more complex shapes cut at the quarry? How much was left to the masons on site? A large part of the answer has come from one cargo found at Punta Scifo, near Crotone in southern Italy. The wreck was discovered and described early this century, but only recently has the Italian archaeologist Patrizio Pensabene correctly identified its cargo.

Some objects consist of white marble from Proconnesus and Synnada, respectively in northern and central Asia Minor; other objects of peacock-colored marble (*pavonazzetto*) came from Synnada. This varied collection included columns, capitals, bases, and large blocks for architectural use; basins and stands; an altar; and even a sculptured group depicting Cupid and Psyche. The finish of these items ranges from complete, except for final detailing and polishing, through half finished (the

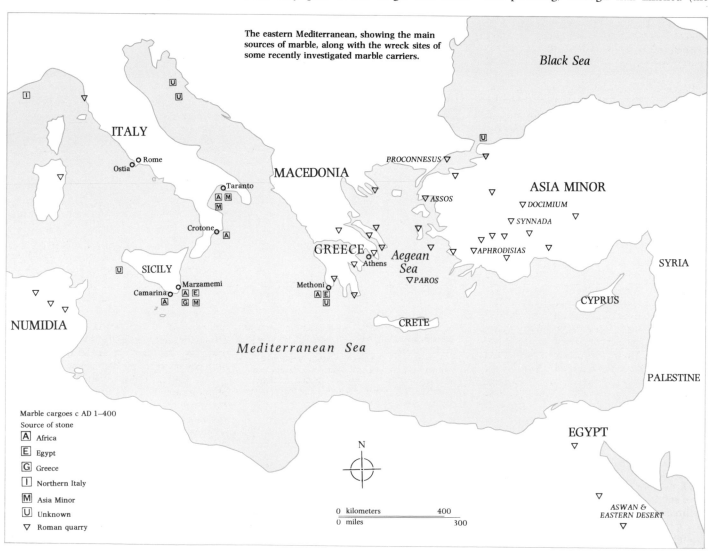

The eastern Mediterranean, showing the main sources of marble, along with the wreck sites of some recently investigated marble carriers.

Marble cargoes c AD 1–400

Source of stone

A Africa
E Egypt
G Greece
I Northern Italy
M Asia Minor
U Unknown
▽ Roman quarry

columns), to merely roughed out (the blocks). This shows that manufacturing finished items involved both the provincial quarry workshops and Roman masons in Italy.

When we turn to sunken cargoes of sarcophagi, however, we find that the provincial workshops had evidently played a relatively smaller part. Thus stone coffins that sank off Methoni in southern Greece on their way from Assos in northern Asia Minor bore merely roughed out garlands. The sarcophagi found at San Pietro were likewise "raw," even though they probably came from Aphrodisias in western Asia Minor, where there was a well-developed school of sculptors.

The San Pietro wreck lies in 3–6 meters (10–20ft) of water, 110 meters (360ft) from the coast southeast of the south Italian port of Taranto. First reported in 1960, the wreck was partly excavated by Peter Throckmorton (p. 32) in 1964. He surveyed a total of 23 sarcophagi that he found lying tumbled on a firm bedrock covered by mobile sand. Their positions must reflect the final alignment of the ship, which had sunk about AD 200–250. Here, as elsewhere, though, there may have been some disturbance from unsuccessful salvage attempts soon after the shipwreck happened. Only scanty remains of the ship herself survive: two frames, a piece of lead sheathing, and some pottery. More remains may be found if excavations are resumed.

Throckmorton found that the sarcophagi were still in a very rough, unfinished shape. In three cases, a block large enough for two sarcophagi had been left undivided, although masons had hollowed out the inside

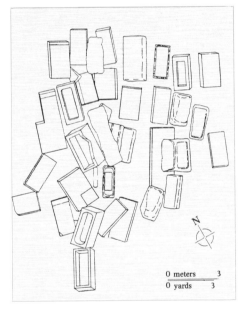

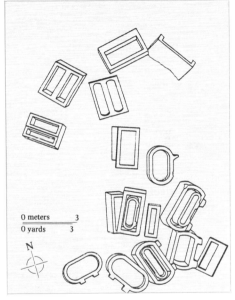

Above: Plans of the cargoes of sarcophagi found at Torre Sgaratta (left) and San Pietro (right), both in southern Italy.
Top: A Roman marble sarcophagus of the third century AD, showing Dionysus, the Seasons, and other figures. This is a particularly fine surviving example of the type of container in which wealthy Romans were buried.

of each prospective unit. Three of the individual sarcophagi still had a piece of stone attached to one side, presumably for future use as a lid. Most importantly, several sarcophagi each had a pair of shapeless projections: bosses presumably left to be

carved into lions' heads or some other decorative feature. Here it certainly seems that the masons back at the quarries had little say in what the final object looked like.

The way in which several smaller sarcophagi nestled in larger ones reminds us that the Romans fully utilized space in their stone-bearing ships. In the contemporary shipwreck at Torre Sgarrata, near Taranto, dockers had crammed thin veneer slabs in the space between the sarcophagi and blocks of stone, and the spaces inside some sarcophagi had served as storage for blocks of expensive alabaster. Archaeologists are still investigating whether the Romans actually built especially strong merchantmen to cope with these heavy cargoes.

A ships' graveyard off Sicily

One of the few Mediterranean areas intensively searched for ancient shipwrecks lies near the village of Marzamemi, at Sicily's southeastern tip. Here, since 1959, Italian, German, American, and British divers (organized by the German archaeologist Gerhard Kapitän) have carried out a wide-ranging search of the relatively shallow inshore zone. In 1975–76, I led several expeditions from Bristol and Oxford universities to search for new sites, and verify earlier reports. The survey is still far from complete, but we now have something close to a sample of this stretch of coast. Altogether, we know of 14 wrecks, and rumors of at least another two, although so far no archaeologist has seen them. Of the 14, 4 are Greek, 5 Roman, and 5 Byzantine. The high proportion of Byzantine sites doubtless reflects the fact that southern Sicily remained part of the Byzantine Empire after much of the rest of the west had fallen to barbarians. In this, southern Sicily contrasts, for example, with the southern French coast, where there is a preponderance of Roman wrecks.

Most of Marzamemi's wrecks lie in less than 15 meters (50ft) of water and are scattered. Few have produced any timbers or complete amphorae. Of the stone cargoes found here we have already mentioned Marzamemi A. Marzamemi B is the well-known "Church Wreck," comprising the pulpit, sanctuary screen, capitals, bases, and some columns of a small basilica of a type widely built in the Byzantine Empire

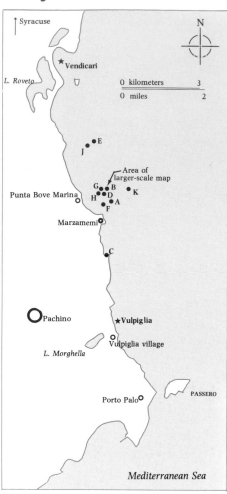

under Justinian I (AD 527–565). Much of the cargo and other material from the ship have now been excavated, but some small column drums still lie on the site. The reason for the wreck is clear: fringed by a white, sandy beach, the bay north of Marzamemi appears to a ship out at sea to offer a safe refuge in a storm. In fact, the bay is a trap. In the center lurks a rocky shallow that shoals to only 3 meters (10ft) deep at a point 100 meters (330ft) southeast of the Church Wreck. This shoal was plainly a serious hazard in antiquity, for here more than one ship struck the rocks and went down.

Marzamemi D, a Roman amphora cargo, was partly excavated in 1964. At the same time, divers discovered nearby what appear to be fragments of metal fittings from a modern sailing ship; if this vessel ever had any cargo it has all been salvaged. In 1975, survey revealed another old wreck, labeled Marzamemi G. This consists of a smashed cargo of Hellenistic amphorae, datable to the mid-second century BC. Nearby on the rocky limestone seabed lies Marzamemi H, first noticed in 1964, and studied in detail

Left: The southeastern coast of Sicily, showing the locations of the many wrecks off Marzamemi and neighboring shores.
Below: A detailed map of an area of seabed off Marzamemi, onto which at least four vessels sank in classical times. Items, mostly potsherds, from four different centuries are indicated separately, thus demonstrating the overlap of the four wrecks (designated B, D, G, and H.)

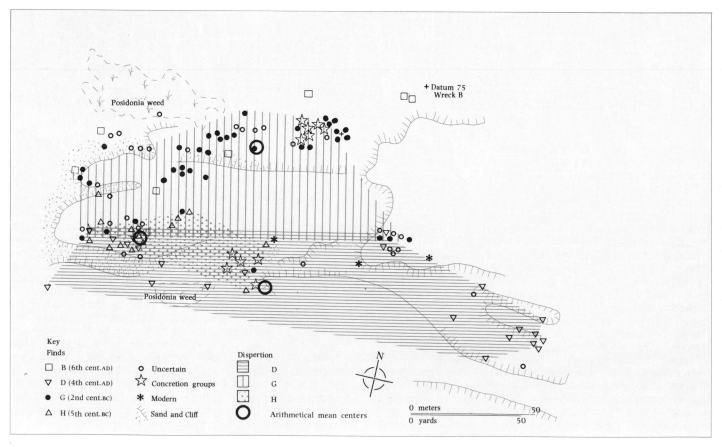

Key
Finds

☐	B (6th cent. AD)	○ Uncertain
▽	D (4th cent. AD)	☆ Concretion groups
●	G (2nd cent. BC)	✳ Modern
△	H (5th cent. BC)	Sand and Cliff

Dispersion

D
G
H

○ Arithmetical mean centers

0 meters 50
0 yards 50

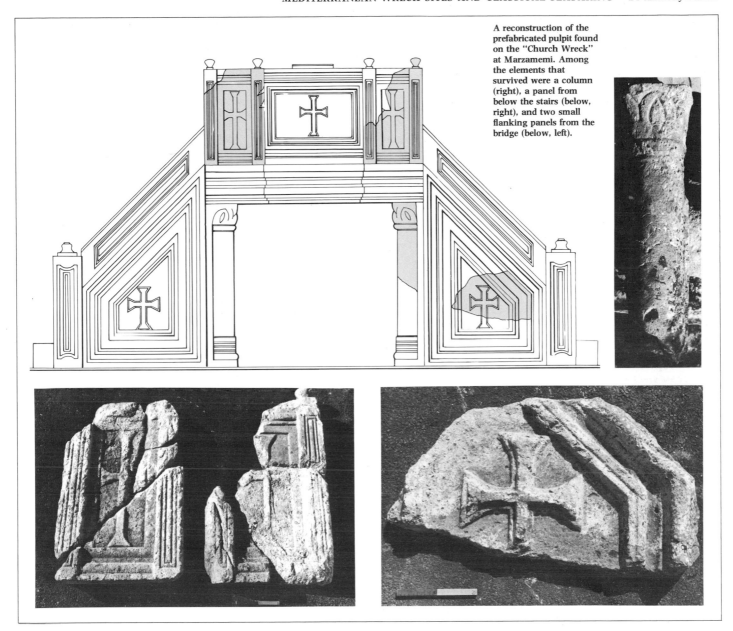

A reconstruction of the prefabricated pulpit found on the "Church Wreck" at Marzamemi. Among the elements that survived were a column (right), a panel from below the stairs (below, right), and two small flanking panels from the bridge (below, left).

in 1975. These cargoes lie close together and in places overlap, so that only methodical survey has finally sorted them out.

The survey was impeded by the concealment of many fragments of pottery by rocks or marine growths. Our divers patiently and systematically covered the area, measuring from base lines with tapes. I classified the identifiable finds in five periods, and plotted them accordingly on the survey plan. From this we can see that the Hellenistic (G) and the Roman (D) cargoes are grouped around nuclei formed by dense masses of concreted amphora sherds. The classical Greek amphorae (H), however, are all scattered. Moreover, the dispersion of these three sites, indicated by drawing "least polygons" around the outlying objects of each class, shows that G and D scarcely overlap, but that H underlies both. Fortunately, the presence of two characteristic Greek grinding stones in the easterly part of the scatter

confirmed that the amphorae of site H really did represent a shipwreck. I have plotted the frequency of finds from each cargo in four standardized diagrams and these enable us to judge the lie of the four wrecks: B, D, G, and H.

It appears that each of the four ancient ships came in from the east. Ship H probably struck the summit of the reef and sank in a fairly small area toward the west of the site. The cargo of ship G is more widely scattered; possibly she came to rest on one side, with cargo spilling shoreward as the hull broke up. Ship D came in more from the southeast, and, striking the high part of the reef, broke into two or even three pieces. This is a reasonable guess, for the cargo lies scattered over a track that extends about 200 meters (about 660ft). Ship B, by contrast, must have gone straight down: the remains of the church lay in an area only 40×25 meters (130×80ft) and a mere handful of

pots rolled away shoreward from the wreck.

The value of these scattered, badly broken shipwrecks lies less in individual detail (not much of that survives) than in the fact that they contribute just as much as well-preserved sites to the statistics of ancient seaborne trade. Scattered wrecks in shallow water account for one-fifth of all recorded sites, so that ignoring them would greatly reduce the value of any statistical summary. Broken and mixed up though these so often are, their cargoes still provide a mass of interesting information. In the Marzamemi area, for example, we have learned that some of the shipwrecks listed here are roughly contemporary, yet no two contain similar types, or groups of types, of amphora. The hundreds of sites known in the western Mediterranean as a whole thus form a store of immensely useful archaeological information on which scholarship is only now beginning to draw.

European Shipwrecks over 3000 Years

Our second thematic section moves chronologically through the history of seafaring in European waters north of the Mediterranean. Lack of sites on land or under water means we have no clear picture of prehistoric developments, but a few sites in the English Channel point the way to future progress. In the first six pages the general editor reviews the potential of this field.

Next, Angela Evans considers developments in the early centuries AD. A similar lack of underwater finds is here counterbalanced by a number of discoveries on land. Miss Evans's own work as an assistant keeper at the British Museum has involved

her in the study of the famous ship-burial at Sutton Hoo in Suffolk.

Miss Evans's consideration of Viking ships in Scandinavia paves the way for Dr. Carl Olof Cederlund's contribution, which examines the special challenges posed by archaeology in Baltic waters. His topics move chronologically from the Middle Ages through the eighteenth century, as well as following the same order as the site investigations, which illustrate advances in techniques and procedures since the 1930s. Dr. Cederlund is keeper of maritime archaeology at the National Maritime Museum in Stockholm, and has been intimately in-

volved in research and reconstruction on the seventeenth-century *Wasa* since the early 1960s.

This section ends with Colin Martin's survey of wreck-site evidence of shipping in western Europe after 1500. His contribution chronologically overlaps and complements Dr. Cederlund's final pages. Since 1968 Mr. Martin has been a leading researcher into the archaeology of the Spanish Armada of 1588, and he uses material from this work to illustrate a number of themes. He is the founder and director of the Institute of Maritime Archaeology at St. Andrews University in Scotland.

Early cross-Channel shipping

There is a big difference between studying the trade routes and cargoes of the classical Mediterranean world and studying prehistoric exchanges across the English Channel. We know much about the political and economic structures of the classical world from a wealth of old writings and archaeological material. But we have far fewer archaeological finds and no written records from the barbarian societies to the north before these entered Rome's imperial orbit. Thus we glimpse the barbarians' political and social systems only indirectly and vaguely. We know equally little about their economies. Because these people lacked coinage, you could argue that they never traded in the same sense as those of the cash-based economies farther south. Most of what transactions there were probably involved only goods – bartered, confiscated or seized as a tribute or tax payment. In this section, then, we give the word "trade" the simple meaning of the transfer of goods from one group of people to another.

One of the most direct ways of investigating past trade is via a study of wrecks and their cargoes (p. 24). But before we consider some sites along the English Channel coast that may shed new light on prehistoric trade, we must consider two things: first, the waters on which prehistoric vessels sailed, and second, the kinds of craft involved. So far as the Channel is concerned the main fact is its clear division into two parts. The eastern end is narrow, only 40 to 50 kilometers (25–30mi) wide, while the main section, from Dungeness westward, is 100 to 140 kilometers (60–80mi) across. Furthermore, the whole Channel is no calm, untroubled stretch of water, but scoured by strong tidal streams, and open to gales that blow from the southwest. A dogleg, often extending the trip to over 160 kilometers

(100mi), is frequently the quickest and safest way of getting across.

This implies that men must have learned to build fairly sturdy craft before they could make frequent, regular crossings. Unfortunately, we know little about the types of vessels available to prehistoric mariners. Craft formed by hollowing out a tree trunk appeared in northern Europe possibly by the seventh millenium BC, certainly by the third. Otherwise, the earliest known boats are three from the later second millenium BC found at North Ferriby on the Humber estuary. Each was constructed of planks sewn together and elaborately caulked. Neither type of craft could have survived well in an open sea.

The probability is that until bronze tools became plentiful in the middle Bronze Age (say, about 1500 BC), building a seaworthy vessel was just not worth the effort involved.

However, as the demand for and use of bronze tools increased, people not only gained the technical ability to produce seagoing craft, they *needed* to make them. Only seaworthy vessels could carry copper and tin – the basic ingredients of bronze – between places cut off by sea. Increasing long-distance exchange shows up in the archaeological record for this period, but until the late 1970s there were no discoveries of northern Bronze Age shipwrecks. This absence can be explained principally by considering the seafloor in the areas concerned. As the map shows, most of the Channel seabed is surfaced with loose sands and silts. This is especially true of the Narrow Seas, where most of the regular voyaging almost certainly happened. A sunken boat and her cargo might be well preserved within these sediments, but she would leave no visible clue to her

presence. Additionally, suspended particles cloud the water, reducing visibility to a few meters. Not many divers swim in such areas for pleasure and those who do see only a small part of the seabed. Thus few prehistoric sites have been found to date in the English Channel.

Nonetheless, two probable middle Bronze Age wreck sites have come to light off the coast of southern England. The first was found by club divers at Langdon Bay, near Dover Harbour and below the famous white cliffs. During 1974, members of the local sub-aqua club began finding bronze objects in chalk gullies in 8–12 meters (25–40ft) of water. All told, they found no fewer than 95 pieces. Uncertain what these were, they consulted the local museum, where staff identified them as tools, weapons, and ornaments derived from Bronze Age France. Experts published short papers about the finds, and the bronzes went to the British Museum. Meanwhile, archaeologists lost contact with the club·divers. Early in 1978, developments at Moor Sand (the next site described in this atlas) led me to enquire about the circumstances of the Langdon Bay finds. I was astounded to learn that club divers were still discovering objects. I was even more amazed when I dived with them and saw dozens of artifacts on the seabed. I quickly sought designation for the site under the Protection of Wrecks Act, 1973, and began making plans with the club for systematic investigation. As I write, the work at Langdon Bay has only just begun. But already scores more bronzes have been plotted and lifted from the site. As a collection of items apparently en route for Britain on just one day, the find must add significantly to our understanding of Bronze Age trade. Meanwhile, low visibility, strong tides, and rough weather make excavation a challenging task.

Below: A map of the English Channel, showing the Bronze Age sites mentioned in the text, with (opposite) a view across the eastern docks at Dover. Langdon Bay lies beyond the outer harbor wall, the Bronze Age site being 500 meters offshore.
Right: A model of the Bronze Age boat found at North Ferriby in Yorkshire. It is likely that this craft was built to operate only in and around the Humber estuary.
Right: A diver inspects a bronze ax as found on the site at Langdon Bay. Usually, it would not be possible to see either diver or ax so clearly. The photographic scale in this picture, and that to its right, is graduated at 5-cm (2-in) intervals.
Below: The bronze being inspected by the diver in the picture to the left. It is a median-winged ax lying on its side and it is shown as found.

Below, right: The collection of 62 bronzes recovered from the Langdon Bay site during July and August 1979. Nearly all these objects were found lying on the surface of the seabed. Many of them are broken, but among the complete artifacts the median-winged axes (for examples, nos. 11, 22, and 30) and the rapiers (nos. 47 and 48) are noteworthy.

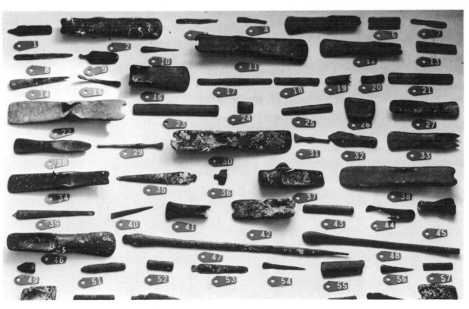

Bronze Age weapons from the sea

In July 1977 further apparent remains from a Bronze Age wreck turned up in the English Channel, this time near Salcombe in south Devon. The second such site to be found, this was the first to be fully studied from the start, thanks to its finder.

The story began on July 4, 1977, when a diving instructor named Philip Baker was escorting a novice diver. Baker suddenly glimpsed a fine bronze sword with a hook-tang. It lay on a patch of gravel in about 7 meters (23ft) of water. An hour or so later, novice diver John Clark discovered a heavily eroded bronze blade a few meters from the first find spot. A collector of naval swords, Baker knew that the bronze weapons were unusual and probably old. He reported them to the authorities, and eventually I assumed archaeological responsibility for the site, which lay off a beach called Moor Sand.

In what remained of the diving season we had to inspect and photograph the area and to look for more artifacts – clues that might point to a major assemblage. Accordingly, Baker arranged for a short reconnaissance to be made in October 1977. We were lucky, and discovered a third eroded blade. This made it more likely that all three had come from a wreck, and led us to decide to launch a major search and survey.

The British Department of Trade recognized the site's potential importance and agreed to designate the area under the Protection of Wrecks Act. Next, the National Maritime Museum and the British Museum provided cash to support work through June and July 1978. Divers were recruited from a number of branches of the British Sub-Aqua Club, and we begged and borrowed equipment and other aid from a number of organizations.

From an operational viewpoint Moor Sand had problems. The beach lay several kilometers from a secure haven, and no tarred roads came very near. We thus had to ship all heavy equipment on to the beach at the start of the season. We installed a hut on a ledge above the high-tide mark and below the main face of a coastal cliff. We also constructed an aerial flightway to carry equipment from hut to beach.

Our main task for 1978 was systematically searching a substantial area of seabed. The idea was to describe minutely the context within which the first three blades had been found, and to discover any more Bronze Age material that might lie close by. We began where the 1977 finds had been made, just off a small offshore rock exposed at low tide. From there we worked in two directions. We searched toward the coast in case objects had been washed further inshore. We also swept out into deep water toward the south and west, from where prevailing storms and swells might have driven the bronzes inshore. The perfect preservation of the first sword suggested that it had only recently been disturbed from a protected spot, either on the cliffs or, more likely, in deeper water. It certainly could not have lain undamaged for long on the heavily scoured seabed where Philip Baker found it.

By the end of the season, we had covered more than 1.5 hectares (about 4ac) in corridors each measuring 100× 10 meters (328× 33ft). Starting from opposite sides of a corridor, a pair of divers would work toward each other, scouring the seabed below the thick kelp until they met. If they found patches of sand or shingle, they disturbed these by hand fanning to uncover anything buried. At intervals they made notes on the nature of the seabed and its plant life. When they met, the divers laid a line across the corridor to mark off the area already covered. Then each returned to his own side and began scouring the next section of the corridor. Meanwhile, another pair of divers worked from the far end of the corridor. This visual hunt was reinforced by metal detector survey. Altogether, it usually took one and a half to two days to cover a corridor.

Systematic search for artifacts was only part of the investigation. Before the season started, we had made enquiries to discover if recent, local dredging or fishing could have uncovered an underwater Bronze Age deposit. We had also asked oceanographers about the prevailing swell, currents, and tides, and recent movements in local seabed sediments.

Geologists considered recent substantial cliff erosion unlikely. Finally, to assess the site's exposure to disturbance from wave action, we commissioned a leading marine biologist to make a biological survey. From the species present, Dr. Robert Earll of Manchester University concluded that the spot was less exposed than either he or we had expected.

It was four weeks before we found our first Bronze Age object: a palstave (a type of axhead) lying exposed on bare rock more than 100 meters (330ft) seaward of our previous finds. By the end of the season this had been joined by a second palstave, 20 meters (65ft) beyond the first. In the meantime, we had found a severely corroded and unidentifiable blade closer inshore. The palstaves are both of a type known to have been manufactured in northwest France, while the closest parallels for the fine sword come from the Seine basin and eastern France. Together, then, palstaves and sword strongly suggest that all the items had been brought from France, presumably in one ship. Moreover, the differing areas of origin hint at an extensive exchange network across the Channel.

Apart from their French affinities, the main arguments in favor of seeing these objects as the remains of a wreck include lack of evidence for the erosion of a Bronze Age deposit from a nearby cliff face, and lack of later artifacts to suggest that the collection had been lost between Bronze Age times and today. Nevertheless, the evidence remains inconclusive; our future investigations could undermine the shipwreck theory. Whatever emerges from Moor Sand will be the fruits of cooperation between experts in many different fields.

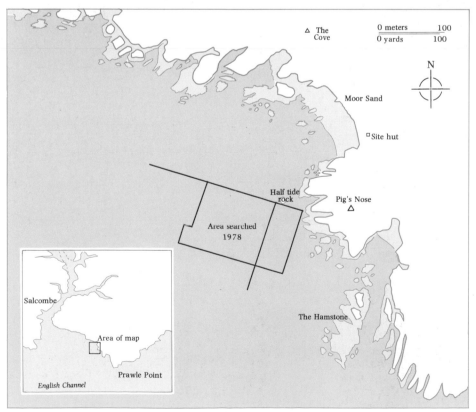

Right: A photograph and drawings of the fine bronze sword found by Philip Baker in 1977.
Below: A generalized map of the area searched in 1978 (see map opposite). As well as seabed topography, it shows the 10-meter-wide search corridors, and the locations of the bronzes found. The first two finds, including the fine sword, came from the area encircled with a double line.
Below, right: John Clark inspects a bronze palstave (type of axhead) he has just discovered. It lies as found except that the surrounding kelp forest has been cut down.

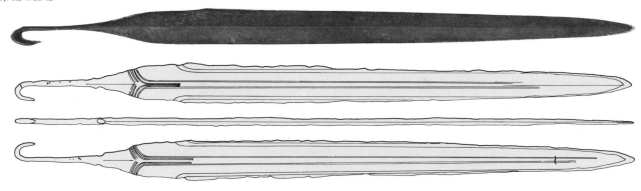

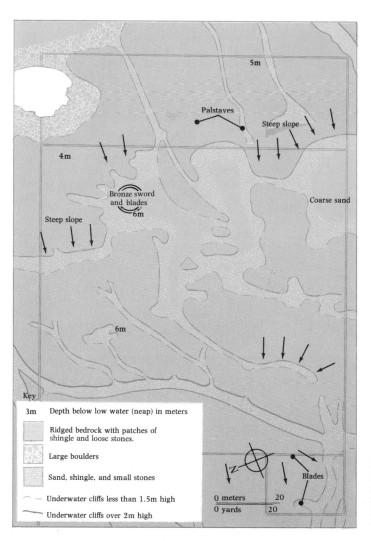

Opposite: A map of the coast around Moor Sand near Salcombe, South Devon, showing the area searched in June and July 1978.
Right: The two small palstaves found in 1978.

Cross-Channel trade after the Bronze Age

Following the brief glimpse of middle Bronze Age trade granted us by the sites at Langdon Bay and Moor Sand, the veil descends again. We can only indirectly assess developments during the first millenium BC. As before, a major reason is sea conditions that obscure old wrecks and their cargoes. Then there is the fact that items not of bronze or similarly valuable metals are less likely to be noticed by those club divers ready to turn an honest coin by recovering scrap. At the same time, wider archaeological studies suggest a reduction in cross-Channel trade at the end of the Bronze Age (800–600 BC). This could be more apparent than real if trade simply shifted toward organic products that on land sites have decayed and left no traces. If so, wreck sites of this period will be particularly valuable, for the seabed can preserve such objects.

However, it seems reasonable to suppose that Britain did become an economic backwater after about 800 BC. Unlike copper and tin, iron occurs in all regions, so one of the principal stimuli to long-distance trade in the preceding period would have disappeared. Furthermore, fine luxury products from the Mediterranean were increasingly being marketed north of the Alps, drawing the attentions of Continental societies toward the south. Their relationship to Mediterranean civilization was analogous to that prevailing between the third world and Europe in the sixteenth to nineteenth centuries AD. In both instances, the end result was colonial subjection of the less advanced societies.

Of course, as time passed, Britain herself increasingly came into direct contact with southern Europe. Her relative isolation was certainly over by the third century BC. Some of the earliest direct imports from the south into Iron Age Britain are found in the extreme southwest, as at Mount Batten near Plymouth, and Harlyn Bay in north Cornwall. Discoveries of objects with Iberian styles of ornament indicate a traffic up the western seaways, but these finds are local enough to suggest only an occasional voyage.

Trade was much more extensive by the end of the second century BC. The main point of entry to Britain had shifted east to a major settlement at Hengistbury Head, near Bournemouth in Hampshire. Pottery finds there and over a radius of 150 kilometers (90mi) show that Hengistbury Head received and distributed wine and other delicacies in amphorae of a type known to archaeologists as "Dressel 1A." Such pottery is absent from sites of this period in northern France, but has been dredged from the seabed off northwestern France. This suggests direct shipments to Britain from southern Europe.

The sheltered waters of Christchurch Harbour behind Hengistbury Head, providing easy access to the hinterland of southern England, and the Channel Islands and Normandy Peninsula opposite, gave Hengistbury Head many natural advantages as a port. But its unusual preeminence in the late Iron Age seems to have been due, above all, to the contemporary political and social situation. Hengistbury Head was probably an independent community flanked by and supplying the two major tribal groups known in Roman times as the Durotriges and Atrabates, or Belgae. Friendly to all other societies, but members of none, Hengistbury's people would thus have oiled the machinery of international trade rather as the Phoenicians before them had done in the Mediterranean.

We know a little about some of the vessels involved in this trade from a description written by Julius Caesar in the mid-first century BC. He was writing of the ships of his opponents, the Veneti, which, he claims, voyaged regularly from northwest Gaul (France) to Britain. Unlike the light and finely carpentered Mediterranean craft that he knew, these ships had heavy oak timbers, upright stems and sterns, high sides, heavy leather sails, and iron anchors with heavy chains. Archaeological support for the use of such anchors in Iron Age Britain appeared in 1882 when one was found in a pit at Bulbury Camp, a hill fort in Dorset. Caesar's account gained further corroboration in 1976 when archaeologists recovered a pre-Roman coin at Canterbury in Kent. Bearing the name of the British ruler Cunobeline, and dated about AD 20, it shows a bluff, high-sided sailing vessel. This suggests that this type was still in use in the eastern Channel nearly a century after Caesar described it. The British ruler probably had it depicted to publicize his commercial relations with the Roman Empire. The thriving trade of the last decades before the Roman conquest of AD 43 is further attested by the wide range of Roman imports found in southeast England.

Naturally, the Roman occupation led to many changes in relationships between Britain and the Continent. The new Romano-British towns represented new markets for entrepreneurs from the south: a large army had to be supplied; and officials moved freely from one province to another. Archaeological proof of intensified cross-Channel commerce includes vast quantities of Samian ware found on British sites. This high-quality pottery arrived from southern and, later, central Gaul in the first and second century AD. All must have come in by sea. Yet so far we know of only one evident wreck from a cargo of Samian ware discovered back in the eighteenth century, when fishermen began dragging up objects from the Pudding Pan Reef off Whitstable in Kent. Dated about AD 160, this cargo serves as a useful chronological marker for studies in dating Samian pottery. Fast tides and poor visibility have prevented detailed investigation by divers.

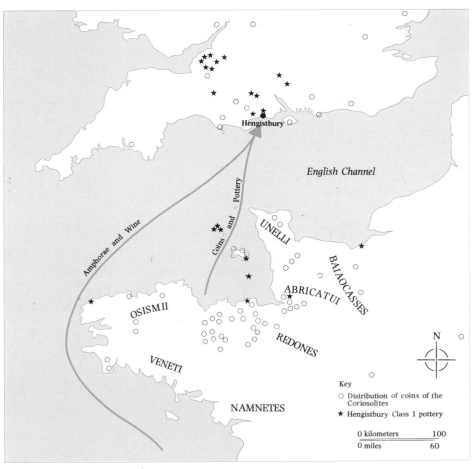

A map of southern Britain and northwest France showing the position of Hengistbury Head at the end of sea routes from the south, and as an intermediary for exchange between Britain and France.

Below: Some of the complete Samian-ware vessels of the second-century AD dredged up from the Pudding Pan Reef off Whitstable, Kent in the eighteenth and nineteenth centuries.
Above: A coin of Cunobeline, found in Canterbury in Kent, and dating from c. AD 20. It shows a sailing vessel that may represent those in use around southern Britain at that period.
Above, right: A view of an amphora of Spanish type lying on the seabed off St. Peter Port in Guernsey. This, and other amphorae in the area, may indicate a Roman wreck buried under the silt. The scale bears 10-cm (4-in) divisions.

This site apart, no other Roman wrecks are known in British waters, although isolated pots have been recovered by divers off Seaford in Sussex, Lulworth Cove in Dorset, and Guernsey in the Channel Islands. Since so much of this material is bright red and easily seen in clear water, this lack of finds is surprising. It may mean a concentration of traffic at the murky, sediment-laden eastern end of the Channel, where sunken objects are so hard to find.

Recent studies of the distribution of other Continental pottery types imported to Roman Britain, and of British pottery exported to the European mainland certainly suggest that the corridor between the Thames and Rhine estuaries was the main route by which Britain communicated with the rest of the empire. A few chance finds under water would do much to confirm this belief, and it must be only a matter of time before they are made.

Shipping in the age of migrations

There are few archaeological clues to the development of ships and boats in northern Europe in the seven centuries (AD 300–1000) that saw independent nations emerge from the former Roman provinces of Britain, Germany, and Gaul. But archaeological finds make it clear that before Rome fell in AD 410 the southern North Sea and the English Channel were alive with boats of raiders and traders. By the fifth century, seaborne migrants from the North European Plain were heading westward to Britain in large numbers. These Germanic groups, known as the Angles, Saxons, and Jutes, between them intensively settled in east and southeast Britain.

It is clear, then, that sea crossings from the European mainland to Britain were everyday events in the Dark Ages. We can guess that most vessels hugged coasts, and used the shortest crossings between mainland Europe and Britain. But we have no details of such routes, and few surviving hulls from either sites on land or those under water from which to assess the vessels' seaworthiness. Any coherent story of boat and ship development in northern Europe must therefore take full account of finds from whatever context.

We can draw further evidence from small objects depicting boat shapes, although all of these are relatively late. For example, ships appear on a series of seventh-century Anglo-Saxon coins called *sceattas*. These show featureless hulls, and stem- and sternposts crowned by knobs. The faint outline of another hull appears engraved on a seventh-century strap end found at St. Germain-en-Laye, in Merovingian Gaul. This engraving shows oars, a steering paddle, and a central mast with stays fore and aft and a fitting of some sort at its head. The boat shape generally resembles that found on the coin of Cunobeline (p. 66). A sword pommel in the form of a stylized boat shape and dating from about AD 700 comes from Sibertswold in Kent. An early seventh-century Anglian urn found at Caistor-by-Norwich in Norfolk bears a free-hand drawing of a boat with a high prow and a steering paddle.

Turning now to actual boat remains, we have at least one fifth-century ship's figure-head, from the Scheldt River at Appels in Belgium. This is a tall post with a basal tenon and a straight neck decorated with ribbon interlace. The head is rounded and has a gaping mouth full of gnashing teeth. A second, slightly smaller, head of much the same date was found nearby at Moerzeke/Mariekerke; this too may have been the finial (crowning ornament) of a stem- or sternpost.

Structural fragments of boats do occasionally survive. A second-century-AD find from Halsøny, south of Bergen in Norway, gives us some idea of the North Sea area's early clinker-built boats (p. 30). Only parts of this boat were recovered, but they

included bits of planks sewn together, one sturdy frame and a well-formed oarlock. These fragments show that, like all craft of the period, this boat was rowed rather than paddled. A similar fragmentary boat find dated almost 500 years later came from Gredstedbro in Denmark. This featured part of a stempost with a horizontal scarf joint secured with iron bolts. There was also an incomplete frame that had been fixed to the planking with wooden pegs.

This last example postdates the period of major Germanic migrations and may not represent craft typical of those times. The earliest complete hull from the period is one of two fine examples ritually deposited in a bog at Nydam, Schleswig, in north Germany, and recovered in 1864. Both were rowing boats with an open, shallow, midships section and low raking stem- and sternposts with deep cutwaters. One of the boats, made of fir, was destroyed in the nineteenth century, although plans still survive. The other — an oak boat 25 meters (82ft) long — provides many details of a well-developed open rowing boat on the evolutionary path

from planked dugout to Viking longship — the finest achievement of the clinker tradition (p. 30).

Dating from AD 350–400, the Nydam oak boat was fairly primitive despite her size, and her construction involved only 15 pieces of timber. Each side featured five strakes, or planks, fashioned from massive pieces of oak 50 centimeters (20in) broad, running the full length of the hull, overlapping each other and held by iron rivets. Inside, the hull was braced by sturdy frames of grown timbers (p. 30), and lashed to projecting cleats carved out of the solid oak of the strakes. The keel was a thick, broad plank projecting only a little into the water. End-posts were equally massive timbers, fastened to the keel by short horizontal scarf joints each held by only two treenails. The boat was steered by a heavy paddle, probably lashed to the hull. Grown forks of oak lashed to the gunwale gave 30 rowing positions. Excavation revealed no decking, but thwarts ran across the hull at the rowing positions. Although apparently typical, this open plan would have made movement inside the boat extremely awkward. The hull's long, narrow shape would have made sailing difficult and there was no trace of a sail or associated fittings.

Despite her open cross section and low freeboard, the Nydam boat was a sturdy vessel, probably capable of making short sea journeys as warship or trader. Boats like her could have ferried immigrants to Britain during the age of migrations. But by the end of the sixth century, new boatbuilding techniques had superseded those of the Nydam boat, and the clinker hull had begun to anticipate Viking ship design.

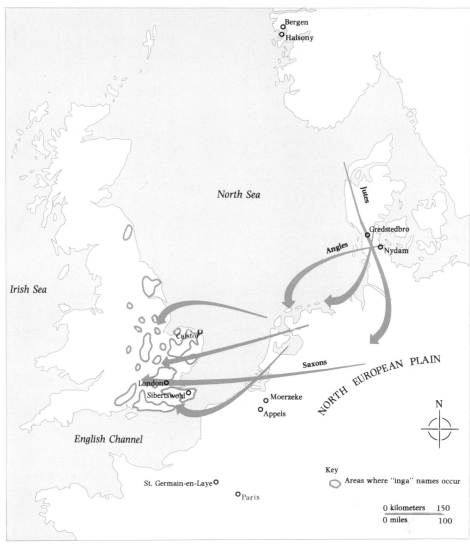

Top: Western Europe, showing the routes open to the Germanic peoples migrating to Britain around the fifth century AD.
Right: The Nydam oak boat displayed at the Schleswig Museum.
Opposite: Ship's figurehead from the Scheldt at Appels in Belgium.
Below: Seventh-century strap end from St. Germain-en-Laye, bearing a representation of a ship.

The grave-ship at Sutton Hoo

Archaeological finds in eastern England show that by about AD 600, people were building sophisticated plank-built boats in the kingdom of East Anglia. Although in the same general tradition as the Nydam boat (p. 69), the East Anglian boats differ in certain details from the Scandinavian mainstream. For example, the frames are shaped to fit snugly against the overlapping planks, to which they are fastened with wooden pegs and iron bolts. This feature is, however, paralleled in Denmark's Gredstedbro boat (p. 69) and anticipates elements in the Graveney boat (p. 76), and the upper parts of the Oseberg and Gokstad ships (p. 72). From East Anglia the remains of three burial boats survive, as well as fragmentary boat timbers laid over cremation urns in the Anglian cemetery at Caistor-by-Norwich.

Of the three excavated boats, the first was found beneath a mound at Snape in Suffolk in 1862. She survived only as an impression in the sand, and was 14.6 meters (48ft) long with eight or nine strakes a side. The other boats both came from burial mounds at Sutton Hoo, across the River Deben from the Suffolk town of Woodbridge. One vessel came from a ransacked mound and survived only as a vague shape in the sand. But enough of the third vessel remained to demonstrate a shipbuilding ability unsurpassed until Viking boatbuilding culminated in the superb ninth-century Gokstad boat.

Excavations at Sutton Hoo began in 1938 when the landowner employed Basil Brown, a local archaeologist, to examine some of the 16 burial mounds. Encouraged by finding the much disturbed remains of a clinker-built boat in one mound, in 1939 Brown opened up the largest mound of all. Inside he found an undisturbed ship burial containing finds beyond the wildest dreams of any archaeologist.

The Sutton Hoo ship lay beneath a large circular mound 3 meters (10ft) high and 30 meters (100ft) across. The mourners had placed her in a ship-shaped trench that hugged her timbers. Then they had filled this trench with sand, so that when the wood disintegrated in the damp, acid soil the sand retained the outline of the hull, with all the iron rivets in position. Amidships stood a burial chamber built of sturdy timbers, with a roof that had been strong enough to withstand the tremendous weight of the mound above for many years. Inside the chamber, hung and carpeted with textiles, the mourners had placed superb gold and garnet fittings, including a jeweled purse containing a collection of gold Merovingian coins that date the burial about AD 625, suggesting that it was the grave of Raedwald, High King of the English and ruler of East Anglia. There were also silver dishes from the eastern Mediterranean; ornate arms and armor; drinking horns; a lyre; a stone scepter; a huge bronze cauldron; and other splendid objects.

To the nautical archaeologist, the most

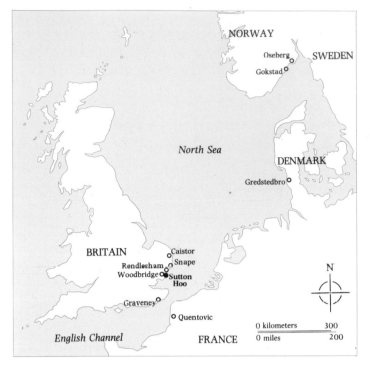

Left: The North Sea area, showing the principal Anglo-Saxon sites in Suffolk, along with related sites on the Continent.
Below: A cross-section and profile of the mound at Sutton Hoo, showing how the mourners had buried the ship, erected a burial chamber within it, and raised a mound over the forward two thirds of the vessel.

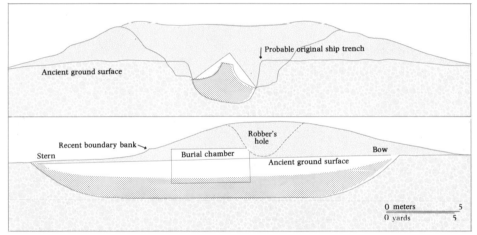

remarkable find was undoubtedly the ship's "ghost." Dark shadows in the bright yellow sand showed, for example, something of the original shape of the plank keel and the stempost. The original wood of the timbers survived only where it had been in contact with the corroding iron of the rivets; thus on the shanks of the rivets and spikes that originally held the timbers together archaeologists could detect the phantom outlines of individual planks and carpentry joins. By piecing together these tiny, perishable fragments, it proved possible to work out the ship's structure; and by adding these details to the lines of the "ghost" ship, surveyed in 1939 where she lay, we formed an overall picture lacking only a few details.

Thirty meters (100ft) long, with a maximum beam of 4.8 meters (15¾ft), the Sutton Hoo ship represented a considerable advance on the rather simple structure of the Nydam boat, although the hull profiles were similar, and we find the same skeleton of plank keel, stem- and sternposts. The strakes

of the Sutton Hoo ship, however, were composite, each consisting of several lengths of planking fastened at their overlap with iron rivets. There were nine strakes a side.

The ship's spine was a long plank keel with a stumpy T-shaped cross section. Traces of this survived in the sand along with the shadow of the stem- and sternposts: long, low, raking posts with a deep and thrusting cutwater. The endposts had perhaps risen 4 meters (13ft) above the keel, but the tops did not survive. Like those of the Nydam boat, the endposts may have been pegged to the keel, but damage to the hull seems to have led to the replacement of the wooden pegs with three iron bolts found joining the ghosts of the plank keel and sternpost. Inside, and strengthening the hull, were 26 heavy frames with a rectangular cross section. The frames pressed tightly against the "skin" of the ship, and were held to it by iron bolts at gunwale level and treenails elsewhere.

Forty oarsmen had rowed the ship, and

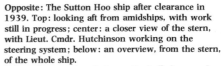

Opposite: The Sutton Hoo ship after clearance in 1939. Top: looking aft from amidships, with work still in progress; center: a closer view of the stern, with Lieut. Cmdr. Hutchinson working on the steering system; below: an overview, from the stern, of the whole ship.
Below: A comparison between the hull shape and planking of the Sutton Hoo vessel (lower) and a contemporary ship from Valsgärde in Sweden (upper). Note how the former has many narrow planks while the latter has a few broad ones.

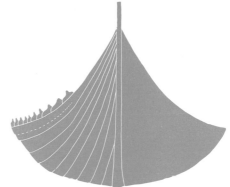

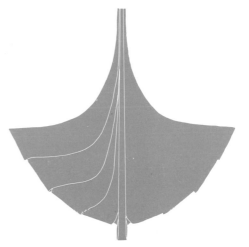

faint traces of the grown timber forks that had acted as oarlocks survived as shadows along the top of the gunwale strake. These tholes had long bases, held to the top of the gunwale strake by pairs of heavy iron spikes. A steering oar hung to starboard and the greatly expanded heads of frames 24 and 25 strengthened the hull at this point. There was no trace of a sail. The amidships area could have supported a mast but was occupied by the burial chamber. Any fittings connected with a sail might have been stripped from the ship before burial, but we have no firm reason to suppose that the Sutton Hoo ship had ever been a sailing vessel.

Possibly a royal barge, the Sutton Hoo ship was exceptionally large and untypical of everyday craft trading around the coasts facing the North Sea in the seventh century AD.

71

Keels, sails, and the coming of the Vikings

We have seen that, in the early seventh century, people in England and Denmark were building double-ended rowing boats, with plank keels and low-raking, plank-on-edge, stem- and sternposts. However, by the end of the seventh century, boat finds in Norway reveal tightly curving stem- and sternposts with lines that were to survive until the twentieth century. Such craft led to the north's first-known sailing ships: seaworthy craft in which Scandinavian seafarers — collectively called Vikings — explored, raided, and colonized lands as far apart as Newfoundland, France, and Italy. Waterborne Vikings also penetrated eastern Europe rivers and traded south to the Black Sea.

A ship and a boat from Kvalsund in western Norway represent the only known complete examples of mainstream northern boat building in the run up to the Viking era. In the late seventh or early eighth century, both vessels were placed in the mud as votive offerings. The larger craft is 20 meters (66ft) long and clinker-built of oak with pine frames. Her broad keel plank has a T-shaped cross section deeper than the plank keels of the Nydam and Sutton Hoo ships (pp. 69–71), and closer to the true keel of the Viking ships. But her most distinctive feature is the tight curve of the stem- and sternposts, a curve creating a ship with a more elegant, seaworthy profile than that of any of her predecessors. Pegs and lashings holding her pine frames to the hull reflect the traditions seen at Nydam and Gredstedbro (p. 69). One especially shaped after frame supports the steering oar, lashed

Below: The hull of the Oseberg ship during excavation in 1904; the ornate carving on her posts is already visible. After recovery and treatment, the ship was reconstructed for display in a special museum in Oslo (right).

to and pivoting against an oak boss nailed to the outside of the planking. The boat is undecked and has 20 rowing positions, but no trace of a mast for carrying a sail. Broad hull, deepened keel, and fixed steering oar would have made sailing possible, but this was probably a rowing boat.

The small Kvalsund boat is similarly built but reflects the shallower lines of the old Nydam style. This small boat has four rowing positions and a fixed steering oar.

Apart from these two examples, we have only fragmentary remains of vessels of comparable date and style. Occasionally, archaeologists find pieces of timber from similar boats, but by far the largest number of relics

consists of "ghost" ships beneath burial mounds. The best known of these lie in the wealthy grave fields of Vendel and Valsgärde in Sweden. Here, over a period of many years, archaeologists have excavated shallow boat shapes with confused rivet alignments. One Valsgärde ghost ship was 10 meters (33ft) long and had five strakes a side; she must have been typical of smaller vessels of the pre-Viking era.

The Kvalsund craft and the fragmentary remains of their contemporaries feature light, highly flexible hulls with an inner framework of widely spaced frames bracing the craft from gunwale to gunwale. The development of a keel, as opposed to the

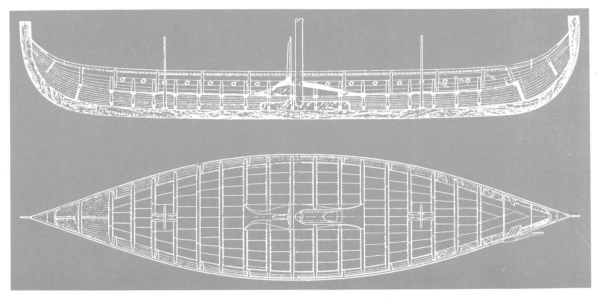

A plan and longitudinal section of the Gokstad ship, showing that she is relatively roomy, despite her sleek lines. Note the massive complex of timbers into which the mast is stepped.
Below: Two views of the Gokstad ship as she stood in a shed soon after recovery. Looking from the bows (left), with the line of shields along her gunwale clearly visible; and (right) the stern of the ship, showing the placement of the massive steering oar.

plank keels of the earlier boats, gives greater longitudinal strength to the hull and, as the keel deepens, scarf joints fusing it with stem- and sternposts turn through 90 degrees and become vertical with horizontal fastenings.

With these changes the evolution of the sailing hull is virtually complete; but the date when the sail was actually adopted in northern Europe remains uncertain. Boats with sails, often with elaborate rigging, appear engraved on the picture stones from the Baltic island of Gotland. But these are difficult to date. The earliest surviving sailing equipment in the north comes from three famous ships found during the nineteenth century near Oslo Fjord in southern Norway.

The Oseberg and Gokstad ships, and a third ship found at Tune, were all burial ships that owed their remarkable survival to the preservative qualities of the blue clay in which the Norsemen had deposited them. The additional protection of a turf mound helped to save most of the Oseberg ship's upper planking and her magnificently carved stem- and sternposts. The style of decoration on these posts suggests that this ship was built about AD 800. The Gokstad and Tune ships date from the last half of the ninth century. The Gokstad and Oseberg ships probably commemorate members of the *Ynglinge* dynasty, rulers of Vestfold (what is now the Oslo region) in the Viking age, but it is not known for whom the Tune ship was buried. The magnificently furnished Oseberg burial contained a woman, and the richly carved vessel may have been a royal barge. The Gokstad ship, with a higher freeboard, is more seaworthy and would have been capable of long sea voyages, as shown in 1893 when a replica was sailed across the Atlantic.

Both the Oseberg and Gokstad ships are large and beamy. The Oseberg ship is 21.44 meters (71½ft) long overall with a beam of 5.1 meters (17ft). She was rowed by 30 oars. The Gokstad ship is slightly larger, 23.33 meters (76½ft) long, and 5.25 meters (17½ft) wide, and has 32 rowing positions. The ship from Tune, now badly damaged, is slightly smaller than the others. All three have steering oars held against bosses on the outside of the hull in the same manner as the Kvalsund ship. But in structural detail the three ships represent a great advance on the earlier examples. In the Oseberg and Gokstad ships, the plank keel has become a true keel with a deep T-shaped cross section. Inside, the frames no longer span the clinker-built hull from gunwale to gunwale, but lie as floor timbers, lashed to cleats in the planks. The ends of the floor timbers rest at the level of the *meginhufr*, a thickened strake on the waterline; cross beams—one for each floor frame—run across the hull, to brace it at that level. Above these cross beams lies the planking of the deck. Strakes above the *meginhufr* are supported by knees nailed to the cross beams and pegged to the hull. Oar ports, running the length of each gunwale, replace the tholes of the earlier ships, although tholes are still used on the Gokstad ship's three boats.

Above all, though, it is these vessels' sailing equipment that marks their major innovation. Amidships each has a mast stepped into a heavy keelson (p. 30), lying across the floor frames. Support for the mast comes from the so-called mast-partner that straddles the cross timbers and, in the Gokstad and Tune ships, is braced by knees nailed to the cross timbers. Few details of sails or rigging survive, but Gotland's picture stones suggest highly evolved square sails, and the Sagas describe sails as colored and striped.

This formidable combination of deep keel, flexible hull, and square sail for generations gave Vikings domination of the northern seas and English Channel.

Five Viking ships at Skuldelev

Splendid as she is, the Gokstad ship (p. 73) represents just one of many types of ships and boats that thronged the coastal waters of Scandinavia during the Viking period. Small craft like her own ship's boats must have been familiar to the independent farming communities that formed the backbone of Viking society.

Viking fleets would have contained many types of fighting ship, including the "snake" ships (so-named because of their narrow, flexible hulls), of which the Ladby ship, discovered in a grave-mound on Funen in Denmark in 1935, is an example. Although the vessel survives only as a shadow in the sand, like the Sutton Hoo ship, her excavators established that she was 22 meters (72ft) long and 3 meters (10ft) in maximum beam, being clinker-built with eight strakes a side. A keel-plank of T-shaped cross section and four shroud rings together indicate that she was worked with a sail. Fragments of a dog-harness with a distinctive style of decoration suggest a mid-tenth-century date for the boat and her contents.

The Icelandic Sagas contain a wealth of information about the different types of Viking vessel, but archaeologists have found very few of these. Thus the discovery of five late Viking ships in eastern Denmark has proved vitally important to the nautical archaeologist, particularly as one ship represents the *knarr* – a type that formed the backbone of Viking trade. Discovery began in 1959 when the Danish National Museum at Copenhagen identified as Viking pieces of a boat found sunk in narrow Roskilde Fjord, off the small town of Skuldelev on Sjaelland Island. For three seasons divers mapped the site. They found not one wreck but several that overlapped. Someone had deliberately filled their hulls with stones to sink them and create a barrier across the narrow channel.

The timbers proved so fragile that the archaeologists decided to build a cofferdam around the wrecks, pump out the water, and excavate as if on land. When the site was drained of water, archaeologists recorded the timbers photogrammetrically. Next, they separately secured each fragile piece to a sheet of hardboard for support, and placed it in an airtight polythene tube for transfer to the National Museum.

Now began the work of conservation. Museum staff cleaned the timbers, fitted them together where they could, then soaked them in tanks containing a solution of polyethylene glycol (PEG). This preservation treatment lasted from six months to two years, depending on the condition and thickness of the wood. Finally, they reconstructed the five boats in a museum especially built to house them at the head of Roskilde Fjord. It was found that the distorted and damaged remains of the five boats represented two warships, two merchant ships, and a smaller vessel, perhaps a ferryboat or a fishing boat. All five hulls

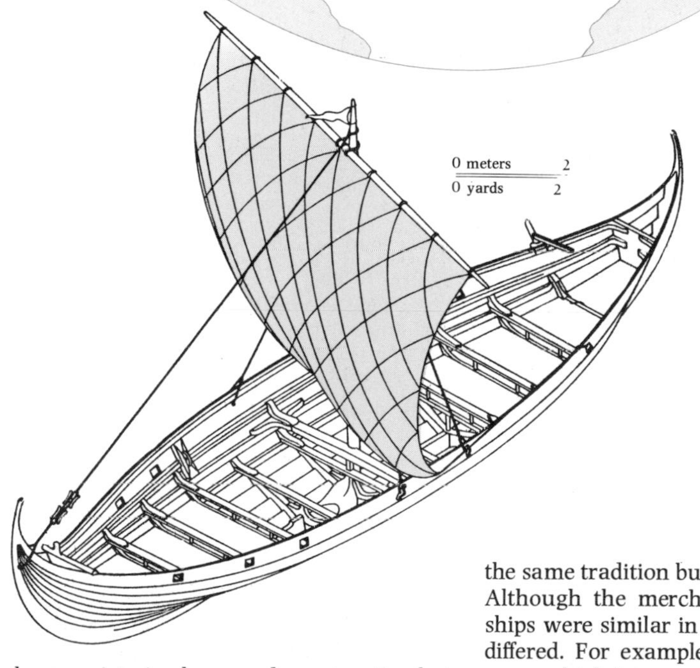

Top: The North Atlantic Ocean, showing the lands visited and colonized by the Vikings, and indicating the main routes they followed. Left: An artist's reconstruction of the coastal trader found at Roskilde.

show variety in shape and construction but clearly belong to the same boatbuilding tradition as the Gokstad ship. All are sailing ships, with light, flexible, clinker-built hulls, T-shaped keel planks, and elegantly curved stem- and sternposts. One novel feature displayed here concerns the stem- and sternposts, which have stepped wings carved in them to accommodate the ends of the side planks, a refinement not found on the Gokstad ship.

The Skuldelev find gave ship archaeologists a first opportunity in northern waters to examine ships built at the same time in the same tradition but for different purposes. Although the merchantmen and the warships were similar in form their proportions differed. For example, the larger merchantman, which has cargo space amidships, has been called "short, squat, and relatively tall" in contrast to the warships' long, low, narrow lines. Her provision for a few oars fore and aft of the cargo hatch compares with the longships' oar ports running the length of the gunwale. Longships were designed for speed and maneuverability in the swift attack-and-withdraw tactics for which the Viking fleets were renowned. Relying more heavily on sail than oars, the merchantmen plied reliably but slowly between ports and across open seas.

The five ships represent different types

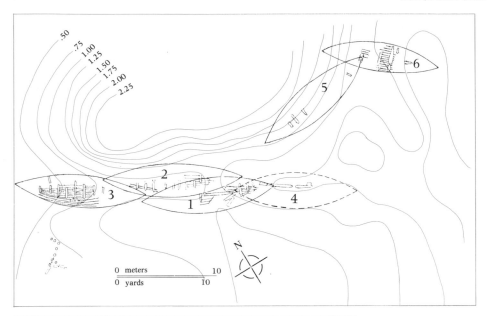

Top: The arrangement of the five ships sunk in Roskilde Fjord to block a shipping channel. The Ship 4 proved to be a misinterpretation; the timbers in that area were a detached part of ship 2.
Left: One of the vessels from Roskilde on display in the new ship museum after conservation.
Below: This illustration from the Bayeux Tapestry, shows a warship of the same type as the smaller one found at Roskilde.

within these two main categories. The two warships are dissimilar in size. The smaller measures 18 meters (59ft) long and 2.6 meters (8½ft) in maximum beam, and had 12 pairs of oars. She probably represents a typical Danish Viking longship. The same type figures in the Bayeux Tapestry, and the reconstruction of a similar vessel based on the Ladby boat reveals a capacity for maneuvering, beaching, and carrying and landing horses. This handy craft would have been the basic fleet vessel, used no doubt in the Danish/English skirmishes of the ninth and tenth centuries.

However, the Sagas also tell of massive ships, symbols of personal power and prestige, and the larger warship found at Skuldelev was surely one of these. Because she lay at the top of the blockade she had suffered more damage than the rest; only one half of her hull survives. She seems to have been at least 30 meters (98ft) long – as long as the great ship at Sutton Hoo (p. 70) – with provision for 26 pairs of oars. Such a vessel could have traveled fast and carried perhaps 60 soldiers in addition to her crew. This fearsome craft represented a cornerstone of Danish maritime defense about a thousand years ago.

The merchantmen stand aside from these swift men-of-war. One vessel, built of oak, measures 13.5 meters (44ft) long and has a beam of 3.2 meters (10½ft), giving a length-to-breadth ratio of 4.2:1 compared with the warships' 6:1 and 7:1. Amidships is an open hold in which the mast was stepped and cargo stowed. Five oar holes lie forward of the cargo space, and two aft. This small ship was probably a coastal trader, familiar on the North Sea and Baltic routes, but also small enough to sail up minor rivers. Stripped of her contents, she could even have been carried overland by her crew from one river to another.

In contrast to this flexible little trader is the larger, sturdier merchantman, 16.5 meters (54ft) long, with a beam of 4.8 meters (16ft). Decked fore and aft, with an open hold amidships, and reinforced by 14 heavy oak frames, this ship was built to cope with heavy open seas. She was almost certainly a *knarr*, the type of broad-beamed, reliable craft described in the Sagas as carrying the questing Vikings over the inhospitable oceans that separated Norway, Iceland, Greenland, and North America.

The fifth boat from Skuldelev is smaller than the rest: about 12 meters (39ft) long, with a beam of only 2.4 meters (8ft). She is undecked and has large, broad thwarts too low to be rowing positions. Archaeologists suspect she was a ferryboat or a fishing boat.

The variety of finds from Skuldelev throws a narrow shaft of light upon the kinds of vessel familiar to Vikings in the tenth and eleventh centuries. The same ship types would have been familiar, too, to Europeans wherever Vikings came to raid, colonize, or trade.

A working vessel from Kent

In the British Isles we lack major boat finds for the three centuries following the Sutton Hoo ship (p. 70). We only have a ship burial at Balladoole on the Isle of Man, where a scattering of iron rivets beneath a stone cairn is all that survives of a Viking boat. This is very different from Scandinavia, where we have seen that archaeologists can trace the slow progress of clinker hull design. However, the discovery of the Graveney boat has thrown valuable light upon the kinds of craft used around the coast of England, about AD 900 to 1000.

In 1970 workers were widening and deepening a watercourse in Kent's Graveney Marshes when an excavator encountered timbers that the driver, Roy Botting, thought might be part of a boat. When archaeologists had cleared the hull of mud they found a shape suggesting a vessel predating the Norman Conquest. Her potential value to archaeology persuaded the Kent River Authority to hold up drainage work for 10 days so that experts could record and lift the timbers.

Despite heavy damage, enough remained to reveal ways in which this boat resembled and differed from her predecessors and contemporaries. Her forward end was missing

projection below, worn and rubbed by beaching. A short horizontal scarf joint held by five iron rivets joins this plank to the sternpost, the lower edge of which projects forward and upward with a sharp angle or heel at the point where the upward rise begins: a feature that separates the Graveney boat from other clinker-built boats. There were three holes in the sternpost, one containing fragments of a rope.

Another unusual feature of the boat was the series of extremely heavy rectangular frames that ran across the hull. Ten of these massive timbers survived, held tightly to the hull by large willow pegs driven from the outside of the hull through holes lined with strips of tar-soaked wool. Inside the hull, the builders had cut the ends of the pegs flush with the upper surface of the frames and had driven little wedges of oak into the ends to prevent the pegs from slipping outward. The frames were composite, with side timbers overlapping the floor frames. None of the side frames survived systematic robbing of the boat and, as the upper strakes

were also missing, we have no details of the gunwale strake. This makes it impossible to say how many oars were used to work the boat, or what kind of steering she possessed. She may once have had a sail: three of the central frames have shallow rebates that could have taken a mast step, but, for some reason, these rebates had been filled making it impossible even to mount a mast and sail.

There is little evidence of this vessel's cargo-bearing role, but two clues found inside her hull give some idea of possible activity. First, hop seeds lay among the debris trapped beneath some of the floor frames and also in the angles between overlapping strakes. Pollen analysis revealed no evidence of hop pollen and the presence of the seeds alone could mean that the boat had carried hops as cargo. But her construction shows that she was built for heavier loads. Investigation within the bottom of the boat revealed fragments of unfinished querns (millstones) made of basalt lava from the middle Rhine, pieces of Kentish ragstone, and fragments of Roman tile. These may

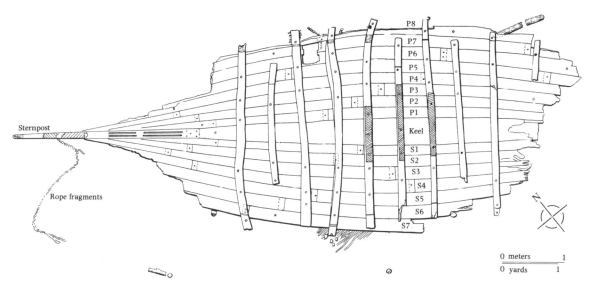

Sternpost

Rope fragments

P8
P7
P6
P5
P4
P3
P2
P1
Keel
S1
S2
S3
S4
S5
S6
S7

N

0 meters 1
0 yards 1

Above: Archaeologists recording the stern of the Graveney boat before attempting recovery. The horizontal fixed lines allow accurate profiles and sections to be drawn. Left: A plan of the hull of the Graveney boat. The map of Europe (opposite) indicates the extent of Viking activity from the ninth to eleventh centuries AD.

altogether and the upper strakes had been systematically removed after she was abandoned in the narrow creek. But we can estimate her original length as being about 14 meters (46ft) and her beam at 3 meters (10ft), giving a ratio of length to breadth similar to that of the merchantmen from Skuldelev (p. 74). The Graveney boat is clinker-built of oak and her hull consists of planks joined end to end by simple tapering scarf joints, made waterproof by wool soaked in a vegetable-based tar and fastened with iron rivets. The boatbuilders had placed wooden pegs in rivet holes before driving home the iron shanks – a method otherwise unknown outside the Baltic. The boat has a broad, flat, heavy plank keel with a stubby

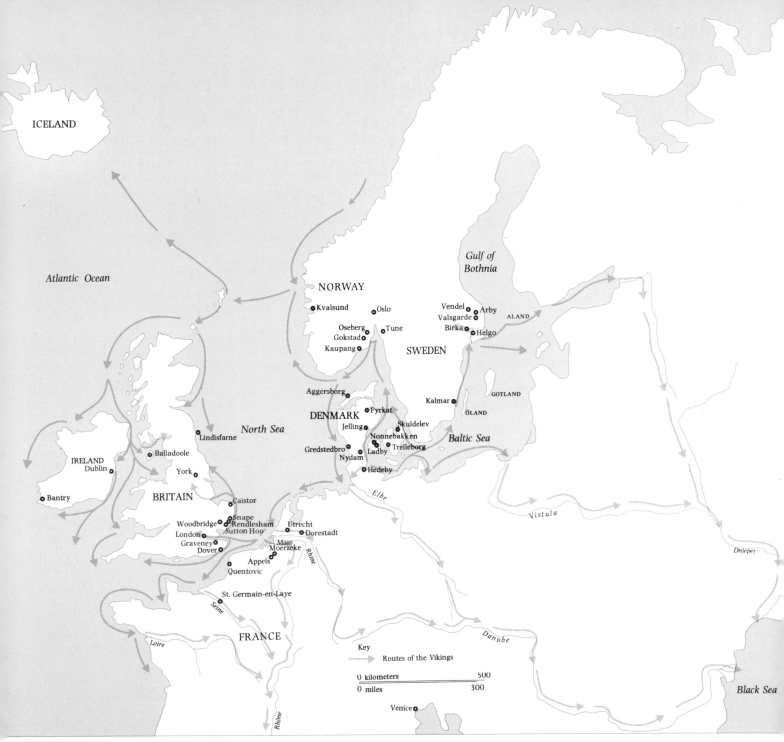

ICELAND

Atlantic Ocean

NORWAY

Kvalsund

Oslo

Oseberg
Gokstad
Kaupang

Tune

North Sea

Lindisfarne

Balladoole

IRELAND
Dublin

York

Bantry

BRITAIN

Caistor

Snape
Woodbridge Rendlesham
London Sutton Hoo
Graveney
Dover

Utrecht
Dorestad
Maas
Moerzeke
Appels
Quentovic

St. Germain-en-Laye

Seine

Loire

FRANCE

Aggersborg

DENMARK Fyrkat
Jelling Skuldelev
Nonnebakken
Gredstedbro Ladby Trelleborg
Nydam
Hedeby

Elbe

Rhine

Rhine

Venice

Vendel Arby
Valsgarde
Birka Helgo

ALAND

SWEDEN

*Gulf of
Bothnia*

Kalmar

GOTLAND

ÖLAND

Baltic Sea

Vistula

Dnieper

Danube

Black Sea

Key

→ Routes of the Vikings

0 kilometers   500
0 miles   300

indicate that she traded across the English Channel, perhaps as far as the Viking trading town of Hedeby (modern Schleswig in north Germany), where archaeologists have found hops and unfinished querns amid a mass of other material. Alternatively, these fragments could be the remains of ballast, and this could suggest a less adventurous riverine and coastal trade.

Whatever her use, the Graveney boat clearly belongs to a tradition of boatbuilding different from that of Scandinavia's light, flexible, clinker-built boats. She appears to have been a more pedestrian vessel, designed primarily for small-scale trading. Sturdy, slow, and reliable, she may have managed the short but tricky crossing of

the English Channel to reach northern Europe's trading depots. But she would not have risked long sea journeys like those doubtless undertaken by the merchant ships from Roskilde Fjord.

One other major find outside the north's main boatbuilding tradition is the boat discovered at Utrecht in the Netherlands in 1930. This vessel has an extraordinary banana-shaped hull without stem- or stern-post – the planks just converge at either end. The hull is about 17 meters (56ft) long and 3.5 meters (12ft) broad, with a huge plank keel almost 2 meters (about 6ft) wide. Heavy closely set floor frames give the boat rigidity. Radiocarbon analysis dates her to AD 790 ± 45, and she resembles ships depicted on

coins struck locally between AD 815 and 840. A "mast" step lies forward of amidships, but because the boat would have been unstable if worked with a mast and sail at this position, it is thought that the step might have held an upright timber used to secure a towing rope. This possibility in combination with the hull shape has led archaeologists to believe that the Utrecht boat worked along rivers rather than out at sea. This vessel is important because she demonstrates the variety of traditions that flourished during this period, although clinker building remained dominant in the north from the Nydam ship to the broad-beamed medieval merchantman from Kalmar (p. 80) and beyond.

Background to the Baltic

Since prehistoric times the Baltic has served as a highway for some of Europe's most forceful trading and military powers. Proofs of its past importance include surviving documents and the old ships that archaeologists have found in its waters. Before we look at some of the most significant of Baltic ship discoveries, it may be helpful briefly to put this north European sea in its geographical and historical setting.

As seas go, the Baltic is small, shallow, and unsalty. It is only about one-sixth the size of the Mediterranean, and its mean depth is a mere 65 meters (213ft). Most of the floor consists of muds, clays, and other deposits dumped by the vast sheet of ice that dominated Scandinavia in the last Ice Age. Since that sheet melted, the area depressed by its weight has been slowly "bouncing" back up—a process that is still going on and changing the shoreline (pp. 132–37). The rising is fastest in the Gulf of Bothnia in the north, where the land rises about one meter a century. The upward movement stops when you reach Öland, a long island off southeast Sweden. Still farther south the land is actually sinking. The known rates at which these geophysical processes happen make them useful as "clocks" for dating old coastal sites by their positions in relation to the present shoreline.

Land rims the Baltic on almost all sides: its present neighbors are Denmark; Sweden; Finland; the Soviet Union; Poland; and East and West Germany. Only a narrow, shallow channel between Sweden and Denmark links the Baltic with the North Sea. This threshhold serves somewhat like a valve controlling the flow of water in and out of the Baltic. Low-density Baltic water, diluted by freshwater inflow from rivers, pours out through the channel, flowing over the high-density, saltier waters of the North Sea, which cannot readily push in beneath. Thus the Baltic remains surprisingly brackish. Its low salt content helps to keep out that marine, wood-boring bivalve, the shipworm. In most of the Baltic, then, submerged wooden objects escape being drilled full of holes and destroyed—the common fate of old wrecks in the open sea.

The Baltic has long played a central role for the peoples of northern Europe and beyond. Since prehistoric times men have sought its fishes, seals, and seabirds' eggs for food. By the Middle Ages, local fishermen and farmers were also using inshore Baltic waters as a highway for shipping local and other produce such as salt, grain, furs, hides, salted herrings, tar, and timber. Early boats were small and vulnerable to the weather. Accordingly, captains hugged the shore, and medieval trade routes followed the ins and outs of bays, estuaries, and archipelagoes that offered shelter from the winds and waves.

Some local shippers simply took their own goods to the market places; others carried freight for merchants, often for the

big companies that sprang up in the growing towns after about AD 1000. In time the Hanseatic League of north German towns came to dominate Baltic trade through offices in coastal towns like Kalmar, Stockholm, and Visby, and others inland such as Novgorod in Russia. Such organizations brought together skilled craftsmen, sailors, and merchants, who between them built, crewed, and supplied loads for ships of growing size, complexity, and number. These changes had important social consequences. In Sweden, for example, between

the Middle Ages and the nineteenth century economic power came firmly under the control of wealthy merchants and the state. Between them these forces largely drove the small, independent traders out of business.

In the sixteenth century a new development emerged when the Dutch replaced the Hanseatic League as the major trading force throughout the Baltic. By the seventeenth century Dutch shipbuilding techniques were influencing Sweden and also Russia, a nation that had hitherto lacked advanced shipbuilders. Meanwhile, Sweden joined the

Right: A two-masted vessel of the second half of the 15th century, engaged in a sea battle. The illustration is taken from a painting in a Swedish church. The ship depicted below has just one mast and a "hulk-shaped" hull. Dated 1450-75, it comes from a Danish church.

list of European powers where people founded companies for transoceanic trade — in Sweden's case with North America and the East Indies (p. 126). Important Swedish companies exported copper, iron, and tar in a new breed of relatively big, oceangoing ships. At the same time, new navigational aids made it easier for ships to strike out across the open sea: only the smaller vessels still hugged the coast for safety.

But merchant ships were not the only kind that shaped the history of Baltic states: warships played increasingly important roles. After the Middle Ages, rival Baltic powers struggled for control of Baltic seaways, partly to control these valuable trade routes, partly with a view to adding to their Baltic territories. Beginning in the sixteenth century, these ambitions unleashed a string of wars. At first the Danes had mastery, and made seaborne assaults on central Sweden. Early in the seventeenth century Sweden's involvement in the Thirty Years' War (1618–48) gave her the upper hand. By early in the eighteenth century Russia's strong young navy shifted the power balance farther east: Peter the Great's fleet was the first big group of warships capable of sailing and fighting among the tricky shoals and skerries of the Baltic's archipelagoes. This new development spurred Sweden to augment her high-sea fleet with a fleet of

vessels as maneuverable as the Russians'. Swedish and Russian fleets clashed in many battles in the eighteenth century, and marine archaeologists have tracked down several of the ships that sank in these encounters: the Russian frigate *St. Nicholas*, for one (p. 84).

In contrast to the centuries before it, the nineteenth century proved relatively peaceful in the Baltic. Nonetheless, its nations went ahead with modernizing warships and naval installations. As elsewhere in the Western world, old-style wooden sailing

ships equipped with muzzle-loaded iron guns gave way to steam-powered ironclads with much more powerful artillery.

Thus the Baltic has had a long history of use by merchantmen and warships. Over the centuries scores of wooden vessels must have sunk in these waters — waters where unusually low salinity affords conditions almost uniquely favorable for the preservation of ships' timbers. It is this combination of historical and geographical factors that helps to make the Baltic so rewarding for the underwater archaeologist.

Above: A prior's seal, dated about 1425; it comes from Denmark and depicts a two-masted ship designed to carry horses. The animals went aboard through the special entrance cut in the hull.

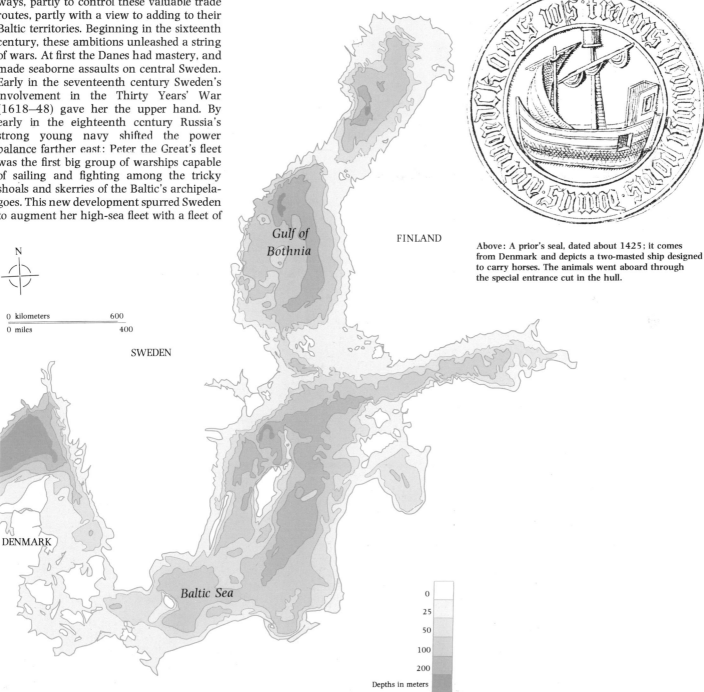

The Baltic Sea, shaded to show the depth of water.

Medieval ships in Kalmar

The first big marine archaeological project in the Baltic took place in the 1930s. This involved the remains of no fewer than two dozen ships and boats spanning several centuries. All lay in Kalmar's old abandoned harbor.

Kalmar stands in southeastern Sweden, facing across a narrow strait toward the long, slim island of Öland. One of the country's oldest towns, Kalmar evidently developed from a small Dark Age harbor and market place. During the Middle Ages, the Danish border ran close by, and in the wars between Swedes and Danes the Danes repeatedly besieged and overran Kalmar; the Swedes responded by building Kalmar's castle and defensive walls.

By about 1200, though, Kalmar was emerging as a leading center for the export trade in Swedish iron, a trade controlled by the German-dominated Hanseatic League, which also largely shaped the town's political affairs. By 1500 the trade in iron had fallen off, and workers were loading other goods on the ships that sailed from Kalmar's harbor. For several centuries, fish, meat, butter, hides, and timber dominated Kalmar's export trade.

During and after the Middle Ages, some of the vessels visiting the harbor came from small, local anchorages used by fishermen and peasants. Other vessels sailed in from larger and more distant harbors of the Baltic and North Sea. The thousands of vessels that used Kalmar harbor made up a complete cross section of the Baltic's medieval trading vessels. But wherever ships collect in large numbers, many sink through fire, storm, or war, or when too old and weak to be repaired, are left to rot on the shore or at their moorings. Thus the seabed at Kalmar became littered with wrecks.

Where harbors stay in use harbor authorities will clear away old wrecks from time to time. But during the 1600s Kalmar's old harbor was abandoned, wrecks and all, and shipping went elsewhere. Soon, all that remained of what had been a thriving medieval port was a shallow pool in the city center just below the castle.

During the 1930s, the citizens of Kalmar decided to drain the area in order to remove this eyesore from the heart of their town. Archaeologists recognized that this would not only remove a nuisance; it was certain to reveal the hulks of many long-forgotten ships, as well as other antiquities. The first stage was for engineers to build cofferdams at the mouths of the harbor and pump it dry. They then removed the mud that in places

Left: The oldest ship excavated in Kalmar harbor, viewed from the stern. Dating from the thirteenth century, she was probably a coasting vessel. In the 1:12 scale reconstruction (above), the darker sections are those based directly on timbers recovered from the harbor muds. A lengthwise section of the medieval ship appears below.

Opposite, top: A map of medieval Kalmar, showing the section of the harbor excavated. Below: A view across the harbor during the excavations, which took place in 1933 and 1934.

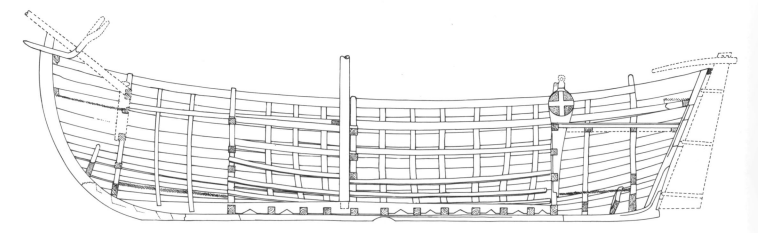

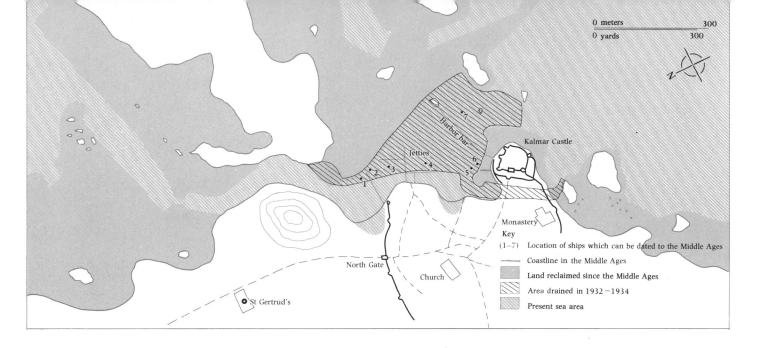

lay as deep as 4.5 meters (14ft 9in). This task involved excavating 50,000 square meters (538,000sqft). Complete and detailed excavation of so huge an area was impossible. Archaeologists had to fix priorities, and one of these was plainly digging out and recording old shipwrecks.

Excavation took place in 1933 and 1934. In that time the excavators found large quantities of items made of pottery, glass, leather, bronze, and tin. They also found the wrecks of 18 ships and boats, and fragments of six more.

A young engineer called Harald Åkerlund led the field-work. Under his direction, the workers first cleared the wrecks of mud. For each wreck, they then stretched a base line from stem to stern, and added further lines at right angles to the first. This grid enabled them to produce longitudinal sections and cross sections of the whole wreck. Åkerlund decided to try to remove and save in their entirety nine wrecks, five from the Middle Ages. He also planned to preserve essential parts of other vessels. Which wrecks got what treatment depended on their age and condition: the oldest ships and the best-

preserved examples of the younger ones received priority.

The same principle guided Åkerlund's preliminary task of recording ships' timbers. From each wreck he selected, Åkerlund measured pieces of wood as soon as he had lifted them from the mud and before they could dry out and shrink. Drawn to scales of 1:20 or 1:10, the resulting plans became a basis for detailed drawn and modeled reconstructions.

Along with the salvaged timbers themselves, these reconstructions give us a good idea of the kinds of boats and ships that had sailed in and out of old Kalmar harbor. Of the five medieval craft, the oldest dates from the thirteenth century, the youngest from the close of the Middle Ages, about two and a half centuries later. All five were clinker built, in the north European tradition (p. 30). All had been small. One was a rowing boat, the others ranged in length from 10 to 20 meters (about 33 to 66ft).

Here we have space only to look in detail at the oldest ship, a vessel famous among naval historians as a well-preserved example of the first stage in the medieval evolution

of ships in northern Europe. Her length and breadth amidships had been 11 meters (36ft) and 4.6 meters (15ft) respectively. She was oak built and double ended, with a curved bow and straight sternpost. Like the other Kalmar craft she had had a stern rudder. A single mast rigged with a square sail had provided propulsion. The hull's reinforcement by "regular" ribs and three crossbeams represented a change in design from the old Viking ships. But although small decks straddled bow and stern, the hold was open.

Apparently, she had been a small cargo ship, supplying goods to the castle, near one of the piers off which she had sunk. It is easy to deduce her origins. The use of oak in construction suggests that shipwrights had built her not much farther north than Kalmar (oak does not grow in lands around the northern Baltic). Moreover, a lump of sandstone used as an anchor weight represented a type of stone common near Kalmar. Very probably, then, Kalmar had been her home port. Archaeologists believe she typified the type of craft in which local farmers, fishermen, and traders coasted around the southern Baltic in the thirteenth century.

Wasa, the big warship

In most areas of the world, old wrecks survive as little more than a mound of pottery or corroded, shapeless lumps of metal; of the actual ships themselves often scarcely any trace remains. Thus in 1961 the world watched with astonishment while Swedish salvage experts raised relatively intact a wooden warship that had been lying under water since 1628.

Called after the ruling Swedish family, the *Wasa* had been built in Stockholm as a significant addition to the Swedish navy. She was a three-masted vessel carrying 1,200 square meters (13,000sqft) of sail, displacing about 1,300 tons, and measuring 70 meters (230ft) from stem to stern and nearly 12 meters (39ft) across the beam. Above the hold rose four decks: successively, the orlop deck, two gun decks, and the upper deck. She also had a stern castle with three decks: lower quarterdeck, upper quarterdeck, and poop deck. She carried 64 guns, 48 of them bronze 24-pounders. This was a very heavy armament compared with most ships of her size.

Badly needed for the Thirty Years' War, she was finished in a hurry and on August 10, 1628, set forth on her maiden voyage to Älvsnabben, a naval base in the archipelago off Stockholm. After little more than one nautical mile the *Wasa* capsized and sank in 35 meters (115ft) of water in the middle of Stockholm harbor. About 50 people drowned in this disaster, simply caused by poor stability due to too high a center of gravity. The lower hull lacked sufficient volume and ballast to counteract a rolling tendency induced by the mass of heavy guns relatively high up in the hull.

The *Wasa*'s rediscovery and raising make one of the most spectacular stories in the brief history of underwater archaeology.

Soon after she sank, divers salvaged many of her guns. But the ship herself remained stuck in the seabed mud until the amateur marine archaeologist and historian, Anders Franzén, rediscovered her in 1956. Soon the Swedish government were backing a massive rescue operation where shore-based archaeologists and engineers directed underwater work by Swedish navy divers. Their objective was no less than raising the wooden warship whole. After much discussion the method that they chose was first to thread cables through the mud beneath the ship, next to attach the cable to pontoons floating on the surface, then to use the cradle thus constructed bodily to lift the sunken vessel.

The first part of this work was dirty, dark, and hazardous. Divers working in conditions of nil visibility used a recoilless water jet to drive six tunnels through the clay beneath the ship. Each tunnel had to be 1 meter (3ft 3in) high and 3–4 meters (10–13ft) wide. Meanwhile, an airline sucked mud to the surface where archaeologists could sift the mud for artifacts. When the tunnels were complete, divers passed

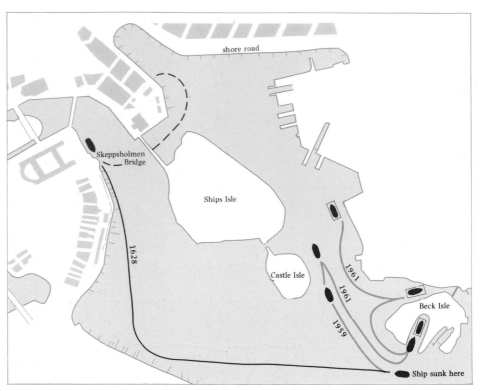

cables through them and attached the cables to two, big, semisubmerged pontoons above. Engineers raised the pontoons by filling them with air. In this way the *Wasa* was gently lifted off the bottom and step by step eased into shallow water. But for two years she remained submerged until the journey to more shallow water was completed and divers had reinforced her hull sufficiently to let her break surface and have her hull pumped out. Next, she was towed into dry dock, mounted on a special concrete pontoon, and protected from the weather by the erection of a capsule that now serves as a museum devoted to this one exhibit.

The next steps were excavation and recording. It took 11 archaeologists plus several assistants five months to clear debris and generally excavate the ship's interior. And for years following the salvage operation, divers were still finding pieces of ship's structure and items of equipment in the course of systematic excavations around the wreck site. All told, archaeologists have listed and described some 25,000 artifacts.

Recording a big seventeenth-century man-of-war posed unprecedented problems. The first thing to decide was the precise objective. Many specialists had an interest in the *Wasa*. Should you seek to satisfy the needs of model builder, ship technician, marine archaeologist, or art historian? The only proper answer seemed to be to document the ship as fully as possible, not just to satisfy all interested parties but as insurance against the *Wasa*'s destruction by fire, war, or terrorism. This meant providing detailed plans, photographs, and other data; enough, in fact, to make it

feasible to build not just a model of the vessel but a full-scale replica should that be ever necessary. By the late 1970s experts had prepared more than 1,000 plans and several thousand photographs, and a great deal of the recording work had been completed.

Recording so large a ship was difficult enough, but restoration was a mammoth

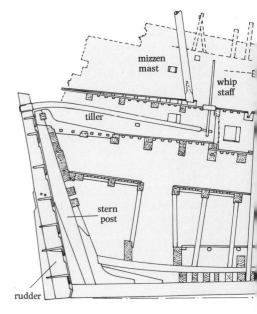

operation too. Originally the *Wasa*'s hull comprised some 14,000 pieces, large and small. Thousands had broken off and lay on the seabed from where divers retrieved them. The main restoration task was using these to rebuild demolished areas of hull, and to replace missing fixtures. The chief affected areas were the upper deck, torn loose by seventeenth-century salvage workers; parts of the lower decks; the three-deck-high stern castle; and part of the bow section.

The present author was responsible for the first stage of restoration: listing large structural objects according to their functions and the places where they had been found. Later, experienced shipwrights helped by museum staff tackled the slow, involved work of finding and replacing thousands of individual pieces of the hull, starting with the structural supports and adding planks and other items later. So successful has this process proved that you can now see ships' cabins reequipped with benches and other furnishings. By the late 1970s the bulk of restoration had been accomplished.

Both as find and archaeological project the *Wasa* is unique. Since her salvage started more than two decades ago, no one has attempted any other project on this scale. The cost, of course, had been colossal, making the *Wasa* among the most expensive of all monuments to Swedish culture, and raising questions of whether we should attempt to raise and save another large ship. At the same time, the ship's display has brought considerable revenue from the public, including many foreign tourists; by the late 1970s people had paid more than

six million visits to the *Wasa*. But for those of us involved in the recovery and restoration project, the resulting surge of public interest in underwater archaeology has been among the chief rewards.

Opposite: Stockholm harbor, showing the routes taken by the *Wasa* in 1628 and 1959-61.
The bowsprit and surrounding structure of the *Wasa* (above), reconstructed by the restoration team since the recovery of the ship. The longitudinal section (below) shows the arrangement of the decks, which all slope up toward the stern. In the hold just forward of the mainmast is the brick-lined galley.

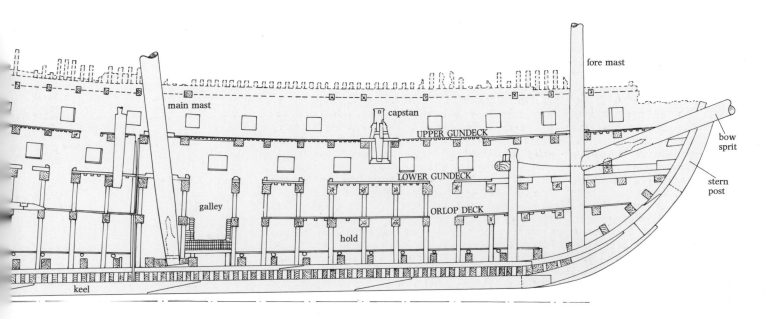

Recording wrecks in Baltic waters

The discovery of the *Wasa* in such a complete condition was an early indication of the archaeological promise of the bed of the Baltic. In the years since her recovery, systematic surveys and chance finds have confirmed the large numbers of wrecks involved, and shed light on their states of preservation. Most lie fairly deep in open, murky water. Although they have been spared the wood-devouring shipworm by the brackish waters of the Baltic, they have faced other hazards. Nails rust under water, loosening the timber structures they held together. Further demolition may follow from underwater currents, ice floes, dredging, or salvage work. Old clinker-built ships seem to have proved more vulnerable to these processes than carvel-built craft: vessels with planks fitting flush at the seams. Among the carvel-built craft that have survived in calm and sheltered waters are both merchantmen and warships of the seventeenth to nineteenth centuries.

Two recent investigations concern sites off eastern Baltic states. One involves the Russian frigate *St. Nicholas*, sunk near Russian territory in 1790 in a Russo-Swedish naval battle. The other is the merchantman *St. Michael*, lost near Bortsö among the islands off Finland. Her cargo included expensive snuffboxes and gilded clocks. Similarly, in Danish water, a large nineteenth-century Swedish frigate has been found in a good state of preservation.

But no one will probably ever be able to finance the study and recovery of such remains on the same scale as the *Wasa*

Above: A surface view the hydrolite in use. Note the tension wires running ashore and to points under the water. Left: A 1:75 scale model of the shipwreck at Jutholmen, built by Sven Erik Nordh. It shows the exceptionally good state of preservation of this wooden hull, as well as its relationship to the team's barge.

Opposite: The distribution of logs – part of the cargo – in the stern of the Jutholmen wreck, shown in plan (above) and in section (below). The position of each log (indicated by a cross) was measured by hydrolite with reference to stations above water and on shore.

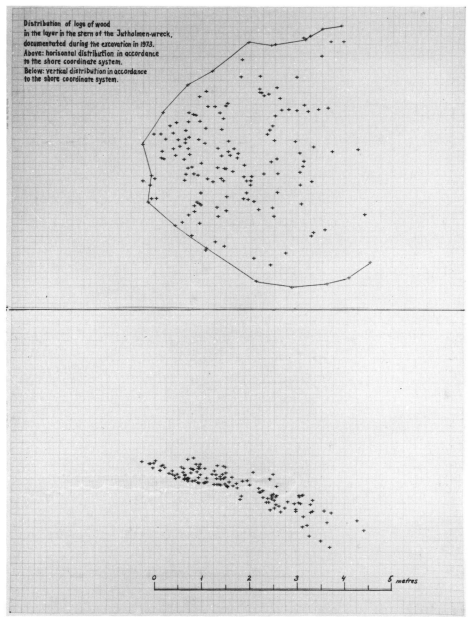

Distribution of logs of wood in the layer in the stern of the Jutholmen-wreck, documentated during the excavation in 1973.
Above: horisontal distribution in accordance to the shore coordinate system.
Below: vertical distribution in accordance to the shore coordinate system.

0 1 2 3 4 5 metres

held not only cargo and equipment but a bed of mud 1 meter (3ft 4in) thick and more.

Our team has tested several techniques to plot objects where they lay. In the first seasons of 1970 and 1971 we plotted horizontal positions in relation to a net with a mesh made up of squares of standard size. Rods marked off in decimeter (4in) units helped us to measure altitudes. We also used photography. Despite poor visibility, we managed to record the larger objects and build a pattern of their distribution. But we failed in the further objective of accurately plotting every find's position to within 1 decimeter.

In 1973 we tried out a new way of plotting positions under water. Developed by the Swedish Road Administration for underwater building work, this technique involved a hydrolite, a tool enabling the engineer or archaeologist to make geodetic measurements as accurately under water as on land. This survey covered 1,500 square meters (16,150sqft) and proved accurate to plus or minus 1 decimeter (4in). It produced a detailed picture of the wreck's size, inclination, and position in relation to the shore and contours of the seabed.

Besides this survey work, our team has explored three ways of plotting the positions of individual finds uncovered in the mud that clogged the inside of the ship's stern. Once again, we used the hydrolite, combining this with photographs of objects as layer-by-layer excavation of the mud uncovered them. The second method was to take overlapping stereophotographs as a basis for computer-produced plans. The third method also used overlapping photographs, but this time for plotting finds, map-fashion, on sheets marked off with grids. The first method proved accurate but somewhat slow; the second, faster and extremely accurate, but costly; the third, fast, relatively cheap, and a little less precise.

Altogether, the 1973 excavation covered an area of about 35 square meters (380sqft) and a volume of 15 cubic meters (530cuft). We worked down through four successive layers of mud and found 1,319 artifacts. Our divers had particular difficulty in plotting in the gloom of the holds the positions of logs that made up part of the cargo.

All this careful underwater work produced a picture of the ship and what she had been doing when she sank. The wood, iron, and tar that she was carrying represented a typical Swedish export cargo. Other finds suggest that she was outward bound for northern Germany, where Sweden had possessions in the seventeenth and eighteenth centuries. Silver and copper coins discovered in the merchantman place her wrecking early in the 1700s.

Her name, owner, and home port remain unknown. However, we shall now see that luck and the study of old documents sometimes reward archaeologists with even that kind of information.

project. With so many finely preserved wrecks along our shores, we in Sweden have thus had to develop methods for studying such vessels while still under water. Since 1970, scholars from the National Maritime Museum in Stockholm have been testing various new tools and techniques on two interesting sites in Swedish waters. The first represented a cargo ship that sank soon after 1700 near the island of Jutholmen, off the small mainland settlement of Dalarö.

The most widespread problem in the central Baltic is poor visibility. Very rarely can you see 10 meters (33ft) under water. Detailed recording is often difficult at distances of more than 4 meters (13ft) and, in the northern and central Baltic, you may have to work as close as 1–2 meters (3–6½ft) to your target. On some sites you must operate where visibility is nil. Other difficulties include the thick layers of mud or sand that cloak many sunken objects in this sea.

This complicates the task of underwater recording of even an almost intact wreck, for the work involves not just measuring the ship's exposed hull, but plotting fragments that have broken off, and scores of individual items from the cargo and the ship's equipment.

The Jutholmen wreck afforded plenty of scope for plotting finds and making other detailed records in the conditions typical of muddy, central Baltic waters. She lay at a depth of 12–14 meters (39–46ft). The sides of the hull rose 3–4 meters (10–13ft) above the seabed, and the stem and stern some meters higher still. The whole vessel measured about 24×6 meters (79×19ft).

Soon after the sinking, divers had sawn up deck beams in order to burrow down into the hold and stern for salvage; pieces of the sawn-up beams still lay inside the hull. Masts and rigging were also broken off and strewn around. Lastly, the ship's interior

Identifying the Älvsnabben ship

The second project undertaken by the team from Sweden's National Maritime Museum involves an obscure eighteenth-century merchantman that sank off the old Swedish naval base of Älvsnabben, in the archipelago off Stockholm. This exercise illustrates the important point that the structure and contents of an old, well-preserved but obscure wreck may help you to discover not only what kind of vessel she was and when she sank, but her actual identity. This kind of information may help you to marry archaeological discoveries about a ship's shape, size, and construction with contemporary records of her building, home port, use, owners, trade, and cargoes carried. Thus you may end up with a far more complete picture of the ship and her career than either archaeology or archives alone could furnish. But, as we shall see, identification is seldom easy and often inconclusive.

The first step is of course recording the wreck's construction in detail. This should give some insight into just how she was built. Next, recording the ship's size and shape gives a basis for working out her displacement, cargo capacity, sailing qualities, and so on. Dating the wreck may involve dendrochronology (see p. 154); radiocarbon analysis; and assessing the age of coins, pottery, or metal objects by their style and methods of manufacture.

Once you have taken this line of study as far as possible, you may turn to oral tradition or archives in order to try to identify the ship herself. Local oral traditions are vague and scanty for wrecks more than two centuries old. On the other hand, archives can present a confusing maze of details into which you should not step until well briefed about your wreck's date, type of construction, equipment, and cargo.

These, then, were the problems involved in assessing the Älvsnabben merchantman –

one of several ships with broadly similar features and cargoes known to have sunk in the same area in the same period. Discovered in 1968, the vessel lay near the main sea route to Stockholm from the south. She had probably foundered when adverse winds had forced her onto rocks near the port entrance. Between 1974 and 1977, archaeologists from the museum did much work, chiefly to secure for posterity a detailed record of the upper parts of her structure, especially the deck. In 1974 we used a hydrolite to measure its main lines and to establish fixed points on the deck. In 1976 the chief task was drawing a plan of the deck and recording constructions below it. The work was made more efficient by the use of cameras, a tape recorder, and a videorecorder. We also recorded details of the sides of the hull, of the rig, and the rudder. Meanwhile, divers began gathering samples of the grain cargo and of artifacts

Below, right: A longitudinal section through the Älvsnabben ship. Based on the results of the archaeological excavation, it shows the disposition of her cargo and stores.
Left: A contemporary drawing of an eighteenth-century galliot, a type similar to the vessel found at Älvsnabben. The photomosaic (opposite, above) of the deck of the Älvsnabben shipwreck shows how the deck has broken up toward the stern (to the left). At the bows a section of mast can be seen leaning against the ship's side.

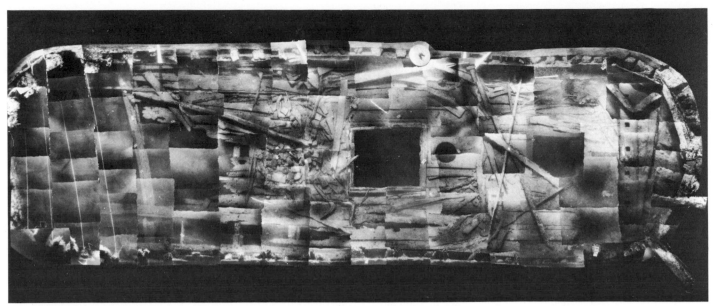

from the ship. Continuing with this in 1977, we found well-preserved pots; plates; glasses; tools; coins; navigational instruments; pieces from a Dutch faience tea set; and many other items. Most came from the stern living quarters, where the deck had long ago been damaged.

From all this, we have built up an image of the Älvsnabben ship. She was plainly a merchantman, for the hold took up most of the inside of the hull. She had measured 18.5 meters (60ft 8in) long, and was 5.3 meters (17ft 5in) across at the mainmast. A tour from bow to stern showed the following features. The bowsprit had vanished but the bow still had a heavy windlass and catheads for hanging the anchors. Two small gun carriages stood forward of the windlass, and aft of it a small hatch led to a boatswain's locker filled with rope. Farther aft a somewhat bigger hatch opened into the fore part of the hold. The mainmast stood forward of this large hatch, just aft of which was the galley. Farther aft still destruction makes it harder to reconstruct the arrangements. But we know the ship's pump was here, and the forward-stepped

mainmast suggests that a smaller mast had stood near the stern, though we did not find one. From surviving equipment we gather that a steersman had worked the rudder tiller from a small raised deck at the stern. Below him lay a cabin with two windows facing aft, and below that another cabin served as a storeroom, loaded by means of an opening in the ship's side.

The ship's size, her rounded stern, and what we can see of her rigging all seem to add up to a type of vessel closely resembling an eighteenth-century galliot – a small, shallow-draft type of merchantman developed by the Dutch. Her cargo had been mainly rye, with smaller amounts of other grains; but there were also traces of many species of weed. All the weeds proved typical of northern Germany, from where eighteenth-century Sweden imported much of her grain. This then implies that when the ship sank she was importing grain into Sweden. Judging by the kinds of coins and other artifacts found aboard, she had gone down some time between 1700 and 1730.

Here, then, were some pointers to the ship's identity. Armed with these clues, a

historian experienced in this kind of detective work began searching the archives. He found that five eighteenth-century ships had gone down off Älvsnabben. No fewer than three had carried grain. But at least three of the five had sunk after 1730 and only one of the others had had a consignment of grains matching the wreck's. What is more, the loading capacities of that ship and the wreck appear to tally, and the records described the missing ship as a galliot. Her home port had been Stralsund in Swedish Pomerania (now in East Germany). From there, with a six-man crew, she had sailed on her last voyage in 1724. Her name was the *Ulrika Eleonora*.

Here, then, surely, was the Älvsnabben wreck. Or was she? Tantalizingly, everything matched but for one small detail: a coin from the wreck postdating by some years the *Ulrika Eleonora*'s sinking. Does this mean we are actually looking at an unrecorded ship loss, or was this coin accidentally dropped on site from a passing ship at a later date? As so often in archaeology, a question had led to an equivocal answer, and there the matter rests.

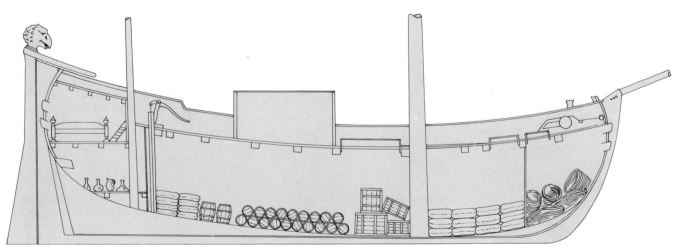

Maritime archaeology in the Baltic

Excavation in the Baltic Sea is still at an early stage, and much remains to be discovered, especially in some places and certain fields of study. But we have at least begun to learn where to look and how best to record it.

For instance, in Sweden, areas most likely to yield Viking and pre-Viking ship remains include former lagoons that could have served as harbors, and past areas of inshore seabed subsequently uplifted and now stranded as coastal marsh or dry land. In Denmark, where the change in level is less marked, several prehistoric wrecks have turned up in shallow, offshore waters.

For medieval ships it has proved worth exploring old harbors or the areas nearby. Some ships sank in harbors that are still in use, while others have been found offshore. But most finds are concentrated near old ports. This is partly because that is where old vessels were most numerous, and thus most likely to have sunk. Then, too, modern dredging and building activities that have revealed ancient wrecks by chance have often taken place in and near old harbor areas.

Collating data largely based on chance discoveries of individual wrecks, however poorly preserved these are, can offer clues to future finds. Thus the known pattern of post-medieval sinkings seems to suggest concentration along the main sea routes, and in the dangerous coastal passages near big ports. In Swedish waters, eighteenth- and nineteenth-century sinkings were especially common off the west coast, in the Sound, and near the Baltic islands of Öland and Gotland. These regions marked major sea-lanes in and out of the Baltic, and we can be sure that hereabouts lie many undiscovered wrecks — or rather bits of wrecks. Paradoxically this ship's graveyard is also the Baltic area least favorable for wreck preservation: off the west coast, exposed to the salty North Sea, the shipworm devours all but buried parts of wooden hulls; in the Sound and at Öland and Gotland drifting sands and strong currents in shallow waters between them seem to destroy or bury wrecks effectively. Similar problems hamper discovery and excavation elsewhere in the southern Baltic. Farther north, old wrecks fare better in the Swedish and Finnish waters sheltered by inshore archipelagoes, and it is in such places that archaeologists have found the best preserved wrecks.

But the remains of old ships are by no means the only evidence of the Baltic peoples' seafaring past. The nautical archaeologist can glean much worthwhile knowledge from living oral and manual traditions. Some old Scandinavian shipbuilding tools and techniques still in use can throw light on how and why men of centuries ago fashioned vessels now known only from their sunken ruins. Often, insight into how yesterday's shipwrights worked comes by questioning the boatbuilders actually using

their forefathers' methods. Indeed, some people argue persuasively that studying living traditions before they die out can tell us more about the past than we learn just by digging up old objects whose use and method of manufacture have slipped into oblivion. There is much truth in this, and research on these lines has already begun in many Scandinavian countries. But while the laws protecting old wrecks and monuments help to provide cash for excavation, governments are less keen to assist research into living traditions, even though these can sometimes add a great deal to our understanding of the objects that archaeologists recover.

Nonetheless, in Sweden scholars have begun to exploit systematically the living, oral, clues to the past. They do so particularly where they know that these may help to save some suspected but yet undiscovered submarine object of historical value. This situation arises where, for example, commercial concerns propose dredging an area of seabed for gravel or sand. Preliminary investigation may suggest that the area holds an old sunken shipwreck or other ancient remains. Before dredging begins, then, archaeologists find out what they can of local coastal tales of ships that sank long ago, or reports of fishermen's nets catching on underwater obstructions. Information like this can be very valuable for the archaeological search and survey that follows: it may pinpoint possible sites in a tract of seabed far too big to be completely combed.

So far we have stressed those clues that help archaeologists to find Baltic shipwrecks, and indeed most of this section focuses upon old vessels. But we must remember that these represented only one element in a much greater cultural whole. You might call this the maritime sector of society, for the ships sailing in and out of the Baltic were simply the tools of the people who used them. At first these were men from coastal farms or fishing communities. Later came full-time sailors transporting cargoes for merchants, and using harbor facilities built and maintained by yet other specialists. Moreover, this maritime sector of society was, and is, part of the still larger economic, social, and political pattern of society as a whole (pp. 24—25).

Shipwrecks, then, are just one of many kinds of evidence that can help us understand how people have lived and worked upon and near the Baltic over the past millenium. Besides ships, other pieces of the jigsaw include old coastal structures like harbors, shipyards, and wharves. Already archaeologists in Denmark have discovered Viking-period and medieval coastal structures ranging from pile defenses to beacons and whole harbors. Elsewhere around the Baltic, people have barely scratched the surface of this field of study. But in Sweden and Finland scholars are now taking the first

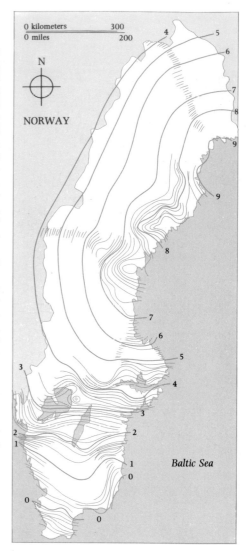

Opposite: Building a fishing boat on the west coast of Sweden in the 1930s. Study of such recent vessels and their construction can shed light on methods and techniques used in earlier periods.
Opposite, top: A rig-maker at work on a mast in the early twentieth century. When this picture was taken, little had changed over the previous 400 years.
Far right: The medieval harbor of Gamlehamn, at Fårö in northern Gotland. A sandy bar has cut off the narrow harbor from the sea, leaving an enclosed lake whose bed may well contain the remains of medieval and later vessels. The potential for maritime archaeological research on such sites is considerable.
Above: A map of Sweden, showing the rate (in millimeters) at which various areas are rising each year. This uplifting results in many coastal sites now being found on dry land. As lines joining places with the same rate indicate, annual movement can be as much as 9mm (0.35in).

important steps of registering material remains and examining oral traditions (even the names of places can be valuable guides to past associations with the sea).

Looking back over the history of Baltic excavation we are still struck by its one-sided emphasis on wrecks. Archaeologists have explored a number since the 1930s. But only since the 1960s have they seriously turned to other aspects of maritime archaeology. From now on, though, this broader view will gain ground. We shall profit from this by a far fuller grasp of how people, products, and processes interlocked to weave the Baltic cultures of the past.

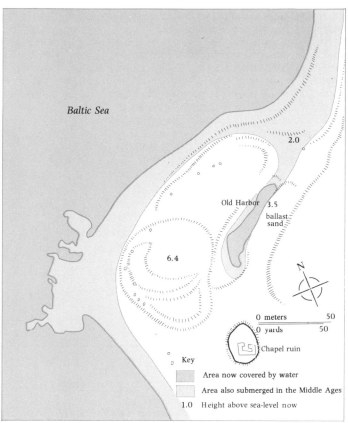

Baltic Sea

2.0

Old Harbor 3.5
ballast
sand

6.4

N

0 meters   50
0 yards   50

Chapel ruin

Key

Area now covered by water

Area also submerged in the Middle Ages

1.0   Height above sea-level now

North European warships (1400-1800)

Archaeology has much to contribute to our understanding of the development of the sailing warship from the fifteenth to the nineteenth century – the period when long-range mobility and concentrated firepower proved key factors in Europe's global expansion.

Our main sources of evidence for this study are wrecks, a number of them from the British Isles, including at least one from the early 1400s. In the mud of the Hamble River, near the southern English city of Southampton, lie the burned-out remains of Henry V's great *Grace Dieu* of 1418. Only the lower part of her hull survives, yet at 41×11.5 meters (134× 38ft) this indicates the ship's considerable size. Limited excavation has also revealed some details of hull structure. Less well-preserved remains of other large ships of the fifteenth and early sixteenth centuries have been identified in England at Bursledon and Woolwich, and smaller vessels have been found at Rye and in Plymouth's Cattewater.

But by far the most important of these early warship wrecks is that of the *Mary Rose*, built at Portsmouth for Henry VIII in 1509 and lost in the Solent during an engagement with the French in 1545. This vessel was one of the first warships to be fitted with lines of continuous gun ports, and we may think of her as a prototype of those heavily armed sailing battleships that were to hold unchallenged sway until the middle of the nineteenth century. The *Mary*

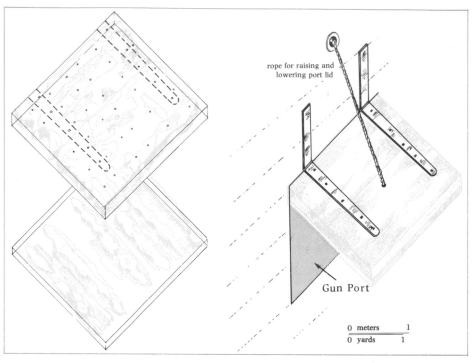

rope for raising and lowering port lid

Gun Port

0 meters 1
0 yards 1

Rose was extensively rebuilt in 1536, and Anthony Anthony's descriptive illustrated "Roll" of Henry VIII's navy of 1545 shows her with an armament including muzzle-loading bronze guns, some of considerable size, as well as plenty of the more old-fashioned wrought-iron breechloaders. This combination of old and new weaponry finds

a close parallel, though on a smaller scale, in the Armada's *El Gran Grifón* (p. 95), flagship of the Armada's supply squadron; the combination seems to be a characteristic of sixteenth-century ship armament.

The Deane brothers, nineteenth-century diving pioneers, discovered the wreck of the *Mary Rose* in 1836, and in 1840 several of

Gonnepowder Shotte of yron Shotte of Stoey and Lehde Sonnes Solbes arrowes Morys Byllys Dacrs

Above: A drawing of a gunport recovered from the site of the *Mary Rose* (1545); it lay just outboard of the port stern quarter. The reconstruction shows how the two layers of planking were nailed together with their grains at right angles to each other, and how the external hinges and lifting rope may have been applied.
Left: A contemporary artist's impression of the *Mary Rose*, included in a muster of Henry VIII's ships known as the Anthony Anthony "Roll." It is probably not totally accurate, but shows very clearly the towering bow and sterncastles of this period.
Opposite: A view along the main gundeck of HMS *Victory* (top). Note the crew's hammocks and mess tables between each cannon. HMS *Unicorn* (below), a frigate launched in 1824, still lies afloat at Dundee, Scotland. The hut-like upperworks are not original, but reflect her recent use as a naval reserve unit headquarters.

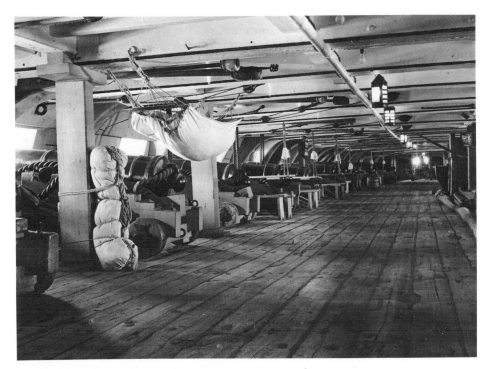

her guns were raised. Alexander McKee, a local historian, relocated the remains in 1965, and since then archaeologist Margaret Rule has directed their extensive investigation. The ship seems to be lying heeled over at an angle of some 60 degrees, with most of the starboard side and the keel preserved in thick mud. The next steps, under active consideration as I write, will be carefully excavating the contents, then raising the hull in much the same way as the *Wasa* was recovered (see pp. 82–83). The problems are immense, but the results in terms of knowledge, together with the preservation of a unique monument, are certain to be worth the effort, expertise, and cost.

Archaeology has so far failed to provide an example of a late sixteenth-century warship to bridge the gap between the *Mary Rose* and the *Wasa* (pp. 82–83). The century that separates these two saw a development away from the *Mary Rose*'s medieval legacy of high castleworks, shipboard infantry, and a hotchpotch of multicaliber armament, and toward the low, unencumbered hull of the *Wasa* with her continuous lines of standardized guns. This new look undoubtedly resulted from the maritime war fought by England and Holland against Spain in the 1580s and 1590s, and particularly the Armada fight in 1588. It was in this battle that the English and Dutch learned to treat

their ships as mobile gun-platforms, rather than as military transports whose main object was to close with the enemy for boarding. The *Wasa*, indeed, is much closer to Nelson's *Victory* than she is to the *Mary Rose*, while Charles I's 100-gun *Sovereign of the Seas*, launched in 1637, could have taken her place in the line at Trafalgar without difficulty.

Naval developments throughout the seventeenth and eighteenth centuries concentrated on refinements of details and organization rather than on fundamental technical change. This stability reflected principally the technical limitations of timber. Single large components, particularly stem- and stern-posts, could only be as large as the timber available, and this in turn restricted the possible size of hulls. Shipboard guns, too, were limited in size to what the gunners could work effectively. Sixteenth-century experiments with 50-pounders and upward had failed, and by Nelson's time the 42-pounder had established itself as the standard heavy gun, although the light-barreled but heavily shotted carronade, mounted on a slide carriage, saw limited service for close-quarter work.

Not all sources of maritime archaeology are sunk or derelict, and Nelson's *Victory*, now preserved in dry dock in the English port of Portsmouth, remains not only a superb monument to the heyday of fighting sail but also an irreplaceable example of wooden ship construction. She has certainly been much repaired and restored during the course of her long life, but she remains, in essence, the same ship whose keel was laid at Chatham in 1759 by Thomas Slade, Senior Surveyor to the Royal Navy.

Another sailing warship that has survived into the present era is HMS *Unicorn*, now berthed — and still floating soundly — at Dundee in Scotland. This ship was launched at Chatham in 1824 during a period of peace that saw a corresponding rundown in the British navy, and she was never fully equipped for service. She had a varied career as a gunpowder depot, drill ship, and, finally, as a headquarters vessel at Dundee; she is now being restored to her original condition. Her survival is particularly valuable to us since she embodies many of the technical innovations that, about a decade after she was launched, helped bring about the revolutionary change from sail to steam.

These innovations owed much to the influence of Sir Robert Seppings, Surveyor to the Navy from 1813 to 1832. They include the introduction of iron knees (brackets), a diagonal method of timbering the hull that greatly increased its strength and hence its maximum potential size, and the replacement of the old and weak square stern with a rounded one that was integral with the rest of the vessel's hull.

The Spanish Armada

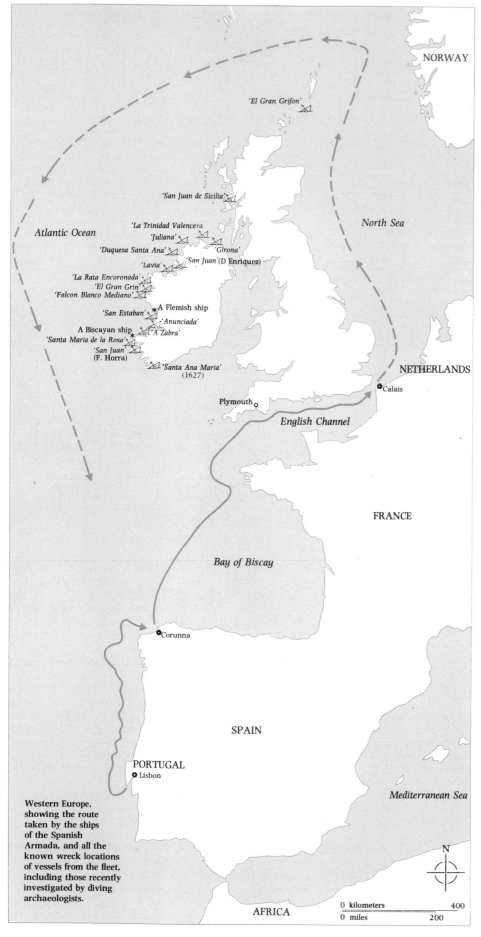

NORWAY

'El Gran Grifon'

Atlantic Ocean

North Sea

'San Juan de Sicilia'

'La Trinidad Valencera'
'Juliana'
'Duquesa Santa Ana'
'Girona'
'Lavia'
'San Juan'(D Enriquez)
'La Rata Encoronada'
'El Gran Grin'
'Falcon Blanco Mediano'
A Flemish ship
'San Estaban'
'Anunciada'
A Biscayan ship
'A Zabra'
'Santa Maria de la Rosa'
'San Juan'
(F. Horra)
'Santa Ana Maria'
(1627)

NETHERLANDS
Calais

Plymouth
English Channel

FRANCE

Bay of Biscay

Corunna

SPAIN

PORTUGAL
Lisbon

Mediterranean Sea

Western Europe,
showing the route
taken by the ships
of the Spanish
Armada, and all the
known wreck locations
of vessels from the
fleet, including those recently
investigated by diving
archaeologists.

N

AFRICA

0 kilometers 400
0 miles 200

The great Armada that Philip II of Spain launched against England in 1588 represented a then unprecedented logistical triumph. Creating this war force involved assembling at the base port of Lisbon 130 ships; 2,431 guns; 30,656 men; provisions for six months; also siege artillery, hand weapons, ammunition, transportation gear, engineering aids and personal accoutrements — equipment for a landing on the Kent beaches and an ensuing blitzkrieg assault on London.

The first invasion wave was to be provided by the Army of Flanders: 17,000 battle-hardened troops under the Duke of Parma, these men would set out from bases along the Flemish coast in a fleet of invasion barges to rendezvous with the Armada, which would then escort them to a beachhead near Margate and cover their landing. The Armada's own troops, amounting to some 20,000 men, including artillerymen, pioneers, and a supply corps, would come ashore as soon as the beachhead had been secured, so turning it into a springboard for the main attack. Meanwhile, the ships of the Armada would secure vital ports in the Thames and the Medway, thus denying their use to the English and opening them to further reinforcement from Flanders and Spain. Once these military objectives had been achieved, Philip reasoned, London would fall, the Tudor regime would collapse, and England would capitulate.

Such, at any rate, was the plan. As everyone knows, it went disastrously wrong. There were delays and frustrations at Lisbon: the huge influx of shipping strained the port's facilities for maintenance and repair far beyond breaking point; there were not enough guns to go round and there was too little ammunition to fit their bewildering variety of calibers; supplies went rotten or failed to arrive; and, worse still, the men became sick and disheartened. That the great fleet managed to sail at all was itself something of an achievement, due in no small measure to the diligence and administrative capabilities of its commander, the Duke of Medina-Sidonia.

At first the size, good order, and apparent strength of the Armada deterred the English fleet from closing in, and Medina-Sidonia was able to sail up the English Channel and reach Calais without serious mishap. At this point he anchored to await word from Parma, only to find that the invasion barges had been blockaded in their ports by the rebel Dutch. The English exploited Medina-Sidonia's confusion by sending in burning fire ships that forced the Armada to cut its cables and scatter. A providential change of wind saved the Spanish ships from grounding in the shallows, but off Gravelines, Flanders, the English attacked at close range and inflicted considerable damage. All hope of achieving the rendezvous with Parma was now lost, and Medina-Sidonia had little choice left but to return to Spain. To turn

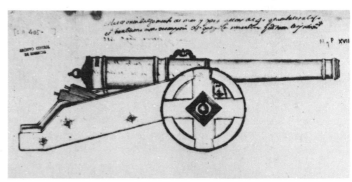

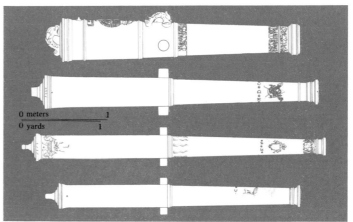

0 meters   1
0 yards   1

about and sail back through the Channel against both the English fleet and the prevailing weather was out of the question, and so the Armada set out on the long haul homeward around the north of the British Isles. It was now September, and the equinoctial gales of that year blew early and particularly fiercely. Caught against the unforgiving lee shores of western Scotland and Ireland, many of the Spanish ships – perhaps 40 or more – were wrecked.

The wrecks of the Spanish Armada provide us with a unique opportunity for studying a wide range of naval, maritime, and social affairs in late sixteenth-century Europe. In the archives of Simancas Castle in northern Spain the voluminous and meticulous paperwork behind the great enterprise survives almost intact, while on the seabed the remains of some of the ships to which these documents refer are now yielding their secrets to archaeologists. Thus we can study physical evidence from the wrecks against an unusually full documentary background; one source complementing and illuminating the other.

This study gains in significance from the cosmopolitan nature of the fleet, whose ships and equipment, far from being exclusively Spanish, were drawn from sources throughout Europe. Some vessels were hired from the Adriatic, others from the Baltic. Many large Mediterranean merchant ships, from places such as Genoa, Leghorn, and Naples, found themselves seized for the campaign when they unsuspectingly put into Spanish-controlled ports. Other merchantmen were requisitioned from the

coasts of Spain and Portugal. Only the King's new royal galleons, the galleys of Portugal, and the galleasses of Naples were warships in the strict sense: the rest were ordinary merchant vessels with cargo capacities making them suitable for conversion into invasion transports.

The varieties of ship types and their diverse origins are well demonstrated by the five Armada wrecks so far found.

Above, left: View of part of the Spanish Armada, derived from a contemporary tapestry that hung in the House of Lords in London until its destruction by fire in 1834.
Above: Bronze guns of the Spanish Armada. The contemporary technical drawing (top), now in the Spanish national archives at Simancas Castle, is contrasted with Colin Martin's drawings (below) of a cannon and three culverins from the wreck of *La Trinidad Valencera* (p. 96).

Ship	Type	Origin	Location of wreck
San Juan de Sicilia (St. John of Sicily)	Argosy (large merchant ship)	Ragusa (now Dubrovnik in Yugoslavia)	Tobermory Bay, Isle of Mull
Girona (Gerona)	Galleass (oared galleon)	Naples (Italy)	Lacada Point, Co. Antrim
Santa María de la Rosa (St. Mary of the Rose)	Merchant ship	San Sebastián (Spain)	Blasket Sound, Co. Kerry
El Gran Grifón (Great Griffin)	Hulk (beamy merchantman)	Rostock (Germany)	Fair Isle, Shetland
La Trinidad Valencera (The Trinity, or Leviathan)	Grain ship	Venice (Italy)	Kinnagoe Bay Co. Donegal

As an historical event the Armada is of limited significance: it failed, and little changed either in England or in Spain as a result. But as a source of physical and documentary evidence of its times, the Armada's potential is large: its wrecked ships and its

documents bring us into direct contact with shipbuilding technology; with the developing science of naval gunnery; with the varied paraphernalia of a sixteenth-century field army; and with many other aspects, mundane and exotic, of contemporary life.

Two Armada wrecks

Over the next four pages we look at three of the Armada ships rediscovered nearly four centuries after they sank in vain attempts to sail around the British Isles.

Santa María de la Rosa

The *Santa María de la Rosa* was the 945-ton vice-flagship of the Armada's Guipuzcoan squadron, a group of 10 ships drawn from the Basque ports of northern Spain. She had been built in 1587 at San Sebastián for Martín de Villafranca, a merchant captain of that town. But before she could enter commercial use she was requisitioned for the Armada, under Villafranca's command. In early 1588 she sailed to Lisbon and there acquired 15 pieces, most of them bronze, to augment her lightweight merchant ship's armament of 12 iron guns, the largest of them stone-throwing 7-pounders. When the fleet sailed she had on board 233 soldiers, 64 seamen, and a general cargo of munitions, stores, and siege artillery.

In a storm that scattered the Armada off northern Spain, the *Santa María* lost her mainmast, and had to have it replaced at Corunna. She sustained further damage in the fighting. The only survivor of her wreck later reported: "This ship was shot through four times, and one of the shots was between the wind and the water, whereof they thought she would have sunk, and most of her tackle was spoiled with shot."

Because of this damage the ship lagged behind the main body of the fleet during the voyage around the British Isles. On September 21, she limped into the shelter of Blasket Sound off southwest Ireland. There she found two Armada ships already at anchor, attempting to ride out a growing westerly gale. An officer on board one of them has left a detailed account of what followed. "The *Santa María* fired a shot on entering, as if seeking help, and another farther on. All her sails were in pieces, except the foresail. She cast her single anchor, for she was not carrying more . . . she held for two hours, but when the tide waned she began dragging, and in an instant we could see that she was going down, trying to hoist the foresail. Then she sank with all on board, not a person being saved, a most

Below: Close-up of the rim of a pewter plate recovered from the site in Blasket Sound. It bears the name "Matute," a senior officer on board the *Santa María de la Rosa*. The plan (below) shows the remains of the *Santa María de la Rosa*, as revealed by excavation.

extraordinary and terrifying thing." In fact, one survivor, the pilot's son, was washed ashore.

In 1968 the British diving historian Sydney Wignall led a determined attempt to discover the wreck. Divers working on swim-lines systematically covered some 10 square kilometers (4sqmi) of Blasket Sound before they finally succeeded. The site proved to be 36 meters (118ft) deep, on a flat patch of seabed 200 meters (660ft) southeast of the submerged pinnacle of rock struck by the ship before she sank. The wreck featured a mound of stone ballast, covering the well-preserved, lower, forward section of the hull. The stern part of the ship, together with the upper decks and all 27 guns, appears to have broken away and drifted with the tide into deep water. No one has yet found it.

In spite of the depth and the difficult tide race in which the hull lies, surveys and limited excavation during 1968 and 1969 have told us much about the ship's structure, and produced a small collection of artifacts. These include two pewter plates bearing the name of Matute, senior military officer on board; a couple of coins; a religious medallion; a balance pan; lead ingots; stone, iron, and lead shot of various calibers; and pottery.

The frames and planks of the lower hull show that the ship was lightly constructed, in line with her planned role as a merchant-

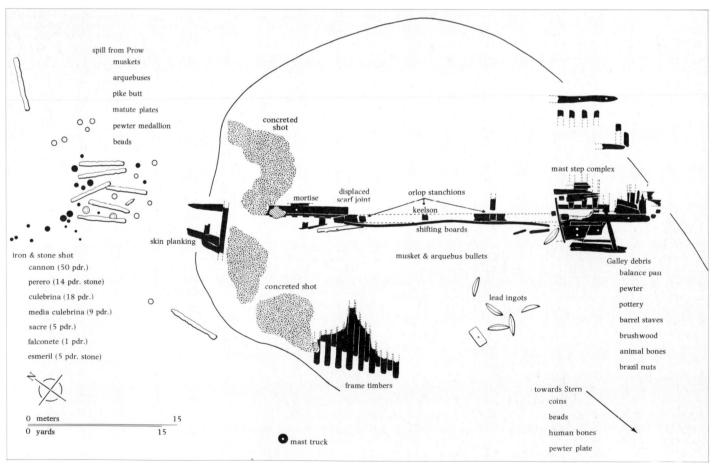

spill from Prow
muskets
arquebuses
pike butt
matute plates
pewter medallion
beads

concreted shot

mast step complex

mortise
displaced scarf joint
orlop stanchions
keelson
shifting boards

skin planking

iron & stone shot
cannon (50 pdr.)
perero (14 pdr. stone)
culebrina (18 pdr.)
media culebrina (9 pdr.)
sacre (5 pdr.)
falconete (1 pdr.)
esmeril (5 pdr. stone)

concreted shot

musket & arquebus bullets

lead ingots

Galley debris
balance pan
pewter
pottery
barrel staves
brushwood
animal bones
brazil nuts

frame timbers

towards Stern
coins
beads
human bones
pewter plate

0 meters 15
0 yards 15

mast truck

Left: An aerial view of Stroms Hellier, the cleft into which *El Gran Grifon* ran in September 1588. Note the encampment on the cliff-top to the left, from which air was piped down to the site to support the divers and their airlift. It was onto this cliff-top that the survivors from the wreck probably scrambled, using the vessel's rigging. Below: the scene 15 meters (50ft) beneath the surface in Stroms Hellier. Excavation of the shingle filling the gully has revealed a large bronze gun, which is here being plotted by a diver using a drawing frame.

man working the Spanish coasts and Mediterranean. Indeed, the well surrounding the vanished mainmast shows that this had been stepped well forward in the Mediterranean fashion.

El Gran Grifón

El Gran Grifón, flagship of the Armada's supply squadron, was a 650-ton hulk on hire from the Hanseatic port of Rostock. When she sailed with the Armada she was under the squadron admiral Juan Gómez de Medina, and carried 243 soldiers and 43 seamen. After a series of misadventures in the Atlantic her crew drove her ashore on Fair Isle, between the Orkney and Shetland islands. The men scrambled ashore but the ship sank in Stroms Hellier, a deep cleft near the southeast corner of the island, where, guided by a local tradition, Sydney Wignall and I found the remains in 1970. That year's work and a season carried out by the Institute of Maritime Archaeology from St. Andrews University in Scotland in 1977 completed the excavation.

Stroms Hellier is a series of deep gullies filled with a constantly shifting deposit of shingle. Severe storms that sweep the site help to explain why no structural remains of the ship survive. But when we began excavation we knew that eighteenth-century salvage had recovered several guns. Encouraged by this, we removed shingle seabed deposits with an airlift powered by a compressor mounted on the overhanging cliff.

Small finds proved few, which suggests that the crew had stripped the ship before she went down. But excavation recovered 400 pieces of shot and more than half of the 38 guns that we know she carried. These finds shed fresh light on the ship's listed armament. We know that when *El Gran Grifón* arrived at Lisbon she carried 30 iron guns of her own. Those from the site range from obsolescent wrought-iron breech-loaders to cast-iron pieces of remarkably high technical quality. They reflect the Baltic's growing iron industry, which was subsequently to assume major economic and strategic significance.

At Lisbon the ship took on eight bronze guns: four demiculverins and four demisakers. These had been cast as part of a crash program just before the Armada sailed. The wreck yielded one example of each type. Significantly, both lacked the normally indispensable royal coat-of-arms; the metal was badly bubbled; and the demiculverin's bore was far out-of-true. All these signs point to the haste with which Spain had equipped her mighty fleet.

A Venetian merchantman off the Irish coast

In 1971 a group of Irish amateur divers from the City of Derry Sub-Aqua Club made what has proved to be the most significant of all Armada discoveries. For two years they had unsuccessfully searched the wide expanse of Kinnagoe Bay in North Donegal for the wreck of *La Trinidad Valencera*, which had gone down after grounding on a reef in September 1588. Then, dramatically, came their reward: bronze guns, anchors, and large guncarriage wheels protruding from a sandy seabed close to the western end of the bay. With the Institute of Maritime Archaeology from St. Andrews University, the Derry club began a major excavation that would continue into the late 1970s.

At 1,100 tons *La Trinidad Valencera* was the fourth-largest ship in the fleet, and one of the most heavily armed. Her own complement of 28 bronze guns had been boosted at Lisbon by four heavy siege pieces complete with carriages for use on board ship and a double set of field carriages for use ashore. The ship herself was a Venetian merchantman, impounded by the Spanish authorities when she put into a Sicilian port for a cargo of grain. When she sailed with the Armada she carried 281 soldiers and 79 seamen, as well as a large contingent of officers and gentlemen-adventurers.

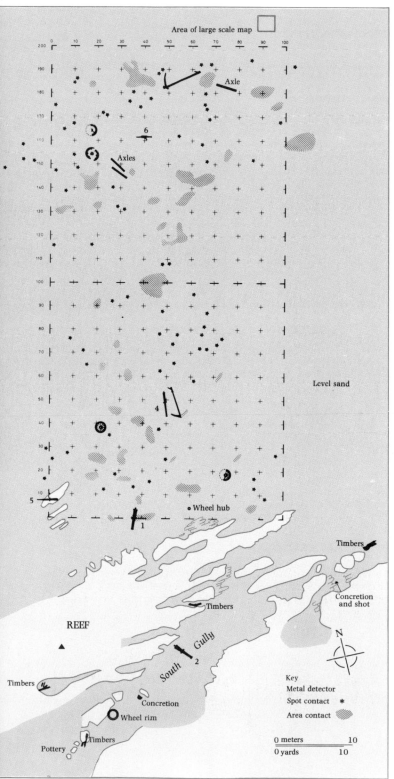

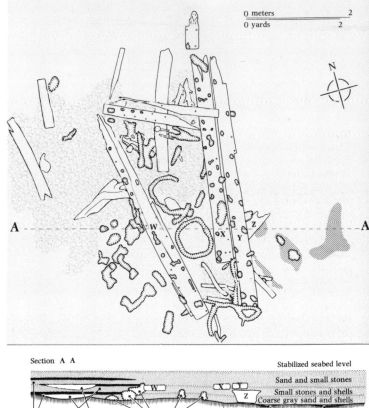

Section A A

Stabilized seabed level
Sand and small stones
Small stones and shells
Coarse gray sand and shells
Lead shot
Clay/sand substratum
Black mud
Organic matter
Iron concretion

The wreck is broken up and scattered, and so far we have found no coherent remains of the ship. Nonetheless, extensive pre-disturbance surveys, followed by systematic grid excavation, have revealed pockets of extremely well-preserved material — including wood, leather, and textiles — buried securely in sand and gravel. Excavation has also revealed a number of isolated hull components, and a study of the fastening holes in them has helped us to deduce a good deal about the ship's construction. Her builders had joined the hull planks to the frames with countersunk iron bolts set with almost mathematical regularity — a point of weakness, this, since the lines of bolts run directly along the grain, so inducing it to split. The use of iron bolts indicates a vessel built with a limited life expectancy, since once the metal began to corrode the hull would have become useless. This combination of preset fastenings and a short-life

Left: The wreck site of *La Trinidad Valencera*, as revealed by the pre-disturbance survey in 1971, including a metal-detector survey.
Above: Plan of, and section through, a part of the site including timbers from the ship and quantities of iron concretion. This area lies at the top right-hand corner of the site map (left).

hull accords well with the historical evidence, which suggests that Venetian merchant ships of this period were mass produced by relatively unskilled shipwrights and designed for an intensive working life of no more than 10 years.

Other finds include two of the ship's anchors, and a 6-meter (20ft) length of cable 13 centimeters (5in) in diameter. Its thickness is significant. Venetian cordage, particularly anchor cable, was manufactured under strict state control: as good businessmen, the Venetians recognized that a merchant's entire investment might literally hang upon the quality of a single length of rope.

Six bronze guns have been recovered. Four have proved to be Italian, presumably part of the ship's original armament. They include a breech-loading swivel piece with a bronze barrel and wrought-iron breech fittings; this gun is fully loaded, with a stone shot some 8.6 centimeters (3.4in) in diameter in its barrel and a twist of hemp in the touchhole to keep the priming dry. The remaining Italian guns are muzzle loaders with calibers of some 12.4, 9.5, and 7.6 centimeters (4.9, 3.7, and 3in). Founders' initials on the guns suggest that one came from the workshop of Zuanne Alberghetti and the other two from Nicolo di Conti. Both of these founders worked at Venice during the second half of the sixteenth century.

There are also two Spanish pieces. These are a magnificently cast matching pair of large-caliber siege guns, bearing the full arms of Philip II and the date 1556. Inscriptions on them show that they were cast at Malines, near Antwerp, by Philip's royal gunfounder, Remigy de Halut. Without doubt these are two of the four siege guns loaded on board the ship at Lisbon shortly before the Armada sailed. Several heavy wheels from their field carriages were with the wreck: no doubt stowed dismantled in the hold, to be assembled when the artillery was brought ashore. Unfortunately, there seem to be no traces of the carriages on which the guns were mounted on board ship, although it is clear that guns of this size — each weighs 2,460 kilograms (5,420 lb) — would have been impossible to work effectively aboard a sixteenth-century merchant ship.

Most of the small finds from the wreck have been of a military nature. They include the well-preserved wooden parts of muskets, arquebuses, and pikes; concreted steel helmets and breastplates; powder flasks; leather water bottles; leather shoes; hemp sandals; fragmentary clothing; basketwork and rush matting (used for consolidating temporary earthworks); scaling poles; handspikes; and palisade stakes — everything, in fact, that a sixteenth-century army needed to carry out a war of sieges. We can identify many other military items, and indeed check them against the original Armada inventories preserved at Simancas in Spain. These objects include bellows; wooden lanterns; shovels, barrels and kegs; mallets; iron tools; a steelyard; weights; as well as basic commodities such as tar, resin, and gunpowder.

The remaining group of finds is domestic in character. Because all classes of material survive on the site, these finds are much more comprehensive than is usual. They

Above: A pair of bellows found intact on the site. Right: Excavation in progress within a trench 3 meters (10ft) wide across the site. The array of wire frames in the foreground is designed to hold bagged artifacts, allowing them to be logged with minimal interruption to the excavation.

range from pottery, which occurs on almost all sites, to wooden plates and bowls, which usually perish. Pewter is well represented, and three of the plates carry English touchmarks — a reminder that trade between Spain and England continued to the eve of the Armada. Most of the finds are plain, but one bowl bears the mounted figure of St. James, Spain's warrior patron.

Copper buckets, brass candlesticks, and a brass mortar remind us of a variety of domestic chores, while simple religious medallions of pewter or brass strike a more personal note. Not all of the personal objects, however, were practical or pious. The troops required entertainment on their long voyage, and the discovery of a tambourine and the fingerboard of a cittern (a kind of guitar) shows that music was a popular diversion.

A composite swivel gun with an iron breech and a bronze muzzle. Note that the breech-block, with its wedge behind it, is still in position. This gun, pivoting on its central iron fork, was principally an anti-personnel weapon.

Insights from Armada pottery

Pottery is one of the most durable materials made by man; once it has been fired, a pot may be broken easily but the sherds into which it shatters remain virtually indestructible. Moreover, although pottery is a widespread artifact, it is far from uniform: pieces show almost infinite variety in terms of the clay used, methods of manufacture and firing, vessel shapes and attributes, and glazing or other forms of decoration. Provided that we analyze them properly, the characteristics of a particular piece of pottery therefore provide an identifiable "fingerprint," revealing the place and approximate date of its manufacture.

But the process of matching pottery "fingerprints" relies almost entirely on the existence of a set of "files" against which to compare them, and the building of such files depends largely on finding pottery in archaeological contexts for which we can determine date and origin. One of the best such contexts is a dated shipwreck, since we can usually assume that all the pottery found with the wreck was in everyday use at the time of the disaster. If we know the ship's origin and ports of call, or can deduce these from other finds, we can often identify the regions that supplied the pottery aboard the vessel. Conversely, if types of pottery of known date and origin turn up on a shipwreck of otherwise unknown date and origin, the pottery provides a valuable clue to its identification.

The main value of the pottery recovered from wrecks of the Spanish Armada is that it provides a unique sample of wares in use in the Iberian Peninsula late in the sixteenth century. Moreover, because documentary evidence had already told us much about the wrecked vessels' pre-Armada movements, we can work out where many of the types of ware aboard originated.

The type of pottery most often found on Armada wreck sites is the so-called "olive jar," a globular container apparently used for the fleet's ration of olive oil and vinegar. These jars were probably made in Seville under contract to the *Casa de la Contratación*. This held a strict monopoly of transatlantic trade, and similar pottery occurs widely on Spanish colonial sites in the Americas. Its occurrence on the Armada ships is not surprising, since the same supply organization provisioned the fleet. For accounting purposes, potters apparently made Armada olive jars to a standard capacity of a half *arroba*, or 6.28 liters (5.5 quarts).

Only one other type of pottery occurs on all the Armada wrecks. This is a well-fired red earthenware: some pieces are unglazed, others covered in a bright green or clear glaze. The fact that this ware appears on every wreck investigated strongly suggests that it was loaded at Lisbon, the only port of call that all Armada vessels had in common. Indeed, we know from documentary sources that the potters of that city accepted a large official contract before the

fleet sailed. The same kind of pottery has turned up in former Portuguese colonies, notably at Fort Jesus in East Africa, and very similar wares are made today in the Alentejo region, not far from Lisbon.

Most of the Armada ships first gathered at Sanlúcar de Barrameda, Seville's satellite port at the mouth of the Guadalquiver River, and this visit is unmistakably revealed by the pottery found on the wrecks of ships known to have called there. Seville had been an important ceramic center from Roman times, and sixteenth-century documents show that that city produced large supplies for the Armada. Much of the ware is cheap and mass-produced — typical "government-issue" crockery — and like the "olive-jar" pottery already mentioned, this

ware crops up widely in the Americas on sites related to the routes of the annual Seville-based treasure fleets. We can recognize examples of this pottery in contemporary paintings of peasant scenes, notably those by Velázquez, who worked at Seville early in the seventeenth century.

A few of the ships, including the *Santa María de la Rosa*, came straight to Lisbon without calling first at Sanlúcar, so it is not surprising that her wreck has yielded no Seville-made pottery. On the other hand, this wreck has produced a type of ware — a well-fired white earthenware with a honey-colored glaze — not found on the other wrecks. Probably this ware originated at or near the ship's home port of San Sebastián.

All these "official" wares are plain and

Above: Western Europe, indicating the main sources of the pottery carried by the ships of the Spanish Armada. Opposite: The route by which Chinese porcelain was brought to western Europe via Central America from the 1580s onward.
Opposite, above: An olive jar lying as revealed by excavation on the *Trinidad Valencera* wreck site. The scale is graduated in inches.
Left: A selection of pottery from *La Trinidad Valencera*.

undecorated, implying that they formed part of large contract orders for general issue to the fleet. But there are also a few examples of more exotic wares, presumably belonging to individuals who had brought their own tableware with them. These items include decorated majolica drug jars and platters, some Spanish and some Italian. A platter fragment from *La Trinidad Valencera*, for example, shows a brightly painted design of fruits and foliage. The discovery of an almost identical platter on the wreck of a late sixteenth-century Venetian merchant ship in the Adriatic suggests that the *Valencera* piece belonged to a member of her Venetian crew.

Most unexpected of all was the discovery, again on *La Trinidad Valencera*, of three pieces of blue on white Chinese porcelain. These can be identified as early imports of their kind — brought to Europe by way of the transpacific galleons from the Philippines to Acapulco in Mexico, from where they were mule-packed across the Isthmus of Panama to connect with the treasure fleet that would have shipped them to Seville. From there they came into the possession of a wealthy Spanish gentleman destined to sail with the Armada on board a ship that foundered in a lonely Irish bay.

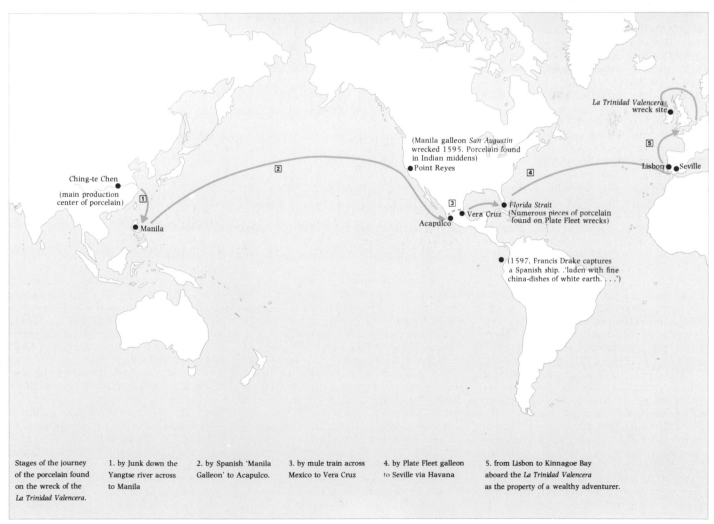

Stages of the journey of the porcelain found on the wreck of the *La Trinidad Valencera*.

1. by Junk down the Yangtse river across to Manila

2. by Spanish 'Manila Galleon' to Acapulco.

3. by mule train across Mexico to Vera Cruz

4. by Plate Fleet galleon to Seville via Havana

5. from Lisbon to Kinnagoe Bay aboard the *La Trinidad Valencera* as the property of a wealthy adventurer.

A standard seventeenth-century warship

On October 9, 1690, the British naval fifth-rate *Dartmouth* sank in the Sound of Mull, on the west coast of Scotland. The Admiralty barely noticed her loss: she was just a small, old, and unimportant vessel in Britain's expanding navy. Today, however, her wreck is providing unique evidence about the service of which she formed so small a part, for her very ordinariness makes her typical of that navy as a whole.

Dartmouth was built at Portsmouth in 1655 by John Tippets, who later became Surveyor to the Navy. She was an early member of a small, lightweight class of warship, loosely called frigates, and designed for dispatch and reconnaissance work. These ships were fast, maneuverable, and well suited to operations in confined waters. Much of the influence behind their design appears to have come from Scandinavia by way of the Low Countries.

In the 1670s the Dutch artist Willem van de Velde the Younger made a drawing of a fifth-rate, almost certainly the *Dartmouth*. We know from documentary sources that the ship underwent a major refit at the Rotherhithe shipyard in London in 1678, and it may well be that the artist sketched her then. In the drawing she appears without masts, and with her guns apparently removed.

In the summer of 1973 a group of enthusiasts from Bristol found the ship's remains during a diving holiday. They were able to identify the wreck as the *Dartmouth* by the discovery of a brass bell bearing the government broad arrow, the letters DH, and the date 1678. The presence of a bell later than the ship's date of building is by no means uncommon, and it may be significant that Willem van de Velde's sketch shows the vessel with an empty belfry. No doubt the bell was replaced during the 1678 refit.

The Bristol group — subsequently reformed as the Bristol Undersea Archaeology Group of the British Sub-Aqua Club — have since investigated the *Dartmouth* wreck in association with the St. Andrews Institute of Maritime Archaeology. Excavations have revealed a substantial part of the ship's hull and plenty of other objects. Although first appearances suggested that the wreck lay scattered and jumbled, research has thrown enough light on the process of break-up and deposition for us to grasp at least something of the vessel's construction and layout. It seems that the ship struck stern first before breaking in two. This allowed the stern part to settle on its starboard side in a shallow gully hard against the small island on which the vessel foundered. Meanwhile, the detached bow section rolled into deeper water where it, too, collapsed on its starboard side.

We identified the bow and stern ends by analyzing the distribution of various classes of artifacts. The stern featured objects like navigational instruments, connected with the executive running of the ship, and objects associated with the gracious living demanded by the captain and his officers. There were also remnants of mica glazing from the stern cabin windows. The more commonplace domestic objects of the forecastle marked the seaward end of the site, while spare rigging fittings and quantities of musket bullets and grenades had come from the boatswain's locker and the armory, both of which lay forward. Between the two ends of the wreck a pile of bricks, tiles, cooking debris, and pottery represented the ship's galley.

Altogether we uncovered and recorded 12 meters (39ft) of coherent structure, involving a run of frames and planking from the lower starboard side. At the after end of this run, 6 meters (20ft) of the keel, including a scarf joint, had survived. Now documentary sources inform us that the *Dartmouth* acquired a new keel 24.4 meters (80ft) long in the 1678 refit and that this comprised three lengths of elm; thus the identification of this scarf joint gives us a fixed point one-third of the way forward from the stern. By recording the curves of the frames, and relating these to the keel, we have managed to calculate much of the hull's underwater shape.

Although the van de Velde sketch well illustrates the ship's general appearance above the waterline, we knew little of the structural details of a vessel of this type until we studied this wreck. The identification of one of the lodging knees from the gun deck has provided evidence for the spacing of the major components, while a number of lead scupper liners (deck drains) demonstrate the thickness of the upper hull timbers.

An important conclusion that we can draw from this work is that *Dartmouth*'s construction differed in many respects from the methods generally held to have been in use at the time. In particular her builders had used considerable ingenuity to avoid using timbers grown into special shapes, reflecting, no doubt, the mounting timber crisis of the mid-seventeenth century.

Locals had salvaged some of the *Dartmouth*'s 36 guns soon after the wrecking, but examples of each of the three types (nine-, six-, and three-pounders) lay undiscovered until the 1970s. They have provided valuable information about her armament.

Sketch made by Willem van de Velde during the 1670s of a Royal Navy fifth-rate vessel, probably representing the *Dartmouth* during her major refit of 1678. The ship has been drawn without masts or guns, and has no bell in her belfry.

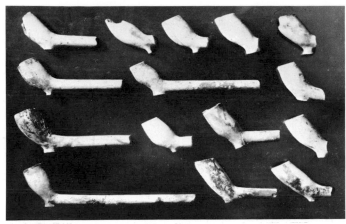

In addition, the site has yielded a large and varied collection of small objects. Navigation is represented by dividers, a protractor, a slate for keeping the ship's log, and part of a backstaff (a tool for gauging latitude); medical equipment by pewter syringes and an apothecary's mortar; and the work of the ship's purser by weights and measures, including a boxwood folding dipstick for gauging spirits in cask. There are also several carpenter's tools, including a wooden caulking mallet, while weapons are represented by a small flintlock pistol and a musket stock.

Most of the small finds, however, are domestic in character, and include several types of pottery, glass bottles, and many clay pipes. Because we can date it precisely, this kind of material affords other archaeologists a valuable reference collection.

All the recoveries from the *Dartmouth*, including a substantial section of the timbers, are now lodged in Edinburgh at the National Museum of Antiquities of Scotland.

Right: The brass bell recovered by the Bristol club divers in 1973. It bears the letters DH and the date 1678, thus confirming the wreck to be that of the *Dartmouth*.
Above: A selection of clay-pipe bowls from the sizeable collection recovered from the wreck of the *Dartmouth*, showing the variety of shapes present.
Below: The Sound of Mull in western Scotland, showing the location of the *Dartmouth* wreck site.
Below: Fragmentary remains of boots and shoes from the site.

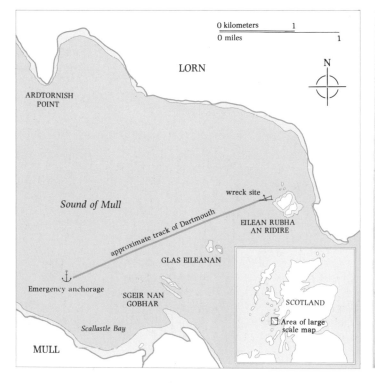

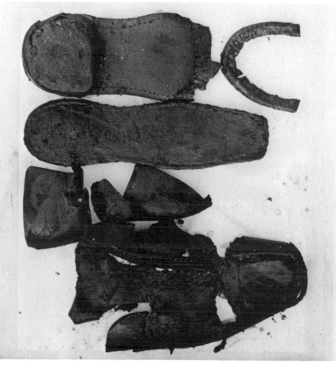

101

Shipwrecks in the Wake of Columbus

This section dwells on the remains of sixteenth- through eighteenth-century European shipping found in American, African, Asian, and Australian waters. The New World comes first, and we open with the search for a Spanish treasure fleet of 1554. Our author is J. Barto Arnold III, marine archaeologist to the Texas Antiquities Committee. The site of one of these wrecks, probably the *San Esteban*, was the earliest in American waters to receive responsible archaeological treatment, and this account lays down the standards that can be achieved.

Unfortunately, many sites in the Americas have received no such respect, as Robert Marx explains in the following 10 pages. The reasons lie in complex legal and commercial considerations; only a few states (notably Texas and Florida) have begun to take steps to protect their archaeological heritage under water. Mr. Marx describes a number of interesting sites he has investigated, and explains how he has tried to maintain acceptable standards despite operational difficulties.

The final 12 pages of this section shift attention from the Americas to the Atlantic and Indian oceans. Jeremy Green considers the study of European trade with the East Indies between the sixteenth and eighteenth century, and provides brief descriptions of more than two dozen wreck sites related to this trade. Once again we see a great variation in standards of excavation, largely reflecting the laws regulating, or failing to regulate, such activities. Undoubtedly, some of the most satisfactory arrangements are those in Western Australia where Mr. Green is curator of maritime archaeology for the state museum. Before taking up that position in 1971. Mr. Green spent several years in the Laboratory for Art and Archaeology at Oxford University, where he developed electronic equipment for underwater reconnaissance.

The fleet of 1554

There are very few sixteenth-century wrecks in American waters. While Columbus himself left four wrecks for posterity, of which two have been located (pp. 110–11), other early sites are very rare. The remains of three ships lost in 1554 off Padre Island on the coast of Texas are thus most important. Moreover, the story of their investigation, from early treasure hunting to recent responsible excavation, mirrors the development of archaeology in American waters.

With his conquest of Mexico, or New Spain, in 1519, Hernando Cortes greatly increased the profitability of New World commerce. Vast quantities of precious metals began to be shipped back to Spain. And as the value of the cargoes mounted, so the numbers of privateers and pirates multiplied along the route. Thus Spanish treasure ships began to sail to and from the Americas in convoy for mutual protection. These flotas (that is, fleets) of merchantmen were also given an escort of warships paid for by a special tax imposed on the cargoes. These escort ships were similar to the merchantmen in appearance, but were supposedly less heavily laden and better armed and manned. But from the *Archives of the Indies*, contemporary commercial archives kept in Seville, Spain, we learn that the warships were frequently so overloaded with cargo that they proved clumsy to handle and were often unable to use their weapons effectively.

The three 1554 Spanish shipwrecks located near Padre Island were part of one of the first regularly organized convoys of the flota system. On November 4, 1552, some 54 ships had left Spain under Captain-General Bartolomé Carreño, of which 16 were bound for Veracruz, in Mexico. In their holds were manufactured goods such as hardware (nails, latches, mallets, and knives), textiles (shirts, fabric, ribbons, and thread), carding tools, soaps, vinegar, and wine. There were also slaves.

The main fleet having been scattered by storms and pirates, the 14 survivors of the New Spain contingent reached Veracruz in February and March of 1553. Of these, only two managed to unload and reload in time to sail for Havana in Cuba with three other ships that had arrived a year ealier. This was partly because Veracruz had been wrecked by a hurricane the previous Sep-

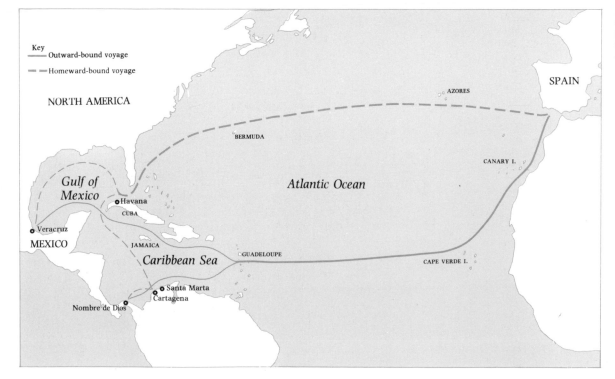

Map showing the outward and return routes between Spain and her Central American possessions.

Key
— Outward-bound voyage
- - Homeward-bound voyage

NORTH AMERICA

SPAIN

AZORES

BERMUDA

CANARY I.

Gulf of Mexico

Atlantic Ocean

Havana
CUBA

Veracruz
MEXICO

JAMAICA

Caribbean Sea

GUADELOUPE

CAPE VERDE I.

Santa Marta
Cartagena

Nombre de Dios

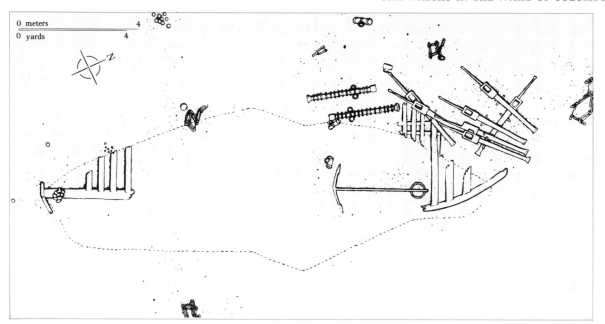

tember. Four other ships waited for over a year before setting out. These were the *San Andres* ("St. Andrew"), Master and Captain-General Antonio Corzo; *San Esteban* (St. Stephen), Master Francisco del Huerto; *Espíritu Santo* ("Holy Spirit"), Master Damian Martín; and *Santa María de Yciar* ("St. Mary of Yciar"), Master Alonso Ojos, and Captain and Pilot Miguel de Jauregui, the ship's owner. The homeward cargo consisted of silver coin and bullion, together with a little gold bullion, valued at over 2,000,000 pesos, or more than $9,800,000 (1975 values). Other merchandise included wool, hides, cochineal, medicinal herbs, and sugar.

On April 29, 1554, all but the *San Andres* were driven aground on Padre Island in a storm. The three wrecked vessels carried about 300 people all told. As many as 200 may have been drowned in the wrecks, leaving the rest stranded on the beach hundreds of miles north of the nearest Spanish outpost. A small group of the survivors probably took a small boat to get help; but the rest, thinking they were only a day or two's march from civilization, decided to walk south down the beach. They fell foul of Indians, and all but twenty or thirty were slain in what became a death march, without food or water.

The authorities in Mexico immediately organized a salvage expedition, which remained at the wreck site from July until September 12, 1554. In water no deeper than 6 meters (20ft), with divers simply holding their breath and working with ropes and grappling hooks, the expedition retrieved rather less than half the treasure.

In recent times the general positions of these shipwrecks have been known locally because of the numerous coins washed ashore. In the fall of 1967, however, a treasure-hunting firm located and exploited one of the wreck sites. The public outcry

Above: A plan of a sixteenth-century wreck in the Bahamas, whose precise identity has never been established. This is one of the few sixteenth-century wreck sites to have been discovered apart from the fleet of 1554 and Columbus's ships (p. 110). On this plan, which was made before any excavations were undertaken, parts of the ship's hull, an anchor, two types of gun, and other remains can be seen.

that occurred when these treasures were removed from the state of Texas resulted in the passage of a very strong Antiquities Code and the creation of an agency, the Texas Antiquities Committee (TAC), to protect cultural resources on state lands and under state waters. One of the most pressing duties of this new agency was scientifically to reinvestigate the shipwrecks of the 1554 fleet. This was accomplished through underwater archaeological field-work in the summers of 1972 through 1976, followed by conservation of the treasure hunters' and state's collections of artifacts, archival research and translation of documents, and intensive study and analysis of the data gained during this project.

Below: Part of a map of the New World published by Sir Robert Dudley in 1646, on which the loss of three Spanish ships is noted (top right-hand corner, inland from "R. Arboledes"). This indicates the continuing notoriety of the disaster of 1554.

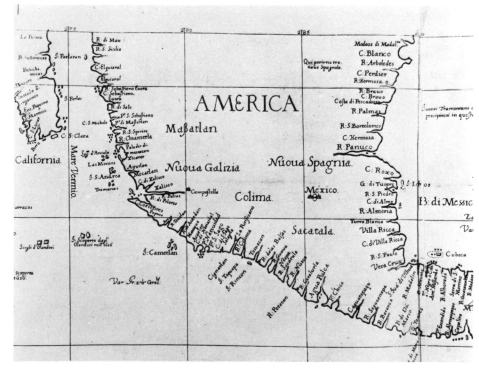

Searching for the *San Esteban*

Any search for wrecks of the three Spanish ships that sank off Texas in 1554 faced some discouraging problems. First was the sheer lack of remains. In the 1940s dredging work had smashed one wreck, probably that of the *Santa Maria de Yciar*. In 1967, treasure hunters had looted another, probably the remains of the *Espíritu Santo*. That left only the third wreck unaccounted for — the *San Esteban*. Spanish documents described this vessel as a *nao* (ship) about 30 metres (100ft) long.

The problem was finding the site off a sandy coast where sediments soon bury sunken objects and the water is so cloudy that a diver can barely see his own outstretched hand. Poor visibility ruled out a visual search. Some kind of electronic survey remained the sole option. Of all geophysical survey instruments available, the proton magnetometer has proved most effective in identifying old submerged shipwrecks. This device measures variations in the local strength of the earth's magnetic field: variations such as those caused by metals, pottery, or stone. In the 1970s we ran several increasingly sophisticated magnetometer surveys along that stretch of coast north of the Rio Grande where the fleet of 1554 had foundered.

The waters in the target area were very

shallows, so we operated from a 10.4-meter (34-ft) aluminum-hulled boat, streaming the magnetometer sensor about 30 meters (100ft) astern, and only 30 centimeters (1ft) or so below the surface. The measurement of the surrounding magnetic field took place at this sensor, which then transmitted a signal along the cable to the craft, for display on a strip chart recorder; we also fed the signal into a small computer aboard ship. The signal recorded any distinctive disturbances, or variations, in the magnetic field. Known as anomalies, these are the main indication of something unusual, perhaps a wreck, immediately below the sensor.

As in so many search exercises, making observations proved straightforward compared with establishing the precise location of every reading. Standard optical instruments may be adequate for many navigational purposes, but for this kind of work they involve too many technical and human weaknesses. Instead, for the *San Esteban* survey, we employed a microwave radar receiver-transmitter linked to a series of shore-based reference stations, already accurately surveyed with respect to each other. For each reading our instruments established 75 distance measurements in less than a second; the average giving our position accurately to within 1 meter (3ft 4in). Our computer then converted these measurements into coordinates on the overall site grid and stored the figures in its memory.

Besides processing data as the survey proceeded, the computer acted as a coordinator, controlling the frequency of instrument readings and correlating them with the locational information. It also supervised the track plotter, and arranged for accumulated data from its memory to

be recorded on magnetic tape cassettes. Back at base we could rerun the cassettes in a machine that used them to produce contoured maps of the site's magnetic field. But we also wanted some immediate indication of major anomalies as we proceeded, so we wrote a special computer program whereby the onboard track plotter would show up significant changes in successive magnetometer readings.

Our survey vessel also had a fathometer, but because its output was incompatible with that from the other equipment, our computer could not integrate the different sets of data. Instead, we produced a separate depth profile along each survey line. By matching this profile against the locational data, we could make detailed contoured maps of the seabed.

With the sensor trailing behind the craft, turning the whole unit was a tricky and time-consuming business. We thus found the most efficient procedure was to make a relatively few long runs parallel to the shore. We kept the gaps between these tracks as wide as we could without risking missing a site. Previous experience suggested that tracks 50 meters (164ft) apart would pass over any ship-shaped anomaly at least twice in the worst possible situation, that is, where the long axis of the site ran parallel to the survey tracks. In the best conceivable situation, where the anomaly's axis lay at right angles to the boat's course, three survey tracks would cross the anomaly. Previous experience also suggested that a wreck in these waters would show up as a large central anomaly (representing the main body of the wreck), with smaller anomalies scattered over a much wider area. Thus tracks outside the crucial two or three might prove fruitful as well.

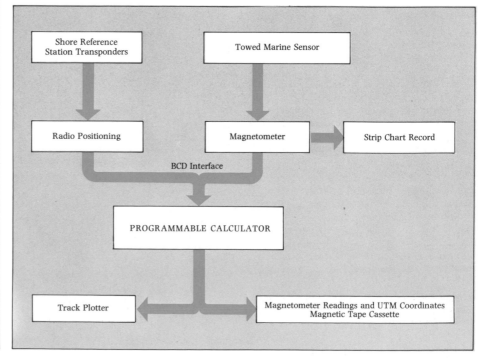

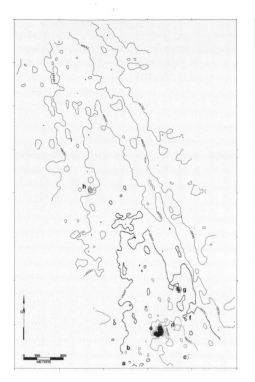

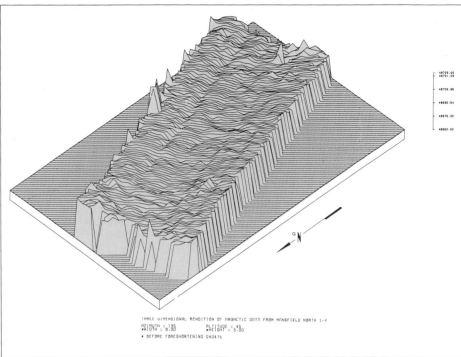

THREE DIMENSIONAL RENDITION OF MAGNETIC DATA FROM MANSFIELD NORTH 1-4
AZIMUTH = 135   ALTITUDE = 45
*WIDTH = 8.00   *HEIGHT = 3.00
* BEFORE FORESHORTENING 040476

Opposite: The Texas coastline north of the Mexican border, showing the location of the wrecks of 1554. The diagram next to it shows how the information from the position-finding instruments and the magnetometer is brought together through the BCD (Binary Coded Decimal) interface and the programmable calculator to produce usable output. The computer plots (right) were produced from data contained on a magnetic tape cassette.

Above, right: Samples of the graphic output from the strip chart recorder, taken from three parallel runs across the site. The major troughs and peaks indicate where the magnetometer head has passed over an area containing iron. The coincidence of such abnormal readings on three runs suggests a major iron feature (such as a wreck) lying across the search lines.

Above: A computer-drawn magnetic contour map of the search area north of the Mansfield Cut. The contours indicate changes in the strength of the local magnetic field as measured by the magnetometer. The same data can be represented by the computer in a three-dimensional image (above, right).

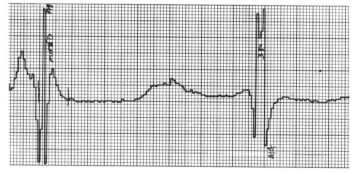

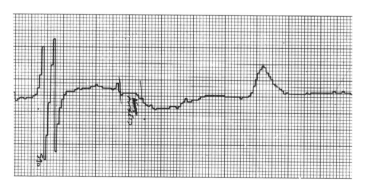

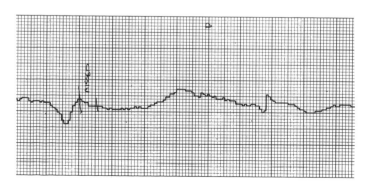

Once magnetometer readings had revealed a site, we performed a more detailed electronic survey of the area. We ran closely spaced tracks across the site in order to build up a highly detailed magnetic contour map. In such areas of poor visibility this information proved invaluable in assessing the extent of a site, and in enabling us to plan systematic excavation. Afterward we found we could match every cluster of objects found with an anomaly that had shown up in the magnetometer survey. The one or two anomalies that we could not relate to wreck material show the need for continuing research into magnetic field behavior.

For the type of water and seabed we worked in and on, the electronic survey I have described was the only possible method of searching. Nevertheless, it probably represents the most efficient initial detection technique in many other situations; at least so our statistics suggest. During the 1974 surveys we achieved an average rate of 13.88 kilometers (8.62mi) of track an hour, representing a coverage of 0.62 square kilometers (0.24sqmi) of seabed searched an hour. A visual survey using divers in reasonable conditions would take about a thousand times longer (compare p. 64 for the Salcombe Bronze Age site search). Against this, of course, is the high price of the equipment involved. Purchased outright, this would have cost about $50,000 at 1974 prices; fortunately, such machines can be hired, and the use of the whole package for a month cost us only $8,500. Bearing in mind the high costs of placing divers on the seabed, this procedure undoubtedly represented extremely good value for money.

The *San Esteban* discoveries

Between 1972 and 1976 we completely excavated the presumed wreck of the *San Esteban* following its discovery in the magnetometer survey that we have just described. Using the contoured magnetic site plans produced by that survey, the divers dealt with each anomaly in turn. Most proved to represent substantial metal objects such as iron cannons, anchors, spikes, and bolts; each surrounded by a considerable concretion of corrosion products. In fact, some 85% of all objects recovered came from such concretions. Storms giving rise to heavy seabed movement had removed almost all trace of light unencrusted objects. Apart from abraded ceramic sherds, the remaining 15% of artifacts were relatively heavy items made of iron, bronze, lead, silver, or gold. It is no wonder, therefore, that our divers complained that all they seemed to do was plot, bring up, and attach numbered tags to encrustations, seldom seeing objects they could recognize. Despite this disappointment for the divers there can be no doubt that the place to "excavate" such conglomerates is not actually on the site but (as the next two pages show) inside the laboratory.

This is no reason for belittling the achievements of the divers working on this site. The mere plotting of each lump in very poor visibility was difficult enough, but items lay buried up to 2 meters (about 6ft) deep in sediments. Accurately pinpointing their positions was an important first step toward a full understanding of what lay where, and this has helped to make it possible for archaeologists and conservators to discuss the wreck in remarkable detail. The resulting report and other scientific papers represent one of the most comprehensive studies in maritime archaeology. Then, too, the actual objects recovered by the divers now form an impressive public exhibition that can tour the state of Texas for the education and enjoyment of every citizen. The finds remain public property and the antiquities market will never scatter them around the world.

The range of objects from the *San Esteban* wreck site proved so extensive that we can only pick out some examples. One of the highlights of the whole collection is the weaponry. Finds include two varieties of breech-loading, wrought-iron artillery, namely, swivel guns and bombards. For these weapons there was ammunition in the form of iron, lead, and stone shot. In many instances the gunners had protected their weapons from damp by plugging the ends of the breech chamber with wood and sealing the touchhole with a twist of hemp. Other surviving weapons include crossbows, one with a well-preserved wooden stock and cocking mechanism.

The official cargo was mainly silver. Silver coins struck by several moneyers at the then newly established Mexico City mint appear in denominations of one, two, three, and four *reales*. There are also a few Spanish silver coins from other mints. Silver bullion takes the form of disks varying in weight from a few ounces to 30 pounds (13.61kg) and more. The upper surface of these disks bears tax, mines', or owners' marks. The only gold recovered consists of two small bars.

Among the personal possessions of the passengers and crew we find a gold crucifix and a broken wooden cross trimmed with gold. Several pewter items, including plates and porringers, bear the English touchmark: the crowned Tudor rose. The pottery is similarly cosmopolitan, including brightly painted majolica wares, and Cologne stoneware. Items for personal use and adornment include a quantity of straight brass pins, as well as brass shoe buckles, a silver thimble, and a fragment of chain mail. More surprising still are the obsidian blades and

Above: Finds from the *San Esteban* wreck included silver bullion, silver coins, and a gold bar (left); a gold crucifix (center); and two inscribed gold bars (above). The pair of silver coins (left) — a two-reales piece and a four-reales piece — also came from the site.

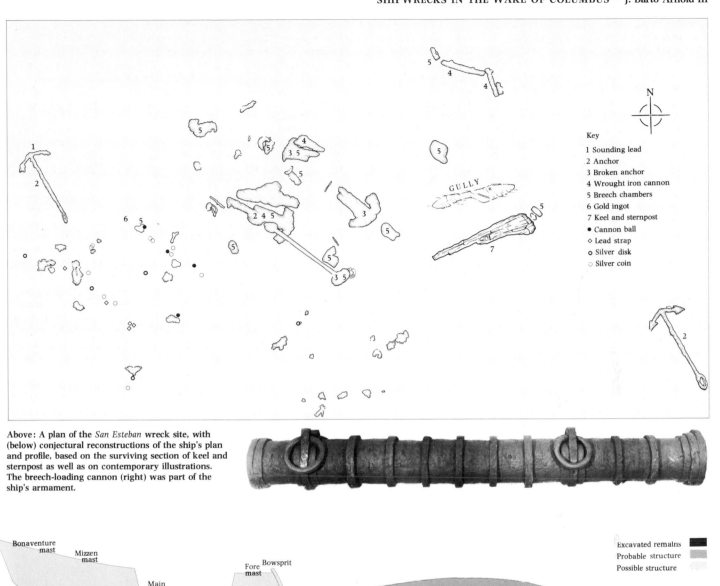

Above: A plan of the *San Esteban* wreck site, with (below) conjectural reconstructions of the ship's plan and profile, based on the surviving section of keel and sternpost as well as on contemporary illustrations. The breech-loading cannon (right) was part of the ship's armament.

Key

1 Sounding lead
2 Anchor
3 Broken anchor
4 Wrought iron cannon
5 Breech chambers
6 Gold ingot
7 Keel and sternpost
● Cannon ball
◇ Lead strap
○ Silver disk
○ Silver coin

Excavated remains
Probable structure
Possible structure

Bonaventure mast
Mizzen mast
Main mast
Fore mast
Bowsprit
Breadth line
Stern post
Stem post
Rudder
Keel

Breadth line

0 meters   10
0 yards   10

a polished iron pyrite mirror, items of American Indian manufacture presumably being taken home by someone as souvenirs. Iron tools and ship's equipment are plentiful, among them bolts; spikes; nails; a sledge-hammer; pincers; a pickax; a gouge and a reamer; caulking tools; chains; rudder gudgeons (sockets) and pintles (pivot pins); and lead sounding weights. Smaller lead weights recovered may have been plumb bobs for gunners' quadrants, instruments used in taking aim. Navigational equipment features fragments of two sets of brass dividers, and three brass mariner's astrolabes, devices widely used in the sixteenth century for accurately finding latitude. Only about three dozen of these early instruments are known throughout the world.

Given the exposed nature of this site, it is not surprising that little remained of the hull of the *San Esteban*. What did survive, however, was the sternpost and a section of the keel, which together can tell us more than any other fragments of equivalent size about this vessel's lines and build.

These finds from the *San Esteban* do not complete the list of preserved relics from the Spanish ships that sank off Texas in 1554. From the wreck destroyed when a dredger cut the Mansfield Channel through Padre Island we have an anchor, a few silver coins, and a pewter porringer — all found on the beach nearby. From the presumed wreck of the *Espíritu Santo* we also have a collection of artifacts looted by treasure hunters in 1967 but sequestered

in 1969 by a U.S. district court acting in the public interest. These finds can tell us far less than they would have done if people had carefully plotted them before recovery, and set about preserving them soon afterward. Nonetheless, they, too, contribute something to our record of the lost ships.

But much the most important evidence remains the *San Esteban* assemblage, representing as it does a unique record of many aspects of culture in the middle of the sixteenth century. Together with a wealth of information from old archives, these finds help us to paint a detailed picture of many aspects of Spain's relations with the New World in the first decades after its discovery.

Conservation lessons from Texas

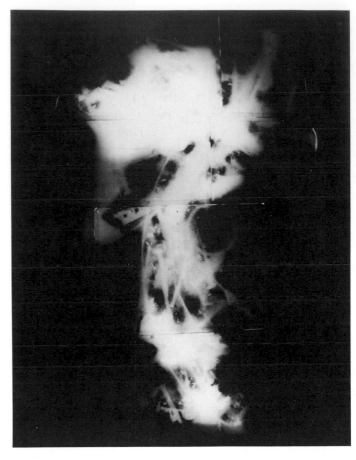

We should have gleaned a bare fraction of what we now know about the *San Esteban* relics without the work of conservation experts. The tasks of cleaning and preserving items from this wreck fell to the Texas Archaeological Research Laboratory, part of the University of Texas at Austin. The laboratory had become involved in conserving objects from the sea in 1969. A court order in that year handed the laboratory temporary custody of material of disputed ownership recovered by a treasure-hunting firm from the supposed site of the *Espíritu Santo*. Empowered to study and preserve these items, the laboratory staff were, however, hindered by the fact that the treasure hunters had crudely hacked away the encrustations from many of the objects.

The handling of material from the *San Esteban*, excavated in a scientific manner a few years later, proved much more rewarding. But it was also very challenging. The collection from the *San Esteban* was unusual in that the great bulk of the material recovered consisted of conglomerates formed around one or more heavily corroded iron objects. During the many decades of submersion in seawater, some of these encrustations had built up to form huge, shapeless lumps incorporating sand and ballast stones, shells and other plant or animal debris, and even other objects belonging to the wreck. For example, the conglomerates surrounding some of the large iron objects, like anchors and cannons, included hundreds of smaller objects and ballast stones. In some instances, especially among the smaller iron objects, corrosion had gone so far that it had totally destroyed the metal artifact, leaving only its ghost in the form of a hollow inside the concretion (see also Yassi Ada, pp. 36–37). Before they broke such concretions open, the conservators therefore photographed them from a number of angles, using natural light and X-rays. The resulting prints showed whether it was going to be necessary to take a cast of the object at the heart of the lump; the prints also served as guides for the technician entrusted with the tricky task of "excavation." Because concretions can be very hard, the technician used a pneumatic chisel for dissecting them. As he opened up each piece layer by layer, he took extensive notes and made a photographic record in order to preserve all information that might prove useful later on. Thus at this point the conservator was actually behaving more like an archaeologist: seeking to interpret the significance of the relationships before him, rather than just extracting objects in readiness for treatment.

Once the conservator and his team had freed each item from concretion they had to treat it according to its constituent material. For most metals, including silver, and iron, treatment meant immersion in an electrolytic bath. Passing a current through the object and the electrolyte in which it hung removed the negatively charged chloride ions from the structure of the metal so that, ideally, it emerged in a pure and stable form. But with iron this process called for careful control, for any chlorides left would combine with hydrogen from water vapor in the atmosphere. The resulting hydrochloric acid would then attack the iron in a self-renewing cycle until the iron had turned into a pile of rust. Small items such as silver coins needed only a few days' electrolytic treatment, but a large iron object like a cannon or an anchor required a year or more. Generally, once chemical tests of the electrolyte showed that all chlorides had been eliminated, laboratory staff removed the object, dried it off, and finally immersed it in a micro-crystalline wax in order to protect it completely from atmospheric corrosion.

Obviously, where an object survived only as a hollow at the center of a lump of concretion, all that the laboratory staff had to do was to clean out the hollow and inject it with some type of latex solution. Once this hardened, they broke away the surrounding concretion, revealing a perfect replica of the vanished original. But this sounds easier than it actually was: cutting through the conglomerate without damaging the hollow called for skill and accurate interpretation of the preliminary X-ray photographs.

Although most of the *San Esteban* artifacts requiring treatment were metallic, there

108

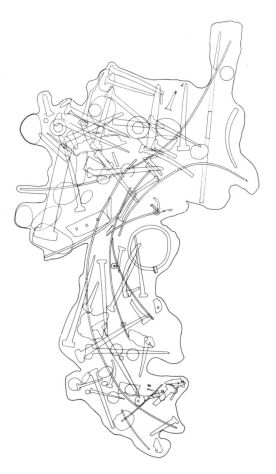

were other substances, presenting other problems. For example, the surviving sections of the wooden keel and sternpost were waterlogged, and drying out would have distorted them. Their potential value for studies on the original hull and as relics to be put on public display meant that the laboratory had to tackle them. The chosen method was total immersion in polyethylene glycol (PEG). This treatment has proved slow and costly, involving years of soaking in vats of permanently heated solution kept circulated by pumps. Similar but less lengthy treatment has also helped save smaller wooden items.

Although firmly based on scientific principles derived from chemistry and the accumulated experience of museum and laboratory staffs over recent years, all this conservation work called for considerable imagination and flexibility. As with archaeological deposits on a site, no two objects or conglomerates were the same, and the conservator had to tackle each one individually in order to extract as much information as possible and to preserve that object for the future. At every stage in the *San Esteban* project, he also had to work closely with his archaeological colleagues, discovering the kinds of questions that we were pursuing, and informing us of better ways to recover, pack, and transport our finds before these reached the laboratory at Austin. This team aspect of archaeology under water was certainly most important.

Various stages in the dissection of a single conglomerate (top, left) from the *San Esteban* site. First, the material is X-rayed in the laboratory. The surface concretions are then removed. Next, the individual artifacts are extracted and conserved, and can be laid out as originally found. Finally, a drawing must be made of the various items. As you can see, the conglomerate was mainly made up of large iron bolts, spikes, and straps, although it contained also 12 coins and an aboriginal polished pyrites mirror.

Discovering Columbus's ships

In May, 1502, Christopher Columbus set sail from Spain on his fourth and last voyage of discovery; four caravels made up his expedition fleet. After reaching the Caribbean, Columbus spent almost a year cruising along the coast of Central America, but found little of importance. Meanwhile, shipworm caused so much damage to his small vessels that he had to strip and scuttle two of them in Panama. His two remaining ships — *La Capitana* and *Santiago de Palos* — were now in very poor condition too; he therefore tried to reach Santo Domingo, hoping to repair both vessels there before he headed home to Spain. A roundabout route seemed the easiest, but between Cuba and Jamaica both ships began to leak so badly that they appeared about to sink. On June 25, 1503, this threat forced Columbus into St. Ann's Bay on the north coast of Jamaica, and he ran both vessels aground about "a crossbow shot from land." With only the fore- and sterncastles sticking up above the water, Columbus and some of his 116 wretched men lived for a year and four days until a relief ship arrived from Santo Domingo.

Contemporary writings, including a book by Columbus's son Ferdinand, closely indicate the place where Columbus beached and left these wrecks. With these documents as guides, the historian Samuel Eliot Morison in 1940 led a Harvard University-sponsored expedition to try to find both wrecks. He failed, but his book *Admiral of the Ocean Sea* included a chart marking both wrecks' supposed locations in the bay: Morison's locations proved to be only a few score meters out.

In March, 1966, the Institute of Jamaica sponsored a new expedition, led by me. A magnetometer survey failed to reveal any clear anomalies in the area, so we laid out a grid system and started using a 3-meter (10ft) metal probe. Forcing the probe down into the soft sediment in order to locate solid objects, we eventually touched something hard at a depth of 2.5 meters (8ft). A test hole produced a fragment of a wooden rib containing treenails. Beneath the wood we discovered several pieces of obsidian, a glassy type of stone that Columbus had mentioned carrying back aboard his ships. We now believed we had located one of the Columbian wrecks, but more than two years were to pass before we could be sure. Meanwhile, my work at Port Royal (pp. 146–47) prevented me from following up the find.

We owed the success of our next attempt very largely to the electrical engineer and inventor Dr. Harold Edgerton of the Massachusetts Institute of Technology. Using his "pinger" and "boomer" — two types of sub-bottom profiling sonar — Dr. Edgerton discovered two sites in St. Ann's Bay within an hour. Sonar graphs indicated that both sites were shipwrecks; more importantly, their sizes and positions matched those we

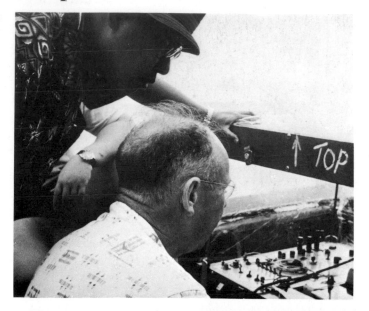

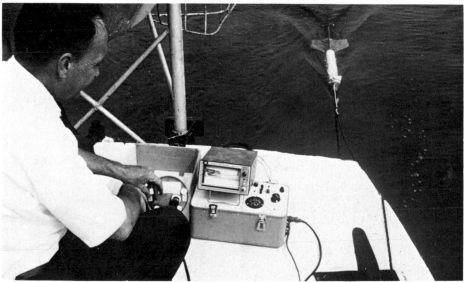

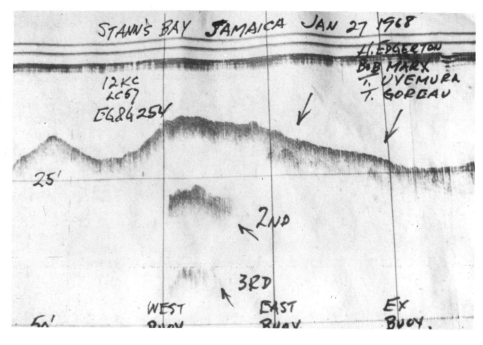

Left: Dr. Harold Edgerton and an assistant watching his sonar unit during the survey of St Ann's Bay, Jamaica.
Center: A fluxgate magnetometer in use on a wreck search.
Below: A print-out from the sonar profiler, showing the run on which the wreck of one of Columbus's ships was discovered. It is indicated by the smudge beyond the arrow labelled "2nd".
Opposite: Robert Marx (far right) with one of the timbers recovered from the site of the Columbus wrecks. Inset: the coring tube being prepared at base camp, and a core-section (below) containing wood from one of the ships.

had predicted for Columbus's vessels. To be on the safe side we made a complete sonar survey of all other likely areas in the bay and found no other sites.

I tried to determine the overall extent of both wrecks by probing with a metal rod. Sonar had indicated that both wrecks lay under 3–3.5 meters (10–12ft) of sediment. In some areas on both sites I was able to reach these levels, and found wood and ballast rock. Elsewhere concentrations of heavy mud obstructed the passage of my probe. Here, I used a special air probe – a tool developed quickly on the spot by Dr. Robert Judd when he saw my difficulty in defining the limits of the site. The Judd air probe consisted of a 6-meter (20-ft) section of 2.5-centimeter (1in) iron water pipe. Compressed air, injected through a hose into the top of the pipe, spurted from the bottom in a stream of bubbles. This tool quickly cut through hard mud and we could readily pull the metal tube out again.

Dr. Judd had really arrived for a different purpose: to operate a coring device sent by Columbia University. This help had been arranged by Dr. George Bass (p. 32), prevented by teaching commitments from joining our important undertaking. Bass and other experts shared my view that taking core samples was better than excavating a series of test holes: these would not only have disturbed the archaeological context of the wrecks, but might have exposed their wooden parts to shipworm attack from which their muddy grave had been protecting them.

Our coring device consisted of a tube 6 meters (20ft) long and 10 centimeters (4in) in diameter. One diver held it vertically while another drove it into the sediment by hitting the top with a heavy sledgehammer. The next step was inserting a rubber plug into the top of the tube so as to maintain suction inside it and stop its contents dropping out when we raised the tube, which we did with an air-filled lifting bag. When we had brought a loaded tube ashore or aboard a vessel above the site, we removed the plug, held the tube almost horizontally, and gently shook it. In this way we recovered pieces of wood, glass, and flint; iron nails and tacks; small ballast rocks; animal bones; ceramic sherds; and beans. This method of recovery also revealed the different depths from which these came.

Analysis by various experts has confirmed the authenticity of both shipwrecks. But lack of funds means that there has been no more work on the sites. To excavate both wrecks properly would mean treating them like the five Viking ships at Roskilde, Denmark (pp. 74–75): in other words, building a cofferdam around the wrecks, pumping out the water, and excavating as you would on land.

Because these are the earliest known European wreck sites in the Americas and relics of the personal endeavors of Columbus, we must hope that the necessary resources will one day become available for such a project.

Spanish ships and wrecks after 1600

So far this section has dealt with Spanish ships that sailed and sank in New World waters in the century after Columbus made his first transatlantic voyage. We move on now to post-1600 ships. Before we look at excavated sites dating from this period, we must review contemporary historical events and developments. We shall also consider the effects of past salvage work on the scope of underwater archaeology.

About 1600 the Spanish system of annual treasure fleets had begun to decline and by 1656 its whole fabric had almost collapsed. Of the many reasons, the most important were: decline in New World silver production; increase in the sale by foreigners of contraband goods to Spain's New World territories; lack of ships and crews for transatlantic voyages; repeated bankruptcy of the Spanish Crown, and hostile powers' attacks on Spanish vessels.

Things became so bad that after 1648 Spain stopped sending out the Tierra Firme flota, one of the three fleets that had annu-

ally sailed to the Americas since 1552. Thereafter, the heavily armed vessels of the armada (the second, armored, fleet) shipped out the small amount of export goods once carried by the discontinued flota. From 1650 onward the New Spain flota and the armada sailed only once every four or five years. Another way of measuring the decline is to compare sailing figures. Between 1570 and 1599 an average of 110 flota ships sailed annually to America; between 1600 and 1610 this number halved; between 1640 and 1650 it halved again; and between 1670 and 1690 sailings slumped to 17. Spain became so weak that in 1661 she used a Dutch fleet to protect her returning treasure ships. During the War of Spanish Succession (1700–13) the French ran the flota system, chiefly using their own ships and crews. Between 1715 and 1736 small flotas sailed to Mexico once every two or three years, but in this same 21-year period only five small armadas sailed to what are now Colombia and Panama. In 1740 the Spanish finally stopped sending out armadas. Thereafter, large, solitary galleons would sail directly from Cádiz to Callao, Peru, and back with the Peruvian treasures. The end was near for the Mexican flotas, too. Between 1754 and 1778, only six flotas sailed to Veracruz. The last New Spain flota returned to Spain in 1778. That year, the Spanish Crown declared free trade throughout Spain's American colonies, and the flota system was extinct. Spanish ships still sailed to the New World with European products and returned with treasure, but not in convoys.

We must not overstress the importance of the decline in treasure fleets. Throughout the three centuries of the so-called Indies navigations single Spanish ships – called *sueltos* – plied between America and Europe. The number annually sailing ranged from a handful to more than 50, according to political conditions.

Whether tackled singly or in convoy, the voyage to and from the New World was hazardous. Treacherous reefs and shallows, and fierce, sudden, tropical storms meant that the Caribbean Sea claimed a particularly heavy toll in those days of dead-reckoning navigation and poor charts, when sail-driven wooden vessels deteriorated swiftly in the tropical climate, and the shipworm turned their hulls to sieves. Thousands of ships were lost at sea. Most sank in storms, others through poor navigation, fire, and battle.

About 98% of those lost before 1825 went down in shallow water where waves badly smashed the sunken vessels, leaving few clues for future archaeologists seeking facts about the vessels' types and methods of construction. But many wrecks suffered much more heavily from salvage.

Contrary to popular belief, early salvage workers were surprisingly efficient, and recovered more than 90% of the treasures

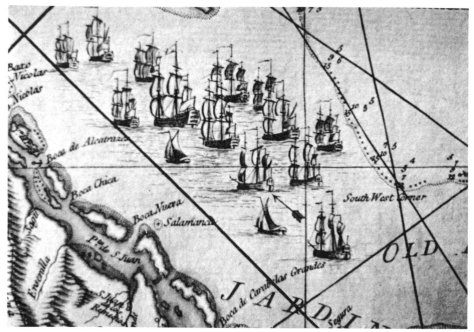

Top: A contemporary picture of a seventeenth-century galleon, with – below it – a chart showing the flota of 1578 passing the coast of Cuba. The Sixteenth-century woodcut (left) shows pearl divers at work off Margarita Island, near the coast of Cuba.

and other cargoes from vessels lost in depths of less than 15 meters (50ft). American Indians had been pearl diving long before Columbus's time, and at first the Spanish used them for this purpose, too; but overwork and disease decimated the supply of local divers. The Spanish accordingly tried using Negroes shipped from Africa. By 1693 as many as 1,000 were diving, many to a depth of 30 meters (100ft).

Meanwhile, salvage had become as great a lure as pearls. In such major ports as Havana, Cartagena, Veracruz, and Panama, teams of Negro divers lived aboard salvage vessels kept ready to sail off quickly on reports of sunken treasures and other goods. Between 1500 and 1800 these divers recovered more than 500 million pesos in lost property and, on more than one occasion, saved Spain from bankruptcy.

In the early 1600s Bermudan-based English privateers began capturing Negro pearl divers and setting them to salvage Spanish wrecks. Treasure-hunting, or "wracking" as the English called it, re-

mained Bermuda's major industry until the middle 1600s. Thereafter, its strategic location near the middle of the Caribbean made newly founded Port Royal the "wrackers'" capital. A Spanish spy who sneaked into this Jamaican port in 1673 reported 50 sloops and schooners seeking treasures from Spanish and other shipwrecks. Later, the "wrackers'" center moved again: to Nassau in the Bahamas in the eighteenth century, and to Key West, Florida, a century later.

In fact, the salvage of old Spanish wrecks has seldom ceased, and modern diving aids have lent it fresh momentum. During World War II "hard-hat" salvage divers seeking to exploit a metal shortage brought up thousands of anchors, cannons, and lumps of metal ballast from old sunken ships. Today, thousands of scuba-diving souvenir collectors and treasure-hunters wreak their havoc too. Add sites destroyed by coastal engineering work, and you find that in the western hemisphere man has done more damage in the last three decades than nature in the last four centuries. The pace of vandalism

quickens, yet governments and scholars do little to protect old wreck sites or to teach amateur divers of the need for conservation. Unless authorities act soon to stop this horrible destruction, a bleak future awaits underwater archaeology in the western hemisphere.

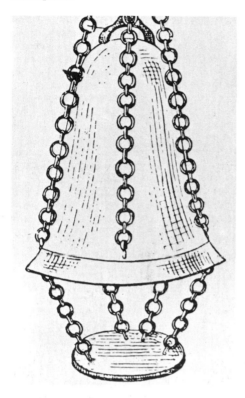

Top, right: A Spanish diving bell of about 1715. Left: Spanish free-divers working on a Caribbean wreck in 1625, a marked contrast to the diving archaeologist (below, right) surveying a wreck of about 1595 off Bermuda.

A Bahamian treasure wreck

On January 1, 1656, an armada of 14 ships left Havana in Cuba for Spain. They were loaded with treasure, for scarcity of available vessels had built up a five-year backlog of shipments from Peru to Spain. Besides picking up a great amount of gold and silver at Portobelo, in what is now Panama, the armada had made an unscheduled stop at Veracruz in Mexico, and gathered several years' accumulated treasures there.

Three days out from Havana, the armada found that navigational error had brought it over the dangerous shallows of the Little Bahama Bank. In the ensuing confusion a ship accidently rammed the *Maravilla*. She sustained a gaping hole in her bow and began taking in water at an alarming rate. The captain decided to run her aground in order to save all the lives and treasure that he could. But the galleon violently struck a coral reef, slid off, and came to rest in 15 meters (50ft) of water. Soon afterward, a violent storm smashed the vessel in three pieces. Of the 650 unlucky souls aboard only 45 survived, and more than 5,500,000 pesos in treasure was lost.

During a three-year salvage effort, the Spaniards managed to recover only about 10% of the treasure before shifting sand buried all trace of the wreck. Over the centuries, other salvagers recovered a small amount of treasure and some of the ship's 58 bronze cannons.

I first became fascinated by the tale of the *Maravilla* in 1960, while doing research in the *Archives of the Indies* in Seville (p. 102). After locating more than 12,000 pages of documents dealing with the ship – including a copy of her original manifest, which listed every item of cargo she carried – I came across a 144-page book published in Madrid in 1657 and written by one of the survivors. The author's exciting and vivid account of the disaster filled many gaps left by the documents. I also located three charts that pinpointed the site.

From the start I knew that this would be difficult to find and work. It lay more than 60 kilometers (40mi) from the nearest land, with no reefs affording shelter from the weather, and in an area where the average current ran at 2 knots (3.7km/h). The one big advantage was excellent underwater visibility – 60 meters (200ft).

Helped by the well-known American oceanographer Willard Bascom, in 1972 I obtained a search permit from the Bahamian government and formed a company to go after the wreck. The expedition that followed taught me a vital lesson: check every buried anomaly and take nothing for granted. Using a magnetometer on our research vessel, we actually located the wreck the very first day: it lay just where the documents and charts had said it should. But debris from a modern wreck also littered the site, and we wrongly assumed that the buried anomaly shown up by our magnetometer was just part of this wreckage. For

three tiresome months we continued vainly searching, covering 78 square kilometers (30sqmi) and finding 20 more shipwrecks. Then we came upon the *Maravilla* by accident. One night we anchored near the known modern wreckage. Next morning we pulled up the anchor, and wedged in it were two Spanish-type ballast rocks.

Diving revealed more ballast rocks, an intact Spanish olive jar, and a large copper kettle, all lying exposed on the reef that the *Maravilla* had struck before sinking. But we soon discovered that just east of the reef part of the wreck lay under 7.6 meters (25ft) of sand. At this time no one had excavated a western hemisphere shipwreck buried to even half that depth. Fortunately, our 23-meter (76ft) vessel carried a powerful blaster, or propwash (p. 116). This was 1.8 meters (6ft) in diameter, powerful enough to work well in deep sand. But besides the sand cover, wreck scatter posed a problem. The center and stern sections lay more than 3 kilometers (2mi) from the bow section, the one we found first, and, as I write, the only section that we have

examined. Even this was badly broken up and spread over an area 180×270 meters (600×900ft); of the hull itself few traces remained.

At first, I considered removing all over-burden and erecting a grid as a basis for methodical work. But because strong currents ceaselessly shifted sand across the site a grid proved impracticable. Instead, I settled for buoys at 6-meter (20-ft) intervals around the perimeter. They served as reference points both for mapping and systematically excavating this part of the site. We started excavation by clearing sand from the northeast corner. There we blasted a hole about 7.6 meters (25ft) across. We progressed by making a series of similar holes. First we worked south, then we moved 6 meters (20ft) west and worked north, and so on. This system ensured that we covered every scrap of the bottom. We assigned a code number to each hole and marked the plot chart accordingly.

After shifting a huge load of overburden we found the remains of the wreck on a hard limestone bottom. Using a wide-angle lens on a 35mm still camera, I was able to take one shot that showed everything where it lay before we removed anything from the hole. When we uncovered a large object such as a cannon or anchor, we attached a buoy and found the object's position by taking bearings from other buoys around the perimeter. We recorded the major artifacts recovered from each hole, and at the end of the day plotted their relative positions on a chart. Photography later enabled me to produce a more accurate chart of the site and a photographic mosaic showing it as if all had been exposed at the same time.

So far we have recovered a good deal of the silver and gold coins and bullion that had made up most of the cargo. We have also discovered many objects probably carried as contraband. These include unmarked gold disks, a three-legged grinding stone, and many examples of unregistered silverware.

After five summer seasons of work on this site we have yet to complete excavation around the bow section, our priority before moving on to the center and stern sections of the ill-fated *Maravilla*.

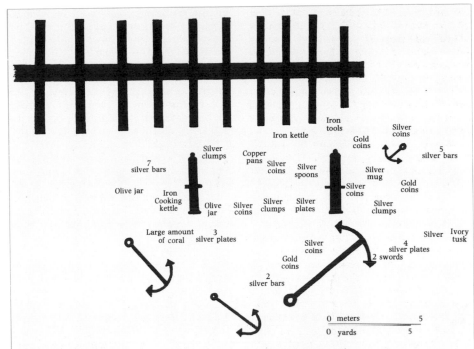

Opposite: A diver excavating around one of the bronze cannons from the *Maravilla*. **Right**: Two complete olive jars from the *Maravilla* (see wreck-site plan above), showing the range of sizes represented in the cargo. The diver (far right) is holding two lumps of concretion made up of silver coins; behind her lies part of the ship's ballast.

Left: A silver bar from the wreck, weighing about 33 kilograms (72lb 3oz). Among the marks are three sets of owner's initials; its weight; a tally number; an assayer's mark; and a seal to show that the royal taxes had been paid.

115

The 1715 treasure fleet

The 12-ship convoy that left Havana at sunrise on July 24, 1715, comprised five ships of the New Spain flota, six ships of the armada from Panama, and a French ship. Officially, the 11 Spanish ships carried 6,486,066 pesos in gold and silver bullion and coin, but we now know that they had aboard an almost equal amount in contraband treasure. Six days out, the convoy was making its way up the Straits of Florida when a devastating hurricane wrecked all but the French ship on the Florida coast. More than 1,000 persons perished: another 1,500 reached the shore by swimming or floating on pieces of wreckage, but many of these died from thirst, hunger, and exposure. Meanwhile, the 11 wrecks were scattered over 80 kilometers (50mi), from Cape Canaveral to 8 kilometers (5mi) south of Fort Pierce Inlet.

Salvage efforts on the wrecks began immediately and by the end of December more than 5,000,000 pesos in treasure had been recovered. By the time the Spanish stopped salvage work in 1719, they had saved more than 8,500,000 pesos. During the next three decades divers from Bermuda and Jamaica also worked the wrecks, but we know nothing of how much they raised.

We find no further mention of the wrecks until early in the nineteenth century, when a surveyor reported finding several hundred gold coins near Fort Pierce Inlet.

In 1948 a building contractor named Kip Wagner found seven silver coins along the beach near Sebastian Inlet. This find was to lead to the discovery of seven of these wrecks, and their exploration by four commercial salvage firms granted leases and supervised by the state of Florida.

Using a World War II metal detector, Wagner first located more coins along other sections of the coast. Then simply by using a face mask to peer under water, he managed to pinpoint several large ballast piles representing wrecks. For years Wagner kept his finds a secret. Then, in 1959, he enlisted the help of a group of amateur sports divers, and they formed the Real Eight Corporation. Working at weekends, and employing only visual search, they managed to locate a great deal of treasure and other artifacts. By 1963 they had graduated to using a water dredge (p. 20). Two other important events took place that year. First, Mel Fisher's salvage firm Treasure Salvors teamed up with Real Eight to work on a full-time basis; second, the state of Florida hired an underwater archaeologist to work closely with both groups. Real Eight gained an exclusive lease to explore 80 kilometers (50mi) of shoreline in return for giving the state of Florida 25% of the finds. State officials aboard each salvage vessel were to record all pertinent archaeological data and ensure that divers used approved excavation techniques.

By the end of 1963 the salvage team had found seven of the 11 wrecks (by the late 1970s the rest still defied discovery). Early detection largely reflected the fact that Treasure Salvors were the first group to use a marine proton magnetometer. They found that all but one of the sites lay scattered over large areas; some encompassed several square miles. In all areas items from the wrecks lay on limestone bedrock, beneath sand 1–3 meters (about 3–10ft) deep and under water varying in depth from 9–18 meters (30–60ft). However, some small items such as coins turned up inshore in water you could paddle in. Underwater visibility on the sites varied from 0.5–10 meters (1½–33ft) depending on the weather. Sometimes cloudy water halted work for weeks at a time.

Realizing that there was always about a

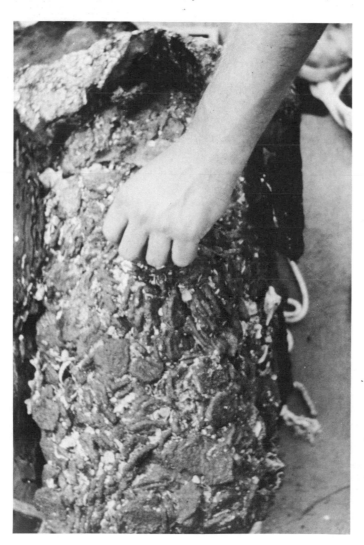

The vast numbers of discoveries from the various 1715 wrecks included the remains of a wooden chest (left) containing 3,000 silver coins; a cannon – which proved to be of English make – shown (above) with a diver removing its coral encrustation; and (below) the inscribed handle of a pocket knife.

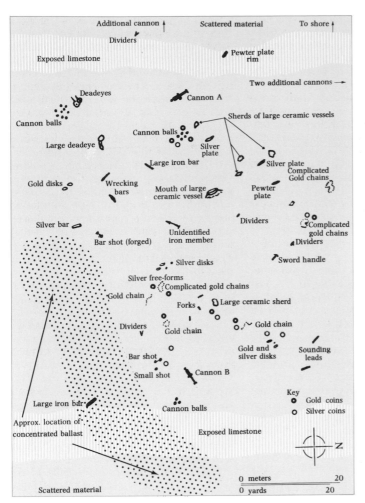

meter of clear water near the surface, the salvagers devised a so-called propwash for pushing clear water from the surface to the bottom. To their great surprise they discovered that this device was a much better excavation tool than the airlifts and dredges they had been using. The propwash, also called a blaster or duster, is simple and inexpensive to construct, easy to operate, and worth describing in some detail. It consists of an elbow-shaped metal tube somewhat larger in diameter than the vessel's propeller. You attach this tube to the transom of the salvage vessel so that the wash from the propeller is forced into the tube and deflected downward to the seabed. It is best to fix the tube's upper end about 0.3–1 meter (1–3ft) behind the propeller, and cover the propeller area with a wire-mesh cage to prevent divers from being cut.

When you are about to use the propwash, you must drop four anchors to hold your salvage vessel in position. Next, you start the vessel's engine, adjusting the propeller's rate of spin according to the depth of water and amount of sediment to be removed. The whirlpool action of the downwash forces water to the bottom at tremendous speed, but the depth at which it effectively drives sediment away depends on two factors: the size of the propwash tube, and the highest speed at which the vessel's propeller will spin. A small propwash on an outboard engine is effective only down to 4.6 meters (15ft). On a large vessel with a 2-meter (6-ft) diameter propeller, you can dig a hole 15 meters (50ft) across in 18 meters (60ft) of water in less than 15 minutes.

The secret of running a propwash effectively lies in using the right speed: fast to remove overburden on the wreck, but slow when you reach the level of the wreck itself. Use too high a speed, and you will smash or blow away artifacts. At slow speeds, however, the sand or other sediment should disperse, leaving artifacts undamaged.

With this revolutionary new excavation tool the wreck hunters increased their work output tenfold and made countless new discoveries. Only one site bore wooden remains of a hull, but other finds revealed a great deal about these ships and the equipment and cargoes that they had carried.

To stay solvent, the divers sold many of the coins they found, but they kept unique items and opened a large museum to display them. The state of Florida has also built two other museums, near Sebastian Inlet and Fort Pierce. Here you can see the state's share of these finds. The complex legal and financial arrangements have prohibited the production of comprehensive site reports, although state archaeologists are studying the material in their care.

Top, left: Plan showing the distribution of material from one of the 1715 wrecks; most of the remains lay in the depression between two submerged limestone reefs running parallel to the shore. Gold jewelry and coins (above) and a silver ornament shaped like a moth (below) were among the many valuable objects raised from the different wrecks.

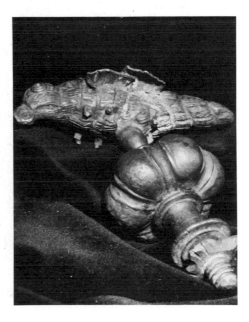

Two eighteenth-century disasters

We end this tour of Spanish New World wrecks with two very different disasters. The first involved another fleet of treasure ships, the second just one vessel.

On July 14, 1733, a hurricane struck the New Spain flota only one day out from Cuba on the voyage to Spain. Of the 17 or 22 ships (records of the total vary) all but one sank or ran aground in the Florida Keys, along a 72-kilometer (45-mi) stretch of coastline. Few people actually perished, and within three months of the disaster Spanish salvage work had refloated several ships and recovered all 13,000,000 pesos of registered treasure and much contraband. But much remained to be discovered. In the nineteenth century, wreckers out of Key West reportedly found gold and silver coins, and divers have subsequently worked most of the wrecks: some people operating under state of Florida leases and control; others working illegally. Results were variable. Divers found a rich supply of coins and other objects within 100 meters (330ft) of the *Capitana*'s ballast pile. But the *San Fernando*'s badly scattered site covers some 30 square kilometers (12sqmi) and is mixed with at least a dozen other wrecks, of earlier and later dates.

Easily this flota's most interesting wreck is that of the *San José*: lost off Plantation Key, discovered by Tom Gurr in 1968, and still yielding finds (to plunderers) a decade later. Not only has this site produced a rich array of interesting artifacts, but the lower hull is well preserved (most of its contemporaries' hulls are not). Excavation has told us how this ship came to grief. First, she struck an offshore reef, then huge seas lifted her intact and carried her about 400 meters (440yd) closer to the shore. On the way she lost five cannons and her rudder, then sank on a sandy bottom in 9 meters (30ft) of water. Gurr found most of the cannons she had carried perched on the 200 tons of ballast sitting on her lower hull. This suggested that the sunken ship had remained sufficiently intact for most of her cargo to remain nearby.

During the first summer's operation Gurr had the help of a team of underwater archaeologists from the Smithsonian Institution and the National Park Service. Accordingly, of all wrecks from the 1733 fleet this alone was first explored by divers using proper archaeological techniques and seeking not just treasure but all the information they could gather. At first, the team used airlifts, but switched to a propwash when they found that sand 6 meters (20ft) deep masked much of the site.

Sand removal showed that most of the site occupied an area only 30×60 meters (100×200ft). This fact facilitated excavation and mapping. When divers had established a datum point they drove pitons into the bedrock surrounding the site and marked them with submerged buoys; this enabled them to plot the finds' horizontal positions. Once they had removed most of the ballast from the lower hull they also photographed the site. Excellent visibility and a wide-angle lens meant that 14 overlapping photographs were enough to build up a complete mosaic. The photographer used a camera mounted on an underwater vehicle with a navigational system enabling him to run a straight course at a constant elevation of 7.6 meters (25ft). The whole operation took only two minutes and the results were excellent. The many priceless artifacts recovered from the *San José* included a number of beautiful pieces of Chinese porcelain; several exquisite glass and ceramic figurines; a complete lead water pump dated 1731; many weapons and tools; more than 2,000 silver coins; 30 gold rings; silver rosaries; various pieces of gold jewelry; and a large collection of silver and pewter tableware.

Unlike the homeward-bound treasure fleets that we have so far dealt with, *Nuestra Señora de los Milagros* ("Our Lady of the Miracles") was a solitary merchant ship, outward bound from Spain to Mexico. She was heading west on the night of February 22, 1741, when she ran aground on the desolate east coast of Yucatán, and quickly broke up in the surf. A few survivors reached Campeche, but high surf hampered salvage and the wreck slipped into obscurity.

A local Spanish place name meaning "Slaughter Point" and a fisherman's chance finds of brass crucifixes and a cannon drew me to the site in 1956. The water was relatively shallow: from a few centimeters deep inshore to 7.6 meters (25ft) deep farther out. But this proved the hardest site I ever worked. For three seasons my small team battled against fierce surf and the cement-hard coral that had swallowed up most artifacts. Using sledgehammers, chisels, and pneumatic hammers, we chopped out and raised big chunks of coral. Then we broke them up to "mine" the articles inside. From one large coral chunk alone we took more than 200 artifacts.

During our third season, more than 100 Mexican divers joined in and a Mexican professional archaeologist took command of what became a massive treasure hunt. In those days, unfortunately, few underwater archaeologists saw the point of meticulously plotting locations.

Nonetheless, our finds proved collectively

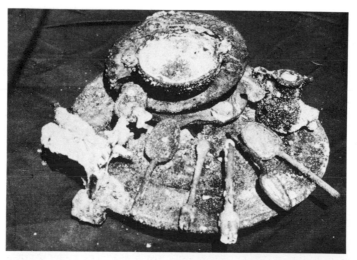

A selection of silver tableware from one of the 1733 wrecks, including a charger (flat platter), plate, porringer, spoons, and forks.

Right: Two divers removing coral encrustations from a cannon.

illuminating. In this third season alone we recovered more than 50,000 items, excluding thousands of pins, needles, and beads. There must have been an insatiable market for trinkets in Veracruz, the ship's destination. We also found more than 5,000 crucifixes; 6,000 belt and shoe buckles; 4,000 buttons; 2,000 knife handles; and several thousand pieces of jewelry such as earrings, rings, necklaces, cufflinks, and bracelets. Other objects included bottles; glass tumblers; window glass; plates; spoons; forks; knives; weapons; tools; musket and cannon balls; flints; thimbles; eyeglasses; and countless other items. The ship must have been stuffed to the gunwales with cargo — hence probably her surprising lack of ballast rock. Such a cargo stands in marked contrast to the treasure in the fleets already mentioned. But archaeology under water should be concerned with the cheap and commonplace, as well as the valuable and spectacular.

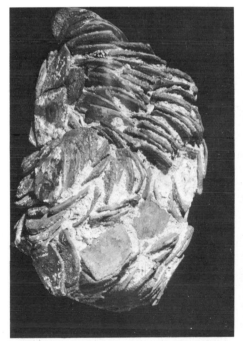

Above: A lump of conglomerate made up of pieces of eight. It was recovered from the *San Fernando's* highly scattered site off the Florida Keys.
Opposite: A photomosaic of the hull of the *San Jose*, showing the keelson and frames.
Right: A detailed view of part of the hull of the *San Jose*, indicating the excellent state of preservation in which it was found.

Europeans in the East (1498-1798)

In 1498, Vasco da Gama reached the port of Calicut (Kozhikode) in western India. His arrival via the Cape of Good Hope marked the first European voyage to the East. For the Portuguese, it was the start of a century of almost undisputed control of sea trade with the East. Sailing ships proved faster, more reliable, and cheaper than the traditional camel caravans of the great spice and silk roads, and soon brought about their decline. The Portuguese quickly established control of the important spice trade, and by the 1570s were doing business in centers as far apart as Hormuz in Persia and Nagasaki in Japan.

But the heyday of Portuguese influence in Asia proved brief. In 1581 Spain annexed Portugal, and soon embroiled her in Spain's wars with England and Holland. Previously the leading transshippers of eastern goods from Portugal to the rest of Europe, the English and Dutch now sailed to the Indies themselves and broke the Portuguese monopoly.

By 1602 each of the two northern nations had chartered a monopolistic trading company to operate in the East. These companies were the (old) English East India Company and the *Vereenigde Oostindische Compagnie* (VOC), or Dutch East India Company. In the first quarter of the seventeenth century, both companies loosely combined against the Portuguese. Otherwise they traded aggressively against each other. From the outset the Dutch company proved the stronger, able to outtrade and usually outfight the English. But each remained more effective than the French, Swedish, Danish, and other East India companies that later joined in the competition.

The first goal of all competitors was simply getting to the East as fast as possible. When the Dutch and English first sailed to the Indies, they followed the route devised by the Portuguese to catch the most favorable winds. They crossed the Atlantic to South America, then swung east to the Cape of Good Hope. From there ships coasted up East Africa then cut across the Indian Ocean, to India, or to the Malay Archipelago. Beyond the Cape the route was slow, unhealthy, and dotted with dangerous islands and reefs. Moreover, East Africa and western India bristled with hostile Portuguese strongholds.

The Dutch and English accordingly learned to avoid the East African coast, and sailed directly to the Indies, stopping only for fresh water at Madagascar and Mauritius. But their ships often wallowed for weeks in hot, still air, so delay and disease bedeviled this route too.

In 1613, the Dutch commander Hendrick Brouwer pioneered a new, fast route to the Indies. From the Cape of Good Hope he sailed south into the Roaring Forties, then headed east until he could turn due north to the Sunda Strait in the Malay Archipelago. The journey proved fast and

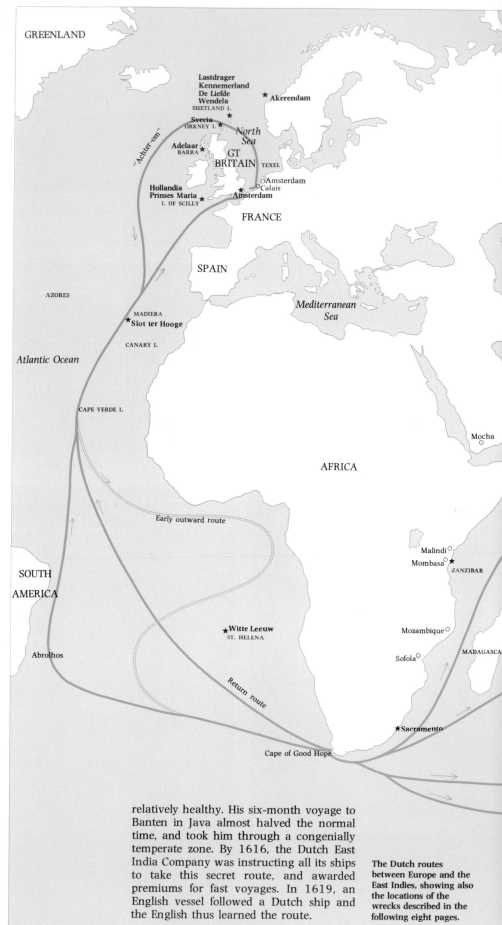

relatively healthy. His six-month voyage to Banten in Java almost halved the normal time, and took him through a congenially temperate zone. By 1616, the Dutch East India Company was instructing all its ships to take this secret route, and awarded premiums for fast voyages. In 1619, an English vessel followed a Dutch ship and the English thus learned the route.

The Dutch routes between Europe and the East Indies, showing also the locations of the wrecks described in the following eight pages.

CHINA

Nagasaki

Ningpo

FORMOSA

Agra

Surat   Hughli

INDIA

Macao   *China Sea*

Goa

Hasulipatnam

COROMANDEL

Calicut   Pulicat
Cochin   Madras

Manila

TRINCOMALEE

Patani

Achin

Malacca

Indian Ocean

TERNATE

INDONESIA
Batavia

AMBON
BANDA

JAVA

Sunda Strait

Early Dutch route

Trial ★

DIRK HARTOG I.   EENDRACHTSLAND

Zuytdorp ★

Batavia ★
Zeewijk ★
Vergulde Draeck ★

ST. PAUL

of Broumer fast route

pany fleets shipped out money and trade goods to buy and barter for Asian products. They also carried equipment and provisions for their Asian trading bases. Shipments of goods like butter, bricks, tablecloths, and tacks served as paying ballast. The companies also discouraged the development of local industries likely to supply and profit from the Europeans' needs. On reaching Java, Dutch ships unloaded at Batavia, their company's headquarters port. There, too, returning vessels took on spices, porcelain, sugar, indigo, silks, cloths, precious stones, and other goods brought in for transshipment by Asian-based Dutch vessels. These regularly combed the East — seeking goods to ship back home, but also dominating seaborne trade between India and the Indonesian Archipelago.

In its late seventeenth-century heyday, the Dutch East India Company had a fleet that ranged from Aden and Persia eastward to Korea and Japan. But for complex reasons, in the eighteenth century the company slid into bankruptcy. In 1798 the Netherlands government took control and the Indonesian sector became part of the Dutch colonial empire. Meanwhile, the English East India Company had virtually mastered India, and ruled there until 1858 when the British government incorporated India within the British Empire. English, Dutch, and Portuguese continued ruling much of southern Asia until World War II, but this section closes with the Dutch East India Company's dissolution.

In the centuries when European fleets of sailing ships were building trade and power in the East, many of those ships inevitably sank or ran aground. So far, divers have found two dozen wrecks of East Indiamen, in two oceans and on the shores of three continents. But this number represents a tiny fraction of the total lost. For example, Dutch East India Company records show the loss of 100 out of 788 vessels sailing to or from the Indies in the 50 years from 1603 to 1653. The list omits ships decommissioned, hulked, or scrapped, at home and in the East. The 100 losses included 56 ships sunk in the Indonesian Achipelago, China, Japan, India, or elsewhere in the East; 14 sunk on the outward or homeward voyage; 10 sunk or captured in battle; and 8 that disappeared. Of the 100 or so Dutch shipwrecks listed for the early 1600s, so far we have found the sites of only three.

The geographical distribution of the two dozen wrecks listed in the following pages is significant. For Europe we give 11 British sites (most from the rocky, often storm-lashed, Shetland, Scilly, and Channel Islands). A mere two sites from safer Atlantic waters farther south contrast with six African sites and five from the dangerous coast of Western Australia. So far, there are no known sites of East Indiamen in the Indies, but we know that many ships were lost there too.

Not only in the Indian Ocean but closer to home, both companies sought speed and safety. For example, the Dutch frequently took the *achter-om* ("round the back") route around the north of the British Isles. This track avoided the particular hazards of the English Channel: headwinds, Dunkirk pirates, and, in times of war, the English.

Each year, the various East India com-

East Indiamen wrecks: early 1600s

Unlike almost every other topic in this atlas, the archaeological study of European trade with the East rests on broad foundations. Elsewhere, we must often generalize on the basis of one or two sites; here we already have more than two dozen, and the list is growing. Among the chief reasons for this plenty is the East Indiamen's reputation as treasure-ships – a reputation that has helped to preserve popular memories of their whereabouts, and encouraged scuba divers to go hunting for them. To stress the wealth of finds resulting from this hunt we shall devote the next few pages to brief notes on a wide range of recently investigated sites.

Unfortunately, no one has so far found East Indiamen wrecks dating from the sixteenth century, the period of Portuguese supremacy in the eastern trade. The first known wrecks date from the first part of the seventeenth century, when Portuguese supremacy was already being challenged by the English and the Dutch. The preponderance of Dutch wrecks faithfully reflects the vigor, even ruthlessness, with which the Dutch worked to dominate this trade. Even so, the wreck of the *Sacramento* reminds us that the Portuguese were still around, especially in India.

In each entry on these pages we give the name of the ship, followed by her date of wrecking; nationality; place of loss; and direction at the time. Where possible we also furnish details of her size and complement.

Witte Leeuw ("White Lion"): 1613; Dutch; St. Helena; homeward bound; 700 tons
This ship sank in an engagement with two Portuguese ships off St. Helena in the South Atlantic. During the battle, the *Witte Leeuw* exploded. After careful investigations in archives and an extensive search in the area, the Belgian underwater archaeologist Robert Sténuit discovered the site in deep water in 1976. It remains the earliest known wreck of any Dutch East India Company ship. Considerable sections of the ship's structure seemed to have survived. Sténuit's excavation recovered three bronze cannons bearing the monogram of the company's Amsterdam *kamer* (that is, branch) and an inscription indicating that Henricus Muers made them in 1604. Diving for artifacts produced a vast quantity of Chinese porcelain and Rhenish stoneware; Indochinese stoneware; personal possessions, and the remains of spices and natural history collections. One of the most engaging finds was an intact boatswain's silver whistle on a chain. The wide range of objects on board shows that the young Dutch trading company was still experimenting with many different kinds of cargo.

Trial: 1622; English;
Western Australia; outward bound; 143 crew
The *Trial* wreck is the earliest known of any English East Indiaman, and the oldest known site in Australian waters. Amateur divers discovered it in 1970 in an area now known as Trial Rocks. Unfortunately, the wreck is archaeologically uninteresting. A brief survey and inspection have revealed only a few, heavily eroded, iron cannons and anchors. Lack of artifacts makes it uncertain that this really is the wreck of the *Trial*. But survivors' accounts indicated that she sank at this dangerous spot, even though the master, Brookes, denied it to avoid prosecution by his company.

Remote, and constantly swept by strong currents and heavy swells, Trial Rocks is one of the most difficult of Western Australian sites to work. Nonetheless, archaeologists hope to identify the vessel.

Batavia: 1629; Dutch;
Western Australia; outward bound; 700 tons; 316 passengers and crew
The *Batavia*'s loss makes grisly reading. One night in 1629 she struck a reef in the Houtman Rocks Archipelago 130 kilometers (80mi) off Western Australia. Leaving 268 passengers and crew safely ashore on nearby islands, Captain Francisco Pelsaert and the senior officers sailed off in a ship's boat, seeking help. They returned about a hundred days later to find that the undermerchant and a gang of followers had mutinied and senselessly massacred 125 men, women, and children. After this and the ensuing executions, only 68 of the *Batavia*'s complement of 316 crew and passengers survived. Surprisingly, perhaps, no one had actually died of thirst or hunger.

In 1963 divers found the *Batavia* wreck in a shallow dip in the coral of Morning Reef in the Wallabi group of islands, one of several groups making up the Houtman Rocks. A short excavation followed. In 1972, the Western Australian Museum launched a four-year excavation program that investigated a great deal of the wreck. Despite the formidable Indian Ocean swell, two and a half years' fieldwork by museum divers completely excavated more than three-quarters of the site. Surprisingly, over one-third of the port side of the ship and

part of the transom had survived buried under many tons of dead coral. From these remains we have learned that the vessel had been massively built, with heavy framing at the stern, and a double layer of planking throughout.

The vast collection of recovered artifacts includes a complete portico facade, almost certainly destined for the new fort at Batavia, and a selection of silverware destined for the Mogul Emperor Janghir. Among the navigational instruments were four astrolabes, a meridian ring for a globe, and part of an *astrolabum catholicum* ("universal astrolabe"). Divers have raised eight cannons made of iron; five of bronze; and two of copper, lead, and iron — a unique composite construction. This leaves 13 cannons still to be recovered.

Sacramento: 1647; Portuguese; Port Elizabeth, South Africa; homeward bound

The *Sacramento* sank near the site of modern Port Elizabeth, while sailing home from Goa in India. Divers found the wreck in 1977 and soon raised 26 of its 42 bronze cannon. There seemed to be 12 iron guns on the site as well. Incidentally, one bronze cannon, bearing dolphin-shaped decorations, had a clenched fist with the thumb projecting through the first and second fingers: a fertility symbol perhaps. Some guns bore the inscription "Antonio Teles de Menezes Governor of India ordered this made in 1640." Almost unbelievably there are reports that badly eroded bronze cannons have now been melted down for scrap. Other finds included Ming china, peppercorns, turmeric, gunpowder, and wadding.

Far left: Divers at work on the remains of the hull of the *Batavia* (1629). After survey, substantial sections of the wooden hull were recovered for study and preservation, including a massive stern "fashion piece", shown here (right) being lifted to the surface. The divers from the Western Australian Museum also recovered many well-preserved artifacts, such as this lidded stoneware flagon (left).
Above: Divers inspecting Chinese porcelain that has just been recovered from the site of the *Witte Leeuw* (1613). Although many such items were recovered intact, others were found broken and had to be restored.

East Indiamen wrecks: later 1600s

By the middle of the seventeenth century the Dutch East India Company dominated the East India trade, and the next half century saw the company's prosperity reach its climax. The English challenge, in particular, had faded; a victim of insufficient capital and application on the part of the City merchants and, later, of the turmoils of the Civil War. Appropriately, then, four of our five wrecks from the later 1600s are Dutch. The fifth, the *Santo Antonio de Tanna*, from the very end of the century, reminds us of continuing Portuguese activity in the Indian Ocean.

Lastdrager ("Load Carrier"): 1653; Dutch; Shetland Isles; outward bound; 640 tons; 200 complement

The *Lastdrager* and most of her crew went down while the ship was rounding northern Scotland. In 1971 evidence in Dutch and Scottish archives led Robert Sténuit to her wreck, which lay at Cullavoe in Yell, an island in the Shetland group. He found that early salvagers had left only a small quantity and range of objects. Furthermore, he established that all had come from the bow section, suggesting that the stern had drifted off somewhere into deep water. Sténuit discovered no substantial sections of structure. But among his small finds were taps;

The contrast between a wreck that settled into the seabed in a sheltered location (opposite), and one dashed to pieces on an exposed coastline and spread over several hundred meters (below). The plan on p. 125 represents the wooden hull remains of the *Santo Antonio de Tanna* (1697), on the bed of the harbor entrance at Mombasa, Kenya. The map on this page shows the distribution of the remains of the *Kennemerland* (1664), spread across the South Mouth of the Out Skerries harbor in the Shetland Isles.

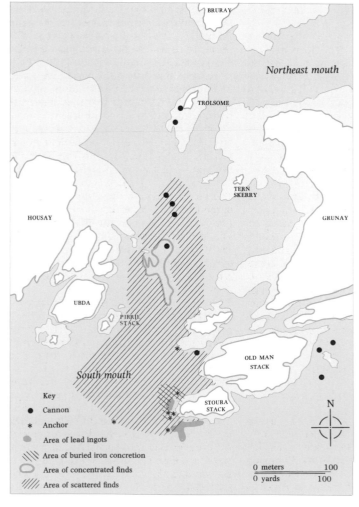

BRURAY

Northeast mouth

TROLSOME

TERN SKERRY

HOUSAY

GRUNAY

UBDA

PIRRIE STACK

OLD MAN STACK

South mouth

STOURA STACK

N

Key
- ● Cannon
- ✳ Anchor
- ⬤ Area of lead ingots
- ⧄ Area of buried iron concretion
- ◯ Area of concentrated finds
- ⧄ Area of scattered finds

0 meters 100
0 yards 100

Right: A close-up of an archaeological deposit, including a pair of scissors, on the *Vergulde Draeck* (1656) site.
Below: Some of the personal items recovered from this wreck.
Top: Using a water jet to remove the gravel overburden covering a concreted deposit on the wreck of the *Lastdrager* (1653) in the Shetland Isles.

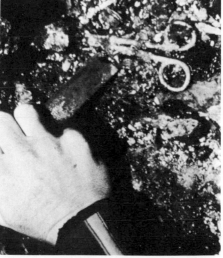

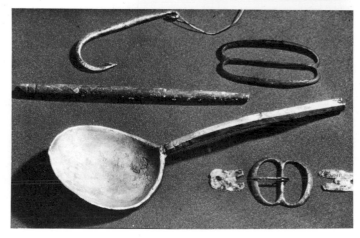

124

spoons; puddles of mercury; navigational instruments; stoneware flagons; clay pipes; and a wide selection of mainly Dutch and Spanish coins.

Vergulde Draeck ("Gilt Dragon"); 1656; Dutch;

Western Australia; outward bound; 250 tons; 190 complement

The *jacht* (trading vessel) *Vergulde Draeck* was on her second voyage to the Indies when she struck a reef off Western Australia. A group of survivors reached Batavia in a

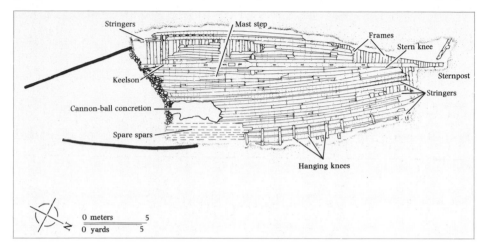

Stringers · Mast step · Frames · Stern knee · Keelson · Sternpost · Cannon-ball concretion · Stringers · Spare spars · Hanging knees

0 meters 5
0 yards 5

small boat. But four subsequent rescue attempts found no trace either of the remaining survivors, left ashore, or of the wreck itself. In 1963 skin divers found it at the base of a low submarine cliff. Unfortunately, looting and vandalism had done much damage before 1972, when the Western Australian Museum carried out a thorough excavation.

Archaeologists found no ship's structure but plenty of items from the cargo, especially examples of the trade goods carried by the Dutch. These included lead, ivory, bricks, amber, and coral beads. Company records show that the annual value of exported goods and supplies could be up to three times greater than the value of exported coins. On this site, though, divers recovered about ten thousand coins – one-quarter of the substantial total carried. Other interesting items include some flawed and leaky stoneware flagons and an iron cannon bearing two monograms, one belonging to the Dutch West India Company, approaching bankruptcy in 1656. On the whole, though, the finds from the *Vergulde Draeck* illustrate its mundane role as a small ship in a vast fleet operating in what had become a regularized and stable commercial system.

Kennemerland; 1664; Dutch;

Out Skerries, Shetland Isles; outward bound; 200 complement

On December 20, 1664, only six days out from Holland, this ship foundered in the South Mouth, a narrow channel in the Out

Skerries. Local people extensively salvaged the wreck soon afterwards. The salvagers hid many finds from the authorities but surrendered the main treasure chests, which a court awarded to King Charles II. The court evidence, plus a lively local tradition concerning the wreck, led a team of student divers to the site in 1971.

There followed five seasons of excavation directed by Richard Price, staffed by volunteer divers, and with Keith Muckelroy as project archaeologist. They found objects spread out over about 500 meters (¼mi) of seabed, with two main areas of concentrated material, reflecting the break-up of the vessel before the southeasterly gale. The area below Stoura Stack, the point of impact, featured such items from the ship's ballast as iron bars and shot; many spare anchors; thousands of building bricks; and 119 lead ingots, each weighing about 140 kilograms (310lb). Farther north, in an area where the surf breaks in rough weather, lay smaller items lost from the ship's stores, and personal baggage, when the ship's upperworks smashed on that dark, stormy night.

Individually interesting finds and groups of finds include the lead ingots, one of the largest surviving collections of seventeenth-century lead. An enigmatic graduated wooden rule proved to be from an early Dutch form of backstaff (a tool for gauging latitude), and a small brass ring had come from the top of a globe. Even though no structure had survived, splinters and fragments reveal that the *Kennemerland* had been planked in oak, with a sheathing of pine. The whole collection is preserved in the county museum at Lerwick.

Prinses Maria ("Princess Mary"); 1686; Dutch;

Isles of Scilly; outward bound; 400 passengers and crew

The *Prinses Maria* was one of the largest Dutch East Indiamen: 48.8 meters (160ft) long; 11.9 meters (39ft) wide; and 5.6 meters (18ft 3in) deep. Built by the Chamber of Zeeland in 1682, she left Texel in 1686 under charter to the Chamber of Amster-

dam, and ran aground on the Isles of Scilly. Scillonians pillaged the wreck, and James II seemingly shared in the plunder, which was pretty well complete before the English heeded Dutch pleas to stop the looting. So far our knowledge of artifacts recovered from the wreck comes solely from auction catalogs.

The *Prinses Maria* site is interesting for its stoneware flagons containing mercury, and the large amounts of mercury discovered. Otherwise, recent diving has revealed few artifacts, mainly because a deep layer of sand makes excavation difficult.

Santo Antonio de Tanna ("St. Antony of Tanna"); 1697; Portuguese;

Mombasa, Kenya

In 1696 Omani Arabs besieged some Portuguese in the port of Mombasa. The Portuguese and their African allies defended themselves in Fort Jesus. The Arabs established batteries around the fort, and guarded the port entrance against Portuguese relief forces that tried sailing in. In a somewhat desultory fashion the siege dragged on for 33 months. Although the Portuguese sent several fleets to relieve the fort, most of their commanders proved timid and ineffectual. A 42-gun frigate, the *Santo Antonio de Tanna*, finally relieved the fort, but, after misadventures, sank nearby at anchor. Documentary evidence indicates that the Portuguese salvaged materials from the ship, and when the fort eventually fell, the Arabs salvaged more.

Divers found the shipwreck in the early 1960s, and preliminary excavation followed in 1970. In 1977 began the first of several seasons of full-scale excavation. Robin Piercy of the Institute of Nautical Archaeology (p. 32) directed an international team working in conjunction with the National Museums of Kenya. Their work has revealed a surprisingly large piece of ship's structure. The port side has survived up to the level of the first deck, a height of about 6 meters (20ft), though the remains of the starboard side are only 2 meters (6½ft) high. Most of the stern structure and transom is missing, but archaeologists have excavated and recorded some flooring and collapsed partitions in the stern section.

By the end of the 1978 season, almost two-thirds of the inside of the hull had been completely excavated. The divers found some ceramics and a huge concentration of cannon balls, plus other small items. But apart from a small bronze swivel gun discovered outside the hull in 1970, they have come across no cannon, and it seems that the contemporary salvage must have been extensive. Huge quantities of ballast stones in the bottom of the ship lay interspersed with crushed barrels, possibly once holding water supplies. The team excavated a pump box around the mast step, and found two pumps still in position.

East Indiamen wrecks: early 1700s

The Dutch East India Company kept up its high rate of sailings into the early decades of the eighteenth century. But losses continued correspondingly high, among them those of five ships dealt with here. The Dutch faced other problems, too. Increasing determination by the English East India Company (refounded in the 1690s); new rival companies formed by other European nations (witness the *Wendela* and *Svecia* below); increasing political and economic stagnation at home; and an acute manpower shortage all conspired to make the East Indies enterprise less profitable for the Dutch. However, effects of the decline became apparent only later in the century.

Meresteyn: 1702; Dutch;
Cape Town, South Africa; outward bound; 200 complement
Since its discovery in 1971, divers have combed this site thoroughly. In 1975 some of the finds were auctioned in London, England. The lots included a breechblock from a swivel gun; a touchhole pricker; a lid to a cartridge container; a musket; a sword pommel and handle; a cartridge case; shoes; chisels; weights; dividers; taps; and spoons. It is a pity that there seems to have been no systematic excavation of the wreck or proper report of the work done and items found.

De Liefde ("The Love"): 1711; Dutch;
Out Skerries, Shetland Isles; outward bound; 500 tons; 300 complement
This ship had set out with the *Mossell* and *Kockenge*, but we know little of her loss (with only one survivor) on Mioness at the western end of the Out Skerries. In the decades after this disaster the Englishman John Lethbridge's newly developed diving barrel made some salvage possible, and the wreck's location passed into local folklore. In the periods 1964–68 and 1974–78 scuba divers recovered thousands of silver coins, a few bronze breechblocks, but little else. In fact the lack of other items strongly suggests that much of the wreck remains to be found. The work and finds are generally poorly documented, and publication covers only the small amount of material now lodged in Lerwick Museum.

Zuytdorp: 1713; Dutch;
Western Australia; outward bound
In the 1920s a stockman discovered coins and other items at the base of a sea cliff about 70 kilometers (44mi) north of the mouth of the Murchison River. In the 1950s a study of the coins showed that many had been minted at Middelburg in 1711. Dutch archives revealed that much of Middelburg's coin output for that year had been aboard the *Zuytdorp* before that vessel disappeared in 1713. This clinched the wreck's identity.

Located below high cliffs liable to heavy battering by waves, and backed by unin-

Above: A diver preparing an iron cannon for lifting from the site of the Danish East Indiaman *Wendela*.

habited bush, the *Zuytdorp* site must be among the world's most difficult to work. Tackling this wreck in the few calm days available each year has involved building a road, an airstrip, and a wire flightway from the clifftop down to a two-ton anchor system, from where a suspended diving platform that doubles as a lift provides divers with a base to work from.

Archaeologists have found the site carpeted with silver coins, almost all double *stuyvers* and *schellingen* minted in 1711. One three-hour dive alone recovered nearly 8,000 coins. Amazingly, such delicate objects as a three-wick oil lamp have also survived battering by waves. But work can only be a salvage excavation in this most dangerous of all known East Indiamen sites to be tackled by the team from the Western Australian Museum.

Slot ter Hooge ("Hooge Castle"): 1724; Dutch; Madeira Islands; outward bound; 254 complement
Robert Sténuit found this wreck with help from archives and a copy of engravings from an old silver tankard. These showed the site and John Lethbridge's diving barrel. (Soon after the wreck occurred, the Dutch had employed that pioneer diver in salvage.) Sténuit found a collection of unique silver bars stamped with the mark of the Dutch company's Zeeland Chamber. There were also coins in great variety; tobacco boxes; pipes; candlesticks; spoons; forks; bricks; taps; and stoneware.

Zeewijk: 1727; Dutch; Western Australia; outward bound; 240 tons; 208 complement
Surviving records of the *Zeewijk*'s loss enabled Catharina Ingelman-Sundberg of the Western Australian Museum to make a three-year study of the wreck site and remains of the Gun Island camps established by survivors. Although scattered over several kilometers, wreck material occurred in two main areas. On the outside of the reef, where the ship originally struck and sank, lay cannons, anchors, ballast and isolated pockets of artifacts. Washed into shallows inside the reef was a second group of articles, including several iron cannons and large quantities of broken glass, Chinese porcelain, German stoneware, and Southeast Asian stonewares. Unfortunately, nineteenth-century guano diggings on Gun Island proved to have removed most traces of the survivors' camps.

Adelaar ("Eagle"): 1728; Dutch; Barra, Hebrides; outward bound; 240 tons
Colin Martin found and excavated this wreck's remains in 1972. Discoveries included lead ingots; bricks; iron cannons; a bronze eight-pounder; and a small bronze swivel gun. There were also some pipes; coins; domestic utensils; and tools. But

there was a general lack of material. This probably reflects extensive salvage work soon after the disaster, and destruction on this rocky and exposed site.

Wendela: 1737; Danish; Fetlar, Shetland Isles; outward bound
Five years after the founding of the Danish East India Company, this vessel came to grief on Fetlar's eastern cliffs while en route for the East with a general cargo and the usual treasure. In 1972 Robert Sténuit found the wreck's remains widely scattered. However, he recovered a large number of coins, many from a variety of European states. This fact reflects the weakness of Danish currency at the time the wreck occurred.

Svecia: 1740; Swedish; North Ronaldsay, Orkney Islands; homeward bound
A few days before the *Svecia* was due in Göteborg, she struck Reefdyke shoal north of North Ronaldsay. Strong tides and heavy

Above: A brass buckle recovered from the wreck of the Dutch East Indiaman *Zeewijk*.
Below: The distribution of the remains of the *Zeewijk*. The ship initially struck the reef shown at the top of the map, but the wreckage was swept on across the shallows for about two kilometers.

seas swept much of the debris far around the Orkney and Shetland isles. But in 1975 a team organized by Rex Cowan found the site itself. Their most notable discovery was large quantities of dyewood from the vessel's cargo.

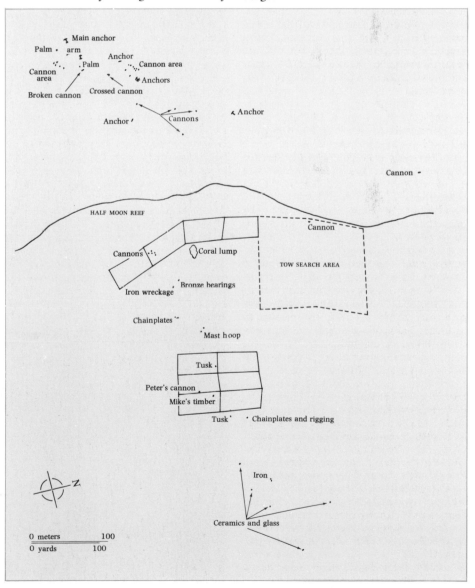

East Indiamen wrecks: later 1700s

In 1781 the Dutch declared war on Britain, supposing her weakened by the rebellion of her American colonies. But the action of the Dutch rebounded badly on them as the Royal Navy rapidly blocked Dutch East India Company trade, contributing to a decline that led the company to bankruptcy in 1798. Before this happened, the company had continued to dispatch substantial fleets and to suffer shipwrecks. Of the four Dutch wrecks considered here the most interesting are the *Hollandia* and *Amsterdam*, for both remain relatively complete. We also include three English East India Company ships; their loss reflects the upsurge in traffic that occurred as the British were establishing supremacy in India.

Hollandia ("Holland"): 1743; Dutch;
Isles of Scilly; outward bound; 220 tons; 276 passengers and crew
The *Hollandia* set forth with the autumn fleet of 1742 but sank with no survivors, and no clue to her precise position. However, in 1971, extensive searching with a magnetometer helped Rex Cowan to locate the site near Gunner Rock. Survey of the wreck revealed a cluster of three anchors, almost certainly from the hold; a number of bronze and iron cannons; small bronze swivel guns; two bronze military mortars; and quantities of military equipment. There were also scraps of Chinese porcelain; small pewter objects; and many coins. One of the few sites in European waters to have escaped the early salvagers, the *Hollandia* wreck represents a unique and complete collection that richly merits detailed publication.

Amsterdam: 1749; Dutch;
Hastings, Sussex; outward bound; 385 passengers and crew
En route for Batavia from Texel, the *Amsterdam* soon encountered storms, lost her rudder, and ran aground on the English Channel coast. Most of the passengers and crew escaped and saved all the chests containing silver. But the ship sank deeply into sand and mud before there could be much further salvage.

In 1969, men working at low water on a nearby sewer outfall used a mechanical excavator to dig into the wreck. Their exploration revealed many artifacts and attracted the interest of several archaeologists. Led by Peter Marsden, a team then conducted test excavations, and surveys with magnetometer, metal detector, probe, and sonar. These showed that the mud concealed a 46-meter (150ft) ship almost intact to the level of her second gun deck. The team also detected a vast quantity of artifacts. For instance, magnetometer surveys disclosed large iron concentrations in the bow and stern, almost certainly the contents of shot lockers. Thus the *Amsterdam* promises to be one of the most interesting Dutch wrecks yet discovered.

The Dutch want to excavate and raise the ship and take her back to Amsterdam. However, excavation in this intertidal zone will not be easy. Plans to raise the ship have included cofferdams, pontoons, and other equally ambitious engineering projects. But, as I write, there is a pause while everyone involved contemplates the millions needed for the project, and watches with misgiving while inflation multiplies the cost.

Doddington: 1755; British;
Port Elizabeth, South Africa; outward bound
The *Doddington* sailed from the Thames for India in a fleet of five ships. Aboard her were 200 soldiers of the Royal Artillery and the English East India Company. She also reportedly carried a treasure in gold coins, and cannons for the army in India. The ship foundered at Bird Island off Port Elizabeth. Twenty-three men survived. For seven months they lived on the island, then built a small boat and eventually sailed to Lourenço Marques (now in Mozambique).

Discovered by David Allen, a South African, the site has now been largely excavated. Finds include coins known as *reals*; domestic mortars; paint; nine glasses; bone and horn handles; brass penknives; combs; mirrors; gunflints; navigation instruments; and four bronze guns.

Nieuw Rhoon: 1776; Dutch;
Cape Town, South Africa; homeward bound
In 1970, workmen building a civic center in Cape Town uncovered the remains of a wreck near the shore. They partly damaged the wreck, but fortunately archaeologists were able to survey and excavate what remained. Because the present low-water mark is about 4.3 meters (14ft) below ground level at the site, they decided the vessel must have been beached in 2.7 meters (about 3ft) of water. Her surviving structure comprised parts of the lower hull on either side of the keel. A plan and profiles made of what could be seen showed the sheathing, frames, ceiling, and keelson.

Among the artifacts found were a large variety of round shot and bar shot, and clay pipes bearing makers' marks that gave a date range for the wreck of 1730–80. Other items included a pottery jar and Kwangtung Chinese porcelain bowls. Such evidence makes it most likely that this site is that of the *Nieuw Rhoon*, which was lost in 1776.

Valentine: 1779; British;
Sark, Channel Islands; homeward bound; 690 tons
Launched in 1767, the *Valentine* was returning on her fourth round trip out East when a northwesterly gale forced her into the Channel Islands and onto Le Neste reef on the west side of Sark. Local club divers began systematically investigating the site in 1975. Their finds include cannons; lead ingots; dyewood; Chinese porcelain; and a large number of worked and unworked agates. Although a very disturbed site in an area of fast currents and heavy seas, this promises to yield an extensive and informative final inventory.

Middelburg: 1781; Dutch;
Saldanha Bay, South Africa; homeward bound
This Dutch ship's commander set her alight when a Royal Navy squadron trapped a Dutch fleet in Saldanha Bay. Fire took hold of the *Middelburg*; she exploded and sank. Since the wreck's discovery in recent years, some commercial work has gone ahead on the site, but no one has published the findings.

Halsewell: 1786; British;
Seacombe, Dorset, England; outward bound
She sank in a southwesterly gale soon after starting her voyage. Club divers have found scattered remains submerged below sea cliffs near Seacombe. They have raised some items, but the area is so hard to work and the material so scanty that any systematic recovery project seems out of the question.

Left: A selection of items from the *Valentine*, wrecked in the Channel Islands in 1779, including Chinese porcelain, glass stoppers, agates, a gunflint, and a brass buckle.
Opposite: A view from the stern of the wreck of the *Amsterdam* (1749), exposed at low spring tides on the beach near Hastings, Sussex. The diagram (below, left) shows how much of the vessel remains buried under the sand.

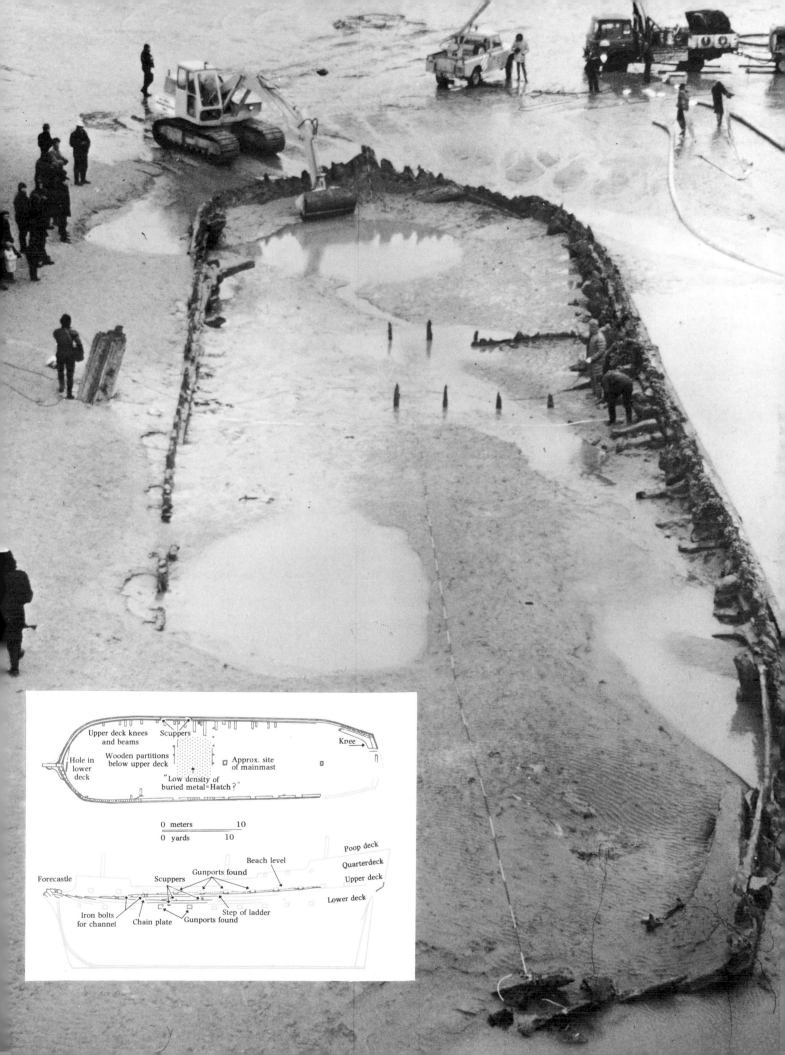

Upper deck knees
and beams   Scuppers

Hole in   Wooden partitions   Approx. site   Knee
lower   below upper deck   of mainmast
deck

                        "Low density of
                         buried metal = Hatch?"

0   meters   10
0   yards   10

                                                          Poop deck
                                      Beach level   Quarterdeck
Forecastle   Scuppers   Gunports found   Upper deck

                                                          Lower deck
      Iron bolts   Chain plate   Gunports found   Step of ladder
      for channel

The archaeology of East Indiamen

The wrecks we have just been describing show a large disparity in number between those of outward bound ships (17) and those of ships bound for home (6). It is difficult to account for this bias, especially as the years spent away from the repair facilities of a home base ought to have made homeward bound vessels less seaworthy than vessels fresh from Europe. Whatever its reason, this imbalance in sites has meant that research has focused on the goods and coins that Europe shipped to the East more than on the Asian products that Europe imported.

Of course, in this research we have extensive documentary evidence to set beside the archaeological data. In particular, lists of items requisitioned from Europe by the agents out East have survived for a number of years, including Dutch lists for the whole of the period 1634–64. So far as coins are concerned, the average for these decades was just under a million guilders a year; for other commodities we can probably gain the clearest impression by looking at the figures for one particular year. Taking 1653 as a typical example, we find that (by weight) the major trade cargoes shipped to the East were: lead (592 tons); vermilion (49 tons);

mercury (29 tons); elephants' tusks (19 tons); amber (3 tons); and coral (2 tons). Other significant items included cloth; leather; sulfur; and curiosities as gifts for local potentates. For the company's staff there were supplies that in 1653 included meat (543 tons); assorted nails (386 tons); bricks (330 tons); beer (329 tons); wine (184 tons); anchors (98 tons); and vinegar (61 tons). You will no doubt have noticed that many of these items have turned up on wrecks described in this chapter. But of course fragile substances such as vermilion seldom leave recognizable traces.

As proofs of the quantities of cargoes shipped, written records will always be more complete than wreck material. But this material is important in two ways. First, artifacts found in wrecks include miscellaneous items omitted from the lists, especially curiosities and objects carried by individual members of the passengers and crew. Thus we know the Batavia had carried a number of ornately engraved silver ewers, chargers, chalices, and bedposts. Featuring oriental scenes, their decorations show how the Dutch attempted to produce acceptable gifts for the local princes with whom they

did business. Equally fascinating is the Lastdrager's large number of pocket sundials, all designed to operate in European latitudes but apparently destined as prestigious gifts for the locals out East, where they would have been utterly useless!

The second way in which artifacts are important is in helping us to learn a good deal about how and when people had made and used different kinds of weapons and tools. A clear example concerns the Batavia's unusual "composite" cannons made of copper sheeting, wrought-iron bands and staves, and a type of lead solder. References to such cannons appear in lists of Netherlands patents for the 1630s, but the Batavia discoveries gave modern scholars their first chance to assess these weapons directly. Scholars have also learned a good deal from the navigational instruments found on these wrecks. For instance, the Kennemerland had carried a relatively crude form of backstaff in 1664, by which time such a design was supposedly obsolete. On the other hand, the Hollandia contained an octant in 1742, only a few years after that device was invented. The Dutch East India Company's supposed resistance to innovation at that

Opposite: A diver exploring the kelp-covered site of the wreck of the Dutch East Indiaman *Lastdrager*. The pair of navigational dividers (below) was one of several found on this site, and was apparently part of the cargo.
Above, right: A cannon from the wreck of the Dutch East Indiaman *Batavia* photographed immediately after being lifted from the site.
Below, right: A horn comb and an ornamental pewter spoon, two items from the Dutch East Indiaman *Kennemerland*.

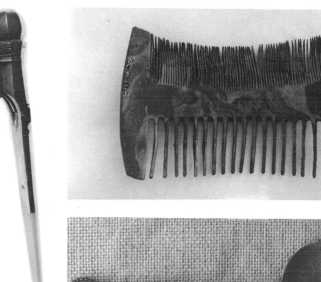

time makes this find especially interesting. We could extend the list of examples indefinitely, to include items of cargo; equipment; clothing; and ships' structures themselves.

Of course, not all East Indiaman sites have proved equally fertile. Each wreck's archaeological value partly depends upon its location. Most of the sites we have mentioned occur in four distinct clusters: around the British Isles; off various Atlantic islands; off the South African coast; or along the shores of Western Australia. Each of these

zones had and has its own political, economic, legal, and environmental circumstances. All these have combined to determine how well wrecks have survived and what people have done with them.

For example, in Western Australia the long powerful swells of the Indian Ocean break dramatically as they reach shallow waters, pounding wrecks into scattered fragments. A rare exception occurred where a depression in a reef trapped fragile material and part of the hull from the *Batavia*, and ship's ballast and coral pro-

tectively covered them. But while the coast here is cruel, at least it has remained free from destructive salvage. On the other hand, along the more densely peopled shores of the British Isles, we find that all East Indiaman wrecks have been more or less subject to salvage except those of ships like the *Hollandia*, which sank in unknown deep-water locations.

Current legal provisions greatly affect the control of work on these wrecks, and the study and publication of what this reveals. The lack of any coherent policy in South Africa or the Atlantic islands largely explains the relative lack of published information about the sites there. The situation in Britain is marginally better, largely thanks to the enthusiasm of excavators who have handed their finds to public museums and published accounts of their work, often at heavy financial loss to themselves. Although British law permits the protection of some sites in British waters, it does nothing to encourage their study, or ensure the preservation of complete collections from wrecks. In this respect Western Australia comes off much better. That state has provided adequate legal safeguards for finds, and set up a museum in Fremantle with a large and experienced staff who can actively direct the investigation of sites in Western Australia.

Until the legal position improves around the world, and more archaeologists record and study material found on these sites, we shall lack the data required for a full archaeological account of the East Indiamen. Meanwhile, these pages have simply outlined some of the chief features of such an overview.

Structures under Water

So far we have dealt with wrecked ships: mobile objects drowned by accident. In this section we consider fixed structures, proceeding from those submerged by chance to those put under water purposely. Dr. Ian Morrison sets the scene in the opening six pages by describing some of the geological and other processes that may submerge terrestrial structures. Dr. Morrison is a lecturer in geography at Edinburgh University, with research interests ranging widely through archaeological and related fields.

Next comes an eight-page contribution on the exploration of submerged prehistoric remains in North America. This is provided by Mr. W. A. (Sonny) Cockrell, since 1972

the state underwater archaeologist for Florida, where he has also helped assert the state's interest in many offshore, historic wreck investigations. There follows Robert Marx's brief account of a much more recent submergence: that of Port Royal in Jamaica in 1692.

Accidentally drowned structures also dominate the following eight pages, where Dr. Ulrich Ruoff describes the investigation of prehistoric villages now inundated by the rise in water level of Alpine lakes. Dr. Ruoff is the city archaeologist in Zurich. Some of the structures that he considers may have been built out over water, which means their bases always were submerged. This is

certainly true of Scottish lake-dwellings, the next class of structure we consider. Our guide here is once again Dr. Morrison.

The final 16 pages of this section take us back to the Mediterranean where, in Section II, our tour of underwater sites began. Dr. Nicholas Flemming's survey shows how much can be learned from intensive surveys under water about submerged coastal settlements and ancient harbors. Dr. Flemming is a principal scientific officer at the Institute of Oceanographic Sciences in Britain. His many research interests include the interpretation of archaeological evidence for sea-level changes.

Many types of submergence

A very wide range of archaeological material apart from shipwrecks may be found under water, submerged by many kinds of natural processes and human activities.

Searchers may discover small objects almost anywhere, in deep or shallow water: fresh, salt, or indeed worse. Victorian scavengers rummaged London's sewers for lost jewelry; excavators of a nineteenth-century American cesspit were recently rewarded (and perplexed) by a bag of dollars and a revolver. English streams only centimeters deep have preserved monastic relics. Deposits in wells have helped archaeologists to work out relationships between medieval pottery styles (and yielded stratified cats, illustrating how domestic breeds developed). The Celts placed severed heads in wells, and more attractive votive deposits have been recovered from the sinkholes (p. 142) and lakes of Central and South America. European pools and rivers have often produced bronzes, notably swords and cauldrons. Some at least of these seem votive, like many of the prehistoric wooden figurines recovered from bogs and springs. Craftsmen who submerged objects for more practical reasons did not always recover their caches. For example, roughed-out Viking-style stempieces found in Scandinavia and Scotland probably reflect the storing of timber in pools, a practice also used by some boatbuilders in modern times.

As well as innumerable types of small artifacts, people have set a considerable variety of large structures in water. These include fish traps; causeways; dams; dock, mole, and bridge foundations; and houses on piles or artificial islands. Eventually, as superstructures decay and foundations subside, their remains may become totally submerged.

Some major shallow-water constructions are intended to be entirely under water from the start. Thus a 2-kilometer (1¼mi) strait

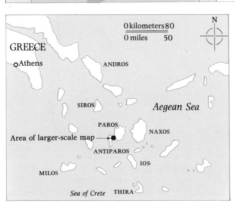

Left: The straits between the islands of Paros and Antiparos in the Aegean are barred by the so-called "Pirates' Wall". This is a barely-submerged blockage invisible to approaching ships, designed to trap them by grounding; an unusual example of a structure designed to be under water.

between the islands of Paros and Antiparos in the Aegean Sea is invisibly blocked by the so-called Pirate's Wall, seemingly a wrecker's ship trap. In contrast, some land-built complexes certainly never meant to enter water have ended up there. As Holderness in eastern England shows, the sea can erode entire villages.

Such erosion by wave attack may involve

no change of sea level. There are many other reasons, natural and human, why archaeologists may find non-nautical antiquities under water. However, such finds sometimes lead people mistakenly to invoke sea-level changes. For example, the submergence of a Roman town in the Adriatic was claimed on the basis of dredged up amphorae, and what seemed from the surface to be parallel streets. Diving showed the "streets" were reefs of natural coralline deposits, while the occasional wine jars appeared to be casual jetsam, like the (unreported) more modern fishermen's "empties" accompanying them.

Genuine changes of level happen for a wide range of reasons, and affect rivers, lakes and the sea at widely varying rates. Some that are so slow as to be imperceptible to the people living through them may, nevertheless, eventually change the entire geography of an area (e.g. pp. 136–37). Sometimes, too, slow trends may generate a critical situation in which a brief event

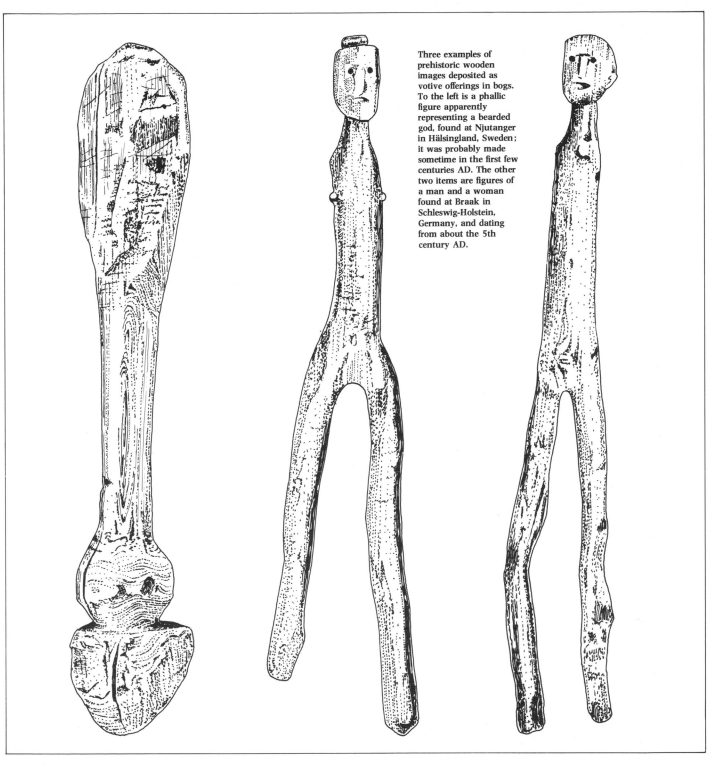

Three examples of prehistoric wooden images deposited as votive offerings in bogs. To the left is a phallic figure apparently representing a bearded god, found at Njutanger in Hälsingland, Sweden; it was probably made sometime in the first few centuries AD. The other two items are figures of a man and a woman found at Braak in Schleswig-Holstein, Germany, and dating from about the 5th century AD.

may trigger a lasting change. A storm surge or seismic sea wave (p. 134) may breach coastal barriers, or a flash flood break river banks, forcing abandonment of low-lying settlements. Landslides and volcanic eruptions can dam valleys, inundating sites so abruptly that they are superbly preserved: even the timber palisade still stands in an early Maori settlement submerged by Lake Okaitina in New Zealand.

Just as natural processes can influence the activities of man, so too is the opposite possible. Human interference with river and lake levels may involve deliberate damming, embanking, or dredging, or it may be indirect and largely inadvertent, as when farming practices alter water tables, runoff rates, and flood susceptibility.

Sea-level changes can also be complicated. Both the land and the sea surface may move vertically, either independently or in interaction. Some land-level changes affect very restricted areas, while others occur systematically over extensive regions, though they are seldom equal in amount or rate from place to place. In contrast, water-level changes tend to be eustatic: uniform and synchronous everywhere. This tendency is not, however, absolute, and does not apply, for instance, to events such as storm surges (p. 134).

With coastal changes, as with rivers and lakes, both slow and abrupt submergences can have considerable implications for archaeology.

133

Changing levels of land and sea

We shall now look at examples of the processes involved in changes in the relative heights of land and sea.

Some land movements are abrupt, and geographically discontinuous. A block of land bounded by geological faults may subside, sometimes amid earthquakes or even volcanic activity. Settlements catastrophically submerged, like Port Royal in Jamaica (pp. 146–47) or Helike in Greece, can prove veritable "time capsules" for the archaeologist, like the most productive shipwrecks. Even though events have generally been much less dramatic, such tectonic activity has submerged a very large number of sites along the geologically active coasts of the world (e.g. pp. 162–67).

More gradual vertical movements of the land sometimes reflect long-term mountain building processes, originating deep within the earth. Others show the response of the crust to loading of the surface with sediment, ice, or indeed water (respectively termed sedimento-, glacio-, hydro-isostasy). Their relative importance differs from place to place. For example, sediment loading is important in areas like Lower Mesopotamia and the Mississippi Delta, while the evolution of Hudson Bay or the Baltic Sea has been dominated by the effects of glacial loading and the upward rebound of the land after the ice sheets melted.

Some sea-level changes (for example, those caused by long-term variation in the volume of ocean basins) are so gradual that they are only archaeologically significant in the perspective of human evolution and the Paleolithic (Old Stone) Age. Others, in contrast, may last only a few hours. Thus storm surges represent rapid local responses to unusual combinations of tides and meteorological conditions, and seismic sea waves (termed tsunami but often misnamed "tidal waves") result from earthquake shocks. These short-lived phenomena cannot be dismissed by archaeologists. The effect on Crete of possible tsunami from the Minoan eruption of Santorin (Thira) in the Aegean is a matter of lively dispute; Holland's history attests the immediate and long-term effects of North Sea storm surges.

In the broad view, however, medium-term changes in sea level have been most important archaeologically. Chief of these have been the variations in world ocean level caused by changes in the amount of the earth's water locked up on land as glacier ice. Since the world's oceans are interconnected, these variations affect all the inhabited coastlines as well as the ice-bound shores.

During the two million years and more of the Quaternary Period, there has been a complex sequence of glaciations and interglacials in which water was repeatedly abstracted from oceans and returned to them. Some land bridges were laid bare and resubmerged many times. Impact varied with terrain. Thus a drop in sea level suffi-cient to link Asia and North America, and to join much of Indonesia to mainland Asia, made relatively little difference to the outline of those parts of the Mediterranean where shores are steep.

When the last glaciation was at its maximum during Upper (late) Paleolithic times, world sea level was perhaps 100–130 meters (330–425ft) or more lower than at present. By 8000 bc, although areas such as Britain were clear of glaciers, substantial ice sheets remained in Scandinavia and northern Canada. (The abbreviation bc refers to dates produced directly from a radiocarbon determination. After correction for certain built-in errors, these can then be expressed as true dates, using BC.) Ocean level accordingly still stood at least 30–40 meters (100–130ft) lower than today. A long history of shoreline changes was thus still to follow, extending into periods of major archaeological interest.

Unfortunately for prehistorians, there is much dispute over the subsequent details. Opinions differ about such basic facts as: when the ocean first returned to its present level; whether or not it has exceeded that level in postglacial times; and even whether the sea-level rise was smooth or irregular.

These problems persist because there seems to be no stable measuring mark against which the history of world sea-level movements may be traced in absolute terms. Land-level movements seem to interact everywhere with the water-level movements.

Where active faults are present, as in parts of the Mediterranean or of the west coast of the Americas, even adjacent sectors of coastline may have quite different histories. The sequence of ocean-level movements is superimposed on individual blocks that tilt or move vertically, sometimes in different directions at different periods.

In some glaciated areas (pp. 135–37), even the rapid ocean rise when the glaciers were melting failed to keep pace with the initial rate of rebound of land freed from the ice load. Thus while the sea was drowning shores remote from the centers of glaciation, it was simultaneously retreating from the rapidly rising land of the most recently glaciated regions.

The problems of working out how events relate in contrasting areas are compounded by such factors as the crust's response to water loading as land is inundated by the sea. It is unfortunate too that the deep "layer cake" sequences of alternating marine clays and terrestrial peats that often offer our most complete records of marine changes are particularly subject to compaction. This additionally falsifies the record of sea-level heights. Relating different types of field evidence to tidal range introduces yet other difficulties, not least in making allowances for former ranges affected by alterations in tidal basin geometry as coastlines changed. And all these are just samples of what may be involved.

However, although the absolute amplitude of changes in world sea level is likely to remain a controversial subject, substantial progress is now being made in locating former coastlines and dating specific changes. Thus the archaeologist contemplating the geographical and chronological patterns of submergence faces complexity, but not anarchy.

Left: The present configuration of the Atlantic seaboard of Europe, as seen from a weather satellite from an altitude of about 450 miles.
Right: Some examples of the differences which a drop in sea-level can make to the shape of land-masses, especially islands. The situations in the Mediterranean (left) and south-east Asia (right) are presented. The upper maps show the position at a low sea-level, the middle maps show the current situation, and the lower ones show the one superimposed on the other.

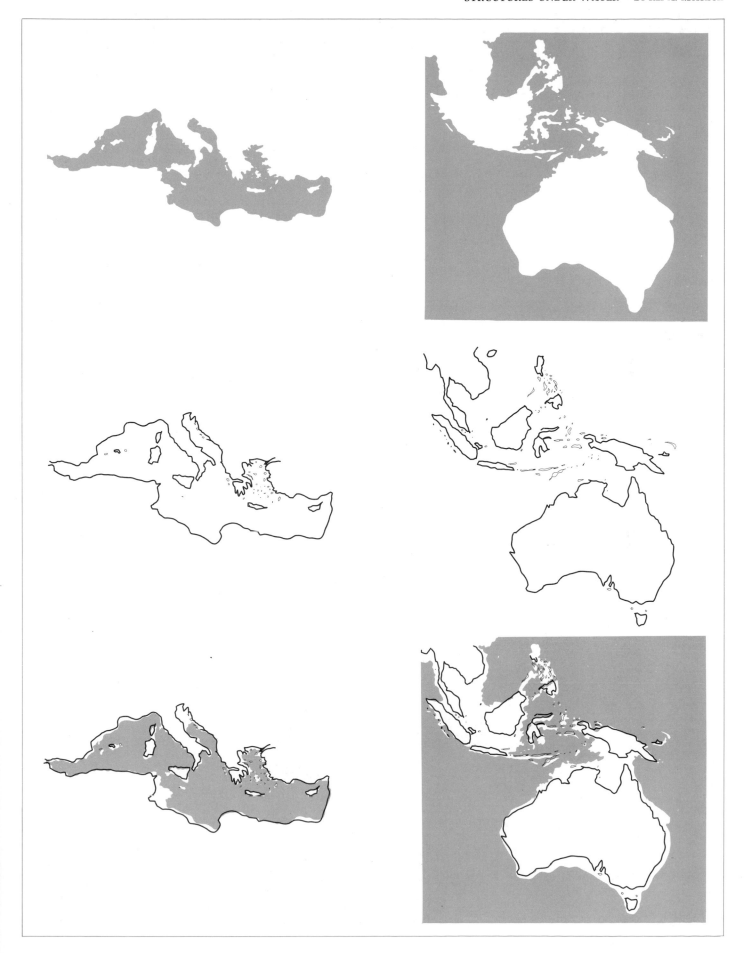

Land and sea in northwest Europe

As we have seen, in some areas active geological faults have disrupted the patterns of coastal change. There, individual movements of crustal blocks may produce quite different sequences of change even on neighboring stretches of coast.

In other areas, however, land movements tended instead to be in the form of continuous warping. In such regions, even when the amount of relative movement has been large, there is some prospect of tracing orderly patterns in the interaction of land- and sea-level movements over extensive areas.

I have experimented with this on the western seaboard of Europe, by making an analysis of the timing of increases and decreases of the area subject to the sea. The radiocarbon dates of these marine transgressions and regressions tend to agree closely right across the wide spectrum of coastal environments and land-movement patterns represented between Arctic Norway and the Bay of Biscay.

For instance, we find that in Scandinavia arms of the sea became isolated and turned into freshwater lakes at the same time that estuarine clays around the North Sea dried out and began supporting peat growth; subsequent burial of that peat beneath more marine clay coincided with intrusion into the lakes of saltwater diatoms (microscopic single-celled plants) that indicate the lakes' reconnection to the ocean.

From the way that the whole range of the evidence tends to show this kind of agreement, it seems that episodes sufficiently marked to synchronize events on coasts of quite different characters have punctuated movements of the world's ocean level.

Analyses involving more than 1,000 radiocarbon dates suggest that something of the order of 20 such sets of simultaneous events are recognizable during the last 10,000 years. Spread fairly evenly through time, they offer a useful supplement to the range of frameworks available for archaeological cross-dating.

Exploiting this still has its problems, however, since even where faulting is not a complication, land movements can still radically alter the original relationships of sites to sea level.

Thus, although world ocean level was considerably lower when early postglacial shorelines were formed, some of those in Scandinavia now stand 300 meters (1000ft) above sea level, because of the upward movement of the land there. In contrast, some early shorelines of the southern North Sea are now probably even lower than their original levels.

Where land uplift was greatest, we find

Left: Views of present-day frozen landscapes, giving some idea of the conditions in northwest Europe during the ice ages. The upper picture shows the Muldron glacier on Mount McKinley in Alaska, and the lower an aerial view of the Greenland coast. Oppsite, above: a diagram illustrating the different situations of two sites, A and B, according to the respective rates at which land and sea may have risen since glacial times.

Opposite, below: A map of northwest Europe showing the varying extent of the ice caps and areas of tundra during upper Paleolithic and Mesolithic times. The respective situations are summarized in the three key maps presented here.

Paleolithic

Mesolithic

Present day

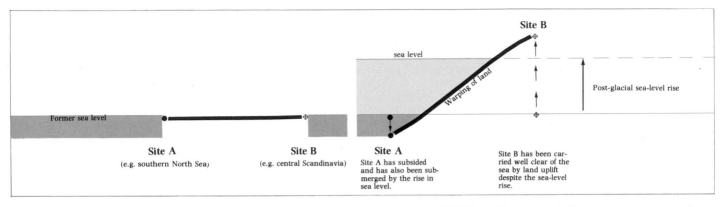

Site B

sea level

Warping of land

Post-glacial sea-level rise

Former sea level

Site A
(e.g. southern North Sea)

Site B
(e.g. central Scandinavia)

Site A
Site A has subsided
and has also been sub-
merged by the rise in
sea level.

Site B has been car-
ried well clear of the
sea by land uplift
despite the sea-level
rise.

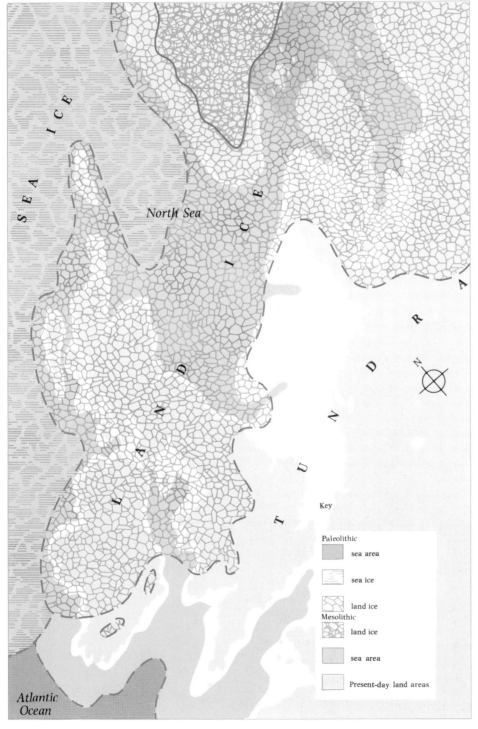

SEA ICE

North Sea

LAND ICE

TUNDRA

Atlantic
Ocean

N

Key

Paleolithic

sea area

sea ice

land ice

Mesolithic

land ice

sea area

Present-day land areas

old coastal habitation sites exposed, or buried under only a shallow covering of marine deposit (laid down during one of the short phases when the rise in sea level temporarily outpaced the rising of the land).

Where the last glacier ice was thin, the rate of crustal rebound was not strongly marked. In parts of Scandinavia and of Scotland, this resulted in a closely matched upward race between land and ocean levels. This persisted until the land eventually drew clear when the ocean completed its main rise, long after the local ice sheets had gone. Thus in such areas later shoreline sites tend to be unburied or subject to only minor marine transgressions, but the early coastal and estuarine tidelines, so important in the economy of pre-agricultural hunters and gatherers, tend to lie hidden beneath thick deposits.

Elsewhere, the processes of land uplift are sometimes absent, or are more than offset by factors such as compaction and other effects of the overlying weight of sediment and water. Some areas, for example around the southern North Sea, are so dominated by subsidence that the highest postglacial shoreline is that of the present day, and all prehistoric coastlines are either submerged offshore or masked by layers of later deposits, or both.

The easily visible (indeed, often spectacular) raised shorelines in regions of uplift have attracted so much attention for so long that it is sometimes difficult to assess just how far widely accepted concepts about them rely on observations that predate modern research standards. Outside those areas, the inaccessibility of the buried and submerged evidence hampers first-hand investigation. In both situations, the complexity of the factors involved in land- and sea-level movements makes it difficult to use theory to reconstruct their interplay.

However, scientists of many nationalities are now providing an increasing flow of fresh and detailed information. This soon renders any general map obsolete. Nevertheless, alterations in coastal geography have been so sweeping since Paleolithic times that land archaeologists and their colleagues under water both need to have at least a broad impression of what has happened.

Drowned sites in North America

Submerged land sites are beginning to give us a new grasp of how and where prehistoric peoples lived. This is especially true for the early inhabitants of North America. Before I examine specific sites, most readers may find it helpful if I briefly sketch the time span and the prehistoric cultures we are dealing with.

The time span extends at least 18,000 years – from about 20,000 to 2,000 years ago. Geologically speaking, we begin at the end of the Pleistocene epoch: the so-called Ice Age that started perhaps two million years ago and featured large mammals like the mammoth, mastodon, giant ground sloth, cave bear, saber-toothed cat, and dire wolf. Our time span ends in the relatively warm Holocene epoch that began about 10,000 years ago and in which we live today. (Some scholars believe this epoch is really just a mild phase of the Pleistocene, but that need not concern us here.) When the Holocene began, most of the big Ice Age mammals were already extinct. In Florida a few persisted until 6,000 years ago. As a

warming climate melted ice sheets, the sea level rose, drowning old coastlines and raising the groundwater level inland. This in turn raised the water level in rivers, springs, and caves; low-lying permeable limestone areas like peninsular Florida were especially affected.

We do not know when man first entered the Americas, but it was almost certainly more than 20,000 years ago, at a time when the sea level was much lower than it is today. Most scholars believe that people reached North America from Asia by walking over the Bering land bridge that once linked Siberia and Alaska. That land bridge now lies beneath the Bering Strait. The shores of this strait have yielded little evidence to link the earliest-known human remains from the western hemisphere with finds from northeast Asia. But if the land-bridge migration theory is right, study of the Bering Shelf (the submerged land bridge) should reveal drowned land sites. The edge of the shelf may prove especially fruitful: migrating peoples would have found plenty

of food on the coastal margins of the Bering land bridge. Probably these margins would also have provided an easy glacier-free route into North America at a time when ice cloaked much of the mountainous northwest. In the same way, studies of submerged shelves off southern and southeast Asia might yield clues to help solve puzzles such as how early man reached Australia, and how the small, dark-skinned Negrillos of Africa and Negritos of southeast Asian islands attained their present scattered distributions.

I will call the earliest Americans Paleo Indians. They were Stone Age hunters and food gatherers leading nomadic lives – their wanderings dictated by seasonal changes in the places where they found food most abundant. For many years prehistorians held that Paleo Indians had been basically big-game hunters because their sites (all found on land) featured the remains of large beasts such as bison and mammoth. But we now believe that this picture is distorted by the rise in sea level. About

Some of the large animals hunted by Paleo Indians in North America more than 10,000 years ago are depicted here, although such a variety of species would never have lived together in a single habitat like this. To the left stand two Pleistocene wolves and a pair of mastadon, while a Pleistocene camel occupies the foreground. At the center a Pleistocene horse drinks as a saber-tooth cat emerges from the bushes behind. A giant sloth is browsing on the right, with a glyptodont in front of it.

10,000—14,000 years ago this level stood some 100 meters (330ft) below today's so that any Paleo-Indian coastal sites there were would have vanished under water. The known habits of efficient hunters and food gatherers lead us to believe that many of these early peoples did indeed gain food from the sea.

In time, the early Americans evolved a pattern of life based largely on intensive food gathering, and featuring semipermanent villages with cemeteries. This shift from the Paleo-Indian to the so-called Archaic cultural stage occurred about 7000 BC in the eastern United States and lasted until 500—300 BC. Prehistorians used to maintain that, during the Archaic Stage, peoples on the eastern seaboard had made little use of marine food resources; a supposition based on the fact that no one had discovered coastal shell middens, although they had found upland sites inland. However, geologists have shown that the rise in sea level continued after Paleo-Indian times

and submerged the Archaic people's coastline too. This has led archaeologists to suspect that – like the Paleo Indians before them – Archaic peoples exploited coastal seafood resources, and that their missing shell middens survive under the waters of the Atlantic.

About 3000 BC, ceramic technology reached Marco Island in southwest Florida. The innovation did not radically change Archaic settlement and subsistence patterns. But its method of arrival raises fresh possibilities in the study of drowned land surfaces. The reason for this supposition is that similar pottery (the oldest-known type in the western hemisphere) appeared simultaneously far to the south of Florida, at several sites in northern South America, yet pottery reached Mexico and the United States outside Florida only considerably later. This suggests that pottery making spread directly across the Caribbean Sea from South America to Florida. Five thousand years ago the sea level may have been

as much as 10 meters (33ft) lower than now, creating a Caribbean land route broken by relatively short water gaps.

Between 500 and 300 BC fresh cultural changes in North America marked the end of the Archaic cultural stage and the start of the Formative Stage. New ideas and technology and, possibly, peoples moved north from Middle America, giving rise to ceremonial structures and maize horticulture. It was then that the Indians of eastern North America developed those social and economic patterns that persisted until the Europeans arrived. By the start of the Formative Stage, the sea level had reached its present height, so that Formative coastal sites are less liable to have been drowned than those preceding them.

Theorizing about North America's submerged land sites is one thing; proving they exist is something else. We shall now see something of the barriers of belief that made this difficult, and how I and my fellow diving archaeologists have recently broken them down.

The belated recognition of inundated sites

An artist's impression of Paleo Indians attacking a cave bear during the Pleistocene period.

Until the 1970s hardly anyone had explored drowned land sites known to be that. At one time lack of diving equipment had made such work impossible. This no longer held true after the advent of diving gear. But while early hardhat and scuba divers no doubt found submerged terrestial sites, they failed to grasp what they saw. The reason was simple: accepted geological and archaeological theories suggested that, with local exceptions, such sites could not have existed. A major cause of this error was a lack of communication between the two professions.

One of the earliest papers to correlate current archaeological and geological knowledge and suggest the existence of submerged terrestial sites appeared in 1966. In "Archaeological Potential of the Atlantic Continental Shelf," K. O. Emery and R. L. Edwards of the Woods Hole (Massachusetts) Oceanographic Institution matched studies of early man against known facts about past changes in sea level, and reached a simple but momentous conclusion: that submerged archaeological land sites probably lay on the Atlantic Continental Shelf. I was then a graduate student in anthropology, and I attended seminars where we enthusiastically explored the new theory. Those discussions, and my present position in Florida, led to many of the concepts and discoveries set forth in these pages.

My practical introduction to submerged sites came in the early 1970s, when I was invited to examine the deposits at Warm Mineral Springs, a natural limestone well 15 kilometers (9mi) inland in southwest

Florida. The Springs' known archaeological value dated from 1959, when amateur archaeologist and expert diver Colonel William Royal had encountered a human cranium with intact brain material. It lay buried on a ledge 13 meters (43ft) below the surface of the warm, anaerobic waters. At the time the scientific community refused to accept that such a find was or could have been made so far under the water.

Two archaeologists had preceded me into Warm Mineral Springs. One said that the remains were indeed Indian, but could be no more than 500 years old; the other, a marine archaeologist, decided that this was no drowned terrestial site: just a pool into which people had fallen and sunk to a ledge where sediments eventually covered their remains. I believed neither theory. Convinced that the finds had been dry deposited, I left all remains where they were and called in consulting archaeologists and geologists to view the materials before excavation. We gathered a few samples and ran some radiocarbon dating tests. Then we acquired funding, and in 1973 the Warm Mineral Springs project was underway; it continued almost annually through the 1970s. The success of this operation (p. 142) has provided a great deal of information about the people and climate of late Pleistocene times in southeastern North America, and yielded clues for the discovery of similar sites.

Apart from my own, little other systematic work has been done on drowned terrestial sites in the States. One exception is Little Salt Springs (p. 144), an Archaic

Stage site some 5 kilometers (3mi) from Warm Mineral Springs. This second site involves a village and cemetery dating back about 5000–7000 BC. Professor Reynold Ruppé of Arizona State University is researching a third, Formative Stage, site (p. 145) nearby at Venice Beach.

People have reported a number of other North American finds suggesting submergence, but I believe these three projects are so far the only stratigraphic excavations of drowned land sites. And even these have proceeded against entrenched scepticism. Many archaeologists who conceded that land sites could have been drowned by the sea believed that these would have been destroyed by erosion during submergence. My research has demonstrated that this need not be so. In particular, work on the Douglas Beach site (p. 143) showed that a number of factors affect site preservation during and after submergence. Commonsense tells us that an advancing surf line will destroy a beach-front archaeological site. However, studies of primitive peoples today and our knowledge of later prehistoric cultures show that Stone Age peoples would have preferred to live on an estuary or lagoon than on an open beach. This is simply because unspecialized gatherers find more food in shallow estuaries and lagoons than they do on open beaches. Thus we should expect to find their settlements not there but on the inland waterways behind. By the time that a rise in sea level had drowned such a site, accumulating sediments and the depth of overlying water would have been enough to protect it from wave erosion

UNITED STATES

UNITED STATES

FLORIDA

SOUTH AMERICA

Chipola River

Wakulla River *St. Mark's River* *River*

Aucilla

Suwannee River

○ **Hilfiker**

Steinhatchee River

Icketucknee Run

Sante Fe River

Manatee Springs

Atlantic Ocean

St. John River

Gulf of Mexico

Ocklamaha River

Withalacoochee River

Silver Springs Run

Guest ○

Melbourne ○

Vero Beach ○

Saxon-Holland ○

Fish Creek ○

Tampa Bay

Myakka River

Douglas Beach ○

Warm Mineral Springs ○

Venice Beach ○ ○ **Little Salt Springs**

Tarpon Point ○

Lake Okeechobee

Marco Island ○

and bottom surge. This supposition proved itself accurate in the excavation of the Douglas Beach site — a site submerged in the Atlantic Ocean off a coastline pounded by surf for much of the year. Despite wave battering, the site is preserved, even to the Pleistocene tree stumps intact beneath the sand.

Yet another problem faced those considering the archaeological potential of drowned terrestrial sites. A number of archaeologists contended that even if the sites did exist, no one could work them carefully enough to produce archaeologically worthwhile results. I therefore found it necessary to show nondiving scientists that the diving scientists were indeed working to "state of the art" standards. I borrowed or adapted a number of methods and techniques from land archaeology, and invented others. For instance, at Warm Mineral Springs in 1974–75 I pioneered the use of underwater closed-circuit video as a communication and recording tool. By means of the video system we made a complete record of the entire excavation on land and under water. This record proved that stratigraphy could, and did, exist under water, and could be recorded and excavated as accurately as on land. In fact, our excavation technique allowed for a complete three-dimensional reconstruction of the site, with measurements from the surface to 70 meters (230ft) below, accurate to within 1 centimeter.

The following accounts should convince any remaining skeptics that land sites of early man were drowned, do survive, and can be scientifically worked.

A map of Florida showing the locations of the sites mentioned in the text.

Middens and burials under water

The rise in sea level at the end of the last glaciation drowned vast tracts of land off the low-lying southeastern coast of the United States. Here, submerged prehistoric land sites occur in a number of settings: in the sea itself, on drowned coastlines and river banks; and inland, on drowned river banks, lake shores, and sinkholes. Florida, where most of the searching has been done, has yielded Paleo-Indian remains from each of these types of location.

The Tampa Bay area of western Florida is rich in submerged Paleo-Indian remains. For years, commercial concerns seeking construction materials have dredged huge quantities of shells from the floor of Tampa Bay. People used to assume that these shell deposits were simply old oyster beds; but archaeologists searching the piles of dredged up shells have found numbers of Paleo-Indian artifacts, especially projectile points. No archaeologist has actually excavated any of the submerged shell middens but at least we now know they are there.

A number of Florida's river systems have produced reported finds of Pleistocene animal remains associated with Paleo-Indian artifacts. The Aucilla, St. Marks, Wakulla, and Chipola rivers of northern Florida are reputedly rich in fossil human and animal remains; and I have already started research into one St. Marks River site, where a sports diver has apparently found human tools and mastodon bones eroding from a level below the present river bank. In central Florida, the Suwannee, Sante Fe, and Ichetucknee rivers are also promising. Their old lower reaches now lie beneath the Gulf of Mexico, where their levees (raised banks) persist 10–20 meters (33–66ft) below present-day sea level. It would be relatively easy to trace these and find likely prehistoric habitation sites.

During 1978 I examined a number of finds from a lake in eastern Florida. Ranging from 500 to 11,000 years old they derived from the Saxon-Holland site in Blue Cypress Lake, near Vero Beach. The most recent artifacts and human remains came from submerged sites in shallow parts of the lake, the oldest materials from the deeper reaches. This freshwater lake forms part of the headwaters of the large St. Johns River system. We think that these sites occur along now submerged waterways, and that, as the sea level rose, the consequent rise in the levels of rivers forced the inhabitants to abandon old sites for higher ones by the new water-line. By studying this shifting settlement pattern we should be able to correlate rises in the levels of groundwater and sea.

A rise in groundwater level created the most valuable submerged land site yet found anywhere in the United States. Warm Mineral Springs in southwest Florida (p. 140) is an hourglass-shaped sinkhole, or cenote, containing human and animal remains in two layers of sediment on a ledge now 13 meters (43ft) under water.

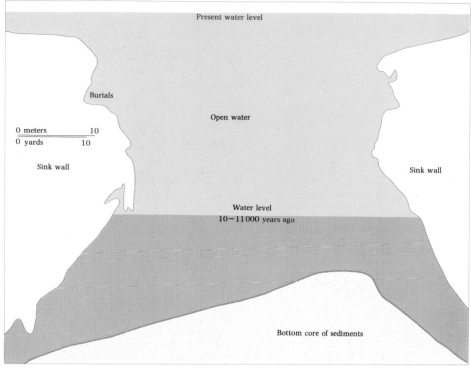

During my years of work on this site with a number of specialist scientists, we proved that both layers had been deposited 17 meters (56ft) *above* the old water level. Apparently, trees growing on ledges in the side of the sinkhole had afforded holds for aborigines who climbed down to bury their fellows. We have recovered the remains of some 20 individuals from the ledge, which seems to have served solely for burials. But land excavations on nearby uplands have revealed a tool "workshop" where early Indians had fashioned stone tools from flakes struck off lumps of imported fossil coral. This upland site also yielded fossil remains of horse and camel. Here, on land, all other remains have been lost by decay.

However, the upper layer of sediment on the sinkhole revealed a shell hook from a spear thrower, interred with a man aged 25–35 who had died about 10,300 years ago. This discovery represents the first known use of compound spear thrower in the western hemisphere. I strongly believe that that tool's introduction had a major effect upon life-styles. By making the spear more effective for killing prey, the spear thrower enlarged man's animal protein supply, thereby reducing the hours needed for food getting, increasing leisure time, and supporting a growth in the size and age span of the family unit. From these changes flowed sexual division of labor, increased accumulation and transmission of cultural skills, and enlarged social groups: at first, big semisedentary bands, and later the village communities of the Archaic cultural stage.

Besides the spear-thrower burial, the 10,000-year-old upper layer of sediment on the ledge at Warm Mineral Springs also

Top: A diagrammatic cross section of Warm Mineral Springs in Florida, showing the relationship between past and present water levels, and the position of the Paleo-Indian burial between the two.
Above, left: An artist's reconstruction of a Paleo Indian (based on the remains of the one buried at Warm Mineral Springs) using a spear thrower like the one also found in that burial.
Above, right: W. A. Cockrell holding the skull of the man found buried at Warm Mineral Springs.

held the remains of turkey, raccoon, cougar, white-tailed deer, opossum, and other animals still found in North America. However, the 11,000-year-old lower layer, of clay, also contained the remains of saber-toothed cat and ground sloth, both now extinct. A human mandible found in this layer is the western hemisphere's first direct evidence that man and saber-toothed cat were contemporaries.

Knowledge acquired at Warm Mineral Springs spurred us to hunt for other Florida sites of similar age. In the nearby Myakka River, at low tide, we encountered a gray Pleistocene clay layer apparently identical to the lower layer on the ledge at Warm Mineral Springs. At this so-called Tarpon Point site we collected fossilized tools: one fashioned from part of an elephant, one from the fossilized earbone of a whale.

We also reexamined the submerged east-coast Douglas Beach site where I had earlier made some discoveries. We collected stone, shell, and bone artifacts, human bone, and well-preserved tree trunks and pollen, indicating that this was once a large marshy area, surrounded by hardwoods. We also found horse teeth and the articulated remains of a mammoth. We are still working on this site to learn more about the dates of these finds.

Two other probable Paleo-Indian sites in Florida are worth mentioning here. One is the Guest site in Silver Springs Run in the northern-central part of the peninsula. Limited research in the early 1970s indicated probable Paleo-Indian tools associated with the remains of a small mastodon, washing out of a bank several meters under water. The other intriguing location is the Fish Creek site in the Tampa Bay region. Here beach erosion has revealed projectile points dating from the end of the Paleo-Indian Stage, as well as a number of projectile points and other tools from the ensuing Archaic Stage.

More drowned sites in North America

I shall end this brief survey of drowned prehistoric land sites in North America with some more Paleo-Indian examples, and finds from the ensuing Archaic and Formative cultural stages.

Outside Florida we know little about submerged Paleo-Indian sites. Intriguing possible exceptions are lower Alabama river sites reported in 1976 by an Alabama archaeologist. Wherever it outcrops on the submerged river banks, a gray clay deposit reveals the remains of people and big Pleistocene mammals; a remarkable parallel with what we discovered in Florida.

One potentially significant location in the Gulf of Mexico is the McFaddin Beach site off the mouth of the Sabine River in Texas. A surface collection from the beach has produced Paleo-Indian points, and the remains of large, extinct mammals. The associations are uncertain but the re-

searchers feel that they have strong evidence of submerged terrestrial sites in this area.

Before leaving the topic of the Paleo-Indian Stage I should mention that the Vero Beach and Melbourne sites in Florida contained human remains and those of large, extinct, Pleistocene mammals. Ever since these discoveries were made in the early 1900s, experts have argued about the age of the human remains. Comparison of the human types from Vero Beach, Melbourne, and Warm Mineral Springs sites with probable Paleo-Indian skeletal collections from southern California shows closely similar physical types, suggesting that all these groups were certainly early.

Evidence for submerged Archaic Stage sites comes from three places in Florida. The most significant is the Little Salt Springs site near Warm Mineral Springs in the south-

west. In the late 1970s, marine archaeologist Carl Clausen found conclusive evidence of a submerged Archaic cemetery on the banks of this water-filled, collapsed, limestone sinkhole. Clausen has reported a number of human burials on a shallow ledge sloping down to 10 meters (33ft) below present water level. The physical types of the skeletons and radiocarbon dating make these finds 5,000–7,000 years old, placing them firmly within the eastern Archaic Stage.

The Hilfiker site in northwest Florida at extreme low tide produces Archaic artifacts

Below: A selection of stone and bone tools from the site at Warm Mineral Springs, including two projectile points (center, left) and the shell spear thrower (below, right). The map of North America (opposite) contrasts the present coastline with that which would have existed in the past when the sea level was 100 meters lower. Submerged Paleo-Indian and Archaic sites from outside Florida are also shown.

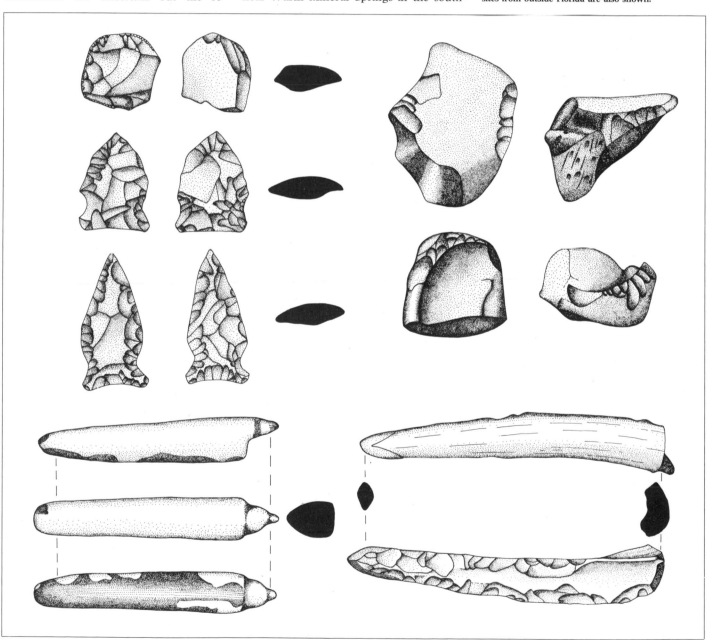

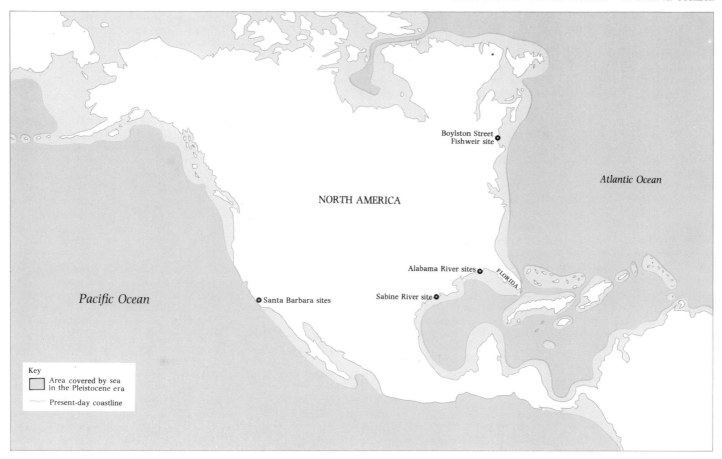

from a stratified peat-type deposit in 1 meter (about 3ft) of water.

My own research at Marco Island off southwest Florida produced intriguing negative evidence for submerged Archaic Stage sites. The tops of old sand dunes on this tiny island contain a number of Archaic Stage seasonal camp sites where only half of the resources that the people had used had come from the sea. With the absence of nearby coastal Archaic Stage sites, this fact suggests that the dune-top sites once stood much farther from the sea than they do now. In fact geological studies show that about 3000–1500 BC the coastline lay 10–15 meters (33–50ft) below today's level, which would have put these sites 20–30 kilometers (12–19mi) inland. This evidence strongly indicates that we should find late Archaic sites (1500–300 BC) submerged in up to 15 meters (50ft) of water off Marco Island.

There is little published evidence on any other submerged Archaic sites elsewhere in North America. However, in the west, divers working off the southern Californian coast near Santa Barbara have found stone vessels and stone tools. At least some of the stone vessels seem to have come from drowned camp sites.

On the northeast coast of the United States, the Boylston Street fish weir in the former Charles River estuary at Boston was a structure built 4,000–6,000 years ago. This fish trap provides clear evidence of submerged late Archaic Stage sites in the New England region.

We have far less evidence of drowned sites from the Formative Stage, beginning about 500–300 BC in the southeastern United States. Presumably this is because sea level had risen to its present height by the time that stage began. Nonetheless, in southwest Florida Professor Ruppé of Arizona has shown that at least part of a shallow stratified Formative midden (the Venice Beach site) lay for some time under water. About 2,000 years old, this midden extends from the beach to 2 meters (6½ft) below sea level. Its submerged deposits are certainly primary (not redeposited), and they contain pollen, which helps us to determine past climatic conditions.

On Marco Island I found seashore Formative Stage shell middens showing that these people had obtained nine-tenths of their food from the sea.

A number of caves and other water-worn holes in the limestone rock of peninsular Florida contain promise of proofs of Formative Stage aboriginal activity. Cave divers have described sightings tantalizingly suggestive of hearths, tool-chipping stations, and pottery in caves as much as 10 meters (33ft) below present groundwater level. But only further investigation will confirm or deny these diagnoses.

From all I have said over the past few pages, the reader will have gathered that there is indeed strong evidence for drowned prehistoric land sites in North America, from the Paleo-Indian through the Formative Stage. But we have only begun to scan this potentially vast and very rich archaeological field. Once archaeologists begin to explore shallow waters we can expect them to find submerged features of many coastal Formative Stage sites. Paleo-Indian coastal sites will prove harder to find. This is partly because Paleo-Indians were scarcer than their successors and left fewer remains. Moreover, early Paleo-Indian coastal sites will be difficult to locate in the ocean where they must now lie under 80–100 meters (260–330ft) of water. The hunt for Archaic Stage sites holds the greatest promise of all. First, Archaic people and their products were relatively plentiful. Second, unlike their nomadic predecessors, these early Indians lived concentrated in seasonal semi-permanent villages. Third, Archaic coastal sites now lie in shallower waters than the coastal sites of the early Paleo Indians. Lastly, submerged Archaic sites have escaped the decay and destruction suffered by many of the later coastal sites, which were not swamped by the sea.

Archaeologists have already done enough work on drowned land sites to revise our picture of how North America's early inhabitants lived. We are now sure that at least some Paleo Indians gathered seafood as well as hunting big game, and that their successors found much of their food at the sea's edge.

The sunken city of Port Royal

Exceptional local geophysical events can submerge settlements and other remains much younger than those in Florida. A perfect example is Port Royal, near Kingston, Jamaica. Founded in 1655, when the English captured Jamaica from Spain, the city soon grew phenomenally rich on trade and piracy; then, on June 7, 1692, it dramatically slumped into the sea. Within minutes of an earthquake shock followed by a giant wave, nine-tenths of the city's 2,000 buildings disappeared, and more than 2,000 persons perished. The toll in property was incalculable.

However, no part of the site lay more than 18 meters (60ft) deep, and salvage started straightaway. Free divers and people using grappling hooks, nets, and poles with tarred ends soon recovered much sunken wealth. But far more remained undiscovered. Port Royal thus became the submarine equivalent of Pompeii – a city preserved by the disaster that had overwhelmed it, and a site with immense promise for the underwater archaeologist.

That promise remained unproven until 1965, when the Jamaican government asked me to direct a large-scale excavation project. There was some urgency about this task because planners proposed a new deepwater port, and its construction would mean dredging liable to destroy over half the sunken city.

The rescue "dig" ran continuously from November 1965 to June 1968. Volunteer aid and donations of equipment and preservation materials helped to compensate for lack of cash, but this prevented the use of costly, sophisticated, surveying instruments. At the end of the project, though, Dr. Harold Edgerton (p. 110) generously used his own sonar to map the entire site.

Several factors made the initial four-month survey slow and difficult. Underwater visibility was never better than 1 meter (about 3ft). Our team had to clear over 50 tons of modern debris from the seafloor. We had only a long metal probe to locate the walls of buildings beneath the sediment, and a hand-held metal detector to find large metallic concentrations.

The survey revealed that the entire site encompassed some 140,000 square meters (1,500,000sqft), three-quarters of it in water less than 10 meters (33ft) deep. We concentrated on clearing and mapping only that section threatened by dredging. Pre-excavation cleaning largely involved removing silt up to 1 meter (about 3ft) deep, and a lower layer of mud and coral fragments up to 1.8 meters (5ft) thick, in turn overlying black sand and coarse gravel.

For the job of excavation, we tested several types of air jet and water jet, including two types of propwash. We finally favored an airlift 25 centimeters (10in) in diameter, with a screen on the bottom to prevent any artifacts larger than a small coin being sucked up the tube. (Other excavation tools, including airlifts with wider tubes, damaged artifacts.) The sediment was pumped onto a barge and passed through a fine-mesh screen where the smaller artifacts were recovered. Divers collected larger artifacts on the bottom and sent them up in buckets for tagging.

Airlift work took at least three divers on the bottom: one to hold the airlift tube; one to send or carry artifacts to the surface; and one to dismantle the submerged brick walls. More than 650,000 bricks were recovered in this manner. After several divers had been trapped beneath fallen walls caused by landslides, the team abandoned scuba equipment in favor of a surface demand unit (p. 12). Thus a diver trapped by sediment or a falling wall was unlikely to run out of air and suffocate before he could be rescued. Since the water was shallow, divers needed to lose no time in decompression, and individually averaged 55 hours a week under water throughout the excavation.

Poor visibility and the caving in of thick sediment ruled out the precise visual measurements made by archaeologists on land and at many underwater sites. Our divers blindly worked by touch. We recovered most artifacts from the first 3 meters (10ft) of sediment, but excavated to a depth of 5 meters (16ft). Horizontal control was maintained by two different methods. Four buoys marked the square to be excavated each day, and the men on the barge recorded the position of the airlift in relation to these buoys when major artifacts were recovered. Also the Jamaican Survey Department set up shore markers and plotted them on special grid charts. A member of the surface team established the precise position of each find and (at half-hour intervals) each area under excavation by taking compass bearings from three or more of the shore markers to the top of the vertically positioned airlift tube. He could also measure the depth from which each item was recovered by determining the length of airlift tube above the water.

Altogether, our team excavated a rectangular hole 155×50 meters (509×164ft) to an average depth of 5 meters (16ft). We uncovered only three intact buildings, but found hundreds of fragments of brick walls and tens of thousands of brickbats. Surviving maps and property records showed that the area excavated had contained 30–40 buildings. By checking owners' initials on pewter and silver artifacts with the property records, we could identify many of the sites. Most were private homes, but there were also three taverns; a carpenter's shop; a cobbler's shop; a pewterer's shop; the fish and meat markets; and two turtle crawls

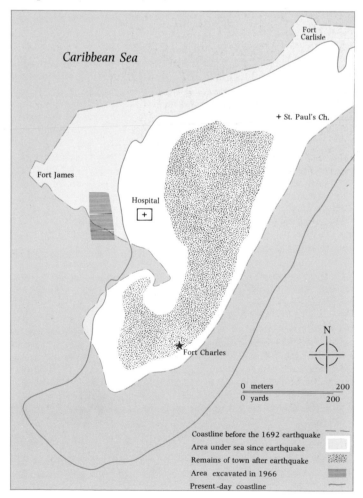

A plan showing the area of the sunken city that was excavated during the first eight months of the project, May to December 1966.

Caribbean Sea

Fort Carlisle

+ St. Paul's Ch.

Fort James

Hospital
+

N

Fort Charles

0 meters   200
0 yards   200

Coastline before the 1692 earthquake
Area under sea since earthquake
Remains of town after earthquake
Area excavated in 1966
Present-day coastline

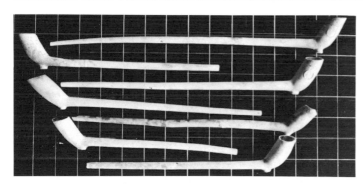

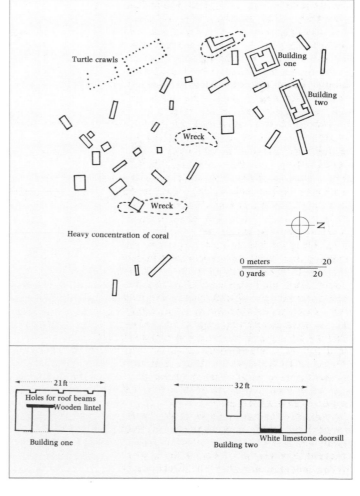

'(pens for holding live turtles imported from the Cayman Islands). The same area yielded two shipwrecks dating from the 1692 earthquake and one lost in a hurricane in 1722.

Divers recovered 3 tons of human and animal bones and (excluding bricks and other building materials) more than 100,000 artifacts. These included more than 2,000 intact bottles; 6,500 clay smoking pipes; over 500 pewter and silver objects; and two large hoards of Spanish silver coins. The whole project generated 32 reports, apart from monthly site reports, yet it had covered only 5% of the entire site.

After the excavation, an official announcement declared the proposed dredging operation canceled, thus lifting a threat from the remainder of the site. Ideally, this should stay untouched until improved financial conditions, tools, and techniques permit detailed survey and excavation.

Top: A selection of the ceramics recovered at Port Royal. Most of the pieces were manufactured in Europe.
Above: Some of the complete clay pipes recovered at the site. Compare these with those lost two years earlier on the Royal Navy frigate *Dartmouth* (p. 101).
Right: Drawings of two of the standing buildings found at Port Royal.

Alpine villages on stilts

In the 1850s the level of Lake Zurich in Switzerland fell so low that large areas along the shore dried out. Exploring the exposed lake bed near Obermeilen, a schoolteacher made some remarkable finds. He discovered a number of wooden posts jutting from the mud and, nearby, numerous prehistoric artifacts. Ferdinand Keller, an archaeologist from Zurich, believed this whole complex to be the remains of a Stone Age village built out over water on a foundation of stilts. Keller doubtless knew about descriptions of contemporary pile structures in New Guinea when he painted this imaginative picture of an early settlement.

The abundance of finds and the intriguing notion that ancient peoples had built over water to avoid their enemies aroused great interest in Switzerland and abroad. People soon reported many more "pile dwellings" from the lakes of Switzerland and neighboring countries, and by 1930 the known total stood at 435 Stone Age and Bronze Age sites.

Investigations made at low water level were mainly crude hunts for finds and in no sense archaeological excavation as we understand the term. When the water level was normal, treasure hunters armed with shovels and grabs fished valuable finds from the floors of the lakes. Others plowed the lake beds with hooks, and even used dredgers. As early as 1854, however, an attempt was made in Lake Geneva to explore such sites by diving.

Meanwhile, people were finding the remains of old settlements in peat bogs as well as in lakes. In 1858 relics turned up in the Robenhausen peat bog on Lake Pfäffiker, north of Lake Zurich; this site gained worldwide renown. A keen interest in all prehistoric lake and bog villages later extended to the so-called Terramare finds of northern Italy and the crannogs of Scotland and Ireland (pp. 156–61). Unfortunately, excessive zeal resulted in all sorts of objects being called pile dwellings, so that significant differences grew blurred.

By the 1920s Hans Reinerth was challenging Keller's concept of pile structures as villages built over water on wooden platforms. Reinerth's own excavations in Sipplingen on Lake Constance led him to declare that the houses had stood on those parts of the lake edge only occasionally liable to flooding, and that the floors had been raised no more than 60 centimeters (2ft) above ground. Twenty years later, Oskar Paret disputed the very existence of prehistoric pile structures over water, but because of several errors in his arguments the new theory won general acceptance only when Emil Vogt's *The Problem of Pile Structures* appeared in 1955. Vogt's own excavations of a bog village at Egolzwill proved particularly convincing, and his findings tallied with those of other Swiss sites, for instance, at Zug and Thayngen. At Zug evidence included late Bronze Age

Left: A clay hearth built on a brushwood mat in the Neolithic settlement at Egolzwill 5, canton of Lucerne, Switzerland. Opposite: A view across the wooden piles of the village at Fiave, Trentino, in Italy. Below: A pictorial reconstruction of a "pile structure", made by the Swiss archaeologists Ferdinand Keller in 1854.

blockhouses of about 800 BC. Thayngen revealed so-called stilt structures comprising houses with floors raised about 60 centimeters (2ft) above the damp ground and resting on joists inserted into holes in the piles.

By the 1960s it had become clear that no excavation had produced firm evidence that any prehistoric village had actually been built over open water. The term "pile dwelling" thus appeared misleading; even at places where the floors of the houses were raised, this special design was intended solely to insulate against damp. In fact, most so-called lake dwellings had actually stood at ground level, as finds of the 1960s helped

to confirm – for instance, those of Neolithic settlements at Portalban on Lake Neuchâtel and on the Utoquai in Zurich. The large number of piles at these sites simply reflects successive building and rebuilding on the same spot. The remains of water plants, freshwater mollusks, and sediments laid down under water indicate only frequent flooding in prehistoric times, not that the piles stood always in water. Indeed, layers of sediment barren of finds show that sometimes floods forced a prolonged spell of abandonment. How these settlements throughout the Alps came to be permanently submerged is a complex question, to which I return below (p. 154).

The problem of the true nature of pile dwellings appeared to be finally resolved through excavations at Auvernier and Yverdon on Lake Neuchâtel. Discoveries here led Christian Strahm to suggest that the Stone Age villages had extended from dry land out to a periodically flooded beach. The houses had stood on piles, with the floors raised at least 50 centimeters (19in). This does not, however, imply a reversion to Keller's concept of stilt construction, since only individual houses, and probably only those located nearer the water, rested on piles. The 1970–71 excavations at Feldmeilen on Lake Zurich led to similar conclusions. Later excavations in the Bay of Auvernier, in Twann on Lake Biel, and at the Pressehaus building in Zurich have reemphasized the occupants' use of the ground surface. On the last-mentioned site, for example, excavators found the remains of a wagon or cart within the settlement area.

However, fresh support for the concept of building true pile dwellings has come from the Trentino region of north Italy. There, in the late 1960s, Renato Perini made astonishing discoveries in the peat bog of Fiave. He found that about 1400 BC a middle Bronze Age village had extended up to 15 meters (about 50ft) into open water from an island in the then Lake Carera. The substructure of the pile dwellings had survived in an unusually impressive manner, and large sections stood exposed. The most important pointer to the location of houses in water was a burned layer on the foundation timbers — obviously the result of a catastrophic fire. The bottom 1.5 meters (nearly 5ft) of the piles bore no sign of fire damage, reflecting their protection under water.

The accumulation of evidence, and especially this last example, should warn us against generalizing too freely about what is evidently a very complex phenomenon.

Discovering drowned villages

Apart from the early diving in Lake Geneva, discoveries from sites under water were at first restricted to antiquities fished up with trawls or grabs. In 1929, however, Hans Reinerth took the bold decision to box off and pump dry 500 square meters (600sqyd) of Lake Constance, near Sipplingen. His dam comprised two parallel wooden walls packed with mud. Seepage was collected in a surrounding trench and fed to a pump. In spite of the fact that average lake level stood 1.5 meters (about 5ft) above the excavation surface, the box withstood the tremendous water pressure throughout a four weeks' excavation period in 1929 and 1930. A similar procedure was employed in 1964–65 in the Bay of Auvernier on Lake Neuchâtel. The aim here was to make a detailed examination of at least a small sector of a vast area of prehistoric settlements before everything was destroyed by land reclamations for a new highway. More recently, in the same bay, a new highway has isolated an area of shallows from open water, enabling archaeologists to work under the protection of a proper dam, as in a polder. This proved a godsend, for it is not easy to wall off a large lake area, especially when floored by soft, deep marl.

Sometimes diving is the only practicable means of exploring lakes and rivers. Hans Reinerth was one of the first to exploit the increasingly popular sport of scuba diving. Later, skin divers searched for medieval relics in the Dvina River near Wolin in northwest Poland. At the same spot, researchers repeatedly lowered reinforced-concrete caissons to allow them to examine parts of the port and a bridge. Around 1960, there was a marked upsurge in attempts to carry out diving research in fresh water. The first topographic survey under water was that of the Gran Carro Bronze Age settlement in Lake Bolsena – a central Italian site probed in the early 1960s. A Salzburg subaqua club has subsequently surveyed a lake settlement in Austria's Mondsee, and a sports-diving group from Neuchâtel and an amateur diver in Zurich have been similarly active in Switzerland.

Freshwater sites hold many obstacles to proper excavation. The most serious are the clouds of mud that swiftly shroud a diver in darkness if he even slightly disturbs the light, fine particles of sediment. In addition, rapid growth of algae begins with the first warm spring days, so that detailed work is impossible in the summer months.

These problems and the urgent need for improved methods of rescue excavation impressed themselves upon me when, in 1963, I joined a Zurich archaeological diving club. It was four years before we reached the point where we felt we could tackle our first underwater dig with our own professional diving team. We have gained much practical knowledge since then. A "water-curtain," usually powered by an electric pump, has proved the most

Above: A diver drawing an archaeological section exposed during excavations on the remains of a Neolithic settlement at Erlenbach-Widen, near Zurich, Switzerland. The underside of the water surface can be seen at the top, showing how shallow the site is.
Right: A diver using a trowel to excavate carefully a Neolithic horizin on the "Kleiner Hafner" site in Zurich (p. 154).

Diagrams demonstrating the construction of the excavation box used by Hans Reinerth in 1929 and 1930 to allow him to excavate some 500 square meters of the floor of Lake Constance, near Sipplingen. The overall plan of the site is shown at the top, with a section through it in the center. At the bottom, one corner of the box and a section through the retaining wall are shown in detail.

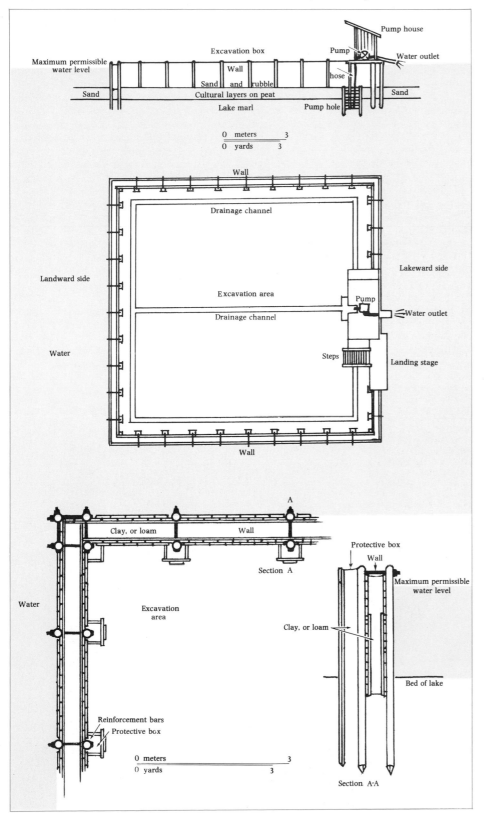

useful aid that we developed — one since adopted by most other underwater archaeologists working on similar sites. The idea is to direct several jets of water away from the place of work. These set up a gentle current in their wake, which moves evenly over the bottom, bearing all light silts toward the curtain, and away from the workers.

For the removal of overburden on site we are increasingly coming to rely on a suction dredge, powered by the same electric submersible pump as we have used for the water curtain. Because suction depends on injection this tool's efficiency remains good in shallow water, where the conventional airlift performs poorly.

Other useful aids in underwater research include sheets of plastic onto which we can trace features at full scale using wax crayons. In recording, we also use a double-clamped drawing grid, which we can easily level; this corresponds to the apparatus widely used on land. Of course the quality of underwater photographs depends on the degree of clarity of the water, but ultra-wide-angle lenses or front-lens attachments can bring about a marked improvement in the results. Color photographs generally show more detail than black and white. Some teams have achieved good results with photographic mosaics. In Lake Bolsena, divers took consecutive exposures with a camera suspended at set distances from a floating rail with an adjustable height and level.

For the initial mapping of extensive lake sites, archaeologists in Switzerland have widely used theodolites fitted with range finders or, more precisely, base reduction tachymeters. Cylindrical buoys may serve as targets for determining distance and bearing from survey stations on shore. It is often simpler and quicker to follow the movements of a diver swimming from one point to the next than to use more conventional fixed targets. Thus the Haag diving group in Austria has produced contour maps using only a plumb suspended from a buoy and towed by a diver. On Lake Neuchâtel, Michel Egloff has established the extent and basic structures of a number of settlements by means of aerial photography.

Archaeologists now agree that any study of old settlements, whether above or below water, should involve careful layer-by-layer removal of the soil or sediment in which the remains lie wholly or partly buried. Where there are thick deposits of prehistoric material, the site director may have to define intermediate excavation levels. It takes much experience and intuition to follow the dividing line between two different layers. If one peters out, there is a risk of overlooking this and continuing to dig until you reach the surface of a deeper but similar layer. You can avoid such mistakes only if the excavation team consists of experienced divers who have collaborated closely for long periods. These divers should have a genuine interest in archaeological problems, and not just the urge to make discoveries. Short-term volunteers are best employed on search and survey tasks. Thus we hope to emerge with our underwater sites dissected, recorded, and interpreted to the same high standards as land-based archaeologists expect.

Landscapes, villages, and houses

A major value of lakes for the archaeologist is the fact that their soft, submerged floors preserve organic substances that would quickly perish on land. Examples include not only the remains of wooden buildings and implements, but also traces of long-dead plants and animals. Getting the most from these relics means taking samples intelligently. For instance, it makes sense to collect samples from the center of a lake settlement and to compare these with others from the settlement's landward and lakeward edges, and even from outside the inhabited area. This helps you to recognize the special features of a settlement and to discover which objects were brought in by man and which arrived as natural deposits.

Pollen grains from successive levels of occupation provide valuable information on the development of local vegetation. Conditions for this type of study are especially favorable in the lower basin of Lake Zurich. Within a relatively small area this contains the remains of nine settlements, some with up to five superimposed cultural layers from various phases of the Neolithic and late Bronze Age. Intermediate layers of lake marl disclose clear gaps between periods of occupation. Analytical studies of pollen from some of these sites help us to picture the changing landscape from Neolithic times onward. During the Neolithic period forests of mainly oaks, with elm, ash, and lime trees predominated in the Zurich area, as elsewhere in central Switzerland. Forest probably extended almost to the shore.

There were no large reed beds or belts of marsh near the lakeside settlements. The Neolithic settlers seem to have accomplished no major clearance of forest, since plant pollens that would indicate open meadowland are relatively rare. But by late Bronze Age times certain changes had occurred. Beech had become the dominant species of tree, and pollens show signs of more extensive clearings. Pollen samples taken from early Iron Age deposits indicate an increasingly damp climate and flooding.

Just as important as pollen grains are the larger botanical items — especially the timbers and branches used in the settlements for building and fuel. These, too, throw light on the kinds of trees that grew locally. Here are just a few examples, drawn from the Horgen Jetty settlement on Lake Zurich, where underwater rescue excavations took place in 1966. The exceptionally high proportion of fir twigs and needles in all cultural strata confirms the natural spread of firs in the forests surrounding the lake and suggests that the leafy twigs served as floor covering or bedding. People also brought the branches of deciduous trees into the settlement. We know they usually did this in summer, for at least 75% of the branches had been cut in the growing period, and the last annual growth ring is incomplete. Bracken and lichen were gathered, too, although neither grew very close to the village.

Samples of edible plants included various species valued for food, for example, apples, raspberries, and blackberries. The inhabitants also grew flax, probably for its fiber and vegetable oil. Lakeside and swamp village sites abound in hazelnuts and charred halves of little apples that had apparently fallen into fires during drying. Considerable quantities of carbonized grain are also usually found.

Generally speaking, animal bones have also survived well preserved. In many Neolithic sites more than 50% are those of wild animals, which tells us that hunting played a major role in nutrition. If we are right in thinking that settlers in this region were not hacking pastures out of the forest before the Bronze Age, it seems likely that animal husbandry played a small role until there were fields big enough to support large grazing mammals. The distribution of bones in a settlement enables us to draw interesting conclusions about the activities of the inhabitants. At a site in Auvernier, archaeologists found more than 800 small fragments of bones in one place; 518 of these were martens', suggesting that someone had been processing their pelts for furs.

As for the lakeside settlements themselves, lack of surviving floors means we must try to deduce structures from the distribution of piles. Often, people settled a locality several times, and during each phase renewals took place; but the parts of earlier piles surviving below ground level were generally left undisturbed, especially where the floor was subsequently raised above repeatedly flooded ground. Here and there, however, when a

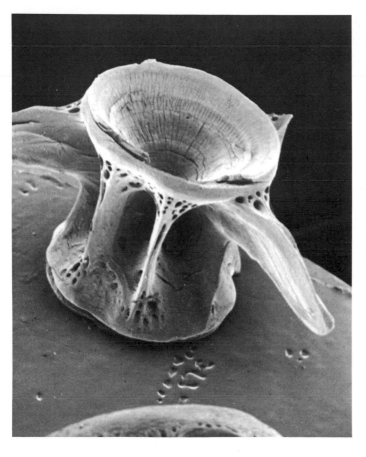

site was resettled, people took out the older piles. Finally, through the compaction of layers, we often find that relatively recent sediments have sunk below the level of older pile heads.

In spite of painstaking and detailed excavation work, there are bound to be occasional failures to allocate all the piles to specific cultural layers, let alone to individual building stages. Many a site has thousands of piles and 10 per square meter (roughly 1 per sqft) is nothing unusual in shore settlements on Lake Zurich. Sites inhabited for only short periods are, of course, those most responsive to analysis.

Sometimes we can identify individual structures. One technique is to plot only those piles that show the same features, for example, all cleft-oak piles. Using this method in layer III at Feldmeilen on Lake Zurich, archaeologists identified four rectangular outlines of houses, each with one row of roof ridges. But two ground plans are superimposed, and we cannot be sure which is the older. Cultural layer I also revealed regular, parallel rows of oak piles, although here specific houses proved hard to isolate. In spite of regular patterning, the same difficulties arose in allocating piles to individual buildings for the latest occupa-

tion layer of the Pressehaus sector in Zurich.

But piles are not the only clues to the sites of individual buildings. Archaeologists often find dish-shaped clay surfaces, which they have interpreted as the remains of fireplaces and house floors. The number of such surfaces may indicate the number of dwellings in a settlement, but we can never be certain.

The detailed study of such sites is thus useful in two ways: first, it can tell us how prehistoric lakeside villagers lived; second, it reveals the size and layout of the village communities. We must now consider some of the wider implications of this evidence.

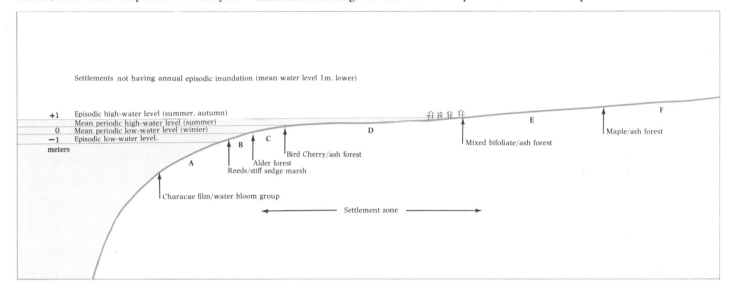

Settlements not having annual episodic inundation (mean water level 1m. lower)

+1   Episodic high-water level (summer, autumn)
    Mean periodic high-water level (summer)
0   Mean periodic low-water level (winter)
−1   Episodic low-water level.
meters

A   B   C   D   E   F

Maple/ash forest
Mixed bifoliate/ash forest
Bird Cherry/ash forest
Alder forest
Reeds/stiff sedge marsh
Characae film/water bloom group

← Settlement zone →

Opposite, far left: A much enlarged photograph of a fish vertebrae, barely 1 millimeter (3/64 in) high, recovered from a lake sediment by fine sieving.
Opposite, Left: A view of a section through the deposits exposed during excavations on the "Kleiner Hafner" settlement in Zurich. It is 3 meters (10ft) high overall, and the organic remains of a Neolithic and Bronze Age settlement can be seen as a dark band running across the section, sandwiched between clean levels of lake-bed marl.
Above: A diagram distinguishing the six types of lake-side environment, ranging from that which is always submerged (A) to that which is never flooded (F). The optimal zone for settlement is shown to be in the range C, D, and E.
Right: Timber exposed during excavations on the "Grosser Hafner" site in Zurich.

Dating the lakeside villages

At one time writers often referred to the Pile Structure Culture, as though the remains of settlements found in lakes and swamps around the Alps represented a single independent culture that had thrived everywhere for the same time span. We now know that all these assumptions are wrong. For example, north of the Alps we find lakeside and swamp villages from the Neolithic Age and from the early and late Bronze Age, but the middle Bronze Age seems almost entirely missing (no one knows why). On the southern slopes of the Alps, on the other hand, we do find examples that date from the middle Bronze Age.

However, it seems true that everywhere lakeside and swamp settlements vanished completely early on in the Iron Age. The reason plainly lies in a general deterioration of the climate, confirmed by pollen analyses. We need not envisage a sudden major catastrophe, but rather gradual abandonment of the shores of lakes as flooding intensified and the general level of lake water rose. In many instances, as at the "Kleiner Hafner" settlement in Zurich, further flooding may have resulted from local subsidence and landslides.

Even before this happened occupation was rarely if ever continuous at one site throughout a whole cultural period. Because the timber structures soon rotted in damp shore areas, any extra problem was likely to persuade the inhabitants to leave a settlement. Thick burned layers at many sites point to disastrous fires. More often, however, floods repeatedly drove people from low-level villages. Sediment "sandwiches," where culturally barren layers alternate with layers bearing traces of occupation, show that one period of settlement in a village was actually divided into a series of separate phases.

But do sharp differences between the contents of adjacent layers indicate some swift, shattering disaster or a long-drawn-out development of which we are seeing only signs of the beginning and the end? The solution to this problem often lies in dendrochronology – dating different timbers by correlating the rings of growth annually added to different trees before men chopped them down. Fortunately, lakeside sites abound in wooden objects. Recently, a laboratory in Neuchâtel and our own laboratory in Zurich have been engaged on such an analysis of piles and other timber finds from lakeside settlements.

Dendrochronology works like this. The width of any tree ring depends above all on the weather during the relevant growth period. If, then, you accurately measure sequences of such rings, you can plot these on a graph to produce a curve that reveals climatic changes. It is obvious that there will be a good match between the curves for woods originating in the same period, provided they are of the same kind and come from the same climatic area. Thus the dendrochronologist superimposes the curve for one set of growth rings on that for another to see if at least part of one curve fits part of the other. If it does, the matching parts of both sets of growth rings are of the same age. If, for both specimens, the last ring underneath the bark is present, straightforward counting of those annual sections that do not match establishes how many years elapsed between the felling of both trees. Eventually a number of specimens may yield a whole series of graphs with overlapping parts that correspond – a series representing several centuries. The dendrochronologist can then accurately place inside this time scale any other contemporary piece of timber he may find.

Study of timbers found in underwater excavations near Charavines in southeast France provides a good example of the detailed knowledge to be won from such analyses. As much as a year before they took up residence, the first settlers appear to have felled timber and made it ready. The following summer they built a house measuring 12×4 meters (39×13ft). Next year they built a second house, parallel to the first. After seven years, it became necessary completely to rebuild the first house. The builders retained the old shape but slightly reduced the width. The hearth stayed where it was. Nine years later they replaced both houses in a fresh burst of rebuilding. We do not know how long this second phase lasted, although it is unlikely to have exceeded 15 years. On the other hand, tree-ring dating plainly shows that people reoccupied the settlement 93 years after the first felling of timber, or some 60 years after abandonment. Of course, not all settlements were so short lived; for example, the older settlement at Zug appears to have lasted for 150 years, admittedly with a number of new phases.

Besides revealing year-by-year building events at a single site, tree-ring dating can prove immensely useful in showing whether separate prehistoric communities flourished at the same time. Thus we now know that there were contemporary late Bronze Age villages at Zug and on lakes Neuchâtel and Zurich. Such correlations are especially significant where they cut across the boundaries of different cultural areas. In a few years we should have enough data to draw a tree-ring curve back into Neolithic times for widely separate Alpine areas. We shall then have certain dating, accurate to within one year. At the moment, all we have are radiocarbon dates whose precise interpretation still arouses controversy.

Even so, we now know that the earliest lakeside settlements go back 6,000 years and the most recent date from about 750 BC. We know, too, that these villages were simply elements in various regional settle-

ment patterns, and probably not even very important ones. To the archaeologist though, they hold a special value for preserving underwater materials that give us glimpses of life styles spanning more than three millenia.

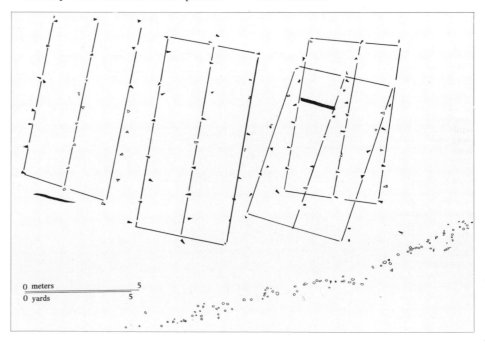

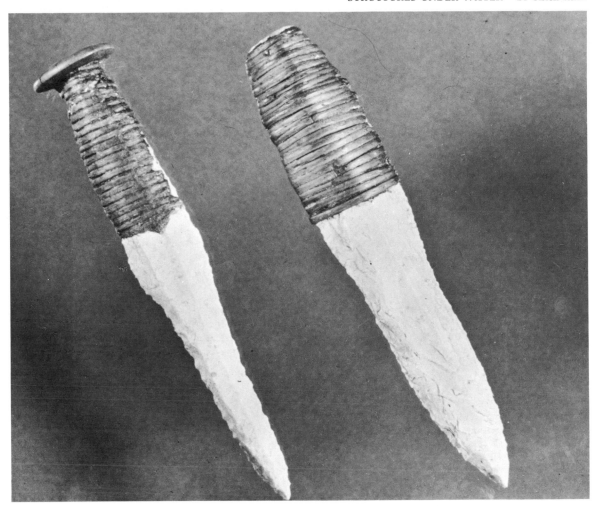

Opposite, below: The ground plans of three Neolithic houses (c. 3000 BC), uncovered by excavations at Feldmeilen, in the canton of Zurich, Switzerland. The house to the right has been razed and rebuilt on a slightly different alignment.

Below: A graph showing a series of dendrochronological curves synchronized within the period 950–1250 BC, derived from timbers recovered from settlements in lakes Zurich and Zug, Switzerland. Each curve records variations in the thickness of tree rings year by year.

Opposite: Neolithic pots (c. 4000 BC) from the "Kleiner Hafner" settlement in Zurich. It is most unusual to find such early pottery so well preserved.

Right: Two flint diggers from the site at Charavines, France, with their original organic handles still in place. There are very few other examples of blades and handles being found together like this.

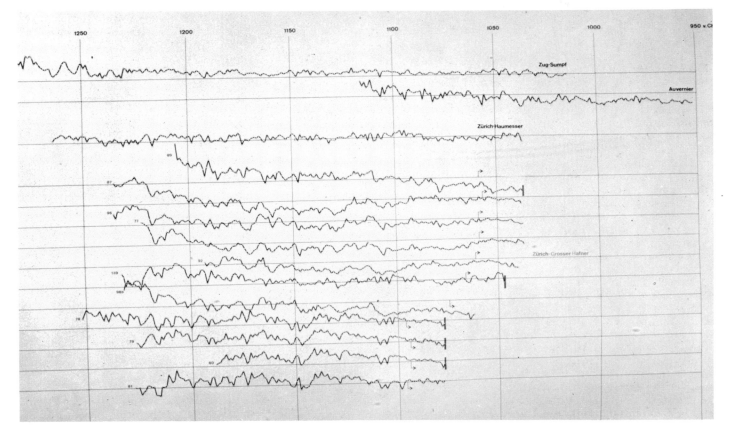

Man-made islands in Scottish lochs

The word crannog is derived from Gaelic. In Scotland and Ireland people use it to indicate a small island that men have built or augmented to support one or more huts. Like the prehistoric lakeside villages of the Alps (pp. 148–55), many crannogs have now become totally submerged, but unlike most of these villages, the crannogs were originally built to exploit the protection of being surrounded by water.

Artificial islands are by no means unique to the British Isles. They are indeed still used by people as different as the Cuna Indians of Panama and the Marsh Arabs of south-eastern Iraq. They occur in most continents, and show considerable variety in siting, construction, and date. This diversity is also characteristic of the Scottish examples.

For instance, although most crannogs are sited in lakes, some stand in shallow and sheltered arms of the sea or in estuaries. There are marine crannogs at the head of the Moray Firth, and estuarine crannogs in the Clyde.

There is variety too in the construction of the islands themselves and of their superstructures, though the word crannog tends to be used only for those that originally had wooden buildings. Thus stone-built duns (forts) and brochs (Iron Age towers) are often sited on islets, notably in the lochs of the Hebrides, and of the Orkney and Shetland islands. However, archaeologists have generally considered these as separate classes of monument, although not all of their islets are necessarily fully natural. Their dates and sizes overlap with those of the crannogs, while their characteristic locations beside patches of farmable land may suggest similar social functions.

So although we shall accept it here for convenience, the conventional distinction between crannogs and other small island habitations perhaps reflects little more than alternative technological response to what different landscapes had to offer. Stone was more readily available than timber in much of the north and west, and there too the ice-molded ancient rocks provided many natural islets offering solid foundations suitable for heavy stone superstructures. Furthermore, detailed fieldwork now under way in several areas suggests that the pattern of island sites complemented the pattern of small fortifications on land around the lakes. It seems that when people needed a secure settlement close to a patch of worthwhile land, a crannog was a common option in Scotland's loch-strewn landscape.

Crannog sites are certainly numerous. No one knows how many there are in Scotland, for although many still appear above water level, many more are now wholly submerged. Reasons for this include the decay and erosion of superstructures; the collapse of piling; internal compaction; subsidence of foundations; as well as changes in the levels of some lochs.

There are several hundred casual reports of the discovery of crannogs during the agricultural drainage schemes of the eighteenth and nineteenth centuries, but such sites were generally destroyed without

any detailed descriptions being made. Even the geographical pattern of these reports is of limited archaeological value. Rather than offering a picture of the original distribution of lake dwellings in Scotland, it tends to reflect merely where enthusiastic antiquaries were operating.

For this reason it seems likely that the old reports under-represented the crannogs in the innumerable lochs of the Scottish Highlands. That formidable priest, the Rev. Odo Blundell (surely one of the earliest archaeologists to dive for himself) started to confirm this in Edwardian times, but little more underwater work took place for another half century. Recent systematic searches by myself and diving colleagues have borne this out. For example, lochs Awe and Tay (previously thought to have only a few crannogs) together have proved to contain at least 40. We thus have evidence that remains of crannogs and other small island habitations occur in lochs in almost all parts of Scotland. From the literature and our sample surveys it now seems possible that eventually we may have to consider as many as 1,000 sites. Clearly a great deal of underwater work is needed to establish their distribution, superficial characteristics, and potential for a logical program of excavations.

That this large number of sites occupies a wide time span is already clear. Very few directly relevant radiocarbon dates are available so far, but those from a crannog in Milton Loch, Kirkcudbrightshire, put its construction around the fifth century BC.

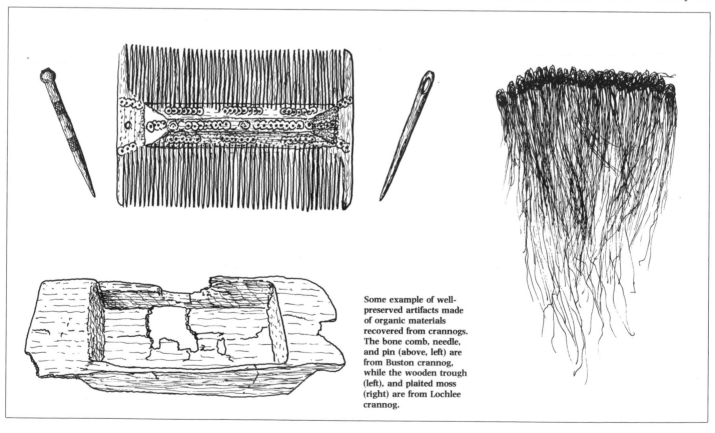

Some example of well-preserved artifacts made of organic materials recovered from crannogs. The bone comb, needle, and pin (above, left) are from Buston crannog, while the wooden trough (left), and plaited moss (right) are from Lochlee crannog.

A plan of the crannog at Buston in southwest Scotland.

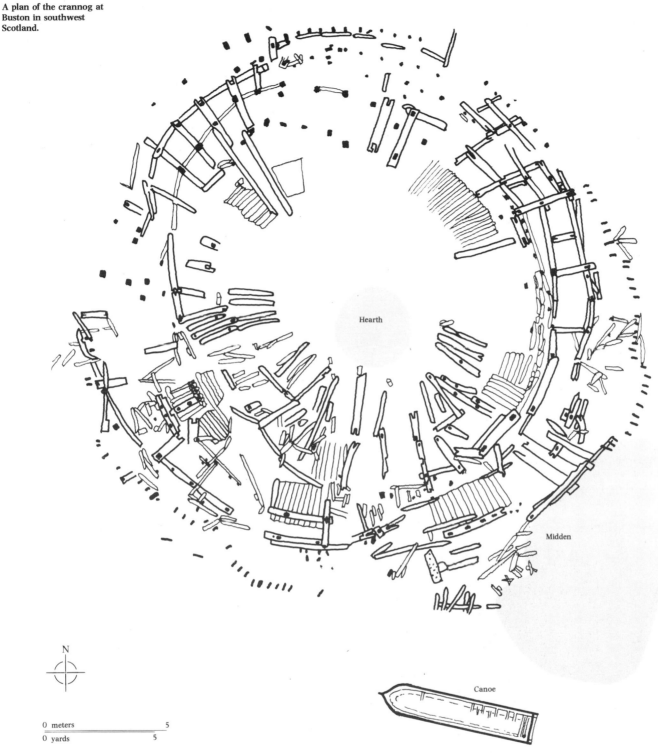

Hearth

Midden

Canoe

N

0 meters _____ 5
0 yards _____ 5

This one was of a well-developed type (p. 159), and seems unlikely to be among the earliest in Scotland. We thus have to consider the possibility of Bronze Age or indeed earlier crannogs. At the other end of the time scale, they were still being built on the threshold of the seventeenth century AD, and some were even occupied by fugitives in the 1745 rebellion.

Crannogs are thus more widespread and cover a greater time span than most people realize. They add an intriguing extra dimen-sion to the archaeology of settlements in Scotland. The cold, dark, peaty waters of the lochs have hidden them from past and present looters, and often preserved their contents from decay to a remarkable de-gree. As even the imperfect old reports sug-gest (and our current diving work confirms), these conditions give an excellent chance of survival to materials generally lost to excavators of land sites. This is so not only for large-scale wooden structures, but for small and fragile items. Along with nor-mally perishable artifacts of wood, leather, or wickerwork, one can hope to find food refuse and other organic clues to the economy of the settlement. What is more, midden deposits and other outfall from crannogs are sometimes sandwiched within layers of naturally accumulating lake muds. Study of the pollen these contain offers a chance of tying in the occupation phases of the crannog with the climatically and man-induced changes in the vegetation of the landscape around the loch.

The nature and construction of crannogs

The remains of crannogs vary enough to make it difficult to identify some of them by shape alone. Indeed, certain natural hummocks of glacial deposits are more regular in form than some crannogs. Furthermore, by no means all the artificial features on the beds of lochs represent ancient lake dwellings. For example, I was recently asked to help decide whether roughly circular deposits of stones discovered by sidescan sonar in Loch Ness might be crannogs, some other form of antiquity, or perhaps stone patterns formed by the freezing and thawing of the ground at the end of the last Ice Age. Diving showed that the features were artificial but not structural. Archival research suggests they probably represent spoil dumped from the hopper barges of the very early steam dredger *Prince Regent*, when the Scottish engineer Thomas Telford was cutting part of the Caledonian Canal, around 1820.

On first inspection, many crannogs seem just boulder mounds. But while woodwork at or above the surface has often rotted away, diving frequently discloses structural timberwork surviving under water. However, waterlogged trees sometimes accumulate around the bases of natural mounds, and in the initial stages (when he is surveying sites without disturbing them in any

foundations into soft lake beds and actual changes of water level, the internal compaction of these layers helps to account for instances where crannogs were heightened during habitation, as well as for the common submergence of their remains after they fell out of use.

So far there have been too few proper excavations to give us a picture of how crannog building evolved or varied in different regions. We do not yet know how far the builders used standardized techniques. Sometimes the timberwork seems to follow a gridiron pattern; sometimes it is radial; and the use of piling varies. It would be interesting to know whether the engineering skill demonstrated by some of the work (for example, the heavier pile driving) was common knowledge, or implies a specialized corps of crannog constructors. Certainly the actual technology employed is worth further study.

If natural foundations were available in suitable locations, people used them of course. Scotland's heavily glaciated landscape abounds in rock knobs, hillocks of boulder clay, and mounds of sand and gravel, so sites cover a spectrum from wholly natural to wholly artificial islets, with various degrees of addition and modification in between.

often a lobe suggesting a jetty foundation, or one of "crab's claw" shape indicating a canoe dock.

A number of dugout canoes have been found beside crannogs, and the positions of some islets suggest that access was always by boat. Causeways and what seem to be footings for wooden bridges lead to others inshore. Some of the causeways always seem to have lain below the surface, with traps for the unwary.

Because so many features of the crannogs are invisible from the surface, a great deal of underwater survey work is needed. Simple and rapid measurement techniques can produce valuable basic information. In the radial method shown here, distances are measured by tape, angles by compass or plastic sextant, and depths by sounding staff (with a hand clinometer for unsubmerged areas).

This kind of work is necessary to establish such fundamental points as whether there are regional variations in crannog sizes and shapes that may indicate differences between cultural groups or in the uses of the islands. Historical evidence and modern folk-life studies show that traditional societies may build islands for many reasons besides human occupation. Possibilities range from vermin-proof food stores, to predator-proof nesting sites for game birds; from kennels for hunting dogs, to purely decorative islets completing landscaped views from stately homes.

Even where surface finds such as querns (millstones) and midden material confirm that islands do represent dwelling sites, it is often still difficult to establish without excavation whether the larger crannogs were islands shared between several households, or single steadings with secure accommodation for the farmer's beasts as well as his family. Often indeed, we cannot be sure whether the crannog served as permanent dwelling, temporary refuge, or seasonal fishing and fowling station. The answers to many problems of use, construction, and dating must await a considerable program of excavations.

So far, very few digs indeed have been carried out to anything approaching modern standards. All of these have been restricted to sites exposed by drainage operations, and the use of diving techniques for controlled excavation below water level in Scottish lochs is only just beginning.

One of the most informative excavations yet published was that by C.M. Piggott at Milton Loch, about 14 kilometers (9mi) west of Dumfries in southwest Scotland (p. 156). As indicated, the island itself was built around the fifth century BC. But the excavator dated the house, here shown reconstructed, to the second century AD; this suggests that the use and reuse of individual islands, as well as the general practice of lake dwelling, was a long-term feature of the Scottish landscape.

The "radial" method of surveying a submerged crannog. One diver records the depth of features around the structure and their distance from a central point, while his colleague notes the bearing of the survey line at each reading.

way), the diver has to be careful not to be misled. The presence of driven piles or carpentered joints helps in positive identification.

These wooden elements seem characteristic of crannogs, despite their superficially stony appearance. Many appear to be composite structures in which dumped stones were controlled by heavy timberwork, and often bound by layers of brushwood packing. Along with subsidence of

The basic form of a crannog is commonly a low truncated cone, but where the structure stands on a reef of rock, say, this inevitably conditions its shape. Sometimes the builders exploited the layout of the natural material to provide not only a house platform but facilities such as a breakwater or canoe dock. Wholly artificial islands have a roundish outline from less than 10 meters (about 20ft) to well over 50 meters (160ft) across, but there is also

Right: An artist's impression of the crannog at Milton Loch, Scotland, whose remains have recently been excavated. The building has been cut away to show the design of the roof structure and the arrangement of the internal partitions.
Below: A view of the reconstruction of a crannog recently undertaken at Craggaunowen in County Clare, Ireland. An access bridge, defended gateway, and the roofs of two round houses can all be seen.

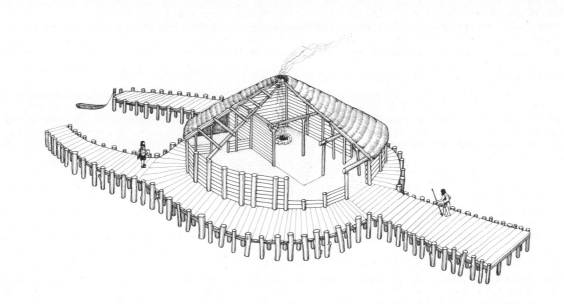

Lake dwelling in the landscape

Crannogs occur not only in all parts of Scotland but also in all types of lochs, from the largest to the very small and shallow. Some indeed seem to have been built in marshes rather than in open water (others that now stand in marsh were, however, built in lakes that have since silted up or been drained).

The practicalities of island building meant that people placed few crannogs in much more than 5 meters (16ft) of water. This fact greatly reduces the areas to be searched under water. But the levels of some lochs have been raised, and a few crannogs (including one partially excavated) now lie nearer the 20-meter (65-ft) mark. On steep sites the fallout of midden material and other debris may extend well below the level of the structure proper.

Distances offshore also vary. Some crannogs lie far out toward the middle of a loch, well protected from shore-based attack. Others, however, are so close to land (and often in such shallow water) that we must question how far defense actually figured in their siting. Castle moats are as narrow, but they are backed by strong stone walls, and these inshore crannogs show no sign of anything equivalent. If their purpose really was defensive, the enemies may have been the four-legged denizens of the forests, rather than archers who might put a fire-arrow in the thatch. Bears, wolverines, and wolves persisted into the Middle Ages in Scotland.

That defense against human adversaries was, however, a major consideration in the siting of many crannogs is suggested by the common preference for locations at the outermost edge of underwater shelves, just where shallows end and lake beds plunge into deep water. In other words, people often built their islands as far from shore as possible.

Another characteristic factor of siting appears to be the availability of cultivable land. This came out clearly in the Loch Awe survey. Toward the northeast end of the loch, there is a cluster of natural islands suitable for a compact lake village. But few of these were used, and at least 20 artificial islands were laboriously constructed at intervals over more than 40 kilometers (25mi) of the length of the loch. Their irregular distribution essentially appears to reflect sites combining farming potential onshore with suitable bottom conditions offshore for island construction. Thus, stretches with bald rocky slopes on land are crannog free, while sizable pockets of soil tend to have crannogs nearby, unless the offshore slope was too abrupt for island building.

The topography and soil availability reflect the glacial history of the area, long before its colonization by crannog builders. However, the early human geography of the region is at least as important as its physical geography, in determining the

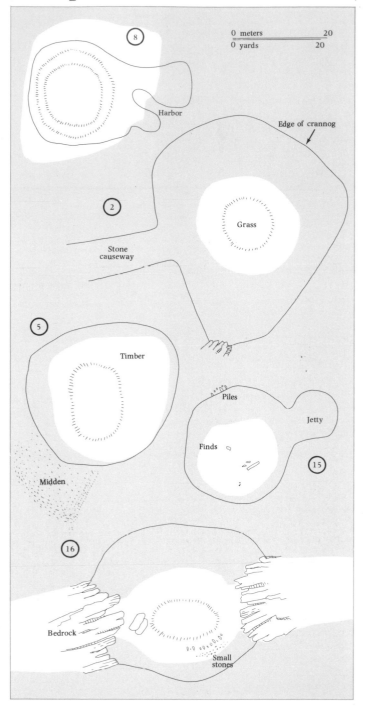

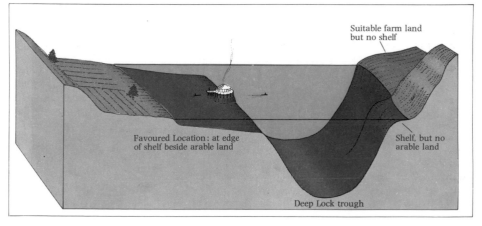

Plans of five crannogs in Loch Awe, numbered as on the map opposite. Note the range of ancilliary features, including a dock, a causeway, and a jetty. Crannog 16 has been constructed so as to take advantage of a natural ridge of rock. Below: A schematic section across a deep Scottish loch, showing how a crannog would be placed to take advantage of both a suitable shallow-water shelf and nearness to good farm land.

pattern of the crannogs in the landscape. For example, in some areas of Loch Awe there is no crannog in spite of a seemingly suitable submerged shelf partnering cultivable land. There, nearby remains and place-names point instead to the use of duns (forts) on shore, in the type of complementary pattern suggested on p. 156.

At Loch Awe we made an extensive survey, looking at many sites in relation to their landscape setting, instead of focusing intensively on the excavation of an individual crannog. A wider perspective of this kind emphasizes the way that the environments of archaeological sites are integrated and constantly developing dynamic systems.

For instance, this approach drew our attention to the way that wind-driven currents in the loch kept some sites swept clear of mud, and buried others deeply. The former are easy for divers to survey, quickly yielding information on shapes and superficial structures. The archaeologist finds buried crannogs initially less rewarding. However, the layers of deposits that have built up around them offer the chance of tracing the natural and man-generated changes that have gone on in the area around the loch during and after the occupation of the crannog.

The wider approach may indeed detect patterns with implications extending beyond archaeology. At Loch Awe, for instance, the height of the crannog platforms varies systematically along the length of the loch. Comparisons with present-day and historical island builders elsewhere suggest that the original height of living surfaces above water level represented a fine balance between two evils: the risk of being swamped, and the sheer labor of building higher. The present height variation along the loch may thus provide insights into natural processes ranging from local wave effects to possible long-term tilting of the loch trough by land movements related to glaciation (pp. 134–35). Crannogs departing noticeably from the overall height pattern raise questions of date or purpose that help us shape the next, more intensive, stage of investigation.

Thus, despite lively interest in Victorian and Edwardian times, the study of crannogs in Scotland is only just recommencing. Properly controlled underwater excavation is the key to many fundamental problems, but that is such a slow and expensive process that it will be a long time before a significant variety of sites can be tackled. Meantime, divers can learn much working with basic survey techniques.

When the sheer numbers of the sites in the lochs and their especially favorable conditions of preservation are taken into account, we need have little doubt that the crannogs have still much to add to our picture of the archaeology and early geography of Scotland.

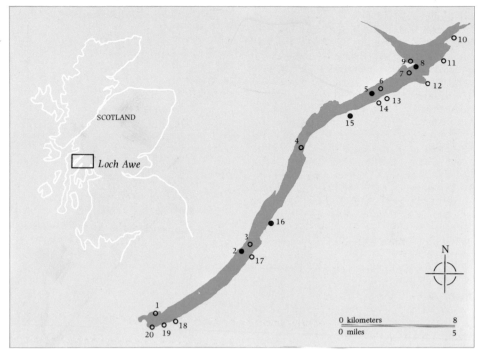

Above: Loch Awe, in western Scotland, showing the distribution of all the crannogs discovered during the systematic survey.
Right: A graph showing the highest and lowest points on each of the Loch Awe crannogs, arranged in ascending order of their highest points. The fact that this order closely mirrors their distribution along the loch indicates the steady uplift of the northeastern end during the past 2000 years, following the retreat of the ice caps.

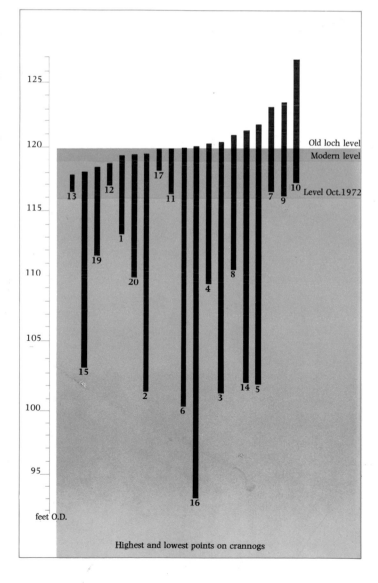

Highest and lowest points on crannogs

161

Cities under the Mediterranean

The Mediterranean is a sea uniquely rich in old submerged, but well-preserved ruins. Hundreds represent the remains of ancient Roman harbors, coastal towns, and villages. Some sites reflect all archaeological periods of the last 5,000 years, and a few sites are even older. To begin our tour of this drowned land, let us first see why so many coastal centers were built, then how they sank, and why their remains survived so well beneath this sea.

There were good reasons why the ancients built so profusely on Mediterranean shores. With the nearby Red Sea and Arabian Gulf, the eastern Mediterranean emerged as one of the chief cradles of seafaring commerce when Neolithic village communities evolved into trading Bronze Age powers about 3000 BC. When the Bronze Age began, the Mediterranean already abounded in anchorages produced by climatic change over the previous 15,000 years or so. During the late Ice Age, when the sea level lay as much as 100 meters (330ft) lower than now and the climate was locally wetter, rivers bordering the Mediterranean had cut deep valleys across what is now the continental shelf. As the sea rose to its present level its waters invaded countless valleys and inlets. Thus, at the beginning of the Bronze Age, every coast was studded with perfect natural harbors.

On much of the Mediterranean coast this sailors' heaven did not last long. As sea levels stabilized, the sea's erosive force and sediments supplied by the rivers and winds between them began to straighten coastlines. The process happened faster to a gently shelving coast with small indentations than to a steep, deeply indented one.

Mediterranean coasts are very unequal in these respects. The southern and eastern shores are the straightest and have the fewest inshore and offshore islands. They also lack big rivers except for the Nile. But they do have hundreds of intermittent streams bringing down plenty of sediment, especially sand from the Sahara and other deserts. The result is that, today, there are few good harbors from Tangier to Beirut.

The northern Mediterranean shore, from Gibraltar to Turkey, varies from stretch to stretch. In general, though, it is steeper and more deeply indented than the southern and eastern shore. Many sizable rivers of southern Europe and Asia Minor enter the sea along this coast. But the continental shelf is so narrow that most sediments washed in by these rivers plunge into deep water, or build only small deltas. Unlike the low southern coasts, the northern coasts have changed little since Bronze Age times, and still retain deep bays, steep headlands, and numerous islands. In many coastal sites local erosion or silting has been too slight to alter the topography much. The major exceptions are on the Rhône, Po, and Menderes deltas, where the coastline has advanced many kilometers in the last few thousand years.

These coastline changes themselves are not enough to explain how scores of Bronze Age and later sites became drowned. By the beginning of the Bronze Age the rise in sea level that had followed the end of the last Ice Age glaciation had just about stopped, and the level has fluctuated little since then (pp. 132–37). Indeed, average Mediterranean sea level relative to coastal land has varied by no more than plus or minus half a meter (1½ft) in the last 5,000 years.

But this is only the general picture. Some parts of the coast have been sharply uplifted and others depressed. Whole harbors have collapsed almost intact into the water in Italy, Greece, Turkey, and Cyprus. General processes of submergence are dealt with on pages 132–37; but here we must take a brief look at the forces that make much of the Mediterranean coast so unstable – the same forces indeed that help to give the north and south coasts their different characters. These forces are the massive earth movements explained by the theory of plate tectonics.

This theory holds that Africa, together with part of the floor of the Mediterranean, is moving north toward Europe at about 2.5 centimeters (1in) a year. Arabia and Turkey are smaller continental fragments that are moving in other directions. Over many million years, Corsica, Sardinia, and Italy have rotated counterclockwise and swung away from France, opening up the Tyrrhenian Sea and narrowing the Adriatic. At the same time, the eastern floor of the Mediterranean has been compressed and foreshortened.

Even in the short span of time since civilization began, earth movements have sparked off volcanic eruptions and also earthquakes that have moved some stretches of coast up, down, or both. As you would expect, the regions of fastest relative plate movements are the regions where earthquakes happen most often. Thus the coasts of Algeria, Italy, Greece, the Aegean, Cyprus, Lebanon, and Israel are much more unstable than others. Research has shown that areas of downward movement are quite widespread, with subsidence of 1–2 meters (3–6ft) in 2,000 years. Areas of uplift have proved to be much more restricted, although movement here may be more rapid: as much as 10 meters (33ft) in 2,000 years. Thus the actual number of submerged cities is far greater than the number of uplifted cities. When you add to the number of cities submerged by earthquakes those submerged by the subsidence of major deltas, and those where harbor remains are under water because they were built there, it becomes clear why the Mediterranean has such a large tally of subsea ruins.

What still needs explaining is why so many structures are so well preserved. In many parts of the world you would not expect a broken stone wall in shallow water to remain recognizable after a few years, let alone after 2,000. However, the Mediterranean is almost like an embalming fluid for ancient harbors. With a few exceptions there is relatively little rainfall and river runoff to cover ruins with sediments; there is no reef-building coral to encrust the ruins; seaweeds seldom grow densely enough to conceal them; and the tidal range is too small to set up erosive tidal currents or to expose ruins to foreshore looting. Although the weather is rougher than many northerners, suppose, storms rarely unleash waves large enough to smash stone buildings made without mortar or cement. Finally, earth movements in this area have drowned hundreds of coastal towns up to 5 meters (16ft) deep – deep enough to escape the force of most storm waves.

Key
Coastline:
Submergence
Uplift
Stable
Plate boundaries
Areas of maximum convergence and subduction
General movement of plate boundaries
Active volcano
Main delta

Above, right: Map of the Mediterranean basin, showing the main geological fault-lines, and the directions in which the various blocks of the earth's crust are moving.
Right: The six main types of natural anchorage identified by geographers. Upper left: a natural embayment, as seen at Sydney, and San Francisco. Upper center: a river estuary, as seen at London, and New York. Upper right: shelter behind an offshore island, as used by early mariners (see pp 166-67). Lower left: bays behind a headland, as used at the Piraeus, and Syracuse. Lower center: shelter in the lee of a promontory; this is effective only during certain wind directions, and so permanent ports do not develop. Lower right: a delta, as seen at Marseilles, New Orleans, and Cairo.

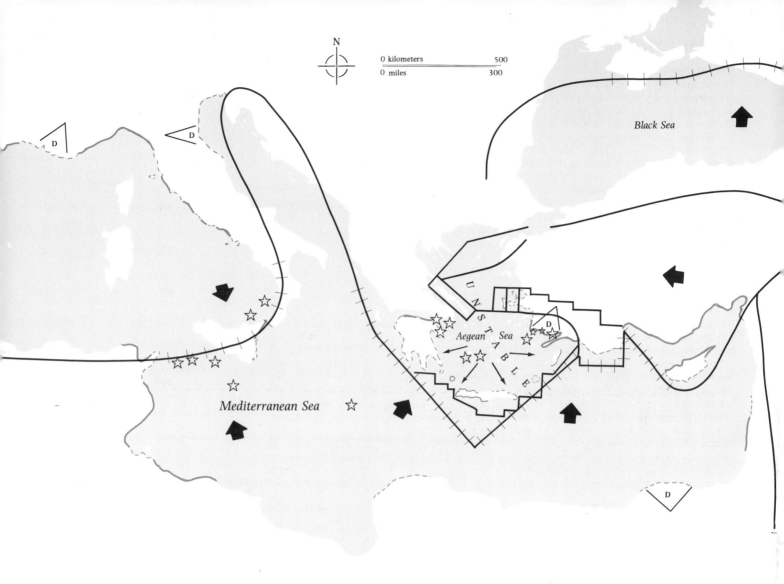
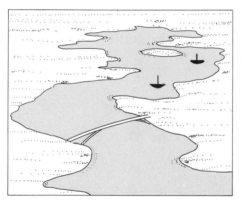
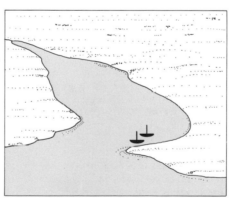
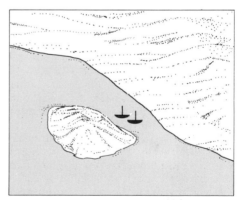
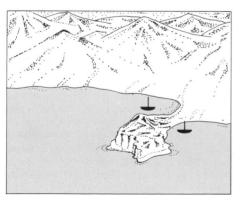
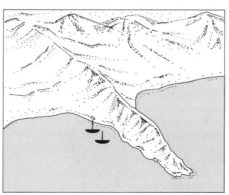
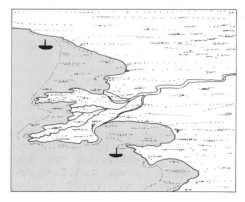

163

A Bronze Age puzzle

The tiny rocky island of Pavlo Petri lies at the northern end of the sandy bay of Vatika in the extreme southeast of mainland Greece. A Bronze Age ship sailing from Crete to mainland Greece would have navigated by line of sight to the islands of Antikythera and Kythera. There she would have hugged the shore to the northern end of the island, before cutting across a strait into the Bay of Vatika. Whichever way she went the ship would then have had to round a headland — either Onugnathos (in order to sail to the fertile lands in the Gulf of Lakonia) or Malea (in order to sail up the southeast mainland coast). For ships on either trip the Bay of Vatika afforded valuable shelter.

In 1967 I discovered Bronze Age remains on the sea floor between the island of Pavlo Petri and the mainland. Next year these were surveyed in great detail by a team of divers from Cambridge University. The oldest remains, dating from before 2000 BC, proved to lie on the island itself; most of the site beneath the sea was of Mycenean Age (1500–1000 BC). Much of its uncemented stone walls remained surprisingly intact. Presumably the town had been

Above: The Aegean Sea, showing the Bronze Age sites mentioned on these pages.
Far left: A line of curbstones on the seabed at Pavlo Petri, clearly marking the course of a street.
Left: A cist-grave on the seabed at Pavlo Petri.
Opposite: A plan of the submerged Mycenean settlement at Pavlo Petri on the southeastern tip of Greece. The main street of the village can be seen running parallel to the coast, with several lanes at right angles to it.

covered by earth and sand after people abandoned it during submergence, and then sank gradually beneath the sea. Waves had merely winnowed away the sand, revealing the patterns of walls, streets, houses, and graves on the sea floor.

An exhaustive search of the underwater site revealed no buildings of any kind more than 3 meters (10ft) down. Thus the ancient shoreline must have been 3–4 meters (10–13ft) below present sea level. Two main streets were mapped, and 15 complete house foundations, each typically revealing

5–10 nearly rectangular rooms. The search also revealed 37 stone, box-like tombs known as cist graves. A major goal of the 1968 survey was to discover the harbor and dockside. It is obvious that the ships would have gained the best shelter in the bay enclosed by Pavlo Petri and the ridge that then connected it to the mainland, but no special buildings of any kind were found. The houses and streets just dwindle away at the ancient waterline.

This illustrates one of the big puzzles of underwater archaeology in the Mediterra-

nean. By 2000 BC many river mouths and small bays had silted up; thus you would expect that by then people had learned to construct artificial harbors. By 1000 BC they surely must have done so. Yet finds of Bronze Age artificial harbors are as scarce as hen's teeth. Archaeologists have mapped or excavated many Bronze Age sites on the coasts of mainland Greece, the Aegean islands, Crete, southern Turkey, Cyprus, Lebanon, Syria, and Israel, but few show signs of man-made harbor structures. Pavlo Petri and nearby Asopos, Mochlos in eastern

Crete, and Aghios Kosmas (near Athens Airport) are among sites with Bronze Age remains now under water. But most of these relics are those of buildings originally erected on land, albeit near or on the beach. The exceptions are some rock-cut features or sculpted reefs that we shall come to in the next two pages.

Let us look now more closely at the puzzle posed by the lack of Bronze Age harbors in what was plainly a flourishing maritime world. Pottery found at coastal sites all around the eastern Mediterranean testifies to active trading between places in what are now Greece, Crete, Turkey, Syria, Lebanon, Israel, and Egypt. The fabulous ship frescoes from Akrotiri on the Aegean island of Thira show sophisticated ships and two coastal towns with houses of several stories. Yet a close examination of the frescoes shows no special waterline features that could indicate harbor works.

To my knowledge, divers or snorkelers have swum and searched around more than a dozen Bronze Age sites in the eastern Mediterranean without producing a single item suggestive of an artificial harbor. In several cases, parts of town walls or pieces of pottery were found in the water. Rarely, there were slim hints of something more: Neve Yam, in Israel, has submerged walls dating from 4500 BC. At Amnisos in Crete a very solid wall extends just below the water but stops abruptly in the surf line, suggesting perhaps a jetty for small boats. The landward side of Tel Nami, a small headland on the coast of Israel, seems to have been built up with a massive wall, but that could have been as much a city defense as a dockside, and there are no signs of artificial breakwaters.

Scholars have often argued that boats were simply dragged up on the beach. This makes sense for military vessels with large crews and oarsmen, especially since a skilled strategic commander would tend to exploit natural shores rather than main ports. But a crew of 3–5 men could scarcely have dragged a heavily laden commercial vessel onto a beach. They could have moored such a ship to the shore with a stern anchor to hold her secure and prevent broaching, but that would have made unloading a cargo a tiresome job of running down a steep gangplank from the bow, or heaving loads onto donkeys, carts, or men standing in the water. Surely the major entrepôts would have had jetties of wood or stone, and breakwaters to guarantee calm water. Wooden jetties – if they existed – would have required frequent rebuilding, and we can hardly expect any traces of such structures to have survived. Slightly more solid jetties of wooden palisades filled with stones would also have left little trace, since the piles of stones would have spread out and become almost indistinguishable from natural rocks. However, Asine near Nauplion in Greece has a ridge of stones suggestive of such a structure.

Thus we are forced to conclude that the Bronze Age mariners of the Aegean, Cyprus, and Israel used headlands, inshore islands, river mouths, and bays more or less as nature had shaped them. Diving investigations have proved almost beyond doubt that even most towns that were certainly trading centers possessed neither man-made harbor basins nor breakwaters. In places, though, a revolutionary change was about to begin, as we shall now see.

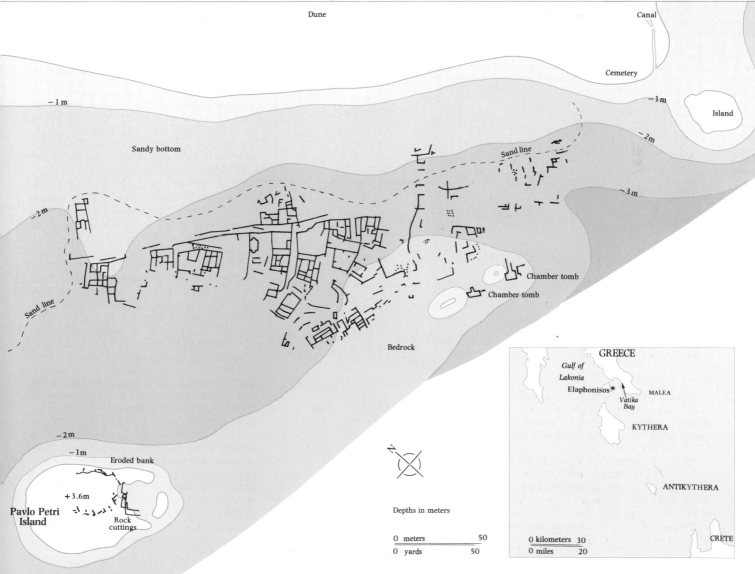

Dune

Canal

Cemetery

Island

−1m

−1m

−2m

Sandy bottom

Sand line

−3 m

−2 m

Chamber tomb

Chamber tomb

Sand line

Bedrock

GREECE

Gulf of Lakonia

Elaphonisos*

MALEA

Vatika Bay

KYTHERA

ANTIKYTHERA

CRETE

−2 m

−1 m

Eroded bank

+3.6m

Pavlo Petri Island

Rock cuttings

Depths in meters

0 meters 50

0 yards 50

0 kilometers 30

0 miles 20

Gigantic harbors in the Levant

The Mediterranean's early sailors used natural anchorages so good that these needed no embellishment. Then, on eastern coasts, changed conditions led to the first artificial harbor works.

We have seen that the inlets used by early Bronze Age shipping largely silted up in the next 2,000 years. This was particularly true on the eastern Mediterranean, or Levantine, coast from the mouth of the Orontes in southern Turkey to the mouth of the Nile in Egypt. This shoreline has been smoothed into an immense curve, with only small kinks, like the Bay of Haifa. There are now no good natural harbors on the whole of this 800-kilometer (500-mi) stretch. The Bronze Age sailors of this coast suffered the unpleasant experience of finding that their ships were gradually and remorselessly excluded from river after river, bay after bay, as sand and mud straightened out the shore. But, meanwhile, shipwrights were building progressively larger vessels – too big to use what creeks survived.

It is not surprising, then, that Phoenician and Egyptian seafarers developed a new approach to sheltering and protecting their ships. In this they were helped by natural offshore sandstone formations. These had their origins in long lines of enormous sand dunes that formed on the ancient sea coast, beyond and below the present position of

the shore. In time calcium carbonate and other minerals derived from groundwater cemented the sand particles together to form a soft kind of sandstone. Streams and small rivers cut their way through the hardened dune ridges, and swamps formed between them. The ridges are not exactly parallel to each other, or to the shore, since they are influenced by the underlying topography and neighboring mountain ranges. Consequently the form of the modern shore and shallow water zone largely depend on the angle at which the sandstone ridges meet the waterline.

In places the ridges form low, continuous hills facing the sea. Elsewhere they jut out as stubby wave-girt peninsulas. Yet other ridges form offshore reefs and islets parallel to the main line of the coast. Some islets are quite large. Arwad, in the north is hundreds of meters long. With Tyre, near the center of the Levantine coast, and Pharos, near Alexandria, Arwad was one of three Levantine islands inhabited in Bronze Age times. Much of what we know about them comes from the collective work of three archaeologists: Antoine Poidebard and Gaston Jondet, active before World War II, and Honor Frost, working in the 1960s. Dating the ancient structures found on and around the islands is difficult, but no one disputes that such structures exist and are old.

Throughout the early Bronze Age sailors must have come to learn a lot about these dangerous offshore ridges and reefs. For instance, in winter storms they would have seen the long line of white breakers about 1 kilometer (0.6mi) offshore – where the

Below: The eastern Mediterranean, showing the Levantine harbors mentioned in the text.
Below, left: A detailed map of some of the submerged masonry discovered off the island of Arwad.

open sea broke over the submerged reefs. Surprised by a storm, or awaiting a favorable wind, early ships with a shallow draft must have sheltered often behind these reefs and small islands. Then, as ships were gradually forced from the coastal rivers, the sailors must have realized that a little improvement could have turned at least some reefs into havens. We do not know just when this happened. Certainly Arwad was inhabited by 1500 BC. It is reasonable to guess that sailors were increasingly adapting reefs to their needs in the next 500 years. How was it done?

The line of reefs and islets from Arwad to nearby Machroud (both off what is now Syria) shows how. At Arwad, air and underwater surveys reveal that the landward side of the island was quarried and flattened to make a quay, while much of the stone removed by this process went to build a masonry wall on the seaward side. This meant that people could build and quarry storm-proof houses and storerooms on the island. Just how durably they built we may judge from mooring stones cut from solid rock, and sea walls recessed into grooves cut in the bedrock so that the impact of waves would not shift them. Parts of the quays and some masonry courses now are under water, and it seems that the island has sunk at least 1–2 meters (about 3–6ft).

At Machroud, 3 kilometers (2mi) south of Arwad, the dry area suitable for construction is now only 60 meters (200ft) across, but underwater mapping suggests

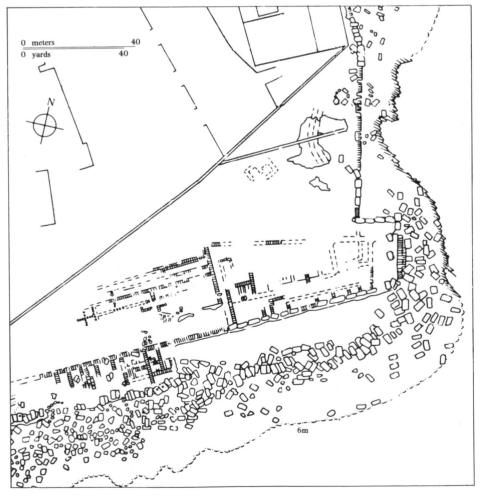

Left: An aerial photograph of Arwad, viewed from the nearby mainland.
Below: An overall map of the ancient harbor installations at Sidon, and a detailed map of the offshore island. Although the bedrock of the island has been extensively cut and refashioned to provide quays and storehouses, this has not impaired the value of the site as a safe anchorage.

never inhabited. The small island known as Pigeon off Magaan Mikhael has some cuttings and stone storage tanks, but no signs of continuous habitation.

Finally, at Pharos, on the seaward side of Alexandria in Egypt, a great submerged protoharbor was reported by Gaston Jondet in 1916. Jondet claimed to have found artificial harbor works along the whole of the reef that runs west for more than 2 kilometers (2.5mi) from Ras al Tin to Abu Bakr. Archaeologists treated his claim with cautious skepticism, and it remains unverified. In view of Honor Frost's more recent discoveries along the Syrian coast the claim is at least plausible.

Some people find it unbelievable that structures as big as these were truly early harbor works. But several factors point to this. First, the linear sandstone reefs off the

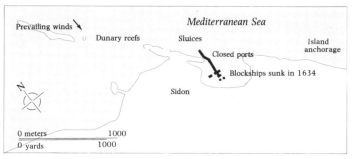

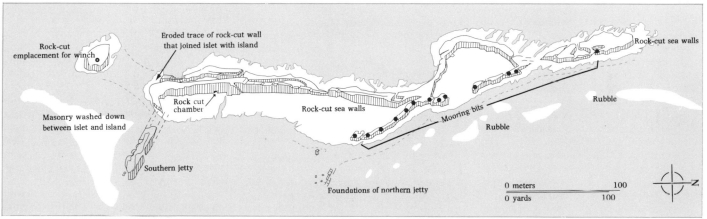

that the island has sunk by 6 meters (20ft). Thus the original usable area would have been larger, and quarries and buildings would have stood well clear of the water. Habbes, Abou Ali, and Nussonie – the three islets between Machroud and Arwad – all show signs of quarrying. Assuming that all this reef was 2–5 meters (6–16ft) higher in the middle of the Bronze Age, we can see that systematic quarrying and construction on the outer edge would have provided an enormous sheltered basin between the reef and the mainland, where there are two Bronze Age towns, Amrit and Tabbat Al-Hammam (p. 168).

At Sidon (now in Lebanon) part of the port was formed by a segment of sandstone ridge projecting from the mainland, and part by reinforcing the natural continuation

of the ridge 1 kilometer (0.6mi) to the north. At Tyre, farther south, the main town was built on a reef-island about 700 meters (2,300ft) across, and 500 meters (1,600ft) from the shore. Submerged reefs extending several kilometers to the south seem to have been reinforced to provide shelter for vessels.

As you continue south the islands get smaller and fewer, but all have been intensively worked in a standard manner: the landward side removed, and the seaward side left as a rampart. The Naohlieli-Sigorion group on the Lebanon-Israel border, and the Achzib group farther south, are very similar in this respect. Today, the quarrying is submerged by only about 1 meter (about 3ft), and as the islands are entirely swamped during winter storms, it seems they were

Levantine coast would have suggested useful shapes made still more useful by reinforcement. Second, the reefs' linearity, and the deep water between them and the mainland, would not have suggested the construction of a round or square enclosed harbor basin. Third, in order to afford good shelter, a linear barrier would have had to be long, otherwise incoming waves would have "bent in" from the ends and met behind the barrier, creating a choppy sea. The reef protoharbors must have served a valuable purpose. But the knowledge won in building them and that already gained from making docks and quays on river banks, soon led to the development of true artificial sea harbors. When this happened, the gigantic protoharbors became as extinct as the *Brontosaurus*.

The first true harbors

Just opposite the Syrian reef-island of Machroud lies the tell (mound) of Tabbat Al-Hamman. In 1940 the American archaeologist Robert Braidwood published a survey of the tell and the neighboring shoreline. This showed that people had lived in the area continuously from the dawn of the Bronze Age to the Byzantine period. The beach at Tabbat Al-Hammam revealed a jetty or breakwater made of massive masonry blocks each about as long as a man. The structure is just over 200 meters (650ft) long and about 15 meters (50ft) wide, and its outer end lies in more than 4 meters (13ft) of water. Correlation with the tell dates it to the ninth century BC. As far as we know, this early Iron Age structure is the world's first artificial freestanding sea breakwater, as opposed to the reinforced reefs of the previous millenium.

The breakwater builders at Tabbat Al-Hammam used dressed blocks, but in the deeper and better protected bays of the Aegean and other northern coasts, people found they could make breakwaters by simply piling irregular rubble blocks into the sea. The first known breakwater of this type is at the Aegean island of Delos; old writings help to prove that it was built in the eighth century BC. During the seventh and fifth centuries BC such breakwaters went up all over the Greek world, which included southern Italy, eastern Sicily, southern France, the Black Sea coast, Aegean Asia Minor, most of Cyprus, and the Cyrenaic coast of North Africa.

Besides the one at Delos, fine submerged rubble breakwaters have been mapped by divers at Salamis in Cyprus; Iasos and Cnidos in Asia Minor; Apollonia and Thapsus in North Africa; Syracuse in Sicily, Piraeus in Greece, Vurgunda on the island of Karpathos. Such breakwaters also form a substantial part of hundreds of other harbors of Greek and Roman date. Apart from the south-coast ports of Apollonia and Thapsus, which we shall look at later, these are all northern Mediterranean ports and of bay-headland type. This type gets its name from the type of site selected as ideal — a so-called anvil headland, which afforded two fine sheltered harbors: one on each side of the city.

Bay-headland ports featured more or less steep fortifiable headlands and promontories, flanked by breakwaters, often continuous with the city walls and designed to narrow the entrances of one or more relatively deep bays. The breakwater builders tipped rubble into water as much as 10–15 meters (33–50ft) deep, and used blocks of several cubic meters, weighing up to 50 or even 100 tons. Quarries supplying the stone usually lay close to the harbor, so there was no problem of long-distance transportation.

The most sophisticated complex of this type was Piraeus near Athens. Before this was built, Athenians had beached their ships at Phaleron, the nearest point on the coast

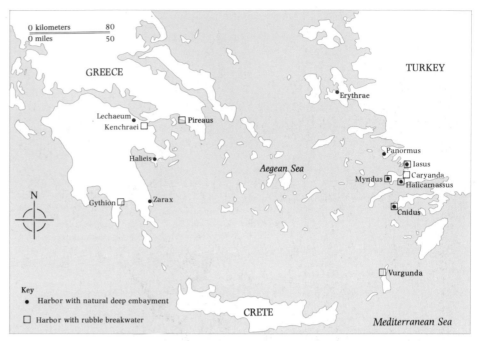

to the city. But in 493 BC they started fortifying the bays on the peninsula of Piraeus. Over the next 50 years they constructed three harbor basins. Each was protected by rubble breakwaters, crowned with masonry walls, roads, and defensive towers. Iron clamps bound the masonry blocks together. Under seaborne attack, defenders could shut out enemy ships by closing the basin entrances with booms or chains. Finally, the whole complex of harbors was connected directly to Athens by defensive walls 8 kilometers (5mi) long.

Within the harbors of Piraeus stood 372 ship sheds with slipways: sloping ramps up which the sailors dragged their trireme warships for storage. Diving and paddling have revealed traces of old slipways and ship sheds at 12 coastal cities elsewhere, but nothing to match the reported complex at Piraeus. Close to each of its slipways stood a storage shed to take a ship's oars, masts, sails, and military equipment; and nearby arsenals held reserve stores for the whole fleet. Unfortunately, later building obscures the slipways at Piraeus, and the only archaeological evidence for them was a glimpse in 1885 when a brief survey was made during building operations. However, we can judge their size and form from the fact that the larger slipways and ship sheds around the Mediterranean seem to have been more or less standardized at 5.5–6.6 meters (18–21ft 8in) wide and 38–47 meters (125–154ft) long. Gradients were 4–12 degrees, sometimes with a central runner or groove for the keel of the ship, and the slipways were roofed to shelter vessels and the craftsmen working on them.

Old Piraeus has been completely built over by a mushrooming modern city and its old harbor basins are modified for big modern craft. Diving archaeologists now have little chance of discovering how its

Above: The Aegean, showing some of the earliest harbors in the area. Places where natural havens were used are distinguished from those where artificial breakwaters were required from the start; in some instances, naturally favoured sites were further improved by the construction of breakwaters. Right: An aerial photograph of part of the Piraeus harbor complex. The circular Zea harbor lies in the foreground, with the head of the Kantharos harbor beyond. The map below shows the full range of natural anchorages available to ancient Athens, together with the fortifications which linked them with the city itself.

slipways, breakwaters, and harbor defenses were constructed. Our knowledge almost all derives from surviving literary descriptions.

This is not true of Syracuse in Sicily. Modern Syracuse is smaller than its classical predecessor. In 404 BC the dictator Dionysius I ordered the construction of a harbor in the bay north of the inshore island of Ortygia, which was joined to the mainland by a sand spit. The bay is about 700 meters (2,300ft) wide, and most of it is only 5–10 meters (16–33ft) deep. However, a sinuous chasm up to 30 meters (100ft) deep winds its way in through the center of the bay. In 1959, teams of divers found that two submerged rubble breakwaters with embedded pottery fragments extended to the brink of the central trough. The outer foundations stood in more than 10 meters (33ft) of water, and beyond each breakwater a mass of loose building blocks, tiles, marble slabs, and carved blocks had tumbled into the trough. There had obviously been a substantial tower on the end of each breakwater.

The southern harbor at Syracuse was too large to be protected by an artificial breakwater, but provided a perfect shelter for commercial vessels waiting to enter the docks and loading bays of the port proper. This combination of one small defended harbor with a second, larger, and undefended basin is the classic pattern. At

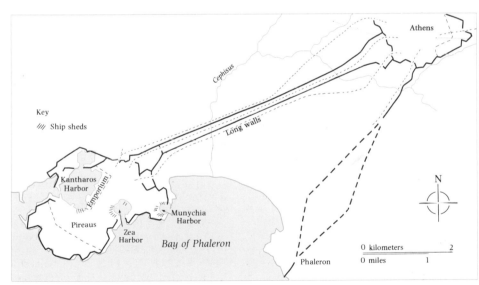

Cnidos in Asia Minor the basin for warships appears to have been shallow and rectangular, while the commercial basin to the south was protected by a rubble breakwater built into very deep water indeed. At both Cnidos and Syracuse the low sandy isthmus joining the headland to the mainland was cut to provide a connecting canal between the two basins.

Building a breakwater from rubble, as the ancient Greeks did, need not be a crude and unsophisticated way of making a wall to withstand wave action. Indeed, rubble breakwaters are the commonest sea defenses built by modern contractors. The stones on the outside, near the waterline, bear the brunt of wave attack, and the fact that there are holes between them, and that the stones can move a bit, helps to dissipate wave energy without sharp impacts or shocks. The lower part of the breakwater and the main core can be built of fairly small stones, while the outer face at the waterline must be made of large blocks. There is every indication that the classical engineers were well aware of this, and used their materials as economically as possible. Provided that the whole mound of stone is stable, road, walls, and towers can be built on top if set back from the seaward slope.

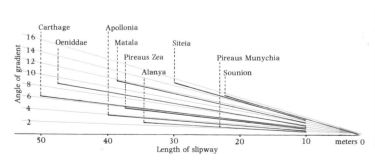

Left: A diagram comparing the lengths and angles of slope of the various ancient warship slipways discovered in recent times around the eastern and central Mediterranean. Considerations of local topography, and of the size of vessel in service, will have been the principle determinants of the various specifications.

169

The Carthaginians excavate their harbors

While the Greeks planted colonies largely on the northern Mediterranean shores, their Phoenician rivals were building in North Africa, western Sicily, Spain, and parts of Sardinia. Sailing westward from bases in the Levant, Phoenicians beat Greeks in the race for Spain's valuable supply of tin. The direct route to Spain lay between Sicily and what is now northeast Tunisia, then along the coast of what is now Algeria. The Phoenician colonies of Carthage, Utica, and Ruscinona (south of the Sicily Channel) and Motya (to the north) made sure that control of that vital section of the route stayed firmly in Phoenician hands. Founded in 814 BC, Carthage soon came to dominate the western Mediterranean. Like their Phoenician forebears, the Punic (Carthaginian) peoples were renowned for their skilled seamanship, canny trading, and military efficiency, sometimes associated with piracy. This makes it especially interesting to see how harbors and harbor technology helped to support the Carthaginians' seaborne success.

We saw earlier that there were few good natural harbors on the North African coast. Those of Carthage itself were probably entirely man-made. The port stood on a large anvil-shaped headland about 5 kilometers (3mi) across — a shape since made unrecognizable by sediment dumped by the Medjerda River. This has thrust the shoreline west of the city forward by nearly 10 kilometers (6mi). The sheer size of the headland may have dissuaded Carthaginian engineers from making harbors on each side, though they did wall off the isthmus to protect the city against land-based attack.

The harbors of Carthage were not in fact built out into the sea, but dug back into the land. This kind of harbor is called a cothon, and Carthaginians were its chief and maybe only exponents. They built a large cothon at Mahdia, south of Carthage; a small one at Motya, in Sicily; and an even smaller one, just a dock really, at Monastir, near Mahdia. These three and the harbors at Carthage are the only known cothons.

Where did cothon-building come from, and why was it used? Clues lie in the Near East. Besides its reinforced reefs, Bronze Age Tyre may have had a closed harbor next to the city and inside its defenses. A stronger hint of cothon evolution comes from Jezirat Fara'un in the north of the Gulf of Eilat (Israel). This island has an Iron Age harbor, possibly of Bronze Age origin. It is a basin totally enclosed within the island. People made the basin partly by excavation, and partly by building up the seaward edge of a natural depression. Another harbor-building tradition pointing toward the cothon could be the large basins dug into the banks of the Nile as berths where ships could load and unload away from the river current and passing traffic.

Given the Phoenicians' and Carthaginians' ambitions in trade and warfare, it seems that the Carthaginians adapted the concept of the harbor within the city's defenses, and took it to the logical conclusion of digging right back from the coast. This meant that no attacker could try to capture the harbor before attacking the city. Naval security was complete.

Archaeologists have excavated two harbors at Carthage. One was rectangular and about 500×300 meters (1,640×980ft). The other was circular and 330 meters (1,080ft) across, with a central island about 120 meters (390ft) in diameter. The harbors provided space for 200 warships, and their slipways, ship sheds, ships' stores and military stores. In the 1970s the British archaeologist Henry Hurst supervised exploration of the harbor area, and groups of divers led by Bob Yorke and David Davidson, British marine archaeologists, have conducted in-tensive surveys in the shallow muddy water.

Carthage was destroyed by the Romans in 146 BC so ferociously that no one can be sure of the full function and form of the harbor areas. But aerial photographs have clearly shown submerged structures in the open sea outside the enclosed basins. Also, work in the circular basin and on the island has disproved the notion that the slipways had been cut from stone and laid out like the spokes of a wheel. We now know that the island slipways extended, herringbone fashion, in two parallel rows from a central backbone. Arranged radially, the slipways would have had to taper almost to a point, leaving no room for ships' prows. The average length of the slipways is 50 meters (164ft). Width ranges from 5–7 meters (16–23ft) and the gradient is 6.5 degrees.

Above: A view across the cothon at Motya in Sicily. Left: Surveying in progress within the cothon at Mahdia in southern Tunisia. This is the smallest cothon known, and is now partially silted up.

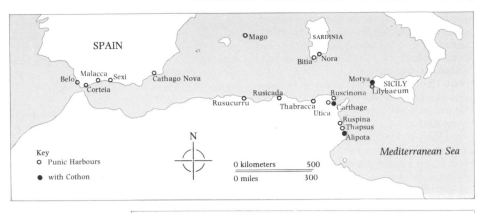

The beds of the slips seem to have been lined with heavy timber, while masonry pillars probably held up a wooden roof.

Divers pumping mud from the circular basin have revealed a series of pier foundations. These seem to have supported a bridge or causeway joining the island to the shore. Their level suggests that the city has sunk about 1.5 meters (5ft) since Roman times. In the open sea, Yorke, Davidson, and John Little (another archaeologist from Britain) have mapped a complex pattern of moles and breakwaters, some of shuttered concrete, some of loose rubble blocks. The concrete structures are probably Roman, but those made of rubble could conceivably be Carthaginian. These finds suggest that the entrance to the rectangular cothon basin probably lay just inside the southern entrance to the outer harbor, in the shelter of the southeast mole.

The cothon at Mahdia is easier to understand than those at Carthage. It is a simple rectangle, 147×73 meters (482×240ft) and cut from solid rock. From near one corner a short straight channel leads out into the sea. Along the sides, lumps of stone were left projecting from the quays as mooring bollards. This superbly simple but effective harbor is now partly blocked by sand, but fishing boats still use it.

About 40 ancient ports stand on the North African coast between the Strait of Gibraltar and the Tunisian border with Libya. Most would have been of Punic foundation, although the submerged remains found today are mainly Roman. Divers have discovered plenty of rubble moles and breakwaters, but no cothons. It seems that the cothon experiment involved only Carthage and the area around. Much later, Rome's vast Trajan harbor and part of the Claudian harbor were dug out of the alluvial delta of the Tiber (p. 172). But these were large open basins, quite separate from the Carthaginian tradition of closed military ports. Thus, for all its planned impregnability, the cothon started no trend.

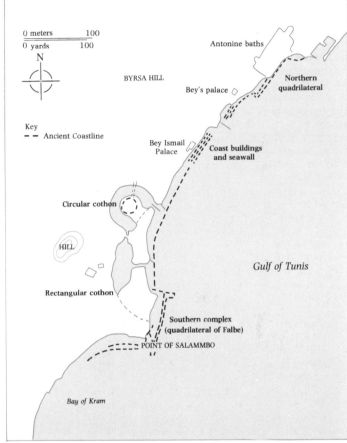

Below, left: The situation of the peninsula on which the Punic city of Carthage stood has changed since classical times because the bay to the north has silted up. But within the city, it is still possible to identify the two enclosed harbors, together with various maritime structures that are now submerged (right). The view across the round cothon (below) shows how shallow it has become, and how the surroundings have been built over in recent years.
Top: The western Mediterranean, showing the principal Punic cities, all of which lay on the coast.

Technical advances under the Romans

Between 100 BC and AD 100 the Romans refurbished and expanded most Mediterranean harbor constructions of previous periods, and founded many new harbors on previously inaccessible coasts. This engineering and architectural achievement was so complete that almost every old harbor that divers try to survey is dominated by Roman constructions. Earlier remains have to be searched for under the relatively much larger Roman structures; newer ones are usually feeble adaptations or modifications of Roman grandeur.

Most Roman harbors featured large rubble breakwaters that differed from their predecessors only in scale. However, there were also a number of major technical innovations. These included shuttered concrete that would set under water; arched breakwaters or moles to allow water circulation and prevent silting; extensive building of stone lighthouses; masonry bonded by multiple keys between every block; and a mastery of design that enabled engineers to construct the largest harbors on straight, exposed coasts lacking natural advantages.

Let us start with the rubble breakwaters. In 1966 divers found the largest breakwater of all off the site of Thapsus in eastern Tunisia. The breakwater extends seaward

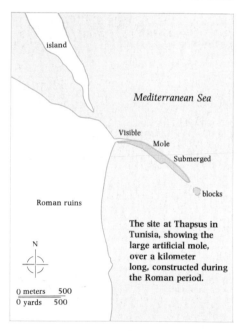

The site at Thapsus in Tunisia, showing the large artificial mole, over a kilometer long, constructed during the Roman period.

for 1 kilometer (0.6mi) in more than 10 meters (33ft) of water, and is 100 meters (330ft) wide at the broadest part. Calculations of the volume of stone in this colossal construction suggest that the Romans never actually finished it, since the volume seems insufficient to have raised the whole length above water. However, the structure may have sunk as its great weight compacted the seafloor.

At Caesarea Maritima on the Israeli coast lie the remains of a large port dating from soon after 25 BC. It was built with Roman assistance by Herod the Great, king of Judea. The coast here was originally straight, although one or two small creeks enter the sea nearby. Architects designed city and harbor as a unit, starting with the drainage and sewerage system. The two breakwaters enclosed a semicircular basin more than 300 meters (980ft) across, with its entrance on the north side, away from the movement of sand along the beach, and protected from the direct onslaught of the dominant west winds. On each side of the entrance three huge statues crowned columns standing in the water. At least one of these monuments probably served as a lighthouse.

Divers have mapped underwater Caesarea intensively, to try to settle a lively controversy as to whether or not its buildings have sunk. In fact most of the shore buildings now stand at the levels for which they were built, or have been slightly uplifted. They include a magnificent fish tank, storehouses, a large sluice gate for seawater, and a sewer. But much of the Herodian rubble breakwater is submerged. Archaeologists could not be sure that it had been built in water of the present depth: 5–10 meters (16–33ft). Accordingly, in the 1960s and 1970s three teams made exploratory dives with some excavation. The organizers were Ed Link, an American pioneer in saturation diving, in the early 1960s, the Israel Undersea Exploration Society in the late 1960s, and the University of Haifa and the Israel Geological Survey, which combined to produce a detailed survey in 1976.

In this last survey, divers cleared away sediments with propwashes – powerful water jets produced by downwash of a ship's propeller. They found several submerged quay surfaces and structures of carefully laid stones on the inner side of the breakwater. These all indicated submergence by 4.5–5.0 meters (15–16½ft). There were also mysterious blocks of masonry or concrete with rectangular recesses, perhaps designed to take wooden beams (an earlier survey had found blocks of stone held together with lead dowels). While the divers worked under water, a launch equipped with an echo sounder and precision navigation equipment generated a detailed bathymetric map of the site. This map plainly reveals the layout of the collapsed breakwater, and how waves have dispersed it.

But the oustanding discovery was the harbor's bisection by a discontinuity, or geological fault. Seaward of that line the breakwater and quays are submerged; landward of that line they remain undisplaced, or are even slightly uplifted. In the late 1970s geological borings confirmed the offset of underlying strata of rock, indicating that the movement is probably due to an active fault.

Other Roman harbors massively built on economically or militarily important sites with few natural advantages include Soli Pompeiopolis in southern Turkey, Seleucia Pieria on the border of Turkey and Syria, Leptis Magna in Libya, and the Claudian and Trajan harbors at Ostia in Italy. In some cases the Romans undertook truly enormous engineering works to ensure that nature did not undermine them. For instance, at Seleucia Pieria they tunneled under a mountain to divert a steep river carrying sand and pebbles liable to make the harbor silt up. They were not always that careful. Thus they failed to take adequate precautions at Leptis Magna, and the harbor there filled up with sand almost before it could be used.

The most intensively developed series of ports in the Roman world were, not surprisingly, north and south of Rome, from Centumcellae to the Bay of Naples. On this stretch of about 200 kilometers (125mi), 20 major ports catered for the military, commercial, and recreational needs of the hub of the empire. In modern terms this was a blend of Rotterdam, Portsmouth, and the Côte d'Azur. The principal military basin was at Misenum, where divers have surveyed a breakwater of rectangular concrete blocks. Nearby, at Puteoli, stood a famous arched breakwater that survived until the first year of the twentieth century, only to be covered by rubble for a modern harbor.

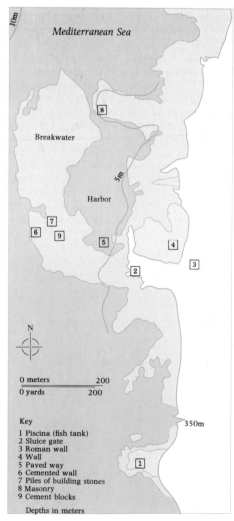

Key
1 Piscina (fish tank)
2 Sluice gate
3 Roman wall
4 Wall
5 Paved way
6 Cemented wall
7 Piles of building stones
8 Masonry
9 Cement blocks

Depths in meters

STRUCTURES UNDER WATER · Dr Nicholas C. Flemming

Dotted along the shore lay pleasure beaches with villas and palaces on concrete platforms jutting out into the sea. Many such dwellings had marine fish tanks, recently rediscovered and mapped by paddling and diving archaeologists.

The chief trading port of the empire was Ostia, near the city of Rome. To Ostia each year came countless shiploads of grain from North Africa. Rome itself depended completely upon this lifeline. The earliest harbor at Ostia stood on the Tiber River where it curved just before entering the sea. As the volume of trade grew, Rome needed a larger basin, and during the reign of the Emperor Claudius (AD 41–54) workers raised breakwaters to enclose a huge area just north of the river mouth. But by then sediments dumped by the Tiber were already blocking the original harbor, and building a delta out to sea at nearly 1 meter (3.3ft) a year. Under Trajan (AD 98–117) navvies quarrying into the alluvium dug out an artificial hexagonal basin connected by canals to the river and to the Claudian harbor. But, eventually, both harbors silted up and the shoreline advanced 5 kilometers (3mi) westward. Today Rome Airport partly covers the site of these ports.

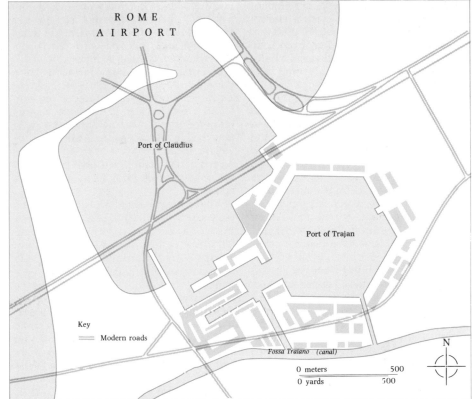

Left: The offshore remains at Caesarea on the coast of Israel. The site is dominated by the arc of masonry collapsed from the massive breakwater which encircled the artificial harbor.
Above, right: A plan of the Claudian and Trajanic ports at Ostia, the ancient port of Rome. Superimposed over them is the modern road system under which they now lie. The aerial photograph (below, right) taken before these modern developments, shows how the mouth of the River Tiber has pushed forward the coastline since Roman times. The lines of successive coastlines can be clearly seen within the coastal dunes. The Roman harbors lay buried at center-right of this photograph.

Apollonia, a model harbor

Apollonia on Libya's northeast, or Cyrenaic, coast is a textbook example of an ancient harbor, and by chance it was the first that I explored. In 1958 my team of divers from Cambridge University discovered a wealth of buildings and other structures that have served as a touchstone for my studies ever since.

Tradition places the city's foundation in 631 BC. There are few detailed references to it in classical literature, since it was only the port for Cyrene, a big inland city that took all the local historical glory. Today Apollonia is ruined and much lies 2.0–2.5 meters ($6\frac{1}{2}$–8ft) under water. The site is similar to many on the Levant coast farther east. A sandstone ridge produces reefs and islands 200–250 meters (650–820ft) offshore, but forms promontories where it clips the shoreline. From west to east, the so-called Grotto Reef, West Island, and East Island all played important roles in harbor construction. Greek colonizers connected the western end of the city wall to the Grotto Reef with a rubble embankment, then built a freestanding rubble breakwater between the reef and the West Island. This created a bay with the mainland forming the southwest and south, and the mouth facing east. This mouth was narrowed by a broad wall of dressed masonry, possibly on a broader rubble foundation, built from the mainland northward toward the West Island.

The rim of this harbor revealed an extraordinary range of structures. On the inner slope of the West Island lies the best preserved set of ancient slipways in the Mediterranean. All 10 are almost un-damaged, but completely submerged in the lee of the island. Curiously, later builders eventually covered them with stone-walled houses or huts. To the west, the break-water bridges the gap to the Grotto Reef, where extensive quarrying in ancient times has left rock masses with precise but now unknown functions. No one has yet produced a detailed map of the reef's maze of defensive works, passages, tunnels, and quarries. In the lee of the Grotto Reef lie strange parallel rock cuttings with floor recesses. They look a bit like slipways, but are quite different from those on the West Island.

The landward side of the basin had many land-based structures: presumably storehouses, sheds, offices, taverns, "rest houses" for sailors, and so on. At one point three differently aligned layers of masonry indicate successive building periods, not yet worked out. In the southeast corner stand nine parallel quays or docks, too narrow for warships. These quays, too, pose a puzzle.

Completing the harbor circuit is a massive wall of dressed blocks, some joined with lead dovetailed dowels. This wall runs from the mainland out to the entrance. The entrance itself is a long narrow channel, flanked by and guarded by two solid towers of stepped masonry. It would have been easy to defend such an entrance, since any enemy ship trying to break into the harbor would have had to pass between rows of defending troops. So much for this harbor. But exploration revealed a great deal more. On the seaward face of the West and East islands divers found that the rock had been quarried to leave residual barriers 10–20 meters (33–66ft) out from the cliff to make wave traps. These wave traps still work, in spite of the change of sea level. Similar structures from the Levant suggest that the Phoenicians may have had a part in Apollonia's construction.

Outside the harbor a rubble breakwater blocked the gap between the islands, and the foundations of a large round tower on the East Island suggest that a lighthouse stood there. From the eastern end of the city a large breakwater runs north, almost out to the "lighthouse." Between them, the two breakwaters enclose an outer harbor basin of uncertain date. The outer end of the second breakwater is now in 8 meters (26ft) of water, and huge squared blocks scattered nearby on the sea floor suggest the remains of a large tower guarding the entrance.

At the foot of the mainland's acropolis hill, and just inside the landward end of the eastern breakwater, divers discovered a well-preserved piscina, or fish tank. The pool measured 50×20 meters (164×65ft) and had dividing walls, multiple channels, and sluices to control the water flow; a bordering pathway; a flight of steps; and little artificial islands presumably connected to the sides by wooden catwalks. In 1959 we found a marble statue of a faun buried in the sand, confirming the literary evidence that piscinae were liberally decorated. About 40 piscinae have now been discovered around the Mediterranean, and there are presumably many more. In the shallow water between the piscina and the central masonry

A plan of the city of Apollonia drawn up by Captain F. W. Beechey of the Royal Navy in 1827, showing the offshore remains in general terms, and indicating that in some places fewer remains were under water at that time. Opposite: A plan of the ruins now visible both above and below water at Apollonia. On the basis of this evidence, maps have been drawn to show the disposition of structures around the harbors in 200 BC and AD 600 (above, left and right).

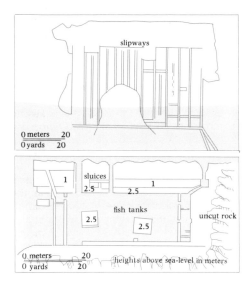

breakwater are relics of numerous land-based buildings, including beehive-shaped grain-storage silos cut into the rock. Silos like this are common near the waterfronts of other ancient Greek ports, and crop up as far apart as Syracuse in Sicily and Kas in Turkey.

The small buildings overlying the slipways, and the superimposed warehouses and apsidal buildings on the southeast side of the inner basin, suggest there were several periods of reconstruction at Apollonia, during which the two basins considerably changed in appearance and use. As ships grew bigger, and the grain trade with Rome became all important, the outer basin emerged as the commercial center, while the inner basin sank to the status of fishing harbor.

Studies of present and past water depth at different places give paradoxical findings. The slipways were almost certainly built centuries earlier than the piscina, and yet are submerged less deeply. One can only conclude that earth movements have tilted the site, or that the sea level was relatively lower when the piscina was built, which is just possible.

Apollonia was revisited by Bob Yorke and David Davidson in 1972 during a survey of other ports in Cyrenaica. The more we learn about other harbors and ports around the Mediterranean, the more clearly we see that Apollonia is exceptionally well preserved. A really thorough survey there today might answer dozens of questions that we were in no position to ask in the 1950s.

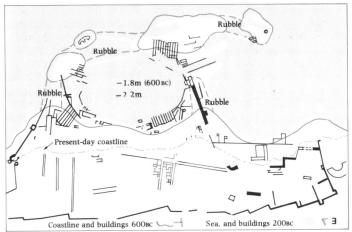

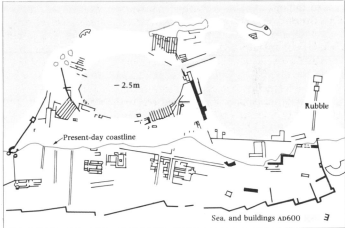

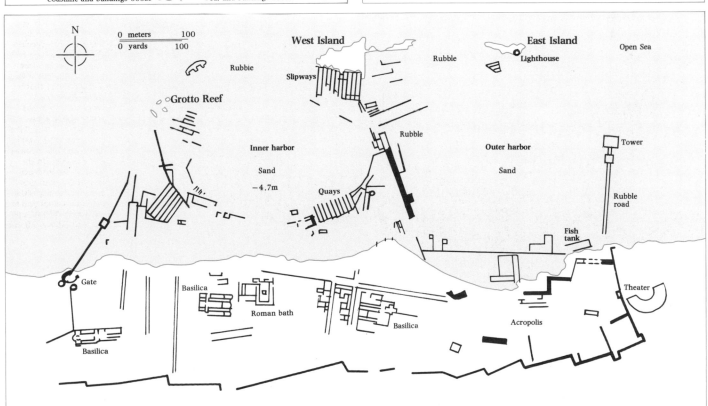

Harbors and sea-level changes

We end this chapter with a broad look at the distribution of Mediterranean ports in their classical heyday and at their subsequent patterns of uplift and sinking.

Between them, the Mediterranean and Black Sea held about 1,000 active harbors in Roman times. For the Mediterranean's western basin that meant on average one harbor for every 35–45 kilometers (22–28mi) of coastline. If we ignore barren stretches, the figure was one every 18–25 kilometers (11–15½mi). In the eastern basin the Aegean's hundreds of harbors rimmed the convoluted coasts of a small sea at an average interval of only 15–20 kilometers (9–12mi). The shores of what are now southern Turkey and Israel had a similar density. But Bronze Age Israel had had coastal settlements only some 10 kilometers (6mi) apart, and by Roman times, the number of active harbors in the Levant as a whole had fallen. The North African coast from Alexandria to Leptis Magna was the stretch least well endowed with Roman

or indeed other early ports. In the Gulf of Sirte coastlines hundreds of kilometers long show nothing worth calling a port. This is largely due to the sandy, unproductive hinterland; shallow, sandy, coastal waters; and onshore winds dangerous to shipping. In contrast, the hilly and mountainous country of Cyrenaica was then very fertile and rich. Cyrenaica's shores held most Roman ports of eastern North Africa.

In Roman times builders left less of a mark around the Black Sea than around the Mediterranean. There were probably 10–20 major ports in the 1,000 kilometers (620mi) of northern Black Sea coastline. However, the southern shore was fairly well developed.

The amazing upsurge of Roman port building and modernization between about 100 BC and AD 100 proves that ports played a vital role in the success and stability of the empire. Trade, administration, and troop movements all relied on a network of sea routes served by ports kept safe from weather and piracy. Emperors and provin-

cial administrators clearly recognized this, and harbors were prestigious structures, laden with civic and religious symbolism, and planned with care. The standardized building techniques used for harbors throughout the Mediterranean tempt us to guess that Rome had a corps of harbor engineers, rather like the US Army Beach Erosion Board. Also, so many big harbors were built in so short a time that we can hardly credit them to a few brilliant individual designers. We must assume that the "Roman Navy Harbor Board" had training establishments and manuals of engineering methods, and that Rome could deploy or hire out trained engineers and their key assistants anywhere in the empire.

Since the Mediterranean has so many ancient harbors, and since we largely know when these were built and used, they form a unique set of evidence for ancient sea levels and earthquakes. The British marine archaeologist David Blackman and others have shown how the original sea

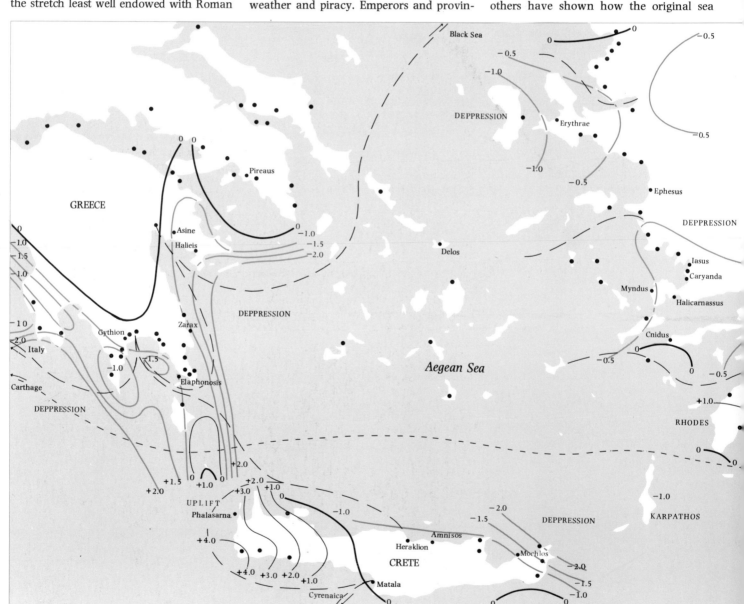

level can be derived from structures such as slipways, quays, mooring stones, fish tanks, and salt-pans. If tidal and atmospheric effects are measured carefully as well, the relative change of sea level at a site can be determined with a probable error of sometimes only 25 centimeters (10in), or more usually 50 centimeters (20in).

Since the mid-1950s, archaeologists have studied the relative change of sea level at hundreds of old Mediterranean harbors. This means that we can show how fast and far change has happened all around the coast since Roman times. Unfortunately, we lack reliable data for other periods except for the Aegean and the eastern shore from Syria to Egypt. These areas also contain significant remains from preclassical, Byzantine, and medieval times. Interpreting the measurements is not so easy as it might appear. There is a statistical problem in separating worldwide, or eustatic, change of sea level from local or regional earth movements or tectonic changes. Without

plunging into any mathematics, we can see that a eustatic change would have been identical in timing and extent for every site, while tectonic changes would have varied from one site to another. It is possible to program a computer to separate one type of change from the other. Even so, the uniform, or synchronous, factor may actually include a steady regional tectonic change indistinguishable, within the limits of the observations, from a eustatic change. Thus any attempts to identify a truly worldwide sea level curve is frustrated. (See also pp. 132–37.)

In the Mediterranean it turns out that the areas of submergence and uplift are quite restricted, while long stretches of coast show no relative movement at all during the last 5,000 years. Also, rather unexpectedly, submergence is much commoner than uplift. In the western basin, submergence has affected the Bay of Naples, southern Sardinia, southeast Sicily, Carthage, and the area around modern Algiers. Of 179 cities,

26 are submerged and two show uplift. Studies of the eastern basin are incomplete; in particular the Adriatic, north Aegean, and Egyptian coasts have not been investigated. In the south Aegean, south Turkey, and Cyprus, of 175 ruins with dated levels 100 show submergence, 43 indicate definite stability, and 32 indicate relative uplift. This last group is concentrated in the islands of the Cretan arc. The south coast of Turkey from Antalya to the Orontes is extremely stable. The coasts of Syria and Lebanon show irregular submergence. Most Israeli sites are stable, but 61 show submergence, and three sites show movements up and down. To conclude, geological and oceanographic theories can help to explain why the levels of the sea and land change as they do, but local effects are so unpredictable that every archaeological site must be treated strictly on its merits. The local evidence for submergence or uplift must be investigated objectively and believed, even where it clashes with cherished theory.

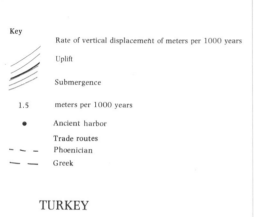

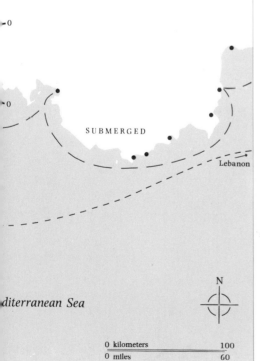

Key

Rate of vertical displacement of meters per 1000 years

Uplift

Submergence

1.5   meters per 1000 years

•   Ancient harbor

Trade routes
- - - Phoenician
— — Greek

TURKEY

SUBMERGED

Lebanon

Mediterranean Sea

N

0 kilometers 100
0 miles 60

Left: A contour-map of the Aegean area. The lines join together locations that have been subject to the same degree of lifting or lowering over the past 2000 years.
Above: Some areas have emerged from the sea rather than been drowned. The rock cuttings an Zinibull (above) are typical of such change – the blue tint indicates the maximum sea level in classical times. A similar situation can be seen with the tombs at Matala (right).

Preservation: Past, Present, and Future

The topic of preservation has recurred throughout this atlas. The evidence available from any site depends entirely on what the site environment has preserved. The potential of any discovery for research and public display depends on what conservators can preserve. The objective of all site recording is to preserve the contextual and other information that excavation will destroy. And the future progress of our subject depends on the success with which legal or other means can preserve unexcavated sites from depredation and vandalism.

By emphasizing the importance of all these aspects of preservation, the general editor draws together in these last 10 pages many of the themes that we have touched on earlier. In the first two pages he considers preservation in the past, or how our evidence has managed to survive until the present. In the remaining pages he discusses the ways in which present actions can preserve this archaeological resource for our study and enlightenment tomorrow.

The survival of archaeological evidence

If archaeology is the study of past peoples and societies through their material remains, its scope and potential must hinge chiefly on how far these remains have survived. We can say so much more about ancient pot-making than we can about ancient cookery for just this reason. Amazingly, early archaeological writings widely ignored this simple truth, although it figures throughout this atlas, and most branches of modern archaeology accord it recognition. In fact, much of this book involves accounting for the survival of what has been found, and reconstructing what is now missing — whether on one site, as with parts of a Byzantine freighter (pp. 36–37), or over a whole trade network, as with Bronze Age wrecks in the English Channel (pp. 62–65).

There are essentially two aspects to the question of survival. First, where individual objects or groups of objects are missing from a complex like a ship or a lakeside village, we have to determine whether the missing objects were destroyed or removed. Second, we must decide whether the surviving elements have been disturbed and rearranged, or whether they still at least partly reflect their original relationship to each other. As the contributors to this atlas stress repeatedly, it is the patterning of objects and assemblages that gives archaeologists many of their insights.

These principles hold true whether a site is in water or on land. But, as Section I has said, one of the notable properties of underwater sites is their ability to preserve in good condition fragile objects made of wood, leather, skins, or other organic materials. On land such items generally disintegrate fairly fast through chemical degradation and bacterial attack, except where it is very dry (as in the Egyptian desert) or very cold (as in Siberia). In these cases absence of water is crucial. On the seabed, on the other hand, what matters is the absence of free oxygen — oxygen chemically uncombined with other elements. (Most of the destructive organisms and chemical processes cannot operate without both oxygen and water.) Oxygen is absent where the water does not circulate, especially in sediments that remain stable, and in certain very still waters of the ocean deeps. Apart from this, survival depends on a lack of undersea creatures able to feed on the material concerned. For instance, several predatory mollusks and crustaceans may attack wood severely in seawater, but no freshwater creature causes comparable damage. This largely explains why wooden ships and structures survive much better in the brackish Baltic (p. 78), and in inland lakes and rivers (pp. 148–161) than in the open sea.

The particularly good survival rate of wood under water is especially fortunate for maritime archaeology since almost all preindustrial shipbuilding involved little else but wood. If wood rotted readily in water this book would have had scarcely anything to say about past nautical technology. Furthermore, most early societies used wood for land-based structures and artifacts. Where these have come to be preserved in underwater sites they help to show what we have lost on land. Besides wood, sites under water can preserve leather, skins, foodstuffs, and even human bodies, helping us to piece together life in, say, a Bronze Age village in the Alps (pp. 148–155).

Other materials achieve varying degrees of stability under water. Pottery usually remains completely unaffected by long-term immersion. On the other hand, iron may be totally destroyed. With iron, a kind of accelerated rusting can set in as an iron object reacts with the chlorides and oxides in salt water. This may continue until an enormous accretion builds up around the object, of which nothing in the end remains except a hollow cast. Descriptions of the work at Yassi Ada (p. 36) or on the 1554 wrecks off Texas (p. 108) have already demonstrated this phenomenon, and shown how archaeologists can deal with it. Apart from iron, most metals suffer only surface corrosion in seawater. But with silver this damage can penetrate quite deeply, transforming the outer layers of a collection of silver coins, for example, into black silver chloride.

Turning now to the survival of interrelationships on an archaeological site, we can similarly see essential differences between what happens on land and under water. Once more, underwater sites generally come off better. In both environments, disturbance can result from either natural or human agencies. Natural disturbances are probably equally common in both situations, with crabs and octopuses as the underwater equivalents of rodents and earthworms. On

The interior of a pocket sundial recovered from the wreck of the Dutch East Indiaman *Kennemerland* (1664). Even the painted compass card below the dial itself has been preserved perfectly.

Left: A hank of rope uncovered on the *Kennemerland* wreck site (1664). Even though it lay in coarse gravel in less than 10 meters of water, this delicate organic object has remained in perfect condition.

Left, center: A turned wooden bowl revealed on the site of the Spanish Armada vessel *Trinidad Valencera*. This object lay under about 30 centimeters (12in) of sand in a horizon packed with similar organic material. The scale is graduated in inches.

Left, below: A diver excavating with an air lift beside a pile of silver bars on the wreck of the Dutch East Indiaman *Slot ter Hooge* (1724). Buried deeply in the sand, this stack was beyond the reach of contemporary salvors, who recovered the rest of the ship's treasure, and has survived 250 years of submergence in good condition.

many Mediterranean sites home-building octopuses have crammed the mouths of amphorae with a confusing jumble of ancient and modern trash (p. 46).

It is when we look at human interference that the full advantages of underwater sites become apparent. On land, an ancient site may have been plowed over, built on, looted, or even dug away by later generations. But through most of history, man could tamper with the seabed only indirectly, by means of trawls, dredges, or grabs; and even then selectively and in very limited areas. It is only during the past two centuries that he has been able to visit the seafloor himself, and only since the middle of this century with any real freedom of maneuver. It is for this reason that relics untouched for thousands of years have suddenly become vulnerable to destruction by unintentional disturbance, pilfering, or treasure hunting; one of the great strengths of underwater archaeology is thus fast disappearing, at least for sites in less than 60 meters (200ft) of water.

These, then, are the chief factors in the survival of archaeological remains under water. Our responsibility to preserve this evidence for the benefit of present and future generations is heavy. Where possible we must guard these sites from the harmful attentions of man, now that he has free access to the seabed. Where disturbance is inevitable, archaeologists must thoroughly record and as far as possible recover the evidence before it is destroyed. The remaining pages of this atlas consider how our underwater heritage can be effectively preserved for posterity.

Conserving finds

The very value of water in preserving all kinds of objects can create vast difficulties when it comes to treating the finds recovered from a submerged site. This is especially true where a collection includes fragile organic items that quickly deteriorate when exposed to air. Conservation can therefore often cost as much as, or more than, the rest of a project; and a responsible excavator will budget accordingly. Many of the examples in this book help to point up the scope of the problem. In fact, lack of, or too few, conservation facilities may sometimes persuade an archaeologist to postpone a project, or to restrict a program to partial excavation. In particular, this frequently means leaving a wooden hull where it is and simply recovering the cargo.

While conservation is thus a crucial part of any archaeological project involving the recovery of objects, it is not, strictly speaking, a part of archaeology, but a separate and independent discipline. Conservators have their own concerns and responsibilities, requiring many years of specialist training, especially in chemistry and materials science. Unfortunately, conservation plays such an important part in underwater sites that many writers have equated conservation competence with ability to supervise a complete project. From the projects set out in these pages you will have grasped that archaeological research presents more than enough problems for one person to tackle, and that a maritime archaeologist's background and expertise are very different from those of a trained conservator.

Now we have established the true position of conservation as an independent science, let us look at the special problems posed by material from underwater sites, drawing together the scattered references that appear elsewhere in this book. The essential point to remember is that when you remove a substance from a situation where its condition has remained stable for many years, you trigger physical and chemical changes. These may be minor or, unless curbed, may lead to total disintegration of the substance. One extreme is represented by stone, which needs no more than washing to stop unsightly salt crystals forming on its surface. Wood and other organic substances represent the other extreme.

Waterlogged wood is wood with its natural juices and resins washed away and replaced by water. This process need not alter a wooden object's outward appearance. However, if you let such a timber dry out, its cell structure loses internal support and will collapse, so that the piece shrinks and twists, or even crumbles to dust. Thus as the wood loses water, a conservator will try to replace the water with a more stable substance that will allow the timber to be dried off, handled, and displayed without fear of damage. Ideally, the treatment should also preserve the timber's previous appearance and dimensions, along with all carpentry features, inscriptions, and other significant detail.

In practice, all available preservation techniques have drawbacks, and there is so far no universally applicable method. Possibly the commonest procedure is to immerse the object — small fragment, large timber, or even complete vessel — in a bath of polyethylene glycol (PEG), a water-soluble artificial wax. This process involves gradually increasing the concentration of the solution until the cells hold enough wax for them to survive drying out. The technique's disadvantages include the fact that you must keep the bath warm, for maximum wood penetration; and for large timbers treatment can take several years. This makes the method very expensive. Conservators successfully applied an interesting variant of this technique to the Swedish warship *Wasa*: they sprayed her with PEG continuously for more than a decade before achieving results that satisfied them (p. 82).

Otherwise, there is a wide variety of less commonly used ways of tackling wood, most of them useful only for saving small objects. One approach involves swiftly forcing water out of the object, for example, by freeze-drying or placing it in a vacuum chamber, then impregnating with a vaporized wax before collapse can set in. Another recently developed method involves replacing the water in wood with acetone, then impregnating the wood with an acetone-soluble resin. Many of these methods, including the PEG process, apply just as well to other organic substances, such as skins or leather, although here there is often less danger of cellular collapse on drying. Indeed, with leather, the best approach is often simply several washes in fresh water followed by drying and then recourse to the traditional leather workers' treatment: liberal applications of beeswax or dubbin.

Where it has not totally disintegrated, iron from the seabed can present at least as many problems as waterlogged wood. Sometimes removing a piece from the water can lead to an extremely rapid reaction between the metal and seawater salts; one sixteenth-century cannon from the English warship *Mary Rose* (p. 18) was audibly fizzing and felt hot to the touch within half an hour of leaving the sea. The objective in the conservation of iron is to remove all the marine salts in order to stop such reactions; unfortunately, even the smallest residue of oxides or chlorides will set off a gradually spreading corrosion that will in the end engulf the whole object. Treatments available include chemical processing, which can take many years; electrolytic reduction; and (most dramatically) roasting in an atmosphere of pure hydrogen to about 1,000°C (1,800°F). Iron from freshwater environments present different, less tricky, problems.

With non-ferrous metals the difficulties are also less severe, although the conservation aim is similar: to remove all corrosive salts and other corrosion products. Silver responds well to electrolytic reduction,

A view of the hydrogen reduction furnace at Portsmouth City Museum, Hampshire, England. The operator is attending to the ammonia cracker, which provides the hydrogen gas for the atmosphere inside the furnace. To his left is the electrical power control console. Behind him is the furnace, the door being open to show the heating elements.

while chemical treatments work best for bronze.

Whatever the substance, the most important point about the recommended treatment is that it should start as soon as possible after the object has been uncovered. This is why every maritime archaeological project should make adequate provision for conservation in its program and its budget. At the same time, archaeology and conservation must keep their independence and integrity intact: neither is master or servant of the other. The relationship between the archaeologist and conservator should be one of mutual regard and understanding, as between equals (p. 108): a happy situation not easily achieved.

Left: Preservation is necessary from the moment of recovery. Here a ship's timber is being wrapped in polythene ready for transport back to the laboratory.
Right: Great care is often necessary in dissecting severely corroded complex artifacts. Here a chest from a wreck of 1733 (pp 118-19) is being opened by experts from the state of Florida. It proved to contain sail needles.
Below: The Bremen cog of c. 1380 in store in the maritime museum at Bremerhaven, Germany. It is being sprayed continuously with water to prevent drying out and consequent collapse. The conservation of such a large wooden object presents severe technical problems and is very expensive.

Storing and displaying artifacts

It is not enough to record and preserve objects recovered from an underwater excavation, and then to lock them out of sight in a museum basement. This does no good to anyone. Archaeological material that remains accessible is potentially useful long after its original discoverer has finished with it. This usefulness takes two forms. First, some of the objects will always interest society at large, helping us to appreciate how our ancestors lived, and how the modern world came into being. Second, all of the objects will be potentially useful to future scholars, who will be able to reassess the finds repeatedly in the light of increasing knowledge and improved methods of analysis.

It would be unrealistic to pretend that there is no potential conflict here. The demands of public education may require part of a collection to visit another town or country on temporary or permanent loan, while the scholar may prefer the whole collection to remain in one place, with its field notes, analytical reports, photographs, and so forth. Then, too, prolonged public display may cause colors to fade, or incur high risks of biological or physical damage. It is the responsibility of museum staff to reconcile these demands and provide facilities that minimize the risks and inconveniences. Few members of the public casually drifting around a gallery appreciate these problems.

So far as public displays are concerned, enlightened museums avoid cramming display cases with inadequately labeled objects. Displays like this baffle rather than instruct. Current practice is to try to set out individual objects in a sequence related to some central theme, so that, for instance, we can grasp how people used the objects. The display may also tell the story of the objects' discovery and excavation. With our subject, this story can often inspire a most compelling presentation, given the romance and adventure of underwater exploration, and the complex and unfamiliar equipment frequently involved.

The display of complete ships recovered from the seabed presents special problems worth considering in detail. Whatever the conservation method used, such vessels must remain in a controlled environment, with regulated temperature and humidity. This means keeping them indoors. That in turn creates an element of unreality, since ships were made for travel in the open air. Furthermore, their overall lines and conception are usually best appreciated from a distance, a perspective impossible within four walls. One display with a largely effective solution to these problems appears at the Viking Ship Museum at Roskilde in Denmark: immediately behind the vessels themselves, one whole wall of the main gallery is entirely glass, and looks out across the waters of Roskilde Fjord, where the five vessels were originally found (pp. 74–75).

Just how impossible it is to gain an overall impression of a large ship in a museum we can best see by looking at the *Wasa*, preserved in a building only slightly larger than herself. Because of this no one has been able to photograph the whole ship since her rescuers hauled her from the Baltic. This ship also illustrates another difficulty with the display of large multidecked vessels. Because her PEG-impregnated decks are not very wear resistant, and because restricted between-decks height prevents the building of raised walkways, the public can never go inside her. Ironically, this is a penalty to be paid for having a complete ship; the English warship *Mary Rose* of 1545 will present no such difficulties, since most of

her port side is missing, and the public will be able to look into each deck in turn from tiered balconies.

Another regular debate regarding the display of ships concerns the validity of reconstructing missing sections with new wood. Most experts would agree that it depends on how much of the hull is missing, although there may be strong disagreements over where to draw the line. The *Mary Rose* obviously represents one extreme, where absence of one side proves a virtue, and reconstruction would be misleading and prohibitively costly. At the other extreme are craft at least nine-tenths complete; here the few missing pieces would look unsightly and completion with new wood seems

acceptable provided that it is stained a slightly different tone from the old wood. This was done with the Viking grave-ships (p. 72) now on display in Oslo. The varying degrees of survival of the five Roskilde ships presented a special challenge, and resulted in a particularly neat solution. Conservators used only original timbers, and employed thin steel rods to indicate the boats' lines across the missing sections.

Most people judge a museum by its public displays, but its value for posterity lies just as much in stores where interested scholars can see those of the collection's objects not on view. Present-day archaeologists must have the humility to recognize that their techniques and procedures may seem appallingly primitive to their successors, just as we wince when we read of the activities of Victorian antiquarians. Although future archaeologists will never be able to re-excavate the sites we have destroyed, they must have the opportunity of working through and reinterpreting all the objects and samples recovered. This is why all the finds from archaeological sites should go intact and undivided into a public museum, and not be scattered through the sale rooms to all parts of the world. Private museums are generally unacceptable since they cannot guarantee the necessary public access or long-term custody.

The proper storage and display of excavated material is as much an essential element in a project as conservation or publication, and provision for it should be made before an investigation starts. As with conservation, the skills and expertise involved are those of an independent specialist, this time the museum curator. At all stages in the work the project archaeologist should liaise with him or her on a basis of equality and mutual respect. This applies whether the material is joining an established collection or going to a special museum set up to show the findings of a major "dig." The projected Tudor Ship Museum at Portsmouth, planned to house the *Mary Rose* and her contents, seeks to epitomize all the ideals of public display and research facilities that we have just described.

Opposite: The Swedish warship *Wasa* within her specially constructed home in Stockholm. The walls and roof hem the vessel in quite closely, for good technical reasons. But this makes it difficult to appreciate the ship's full grandure and scale. Three solutions to the problems of displaying the moderately sized vessels of the early medieval period in northern Europe. The Nydam boat (top) is displayed simply in a roomy hall with access on all sides. The Viking ships at Oslo (center) are housed in a specially constructed ship museum; here the plain vaulted galleries give an illusion of spaciousness and a lack of restricting perspectives. The most modern attempt to solve these problems is represented by the Viking Ship Museum at Roskilde (lower). The vessels are displayed in spacious galleries here, with one wall of glass (to the left in this picture) offering views across the fjord. The wooden hull remains are left incomplete, the ship's lines being indicated by metal rods.

Presenting information

Conserving, storing, and displaying artifacts is not the end of the story, since finds represent only part of the archaeological evidence gathered during excavation. Equally important are the site plans and records. These should show as far as possible the context of all objects recovered (p. 28). Once he has processed and studied this information and drawn conclusions from it, an archaeologist has a duty to make his findings available to everyone interested in the work. For, as one writer has put it: "An unpublished excavated site has been destroyed or mutilated as surely as if it had been bulldozed."

As with museum presentation, publication should be on two levels: one for the general public, and another for scholars. The popular level may involve articles in the press, features for radio or television, and contributions to popular archaeological magazines. It is vital that all these bear the stamp of authenticity and accuracy that can come only from the archaeologist involved. The public has a right to expect authoritative and up-to-date summaries of current research. After all, directly or indirectly the public has often helped to pay for it. Archaeologists too lazy or fearful of losing face to meet this demand fail in their social and academic obligations. This book

is itself intended as a contribution to general knowledge from a group of diving archaeologists.

To the general reader, the average site report in an archaeological journal seems wordy and overburdened with undigested facts. To the appropriate specialist, however, it may be a gold mine to pore over for hours. The difference lies, of course, in each person's starting point. We cannot pretend that site reports make lively reading, but we can at least show something of why archaeologists find them indispensable.

The starting point for any report is obviously the previous state of knowledge, generally indicated by references to the appropriate literature, rather than by a complete résumé of the topic. Depending on the period concerned, this established knowledge may come just from archaeological studies, or from documentary or ethnographic evidence as well.

Next, the report should carry a simple description of the material or site studied, and an explanation of why the archaeologist undertook the project. This explanation should set forth what he expected to find on a site and which questions he hoped his project would answer.

The detailed description of working

methods and techniques that usually follows is important for a number of reasons. It shows how the questions posed helped to shape an excavation strategy. It also serves future excavators as a guide to procedure and as a warning of some of the pitfalls. But above all, this description enables the reader to assess the quality of the work, and to interpret the evidence given and conclusions suggested. What an observer notes depends chiefly on the kinds of things that he is looking for. Thus if his report makes no mention of animal bones, this may mean that he found none, or that bones were there but he considered them not worth noting. His statement of aims and methods is a strong clue to the likely state of affairs.

Next, we come to the heart of the report: detailed facts about the site and its contents. The accent here is an objective description, and there should be no expressions of opinion or belief. This section will often have three parts: first, a feature-by-feature account of the site itself; next, a descriptive catalog of finds; and, last, appropriate specialist reports from geologists, botanists, analysts, and so forth. At some stage there should also be an indication of the conservation treatment given, and of the present whereabouts of the finds and site records.

Left: To many people, wreck excavation means only one thing – treasure, such as this hoard of silver ducatoons from the Dutch East Indiaman *Hollandia* (1743). But, as this book shows, archaeologists are proving that the underwater world can offer more significant and exciting discoveries.

Opposite: A flow-diagram depicting the way in which the discovery of a site, and its subsequent investigation, can combine with previous knowledge to expand our understanding of the past. Within any project, the main stream of progress runs from top to bottom; but, as this diagram shows, there should also be a considerable feedback of ideas and theories from later stages to earlier ones.

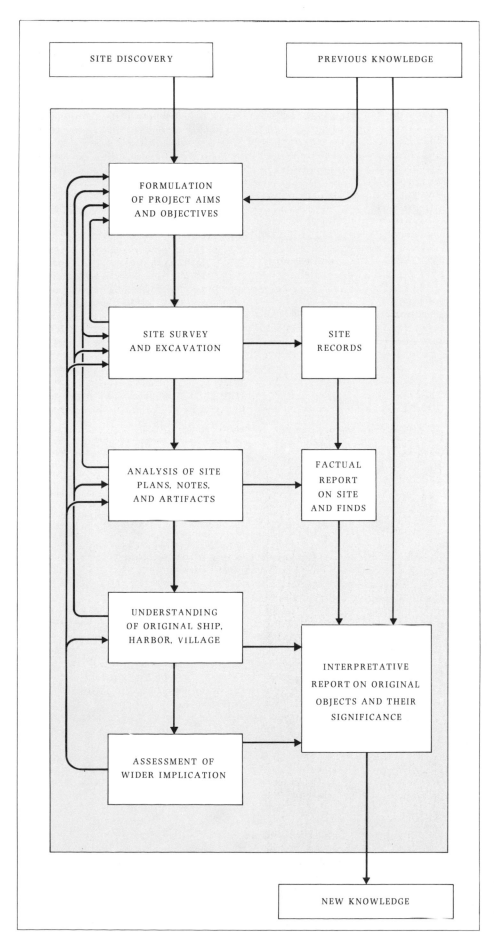

SITE DISCOVERY

PREVIOUS KNOWLEDGE

FORMULATION
OF PROJECT AIMS
AND OBJECTIVES

SITE SURVEY
AND EXCAVATION

SITE
RECORDS

ANALYSIS OF SITE
PLANS, NOTES,
AND ARTIFACTS

FACTUAL
REPORT
ON SITE
AND FINDS

UNDERSTANDING
OF ORIGINAL SHIP,
HARBOR, VILLAGE

INTERPRETATIVE
REPORT ON ORIGINAL
OBJECTS AND THEIR
SIGNIFICANCE

ASSESSMENT OF
WIDER IMPLICATION

NEW KNOWLEDGE

The final section of a report naturally contains the investigator's conclusions and suggests how these may modify previously held theories or ideas. As our flow diagram indicates, these conclusions may involve three levels of assessment: first, study of the development of the site (how it came to survive as it did); second, study of the ship, harbor, village or other unit from which the site derived; third, study of the broader cultural system of which the excavated unit was a part. In maritime studies this may be a trade route, tradition of naval architecture, war fleet, or coastal settlement pattern. Only by looking at this general context can archaeologists help to make specific sites illuminate broad trends and patterns of the past.

Preparing a comprehensive report on a major site involves the labors of many scholars and research assistants and can take several decades. A good example is the investigation of the seventh-century-AD wreck at Yassi Ada (p. 36), first excavated in 1961: the final report was due in 1980. In such situations it is usual to fill the long information gap by issuing an interim report after each main period of work. These reports briefly outline what has been done, and make preliminary observations on the discoveries. For underwater projects, the main vehicle is the *International Journal of Nautical Archaeology*, published quarterly in Britain and the United States by Academic Press for the Council for Nautical Archaeology.

The fact that underwater archaeology is a relatively young subject and that a long gestation period is required for final reports means that there are, so far, few final reports to which we can refer the reader. An early example is Fernand Benoît's report on the excavations at Grand Congloué (p. 52). Published in 1961 as a supplement to the French journal *Gallia*, this clearly demonstrates the strengths and weaknesses of underwater work in the Mediterranean in the 1950s. The first substantial and authoritative report appeared in 1967 when the American Philosophical Society's series of Transactions featured a report by George Bass and five principal collaborators on the Bronze Age wreck at Cape Gelidonya (pp. 32–35). Although a relatively small site, this generated a discussion running to 177 double-column pages. For an extensive post-medieval site, the publication demands will be correspondingly enormous, and no truly representative examples have yet appeared. The nearest to date is probably Jeremy Green's report on the seventeenth-century Dutch East Indiaman *Vergulde Draeck* (p. 124). Published in 1977, this account occupies no fewer than 506 pages, and yet makes no claim to be final.

The archaeological report will never be great or compelling literature, but it will remain indispensable as a record of some fragment of the past whose pieces have been irrecoverably separated.

185

Protecting sites

We have shown that archaeology under water has limitations: it is expensive in terms of money, personnel, and equipment, and is still in a primitive and immature state. Three decades or so is a short span for the life of any scientific study, and we can hardly expect ours to have perfected its techniques and procedures already, especially when we remember that each individual project involves complex work and a great deal of time. In no sense, therefore, can we deal with every known site, and those now being excavated are subject to a standard of archaeology that may seem unacceptably low by the end of the century. For these

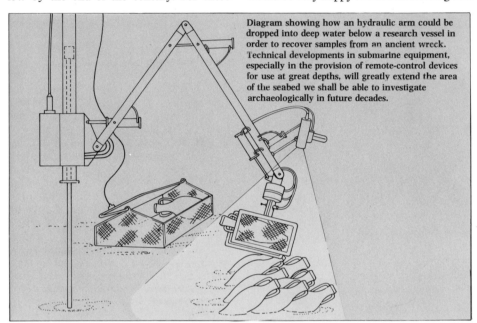

Diagram showing how an hydraulic arm could be dropped into deep water below a research vessel in order to recover samples from an ancient wreck. Technical developments in submarine equipment, especially in the provision of remote-control devices for use at great depths, will greatly extend the area of the seabed we shall be able to investigate archaeologically in future decades.

reasons, many sites not yet investigated should remain intact and undisturbed, since these must provide the material from which tomorrow's archaeologists will re-examine and modify today's theories and interpretations.

We cannot precisely predict future developments in archaeological and diving techniques, but we can say with some assurance that future generations will be far better equipped than our own to extract all the evidence from such sites. At the very least they will have the accumulated experience of our mistakes to guide them. In terms of diving technology, moreover, future excavators will probably be able to go under water with equipment and suits lighter and more convenient than the relatively cumbersome gear that we use now. It may even be possible to adapt man's lungs to enable him to breathe water, and allow him as much freedom on the seabed as he enjoys on land. Alternatively, progress may move in the direction of allowing us to place water-tight spheres around sites, enabling us to work on the seabed in the dry, possibly even at atmospheric pressure. Another foreseeable option, especially for sites in very deep water, would be to encapsulate them and

lift a whole section of seabed to the surface for excavation in a controlled environment.

These few suggestions should be enough to show why we have a responsibility to leave a part of this archaeological resource intact for the future, irrespective of the fact that anyway we lack the means to tackle all known sites at once. Nevertheless, many people find it hard to accept that we should leave obviously interesting sites untouched. If the archaeologists have no time to deal with these sites, goes one argument, why not offer them to commercial salvage concerns or amateur treasure hunters, who would be very happy to raise interesting and valuable relics without any call on public funds? At this point the argument becomes more than a purely academic one, and takes on political or even moral overtones. The fundamental question is whether it is right that the common heritage of mankind should be exploited for private profit, or even just for recreational amusement. I cannot accept that it is, and legislators in most coastal states in the world evidently take the same view.

Turning to how the legal protection of underwater sites should operate, we find many difficulties, but few that do not apply just as much to the protection of monuments on land. While specific provisions must obviously fit into the general legal code of each country concerned, effective conservation must presuppose some basic principles. The most important of these is public ownership of all historic material on the seabed. This provision should have the effect of safeguarding known sites, reserved for future study, and protecting sites as yet unknown from the moment they are found. It is important to avoid any time gap between finding a site and affording it legal protection, for during that interval people could damage the site with impunity.

Having asserted public ownership and control over such sites, it is important that the law be administered in a positive and nonrestrictive manner. There should be efficient procedures for allowing excavation by adequately equipped and experienced teams, and keeping a watch on their progress. Equally, the law should permit non-destructive inspection and reconnaissance of sites by interested and responsible groups in order to maintain interest in such sites and allow continuous assessment of their condition. This is particularly important for club divers, the likely discoverers of many a site; their access to and interest in such sites deserves respect if they behave responsibly, and they should have every opportunity to participate in an investigation when one is organized.

All these ideas depend on the agencies of the state having their own officers to inspect and assess sites, consider their situation, and advise on policy. These officers may advise excavators on techniques or procedures in situations unfamiliar to them. But above all, such officers should be available to advise when a site must be excavated at once, and when it can and should be left intact. There will always be sites where the material is lying around loose on the seabed, a temptation to any visitor, or where natural erosion threatens the remains. These sites need tackling just as urgently as land sites threatened by highway construction or urban development. In such situations, above and below water, rescue excavation needs backing by public funds.

People have argued that lack of police or other surveillance makes it difficult or impossible to enforce legal protection of underwater sites. This is certainly why immediate rescue excavation is sometimes more practicable than long-term preservation. But not always: after all, there are far fewer unauthorized people likely to visit and tamper with underwater sites than with those on land. Also, extensive interference on most sites involves large and conspicuous craft and machinery that are easily spotted.

More of a problem is posed by sites outside territorial waters and subject to no sovereign jurisdiction. International conventions concerning the law of the sea seem particularly difficult to conclude, and enforcement will never be fully effective. But this is no reason for not seeking international agreement.

Underwater sites represent a substantial asset and resource for the archaeologist, and one that he is increasingly able to exploit to full scientific advantage. Natural environmental conditions have preserved that resource up to the present day, and modern archaeological and conservation technology helps us to save for posterity a good part of the material and information from sites now being excavated. But it is up to us to generate the political will to assure preservation for the future of those sites so far untouched.

Notes on illustrations

Further Reading

We list below a selection of the more readily available books in English about archaeology under water. Since the subject involves such a new field of research, the literature relating to it is not extensive, and information about many significant sites and investigations remains unpublished, or available only in specialist journals.

General

Bass, George F. (ed) **A History of Seafaring** Walker, New York; Thames and Hudson, London, 1972
The first attempt to bring together in one work the contribution that investigations under water have made toward various aspects of seafaring in the past. Its contributors include many early pioneers of the subject.

Bass, George F. **Archaeology under Water** Praeger, New York; Thames and Hudson, London, 1966
After his pioneering campaigns Professor Bass wrote this book, setting out the standards and disciplines of excavation under water. Although it is strongly influenced by Mediterranean conditions, it remains an authoritative statement on basic techniques and concerns.

Frost, Honor **Under the Mediterranean** Routledge and Kegan Paul, London, 1963
An account by a diver and archaeologist who was involved with many of the earliest underwater projects in both eastern and western basins of the Mediterranean. Combines a strong narrative with several profound reflections on the nature and promise of the subject.

Muckelroy, Keith **Maritime Archaeology** Macmillan, New York, 1979; Cambridge University Press, Cambridge, 1978
An attempt to review the scope and problems of maritime archaeology in the light of the first quarter-century of work, and to point the way to future progress. It also seeks to accommodate the subject within recent developments in the theory of archaeology.

Taylor, Joan du Plat (ed) **Marine Archaeology** Crowell, New York; Hutchinson, London, 1965
A summary of most of the major underwater projects in the Mediterranean during the 1950s. Gives a useful insight into the state of progress at the end of the first decade.

In addition to the above, the reader should consult the **International Journal of Nautical Archaeology,** published quarterly by the Academic Press, London and New York, for the Council for Nautical Archaeology. This is the only English-language periodical devoted to this subject, and is notable for its many interim reports on projects in hand. Papers or short notes have appeared in its pages on most of the sites mentioned in this book. Indispensable for anyone seriously interested in this field.

Note should also be taken of **Progress in Underwater Science,** the annual report of the Underwater Association, published by Pentech Press, London. This often contains reports on current research projects; important papers on the *Mary Rose*, Madrague de Giens, and Marzememi sites, among others, have been included.

1 Techniques and approaches

Barker, Philip **The Techniques of Archaeological Excavation** Batsford, London, 1977
The best available account of the aims and methods of modern excavations, wherever undertaken. Uncompromising in its advocacy of high standards, it represents a challenge to all field workers.

Bass, George F. **Archaeology beneath the Sea** Walker, New York, 1975; Harper and Row, New York, 1976
The story of Bass's first 15 years as a diving archaeologist. His constant efforts to improve standards and cost-effectiveness emerge clearly, as do the inevitable hazards, difficulties, and frustrations of all diving projects. The writing is both compelling and thought-provoking.

BSAC Diving Manual British Sub-Aqua Club, London, 1978
The BSAC's internationally recognized instructional manual for the amateur diver. Essential reading for anyone taking up diving.

Fowler, Peter J. **Approaches to Archaeology** St. Martin's Press, New York; A & C Black, London, 1977
The best available introduction for anyone wishing to know more about what is involved in archaeology.

Greenhill, Basil **Archaeology of the Boat** Wesleyan University Press, Middletown, Conn; A & C Black, London 1976
The most recent review of the evidence available from archaeological, historical, and ethnographic sources concerning the development of boats. Extensively illustrated, it provides a useful guide through the uncertainties and controversies of this particular speciality.

Wilkes, Bill St. John **Nautical Archaeology** Stein and Day, New York, 1971; David and Charles, Newton Abbot, 1973

A manual of techniques in archaeology under water, heavily dependent on the author's experiences of the harbor sites in the Mediterranean.

2 Mediterranean wreck sites and classical seafaring

Bass, George F. **Cape Gelidonya: a Bronze Age Shipwreck** Volume 57, part 8 of the Transactions of the American Philosophical Society, Philadelphia, 1967
The definitive report on the investigation of this most important site, and on many aspects of the material recovered. Not easy reading, but a model report of its type.

Casson, Lionel **Ships and Seamanship in the Ancient World** Princeton University Press, Princeton, New Jersey, 1971
An exhaustive review of the evidence available concerning seafaring in classical times; very fully referenced.

Parker, A. J. **Ancient Shipwrecks of the Mediterranean and the Roman Provinces** British Archaeological Reports (BAR) Oxford, 1980
A fully referenced list of every known wreck site from classical times.

Throckmorton, Peter **Shipwrecks and Archaeology** Atlantic Monthly Press, Boston; Gollancz, London, 1970
A personal account by one of the pioneers of the subject, including detailed discussion of some important sites of Roman and later periods.

3 European shipwrecks over 3000 years

British Museum **The Sutton Hoo Ship Burial: a handbook** British Museum Publications, London, 1976
General guide to this most important site and its contents; well illustrated.

Brogger, A. W. & Shetelig, H. **The Viking Ships** Arthur Vanous Co., Riveredge, New Jersey; Hurst, London 1951
Extensively illustrated account of vessels recovered from grave mounds between the 1860s and the 1930s; ranges well before and after the true Viking period.

Cunliffe, Barry **Hengistbury Head** Paul Elek, London, 1978 Discussion of the many investigations conducted over the past century on this Iron Age site on the Hampshire coast, with particular emphasis on the evidence for cross-Channel trade.

Fenwick, Valerie **The Graveney Boat** BAR British Series 53, Oxford, 1978
The final report on this 10th-century AD English boat with particularly extensive discussions concerning its original capabilities and uses.

Franzen, Anders **The Warship Wasa** Norstedts, Stockholm, 1966
An account by the man who originally discovered the *Wasa* of the history and recovery of this Swedish warship of 1628.

Martin, Colin **Full Fathom Five: The Wrecks of the Spanish Armada** Viking Press, New York; Chatto and Windus, London, 1975
The investigation of three Spanish Armada wrecks in Scottish and Irish waters. A fluent narrative that conveys the atmosphere of such diving projects particularly well.

Taylor, Joan du Plat and Cleere, Henry (eds) **Roman Shipping and Trade: Britain and the Rhine Provinces** Council for British Archaeology Research Report No 24, London, 1978
A series of papers (delivered at a conference in 1977) reviewing various aspects of contacts between Britain and the Continent during the Roman occupation. Fully illustrated.

4 Shipwrecks in the Wake of Columbus

Arnold, J. Barto III **An Underwater Archaeological Magnetometer Survey and Site Test Excavation Project off Padre Island** Texas Publication No 3, Texas Antiquities Committee, Austin, Texas, 1976
A detailed technical account of the magnetometer survey off the Texas coast.

Arnold, J. Barto III, and Weddle, Robert **The Nautical Archaeology of Padre Island** Academic Press, New York and London, 1978
A presentation of both the documentary and archaeological evidence relating to the wrecks of 1554 and their recent study. Undoubtedly the best account available of all aspects of a modern wreck investigation.

Green, Jeremy N. **The Jacht Vergulde Draeck**
BAR Supplementary Series, 36, Oxford, 1977
Full report on the site of this wreck of 1656 on
the coast of Western Australia, and a
description of the objects recovered.

Marsden, Peter **The Wreck of the Amsterdam**
Stein and Day, New York, 1975; Hutchinson,
London 1974
The story of the early investigations on the site
of this Dutch East Indiaman of 1749, now lying
on a beach in Sussex, England. Gives a useful
insight into the formidable problems to be faced
in recovering entire ships.

Marx, Robert F. **Shipwrecks of the Western
Hemisphere, 1492-1825** David McKay, New
York, 1971
A checklist of known wreck sites in the Americas,
together with a discussion of their main common
features, the ways in which they can be
investigated, and their historical importance.

5 Structures under water

Flemming, Nicholas C. **Cities in the Sea** New
English Library, London, 1972
A personal account of exploration of submerged
towns and harbors around the Mediterranean.
Gives an insight into both the scientific
importance of this work, and the practical
problems posed.

Flint, Richard Foster **Glacial Geology and the
Pleistocene Epoch** John Wiley and Sons, New
York; Chapman and Hall, London, 1947
A basic textbook concerning processes operating
during the Ice Ages.

Marx, Robert F. **Port Royal Rediscovered**
Doubleday, New York, 1973; New English
Library, London, 1973
The story of the author's endeavors to investigate
the site of the Jamaican town submerged in the
earthquake of 1692. A particularly vivid
evocation of the difficulties of such work.

Munro, Robert **Ancient Scottish Lake-Dwellings
or Crannogs** David Douglas, Edinburgh, 1882
Even though it is nearly 100 years old, this
remains the only overall survey of the subject.
It presents the state of knowledge on which
recent diving investigators have tried to build.

6 Preservation: Past, Present, and Future

Bascom, Willard **Deep Water, Ancient Ships**
Doubleday, New York; David and Charles,
Newton Abbot, 1976
A survey of the archaeological potential of deep
waters, and of recent technical developments that
may allow us to operate there; a thought-
provoking read.

Dowman, Elizabeth A. **Conservation in Field
Archaeology** Methuen, London, 1970
A basic textbook on conservation, setting out the
principles to be applied under water.

Hamilton, D. L. **Conservation of Metal Objects
from Underwater Sites: a Study in Methods**
Texas Antiquities Committee, Publication No 1,
Austin, Texas, 1976
A technical report on the experience of the
laboratory conserving the objects from the 1554
wrecks off the Texas coast. Valuable in showing
an awareness of the conservational, archaeological, and museological problems involved.

Index

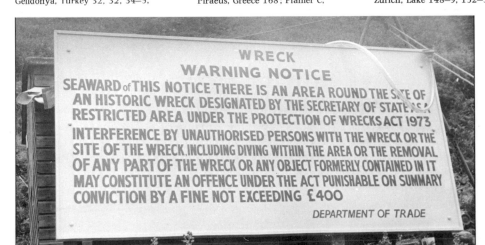